MOSAIK

Deutsche Grammatik

sich
rentieren
be worthwile

MOSAIK

Deutsche Grammatik

CHARLES M. BARRACK / HORST M. RABURA

University of Washington, Seattle

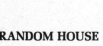 **RANDOM HOUSE** **New York**

This book was developed for Random House by EBI Eirik Børve, Inc.

First Edition

98765432

Copyright © 1982 by Random House, Inc.

All rights reserved under International and Pan-American
Copyright Conventions. No part of this book may be reproduced in
any form or by any means, electronic or mechanical, including
photocopying, without permission in writing from the publisher.
All inquiries should be addressed to Random House, Inc., 201 East
50th Street, New York, N.Y. 10022. Published in the United States
by Random House, Inc., and simultaneously in Canada by Random
House Limited, Toronto.

Library of Congress Cataloging in
Publication Data

Barrack, Charles Michael, 1938-
  Mosaik: deutsche Grammatik.

  Includes index.
  1. German language – Grammar –
1950- I. Rabura, Horst M. II. Title.
PF3112.B37   438.2'421   81-21126
ISBN 0-394-32870-1   AACR2

Text and cover design, book production: Christy Butterfield
Illustrations: Axelle Fortier
Photo research: Lindsay Kefauver
Composition: Jonathan Peck, Typographer

Manufactured in the United States of America

Photo Credits

Foto-Bild-Verlag 72
© Klaus D. Francke/Peter Arnold, Inc.
  1, 306
© Owen Franken/Stock, Boston, Inc.
  138, 246
© Leonard Freed/Magnum Photos Inc.
  269
German Information Center, New York
  55, 67, 82, 107, 127, 160, 180, 187,
  211, 214, 295
Patricia Hollander Gross/Stock, Boston,
  Inc. 193
Fritz Henle/Monkmeyer Press Photo
  Service 29

© Uta Hoffmann 99
© Erich Lessing/Magnum Photos Inc. 269
© Peter Menzel 171, 198, 235, 317
© Peter Menzel/Stock, Boston, Inc. 143
© Press-und-Informationsamt der
  Bundesregierung, Bonn 39
Edith Reichmann/Monkmeyer Press
  Photo Service 286
© Horst Schafer/Peter Arnold, Inc. 280
© Sybil Shelton/Peter Arnold, Inc. 339
Sybil Shelton/Monkmeyer Press Photo
  18

Preface

The Program

Mosaik is an integrated second-year German program for the college level. It consists of three integrated texts: *Mosaik: Deutsche Grammatik, Mosaik: Deutsche Kultur,* and *Mosaik: Deutsche Literatur.* The review grammar, *Deutsche Grammatik,* is the core of the program and is accompanied by a combination workbook and laboratory manual with a tape program. Any of the three texts can be used alone or in combination with the other two, depending on the objectives of the course:

1. *Deutsche Grammatik* and *Deutsche Kultur* present historical and contemporary aspects of the culture of German-speaking countries with a collateral grammar review.

2. *Deutsche Grammatik* and *Deutsche Literatur* can be used together for appreciation of literary texts with a collateral grammar review.

Each of the fourteen chapters of each component is integrated grammatically and thematically with the corresponding chapters of the other two components. The texts are therefore mutually supportive, each one illustrating and reinforcing the same grammatical structures, related vocabulary, and theme.

Mosaik: Deutsche Grammatik

This review grammar reviews basic structures and vocabulary and introduces more advanced material appropriate for the second year. Each chapter of the text features:

1. *Wortschatz.* This thematic vocabulary list provides words necessary for everyday communication at the university, in bilingual careers, and for travel in German-speaking countries. It is followed by vocab-

ulary exercises. To do the grammar exercises throughout the chapter effectively, students should first master the *Wortschatz*.

2. A series of grammatical explanations. Grammar topics are first defined and then their forms and uses are discussed. Grammar necessary for effective conversation and composition at the second-year level is stressed. Attention is consistently drawn to the differences in usage between conversational and formal German. Some grammar sections contain an optional capsule of slightly more advanced material; these sections, labeled *Ein Schritt weiter*, are designed to challenge the curious. Because of their optional nature, no exercises are provided on these.

3. *Übungen*. Each grammatical section is immediately followed by a set of exercises arranged in order of increasing difficulty. The simplest of these (preceded by the symbol °) may be used as oral warm-up drills that the instructor may have students perform with books closed. Every set of exercises closes with an English to German translation and at least one situationalized or personalized exercise designed to spark the student's interest and to enable the student to internalize the grammar of the chapter.

4. *Rückblick*. Each chapter except the first ends with two sets of review exercises in the form of translations from English to German. The first exercise, *Zur Wiederholung*, provides a review of the current chapter; the second exercise, *Zur Gesamtwiederholung*, provides an ongoing review of the four or five preceding chapters. This final exercise is purposely designed to be of greater difficulty in that it ties together the grammatical structures of the current chapter with those of the preceding chapters. The instructor may wish to make use of this exercise not only for review but also as a point of departure to treat more complex structures—for example, the passive voice in indirect discourse.

Following the fourteen chapters is an appendix of the principal parts of strong and irregular verbs (including the modals). A German-English, English-German glossary and an extensive, cross-referenced index close the text.

One special feature of this text is its unique treatment of the subjunctive of indirect discourse. Virtually all first- and second-year textbooks of German relegate the subjunctive of indirect discourse (and, incredibly, even indirect discourse in the indicative, as used in conversational German) to the final chapters. The result is that the student who decides to pursue advanced studies in German is never given the opportunity to master this difficult aspect of the formal written language: The beginning student gets a smattering of this topic at the end of the first year. If students continue with second-year German, they again hear nothing of this topic until the end of the year. *Mosaik*, breaking with this tradition, deals with indirect discourse early in the second half of the text (Chapter 9), a sequencing that provides the student opportunity to review and practice this topic thoroughly.

Arbeitsheft

The accompanying workbook/lab manual provides additional oral and written exercises to supplement those in the review grammar. Teachers will welcome the special section in each chapter on word formation, which should help students broaden their vocabulary. The tape program reinforces grammatical structures covered in the text and stresses pronunciation—especially of difficult words appearing in the corresponding chapters of the review grammar.

Acknowledgments

To Mary McVey Gill for her numerous suggestions on writing situationalized and personalized drills, her coordination and supervision of this entire project, and her inexhaustible optimism and patience. (And we forgive her her attachment to the Romance languages.)

To Maria Biege for her work on the initial vocabulary exercises and adding an idiomatic dimension to the example sentences.

To Helene Lattimore, Toni Schifferl, and Anneliese Wuichet for enduring a myriad of questions on German usage with the patience of Job.

To Eirik Børve for initiating this project and with a surfeit of optimism no less.

A special note of thanks is due to Stephen J. Kaplowitt, University of Connecticut, for his very careful reading of the grammatical explanations.

We would also like to thank the following instructors who participated in various surveys and whose suggestions have proved invaluable in the development of this text. The appearance of their names does not necessarily constitute an endorsement of this text and its methodology.

Waltraud Bald, Ohio University
Lowell A. Bangerter, University of Wyoming
Leo W. Berg, California State Polytechnic University, Pomona
Marianne Bigney, University of Toledo
Mary Lou Coppock, Phoenix College
Otto Dornberg, University of Rhode Island
Ralph E. Ewton, Jr., University of Texas at El Paso
Kirk Follo, Northwestern University
W. Griesbach, California State University, Los Angeles
Walther Hahn, University of Oregon
Todd C. Hanlin, University of Arkansas
Kay Herr, Colorado State University

Klaus Hoffmann, Colorado State University
Robert A. Jones, University of Wisconsin
Duane Keilstrup, University of Texas at Arlington
Dagmar E. Malone, California State University, Long Beach
Kenneth O. Negus, Rutgers University, New Brunswick
Joan Neikirk, University of Delaware
Solveig Olsen, North Texas State University
Michael O'Pecko, Towson State University
Susan Ray, Fordham University
Claus Reschke, University of Houston
Richard G. Rogan, Northern Illinois University
H. Michael Sharpe, University of the Pacific
Harold M. Sommer, Indiana University of Pennsylvania
Carl Steiner, The George Washington University
William Sullivan, Jr., California State University, Sacramento

C. M. B.
H. M. R.

Contents

MOSAIK

Deutsche Grammatik

1
Reisen und Ferien

Am Strand auf der Insel Föhr

The Present Tense

Irregularities in the Present Tense: Weak Verbs and Strong Verbs

The Present Tense: Use and Word Order

The Imperative

Negation

Wortschatz

das Ausland foreign country; **ins Ausland** abroad

die Fahrkarte (-n) ticket

der Fahrplan (-̈e) (train, bus) schedule, time-table

das Fahrrad (-̈er) bicycle

die Fahrt (-en) ride, trip

die Ferien *pl.* vacation (from school); **Ferien haben** to be on vacation; **in die Ferien fahren** to go on vacation

das Gebirge mountains, mountain range

das Gepäck luggage

die Jugendherberge (-n) youth hostel

der Koffer (-) suitcase

die Landkarte (-n) map

das Meer (-e) sea, ocean

die Reise (-n) trip, journey; **Gute Reise!** Have a good trip!

der, die Reisende (-n) traveler

das Reisebüro (-s) travel agency

der Strand (-e) beach

der Urlaub vacation (from a job); **auf (in) Urlaub gehen** to go on vacation

bitten to ask, to request

bleiben to stay

empfehlen to recommend

fahren to drive, to ride, to go

fliegen to fly

gehen to go, to walk

genießen to enjoy

laufen to run

liegen to lie

nehmen to take

raten to recommend, to advise

reisen to travel

reservieren to reserve

sammeln to collect

übernachten to stay overnight

vergessen to forget

wandern to hike

warten to wait

entfernt distant		**nördlich** north	
fertig finished, ready		**östlich** east	
interessant interesting		**schnell** quick	
langsam slow		**südlich** south	
langweilig boring		**westlich** west	
nah close			

A. *Choose the most logical response on the right for each statement on the left.*

1. Mein Gott, bist du immer noch nicht fertig?

2. Mensch, ich weiß nicht, wo wir sind.

3. Ach, ich möchte heute so gerne in der Sonne liegen.

4. Heute muß ich aber wirklich die Fahrkarten kaufen, Rudi.

5. Entschuldigen Sie bitte, ich suche ein Zimmer, habe aber nicht sehr viel Geld.

6. Ich fliege morgen endlich in Urlaub—nach Spanien. Gottseidank!

7. Ach du liebe Zeit, mein Fahrrad ist kaputt.

8. Sammeln Sie auch Postkarten?

a. Gute Reise! Genießen Sie die Ferien!

b. Naja, dann gehen wir eben zu Fuß oder fahren mit dem Bus.

c. Hast du wieder den Fahrplan vergessen, du Idiot?

d. Moment, das können wir leicht herausfinden. Ich habe nämlich eine Landkarte.

e. Geh doch schnell zum Reisebüro und kauf sie dort. Ich gebe dir das Geld.

f. Tut mir leid, aber diese Arbeit hier geht so langsam. Kannst du noch etwas warten?

g. Hast du Lust, zum Strand zu fahren? Da ist das Wetter bestimmt schön.

h. Ach, gehen wir doch einfach in das Restaurant hier. Das sieht doch gut aus.

i. Tja, junger Mann, da kann ich Ihnen die Jugendherberge empfehlen. Die liegt sogar ganz in der Nähe.

j. Darf ich Ihnen die Napoleon-Suite reservieren, gnädige Frau?

k. Ja, aber ich finde das als Hobby jetzt ziemlich langweilig.

B. *Complete the sentences with the opposites of the words in italics.*

1. Er fährt immer *schnell,* aber ich fahre gerne _____.

2. Mein Buch ist sehr *interessant,* aber dein Buch ist _____.

3. In der *Heimat* ist es anders als im _____.

4. Der Strand ist zwanzig Kilometer von hier *entfernt,* aber die Stadt ist

   sehr _____.

5. Dänemark liegt *nördlich* von Deutschland. Italien liegt _____ von

   Österreich.

6. *Östlich* von hier sind die Berge; _____ von hier liegt das Meer.

C. *Replace each of the words in italics with a word similar in meaning.*

1. Wir haben dieses Jahr im Juli *Ferien.*
2. Mein *Koffer* ist noch in Berlin.
3. Was können Sie mir in dieser Situation *raten*?
4. Manche *Touristen* kommen nach Hamburg und Bremen.
5. Die Meyerholds *reisen* jedes Jahr nach Frankreich.
6. Wir *übernachten* bei unseren Freunden.

The Present Tense

The present tense is formed from the infinitive, the form of the verb that is usually preceded by the preposition *to* in English: *to go, to come, to do.* In German, the infinitive ends in **-en** or **-n: gehen, kommen, tun.** This **-en** or **-n** ending is dropped from the infinitive to obtain the stem of the verb; for instance, **geh-, komm-, tu-.** To form the present tense of most verbs, the endings **-e, -st, -t, -en, -t,** and **-en** are added to the stem.

kommen

Singular

First Person:	ich komm**e**	I come
Second Person:	du komm**st**	you come
Third Person:	er ⎱	he ⎱
	sie ⎬ komm**t**	she ⎬ comes
	es ⎰	it ⎰

Plural

First Person:	wir komm**en**	we come
Second Person:	ihr komm**t**	you come
Third Person:	sie ⎱ komm**en**	they ⎱ come
	Sie ⎰	you ⎰

Notice that the verb is the same for the polite **Sie** form (you, singular or plural) and the third-person plural **sie** form (they), as well as for the first-person plural form, **wir.**

It is important to remember that there are no progressive or emphatic forms in German equivalent to those in English:

	English	German
Statements		
Progressive:	Edith is hiking.	Edith wandert.
	Edith is not hiking.	Edith wandert nicht.
Emphatic:	Edith does hike.	
	Edith does not hike.	
Questions		
Progressive:	Is Edith hiking?	Wandert Edith?
	Isn't Edith hiking?	Wandert Edith nicht?
Emphatic:	Does Edith hike?	
	Doesn't Edith hike?	

Verbs with Stems Ending in an /s/ Sound

If the verb stem ends in an /s/ sound (s, ss, ß, or z), **-t** rather than **-st** is added to the stem to create the **du** form; the **du** and **er** forms are then identical.*

reisen	to travel	du reist, er reist
küssen	to kiss	du küßt, er küßt
genießen	to enjoy	du genießt, er genießt
sitzen	to sit	du sitzt, er sitzt

The Endings -et and -est

If the verb stem ends in **-t** or **-d** (**arbeiten, finden**) or **-m** or **-n** preceded by a consonant (**atmen, regnen**), the endings **-et** and **-est** rather than -t and -st are added to the stem. The **e** facilitates pronunciation.

---

*Regarding the use of **ss** or **ß**, there is a simple rule: **ss** is used only between two short vowels (**Wasser, besser, essen, lassen, Flüsse**). In all other situations, **ß** should be used: at the end of a word (**Iß! Fluß, Laß das!**), before a consonant (**Eßt!, Laßt das!**), or after a long vowel or diphthong (**beißen, genießen, Füße**). Of course, in typing, **ss** may be used in place of **ß**.

arbeiten	*to work*	du arbeit**est**, er arbeit**et**, ihr arbeit**et**
finden	*to find*	du find**est**, er find**et**, ihr find**et**
atmen	*to breathe*	du atm**est**, er atm**et**, ihr atm**et**
regnen	*to rain*	es regn**et**

This rule does not apply to stems ending in **-m** or **-n** preceded by **l** or **r**:

filmen	*to film*	du filmst, er filmt, ihr filmt
lernen	*to learn*	du lernst, er lernt, ihr lernt

Verbs with Infinitive Ending in *-ln* or *-rn*; the Verb *tun*

If the infinitive ends in **-ln** or **-rn**, the first- and third-persons plural (**wir, sie**) and the polite form **Sie** end in **-n** rather than **-en**, just like the infinitive.

sammeln	*to collect*	wir (sie, Sie) sammel**n**
wandern	*to wander; to hike*	wir (sie, Sie) wander**n**

The verb **tun** also follows this pattern.

tun
to do

ich tue	wir tun
du tust	ihr tut
er ⎤	sie ⎤
sie ⎬tut	Sie ⎬tun
es ⎦	

Übungen

°A. **Ersetzen Sie die Pronomen!** Replace the pronouns in italics with the pronouns in parentheses and change the verbs accordingly.

Zum Beispiel: Wir kommen morgen zurück. (ich)
        Ich komme morgen zurück.

1. Sie übernachten in Dinkelsbühl. (er, ihr, wir, ich)
2. Genießen Sie dieses Wetter? (du, er, ihr, sie *pl.*)
3. Sitzt er am Strand? (du, ihr, es, Sie)
4. Ich warte auf den Professor. (er, du, sie *sing.*, wir)
5. Wir öffnen alle Fenster. (du, er, ich, ihr)
6. Warum ändert er den Plan nicht? (du, sie *pl.*, man, Sie)

°Exercises preceded by this symbol may be effectively used as oral drills because of their simplicity.

Ergänzen Sie die folgenden Sätze! Complete the following sentences with the appropriate present-tense forms of the verbs in parentheses.

Zum Beispiel: Ich _____ nach Travemünde. (reisen)
Ich reise nach Travemünde.

1. Christa _findet_ Lübeck sehr schön. (finden)

2. Dieser Zahn _tut_ mir weh. (tun)

3. _Wanderst_ du oft in der Schweiz? (wandern)

4. Es _regnet_ mehr in Norddeutschland als in

   Süddeutschland. (regnen)

5. Klaus, warum _reist_ du immer in die Alpen? (reisen)

6. Jürgen _arbeitet_ für seinen Onkel. (arbeiten)

7. Ihr _antwortet_ auf alle Fragen. (antworten)

°C. **Geben Sie die folgenden Sätze im Singular!** Restate the following sentences in the singular.

Zum Beispiel: Wir genießen die Fahrt nach Stuttgart.
Ich genieße die Fahrt nach Stuttgart.

1. Die Amerikanerinnen finden diese Reise langweilig. _Die Amerikanerin findet_
2. Warum übernachtet ihr in der Jugendherberge? _übernachtest du_
3. Die Kinder atmen schneller, wenn sie rennen. _das Kind atmest schneller, wenn sie rennt_
4. Fliegt ihr nach Hamburg? _Fliegst du_
5. Die Studentinnen gehen samstags oft in den Park. _Die Studentin geht..._
6. Ihr sitzt in der ersten Reihe, nicht wahr?
   du sitzt in der erste Reihe nicht wahr.

°D. **Geben Sie die folgenden Sätze im Plural!**

Zum Beispiel: Ich reise nach Berlin.
Wir reisen nach Berlin.

1. Warum wartest du hier?
2. Sie bleibt zu Hause.
3. Er lernt Englisch.

4. Die Frau ändert den Reiseplan.
5. Was tut das Kind im Garten?
6. Ich sammele Postkarten.

E. **Übersetzen Sie die folgenden Sätze!** Translate the following sentences.

1. Pamela, do you sit in front of (**vor**) Rolf?
2. Ulrike and Klaus, why are you opening all the (**alle**) windows?
3. It rains here often.
4. Why is Sophia changing our (**unseren**) Plan?
5. Mrs. Barner, are you traveling to Berlin?
6. Nina and Sylvia, are you staying overnight in Kiel?
7. Reinhold finds the postcard interesting.

F. **Was machen Sie gern im Urlaub?** Tell what you like to do when you are on vacation. Ask one of your classmates if he or she likes to do the same things. You may want to use some of the following vocabulary:

am Strand liegen

angeln (fischen) *to fish*

Baseball, Fußball (*soccer*), Tennis spielen

die Briefmarke(-n), die Postkarte(-n), sammeln *to collect stamps, postcards*

die Familie besuchen

ins Ausland reisen

im Gebirge wandern

kegeln *to bowl*

kochen *to cook*

nähen *to sew*

Rollschuhlaufen gehen *to go roller skating*

Schlittschuhlaufen gehen *to go ice skating*

schwimmen *to swim*

Skilaufen gehen *to go skiing*

Sport treiben *to take part in sports*

stricken *to knit*

tanzen *to dance*

Zum Beispiel: **Ich schwimme in den Ferien gern. Schwimmst du auch in den Ferien gern?**

Ja, ich schwimme im Urlaub auch gern. (Nein, ich schwimme im Urlaub nicht gern.)

Irregularities in the Present Tense: Weak Verbs and Strong Verbs

All German verbs except modal verbs are either weak or strong.

Weak Verbs

Weak verbs are verbs that have past stems formed by adding **-te** to the stem of the infinitive; for instance, **lernen: lernte-**. The only weak verb with irregularities in the present tense is **haben**.

haben
to have

ich habe	wir haben
du **hast**	ihr habt
er	sie
sie **hat**	Sie haben
es	

Strong Verbs with a Stem Vowel Change

Strong verbs are verbs that have past stems formed by changing the stem vowel of the infinitive; for instance, **sehen**: **sah-** Many strong verbs show modifications of the stem in the second- and third-persons singular of the present tense. A complete alphabetical listing of strong verbs and their forms is in the appendix, but here are the major changes that occur in the present tense of such verbs.

Stem Vowel Change from _e_ to _i_

helfen
to help

ich helfe	wir helfen
du hilfst	ihr helft
er sie }hilft es	sie Sie }helfen

Other verbs that follow this pattern are:

brechen	_to break_	treffen	_to meet_
essen*	_to eat_	treten	_to step_
fressen*	_to devour, eat_	verderben	_to ruin_
geben	_to give_	vergessen*	_to forget_
nehmen	_to take_	werden	_to become_
sprechen	_to speak_	werfen	_to throw_
sterben	_to die_		

The verbs **nehmen**, **treten**, and **werden** show other modifications besides a change in the stem vowel:

nehmen
to take

ich nehme	wir nehmen
du **nimmst**	ihr nehmt
er sie }**nimmt** es	sie Sie }nehmen

treten
to step

ich trete	wir treten
du **trittst**	ihr tretet
er sie }**tritt** es	sie Sie }treten

werden
to become

ich werde	wir werden
du **wirst**	ihr werdet
er sie }**wird** es	sie Sie }werden

---

*Since the stems of **essen**, **fressen**, and **vergessen** end in **-s**, **-t** (not **-st**) is added to create the **du** form: **du ißt**, **du vergißt**.

Stem Vowel Change from *e* to *ie*

sehen
to see

ich sehe	wir sehen
du **siehst**	ihr seht
er ⎫	sie ⎫
sie ⎬ **sieht**	Sie ⎬ sehen
es ⎭	

Other verbs that follow this pattern are:

befehlen *to command, order*
empfehlen *to recommend*
geschehen* *to happen*
lesen[†] *to read*

Stem Vowel with Umlaut

schlafen
to sleep

ich schlafe	wir schlafen
du schl**ä**fst	ihr schlaft
er ⎫	sie ⎫
sie ⎬ schl**ä**ft	Sie ⎬ schlafen
es ⎭	

Other common verbs that follow this pattern are:

blasen[‡] *to blow*
einladen *to invite*
fahren *to drive, to travel*
fallen *to fall*
fangen *to catch*
halten *to hold*
lassen[‡] *to let, to leave (behind)*
laufen *to walk, to run*
raten *to advise*
saufen *to drink (said of animals)*
schlagen *to strike*
tragen *to carry, wear*
wachsen[‡] *to grow*
waschen *to wash*

***Geschehen** only occurs in the third person singular: **Es geschieht jeden Tag.**
[†]The **du** form is created by adding **-t** rather than **-st**, since the stem ends in **-s**: **du liest**.
[‡]The **du** forms are created by adding **-t** rather than **-st**, since the stems end in **-s** or **-ß**: **du bläst, du läßt, du wächst.**

The verbs **einladen**, **halten**, and **raten** show other modifications besides a change in the stem vowel:

einladen*
to invite

ich lade . . . ein	wir laden . . . ein
du **lädst** . . . ein	ihr ladet . . . ein
er	sie
sie }**lädt** . . . ein	Sie }laden . . . ein
es	

halten
to hold

ich halte	wir halten
du **hältst**	ihr haltet
er	sie
sie }**hält**	Sie }halten
es	

raten
to advise

ich rate	wir raten
du **rätst**	ihr ratet
er	sie
sie }**rät**	Sie }raten
es	

The Verb *sein*

sein
to be

ich bin	wir sind
du bist	ihr seid
er	sie
sie }ist	Sie }sind
es	

Sein is the only German verb that is irregular in the plural of the present tense. **Notice that there are no irregular *ihr* forms other than in the verb *sein*.** (The **ihr** form is always constructed by attaching **-t**—or **-et** if appropriate—to the stem: **ihr nehmt, ihr wollt, ihr ratet.**)

Übungen

°A. **Ersetzen Sie die Pronomen!** Replace the pronouns in italics with the pronouns in parentheses and change the verbs accordingly.

1. Geben Sie dem Touristen die Landkarte?   (er, wir, du)
2. Nehmen Sie jeden Tag den Bus?   (du, sie *sing.,*ihr)
3. Wir treffen Karla unterwegs.   (sie *pl.*, ich, du)

---

*In conversational German, **einladen** is often used without the umlaut in the present tense. When this is done, the endings **-est** and **-et** are used: **du ladest . . . ein, er ladet . . . ein.**

4. Empfehlen Sie dieses Restaurant nicht?   (du, er, ihr)
5. Was halten Sie in der Hand?   (du, sie *sing*. ihr)
6. Wir laufen morgen fünf Kilometer.   (er, du, sie *sing*.)
7. Raten Sie uns, den Zug zu nehmen?   (du, er, ihr)

°B. **Ändern Sie das Subjekt des Satzes!** Change the subjects and verbs of these sentences from the singular to the plural or vice versa.

Zum Beispiel: Ich fahre in die Ferien.
   Wir fahren in die Ferien.

   Die Studenten studieren deutsche Literatur.
   Der Student studiert deutsche Literatur.

1. Macht ihr eine Reise nach Kiel?
2. Haben die Kinder Hunger?
3. Ich helfe den Touristen, die Koffer ins Auto zu bringen.
4. Essen die Ausländer gern in diesem Restaurant?
5. Gibt er der Frau die Hand?
6. Nimmst du immer ein Taxi?
7. Warum seid ihr so müde?
8. Wann fängt die Reise an?
9. Wascht ihr heute das Auto?
10. Jetzt sehen sie das Hotel.
11. Er vergißt die Koffer.
12. Ist diese Stadt weit von Hamburg entfernt?

C. **Ergänzen Sie die folgenden Sätze!**

1. _bist_ du nicht fertig?   (sein)

2. Zuviel Salz _verdirbt_ das Essen.   (verderben)

3. _Werdet_ ihr müde?   (werden)

4. Wohin _wirfst_ Julia den Ball?   (werfen)

5. Die Freunde _raten_ uns, nach Lübeck zu fahren.   (raten)

6. _Lest_ ihr immer Reisebücher?   (lesen)

7. Warum _läßt_ sie (*sing*.) ihr Fahrrad nicht zu Hause?   (lassen)

8. Wohin _trägst_ du die Koffer?   (tragen)

9. _Siehst_ du das Gepäck?   (sehen)

10. Warum _antwortet_ er dem Ausländer nicht?   (antworten)

D. **Schreiben Sie Sätze im Präsens!** Use the following verb forms.

1. werdet   2. läufst   3. triffst   4. sprechen
5. ißt   6. nimmt   7. haltet   8. rät

E. **Übersetzen Sie die folgenden Sätze!** *Renate, schlägst du diese Jungendherberge vor*

1. Renate, do you recommend this youth hostel?
2. It's getting (becoming) late. *Es wurdet spät*
3. Jost and Sara, do you walk every (**jeden**) day to the (**zur**) university?
4. Is Mr. Diels carrying a suitcase?
5. What are you holding in your (**in der**) hand, Gisela?
6. Hilde and Diana, are you on vacation?
7. Do you sleep here, Mr. Becker?

F. **Greta geht auf Urlaub.** Describe Greta's vacation following this model.

Zum Beispiel: fahren / in die Schweiz
Sie fährt in die Schweiz.

1. haben / viel Gepäck
2. nehmen / ihren Tennisschläger (*tennis racket*) mit
3. vergessen / ihre Tennisbälle
4. bitten / den Portier, das Gepäck ins Hotel zu bringen
5. treffen / eine gute Freundin in Zürich
6. laden / ihre Freundin ein, ins Kino zu gehen
7. werden / müde
8. gehen / ins Hotel zurück
9. schlafen / bis 10 Uhr morgen

The Present Tense: Use and Word Order

The Present Tense: Use

The present tense in German has many uses and many equivalents in English. It can express almost any action except an action that has been completed or finished in the past. It is used for:

1. actions presently occurring

Hans liest jetzt den Fahrplan.
Hans is reading the (train) schedule now. (English present progressive)

2. actions begun in the past and continuing into the present

Hans liest schon seit fünfzehn Minuten den Fahrplan.*
Hans has been reading the schedule for fifteen minutes. (English perfect progressive)

---

*Notice that (**schon**) **seit** with the dative case is used to indicate a period of time. The verb is in the present tense in German since the action is still going on: **Wir warten (schon) seit zwei Tagen.** *We have been waiting for two days.*

3. future actions

   Hans liest den Fahrplan morgen.
   Hans will read the schedule tomorrow.   (English future)

   Vicki, wann bist du in Deutschland?
   Vicki, when will you be in Germany?

4. habitual actions

   Hans liest jede Woche den Fahrplan.
   Hans reads the schedule every week.   (English simple present)

5. emphatic statements about habitual actions

   Hans liest den Fahrplan.
   Hans does read the schedule.   (English present emphatic)

Notice in these sentences that adverbs (such as **schon**, **jetzt**, **morgen**, and **jede Woche**) are sometimes used in German to specify time relationships that must be expressed in English through tense.

The Present Tense: Word Order

Normal Word Order

In typical declarative sentences in German (statements, not questions), the subject with its modifiers immediately precedes the finite verb (the verb with personal endings: **ich singe**, **er kommt**). This is referred to as "normal" word order.

| | Predicate | | |
Subject (1)	Finite Verb (2)	Other Element (3)	Other Element (4)
Herr Benrath	reserviert	das Zimmer	heute.
Die kleinen Kinder	spielen	Fußball	im Park.
Das Wetter	ist	im Juni	schön.

Inverted Word Order

Sometimes elements such as those in the third column above precede the subject for emphasis, a sequence referred to as "inverted" word order.

Other Element (1)	Finite Verb (2)	Subject (3)	Other Element (4)
Heute	reserviert	Herr Benrath	das Zimmer.
Im Park	spielen	die kleinen Kinder	Fußball.
Im Juni	ist	das Wetter	schön.

With either inverted or normal word order, the finite verb appears second in the sentence. Only one element may appear first—either the subject or a single word or phrase from the predicate.

Transposed Word Order: Sentences with a Subordinate Clause

A subordinate clause is a clause that cannot stand alone. For example, the italicized subordinate clauses in the following English sentences would not constitute complete sentences by themselves:

Kurt is studying German *because he is going to Germany.*
Gerhard says *that his sister is becoming a lawyer.*

In German, the finite verb occurs at the end of the subordinate clause; this is referred to as "transposed" word order.

Main Clause	Subordinate Clause		
	Subordinating Conjunction		*Finite Verb*
Kurt studiert Deutsch,	weil	er nach Deutschland	fährt.
Gerhard sagt,	daß	seine Schwester Juristin	wird.

Subordinate clauses are often inroduced by subordinating conjunctions like **daß** (*that*) and **weil** (*because*). Other common subordinating conjunctions are: **bevor** (*before*), **nachdem** (*after*), **ob** (*whether*), and **während** (*while*).*

Word Order with Coordinating Conjunctions

The conjunctions **aber** (*but*), **oder** (*or*), **und** (*and*), **sondern** (*but, on the contrary*), and a few others are called coordinating conjunctions. They do not subordinate one clause to another, and for this reason they have no effect on the word order of the clauses they join.

Ich bleibe heute zu Hause. Morgen gehe ich zur Universität.
Ich bleibe heute zu Hause, aber morgen gehe ich zur Universität.
Ich bleibe heute zu Hause, und morgen gehe ich zur Universität.

Wir reservieren ein Zimmer im Hotel. Wir übernachten bei
    unseren Freunden.
Wir reservieren ein Zimmer im Hotel, oder wir übernachten bei
    unseren Freunden.

Ute arbeitet nicht bei der Bank. Sie besucht die Uni.
Ute arbeitet nicht bei der Bank, sondern sie besucht die Uni.

Notice that **sondern** can only be used after negated clauses.

---

*Any question word can act as a subordinating conjunction: **Kurt hat gefragt, *warum* wir nicht zur Party gehen. Kurt hat gefragt, *wann* wir zur Party gehen.**

Word Order in Questions

In yes/no questions in German, the finite verb precedes the subject.

> Sie fahren ins Ausland. *Fahren* Sie ins Ausland?
> You are going abroad. Are you going abroad?
>
> Klaus übernachtet oft in Köln. *Übernachtet* Klaus oft in Köln?
> Klaus often spends the night in Cologne. Does Klaus often spend the night
> in Cologne?

If a question word—such as **wer, was, wohin,** or **warum**—is present, the finite verb directly follows it.

> Cornelia will etwas. Was *will* Cornelia?
> Cornelia wants something. What does Cornelia want?
>
> Andrea fährt nach Berlin. Wohin *fährt* Andrea?
> Andrea is driving to Berlin. Where is Andrea driving?

Übungen

°A. **Ersetzen Sie die Adverbien!** Replace the adverbs in italics with the adverbs in parentheses and translate into English.

1. Axel studiert *jetzt* Englisch.   (schon seit zwei Jahren, jeden Tag, morgen)
2. Reist du *heute* nach Kiel?   (morgen, jede Woche, nächstes Jahr)
3. Ich mache *morgen* meine Reisepläne.   (heute abend, jeden Tag, jetzt)
4. Daniela liest *heute Nachmittag* den Fahrplan.   (jetzt, morgen, jeden Tag, oft)
5. Besuchen Sie *jetzt* die Eltern?   (übermorgen, jeden Monat, nachmittags)

°B. **Beginnen Sie die folgenden Sätze mit den kursiv gedruckten Wörtern!** Begin the following sentences with the words or phrases in italics and make the necessary changes in word order.

Zum Beispiel: Ich fliege *nächste Woche* nach Travemünde.
Nächste Woche fliege ich nach Travemünde.

1. Matthias fährt gern *mit dem Fahrrad.*
2. Lübeck liegt *nicht weit von Travemünde.*
3. Ich verstehe *den Fahrplan* gut.
4. Es regnet oft *im Norden.*
5. Wir fahren *morgen* auf Urlaub.
6. Dänemark liegt *nördlich von Deutschland.*

C. **Wählen Sie das passende Adverb!** Select the proper adverb or adverbial phrase to complete each of the following sentences.

1. Ich wohne _____ in dieser Stadt.   (letztes Jahr, letzten Sommer,

   vor fünf Jahren, schon seit zehn Jahren)

2. Machst du _____ deine Hausaufgaben? (jetzt, gestern, letzten Dienstag)

3. Karin fährt _____ mit dem Zug. (vorgestern, jede Woche, letzten Montag)

4. Wir reisen _____ ans Meer. (nächste Woche, gestern, letzten Freitag)

5. Marianne fliegt _____ nach Liechtenstein. (vor zwei Wochen, in zwei Wochen, letzte Woche)

°D. **Verbinden Sie die folgenden Sätze mit Konjunktionen!** Join the following sentences with the conjunctions in parentheses and change the word order when necessary.

Zum Beispiel: Der Tourist sagt. . . . Er reist an die Nordseeküste. (daß)
Der Tourist sagt, daß er an die Nordseeküste reist.

1. Mein Vater kommt aus Hamburg. Meine Mutter kommt aus Husum. (aber)
2. Wir gehen nicht in Urlaub. Wir bleiben zu Hause. (sondern)
3. Der Professor sagt . . . . Danzig heißt jetzt „Gdansk". (daß)
4. Flensburg liegt nördlich von Kiel. Hamburg liegt südlich. (aber)
5. Ich bleibe eine Woche in Bremerhaven. Meine Schwester wohnt dort. (weil)
6. Ich weiß. „Auf der Lüneburger Heide" ist ein berühmtes Volkslied. (daß)
7. Rainer fragt . . . . Empfehlen Sie dieses Hotel? (ob)
8. Wir spielen Fußball. Wir gehen nach Hause. (bevor)

E. **Bilden Sie Fragen!** Rearrange the words to form questions.

Zum Beispiel: woher / Sie / kommen?
Woher kommen Sie?

Sie / sprechen / Deutsch?
Sprechen Sie Deutsch?

1. wohin / du / gehst / morgen?
2. Thomas / fährt / in die Ferien?
3. du / kennst / die Stadt Bremen?
4. ihr / spielt Tennis / nach der Schule?
5. wie / Sie / heißen?
6. woher / der Professor / kommt?
7. Flensburg / liegt / in Schleswig-Holstein?

F. **Ergänzen Sie die folgenden Sätze oder Fragen!** Complete the following sentences; make sure to place the verb in the correct position.

1. Hamburg liegt im Norden, aber München *liegt im süden*
2. Ich bleibe heute zu Hause, weil . *du krank bist,*
3. Wir fahren morgen nach Kiel, oder wir *bleiben zu Hause.*

4. Meine Mutter kommt aus Bremen, aber mein Vater *kommt aus Kiel.*
5. Stefan fährt nach Frankreich, aber seine Schwester *fährt nach Italien.*
6. Udo besucht die Eltern nicht, sondern *kommt mit uns.*
7. Ich gehe morgens in die Universität, und nachmittags *mache ich Hausaufgabe*
8. Die Touristin fragt, ob *hier ein Turm gibt.*
9. Woher . . .? *kommst du denn?*
10. Wie lange . . .? *wartet ihr schon.*

G. Beantworten Sie die folgenden Fragen!

1. Wie lange wohnen Sie schon hier?
2. Wie lange fahren Sie schon Auto?
3. Wie oft fahren Sie Fahrrad?
4. Wann haben Sie Ferien? Wohin fahren Sie?

Im Reisebüro

Übersetzen Sie die folgenden Sätze!

1. Konrad has been living here for three years.
2. Next year Petra will travel to Hamburg.
3. I visit my parents every week.
4. We'll see Jürgen and Brigitte tonight.
5. Toni, how long have you been traveling?
6. Next month I'll be in Germany.
7. How long has Volker been on vacation?
8. Günter is asking whether we will stay overnight in the (**in der**) youth hostel.
9. Sara and Erich are going to France (**Frankreich**) because they want to see Paris.
10. I'm flying to Bonn, and Brigitte is flying to Munich.

I. **Schreiben Sie an Ihren Freund (Ihre Freundin)!** You have been visiting your favorite city in Germany during summer vacation. Write a short letter to a German friend in the United States about your trip. Your letter should open **Lieber** (masculine) . . . ! or **Liebe** (feminine) . . . ! and should close **Dein(e)** and your name. Use as many of the following expressions as possible:

in drei Wochen *in three weeks*	morgen früh *tomorrow morning*
jede Woche *every week*	nächste Woche *next week*
jeden Tag *every day*	nächsten Montag (Dienstag, usw.) *next Monday (Tuesday, etc.)*
morgen *tomorrow*	nächstes Wochenende *next weekend*

The Imperative

The imperative is that form of the verb that expresses a command or request:

Kurt, *sprich* lauter!   Kinder, *wartet* hier auf den Bus!
Kurt, speak louder!   Children, wait here for the bus.

In German, the imperative is nearly always followed by an exclamation point.

Du, ihr, Sie

Although there is only one second-person imperative form in English, there are three in German, corresponding to the three pronouns expressing *you*.

(du)   Hans, *sprich* lauter!
(ihr)   Kinder, *sprecht* lauter!
(Sie)   Herr Braun, *sprechen* Sie lauter!

The three present-tense forms meaning "you" are used as a basis for forming the imperative.

sprechen	warten
du sprichst	du wartest
ihr sprecht	ihr wartet
Sie sprechen	Sie warten

The *du* Form

The pronoun **du** and the **-st** ending are dropped from the present tense to form the imperative.

Sprich!   Warte!

If the verb stem ends in **-s, -ß,** or **-z,** only the **-t** is dropped.

essen!	du ißt	Iß!
lesen	du liest	Lies!
genießen	du genießt	Genieß die Fahrt!

If the **du** form of the present tense has an umlaut that is not in the infinitive, the umlaut is dropped in the imperative:

laufen	du läufst	Lauf!
schlafen	du schläfst	Schlaf!

But:

träumen	du träumst	Träum schön!

If the stem vowel of the second-person singular imperative is the same as that of the infinitive, the ending **e** is sometimes added, especially in formal German.

gehen	Geh! *or* Gehe!
laufen	Lauf! *or* Laufe!
lernen	Lern! *or* Lerne!

The *ihr* Form

To form the imperative of the second-person familiar plural, the pronoun **ihr** is simply dropped.

Sprecht!   Wartet!

The *Sie* form

The pronoun **Sie** is placed after the verb to form the imperative.

Sprechen Sie!   Warten Sie!

The First-Person Plural: *wir*

The imperative of the first-person plural (*Let's* . . .) is formed by placing the pronoun **wir** after the present-tense form of the verb.

Gehen wir nach Hause!
Let's go home.

Kaufen wir eine Landkarte!
Let's buy a map.

A construction with the second-person forms of the verb **lassen** is sometimes used in place of the imperative.

Gabi, laß uns nach Hause gehen.
Gabi und Franz, laßt uns nach Hause gehen.
Fräulein Eberhard, lassen Sie uns nach Hause gehen.

Notice that the main verb, expressed as an infinitive, is placed at the end of the clause.

Ein Schritt weiter ────────────────────────────────

The infinitive often appears in public signs as a substitute for the imperative:

Irregular Imperative Forms

The verb **sein** is irregular in the imperative in all forms except the **ihr** form:

Vicki, sei ruhig! (du)
Kinder, seid ruhig! (ihr)
Herr Braun, seien Sie bitte ruhig! (Sie)

The second-person singular (**du**) imperative form of the verb **werden** is **werde.**

Bruno, werde doch Pilot!
Bruno, why don't you become a pilot?

Übungen

°A. **Bilden Sie den Imperativ!**

Zum Beispiel: Du sprichst laut. (drop the **-st** ending)
Sprich laut!

1. Du kommst mit uns.
2. Du antwortest mir.
3. Du gibst Kai die Koffer.
4. Du siehst das Foto an.
5. Du nimmst das Gepäck mit.
6. Du findest den Fahrplan.

Zum Beispiel: Du schließt die Fenster. (drop the **-t** ending)
Schließ die Fenster.

1. Du ißt langsamer.
2. Du vergißt die Landkarte morgen nicht.
3. Du grüßt deine Eltern.
4. Du schließt die Tür.

Zum Beispiel: Du läßt den Koffer nicht zu Hause. (drop **-[s]t** and the umlaut if it is absent in the infinitive)
Laß den Koffer nicht zu Hause.

1. Du fährst langsam.
2. Du läufst nicht so schnell.
3. Du träumst etwas Schönes über deine Reise.
4. Du hältst die Landkarte in der Hand.

Zum Beispiel: Ihr kommt mit uns.
Kommt mit uns!

1. Ihr antwortet mir.
2. Ihr nehmt diesen Bus zum Sankt-Petri-Dom.

3. Ihr besucht uns morgen.
4. Ihr vergeßt den Fahrplan nicht.
5. Ihr laßt das Gepäck nicht zu Hause.

Zum Beispiel: Sie sprechen lauter.
       Sprechen Sie lauter!

1. Sie vergessen das Buch morgen nicht.
2. Sie rauchen nicht im Zug.
3. Sie schreiben die Antwort an die Tafel.
4. Sie laden Martin, Ruth and Michael ein.
5. Sie übernachten in Hannover.

B. **Ergänzen Sie die Sätze!** Complete the sentences with the appropriate imperative form of **sein.**

1. _____ Sie ruhig!

2. _____ brav! (du)

3. _____ Sie höflich!

4. _____ nicht so langsam! (du)

5. _____ vorsichtig! (ihr)

C. **Schreiben Sie Sätze!** Compose imperatives for all three pronouns (**du, ihr, Sie**) from the verbs listed.

Zum Beispiel: sprechen
       Sprich nicht so laut! Sprecht nicht so laut! Sprechen Sie nicht so laut!

1. antworten	2. fahren	3. nehmen
4. vergessen	5. laufen	6. sein

D. **Was machen wir?** Hans and Anneliese are deciding what to do on their vacation. Create sentences, following the model.

Zum Beispiel: in die Schweiz fahren
     HANS: **Fahren wir in die Schweiz!**
   ANNELIESE: **Ja, laß uns in die Schweiz fahren!**

1. nach Zürich gehen
2. in den Alpen wandern
3. den Zürichsee sehen
4. Fondue essen
5. viel Schokolade kaufen
6. in Luzern Toni besuchen
7. Skilaufen gehen
8. in Bern übernachten

E. **Das Kinderhüten (*Babysitting*) ist schwer!** You are babysitting Gerd and Anna, the children of some friends who are on vacation for a few days. Using the verbs listed, give the children instructions.

Zum Beispiel: **Gerd, warte auf Anna!**
    Anna, trink deine Milch!
    Gerd und Anna, geht ins Bett!

Gerd

den Teller (*plate*) nicht zerbrechen

die Suppe essen

der Schwester den Ball geben

dieses Buch lesen

den Ball fangen

das Glas halten

ins Haus kommen

Anna

den Ball werfen

deine Jacke tragen

den Hund nicht ins Haus bringen

das Buch nicht vergessen

dem Bruder helfen

nicht ins Buch schreiben

Gerd und Anna

zu mir kommen

den Kartoffelsalat essen

diese Märchen (*fairy tales*) lesen

Ball miteinander (*with each other*) spielen

auf mich warten

Now add five commands of your own.

F. **Übersetzen Sie die folgenden Sätze!**

1. Vicki, open the window.
2. Petra, let's go abroad.   (Translate in two ways.)
3. Gerd and Monika, don't run so fast.
4. Mr. Dörfling, don't forget the baggage.
5. Hans, eat the bread.
6. Miss Schiller, let's visit Mrs. Eberhard.
7. Children, be careful!
8. Kurt and Georg, let's spend the night in Hamburg.   (Translate in two ways.)

G. **Sie haben Besuch aus Deutschland!** Two German friends of yours, Mr. and Mrs. Päsler, are visiting the United States. Give them suggestions about things they should see and do, and about things you all might do together, using the verbs listed.

Zum Beispiel: Herr Päsler: **Essen Sie nicht in diesem Restaurant!**

Herr und Frau Päsler: **Sprechen Sie langsamer, bitte!**

Wir: **Trinken wir eine Tasse Kaffee! (Lassen Sie uns eine Tasse Kaffee trinken!)**

Frau Päsler

in die Oper (*opera*) gehen

dieses Reisebuch lesen

alte Freunde besuchen

Herr Päsler

Ihren Hut nicht vergessen

einen Regenschirm (*umbrella*) tragen

in die Stadt fahren

Herr und Frau Päsler

diesen Bus nehmen

langsamer sprechen

diesen Wein probieren

morgen ein Picknick machen

Wir

ins Kino gehen

aufs Land (*countryside*) fahren

im Gebirge wandern

Now add five suggestions (imperatives) of your own.

Negation — nicht comes at end except when gern, location or specific items are stressed. kein when negating

Negation is usually expressed by the adverb **nicht** or the adjective **kein.** ein or definite nouns

Nicht + Predicate Adjectives or Nouns

Adjectives or nouns following the verbs **sein** or **werden** are called predicate adjectives or nouns. In negation, **nicht** directly precedes these predicate adjectives or nouns.

Es wird heute *warm.*   Es wird heute *nicht warm.*

Das ist *Frau Dießner.*   Das ist *nicht Frau Dießner.*

Object Nouns or Adverbs of Time + *nicht*

In negation **nicht** usually follows object nouns and adverbs of time.

Wir kennen *den Ausländer nicht.*   (object noun: *Ausländer*)

Ich fahre *heute nicht* in die Stadt.   (adverb of time: *heute*)

However, **nicht** usually precedes other adverbs and prepositions.

Ich gehe *nicht zu fuß* in die Stadt.

Das mache ich *nicht gern.*

Wir fliegen *nicht nach* Frankfurt.

Sie übernachten *nicht in* Köln.

Nicht may precede almost any word for emphasis.

Ich habe *nicht viele* Bücher.
I don't have many books (I have some, but not many).

Kein

The negative form of **ein** is **kein** (*no, not a, not any*).

Das ist ein Auto.	Das ist *kein* Auto.
Marianne hat ein Fahrrad.	Marianne hat *kein* Fahrrad.

Kein is also normally used when there is no other **ein-** or **der-**word preceding the noun.*

Marie trinkt Bier.	Marie trinkt *kein* Bier.
Das sind Landkarten.	Das sind *keine* Landkarten, sondern Fahrpläne.

Doch!

Doch is used as an affirmative answer to a negative question.

Fährst du nicht nach Hause?—*Doch*, ich fahre nach Hause.

Ist das keine gute Antwort?—*Doch*, das ist eine gute Antwort.

Negative statements are also made affirmative by the adverb **doch.** Compare these sentences:

Herr Smith, sind Sie Engländer?—Nein, ich bin Amerikaner.

Herr Smith, Sie sind kein Amerikaner.—*Doch!* (Yes I am!)

Nicht wahr?

Nicht wahr? can be added to the end of a statement to form a question. In conversation, **nicht wahr?** is often reduced to **nicht?**

Sie ist sehr vorsichtig, *nicht wahr?*

Wir sind fertig, *nicht (wahr)?*

---

*Kein is an **ein**-word; **ein**-words and **der**-words are discussed in Chapter 4. Adjective endings used with **kein** are discussed in Chapter 8.

Übungen

°A. **Verneinen Sie die folgenden Sätze!**

Zum Beispiel: München liegt im Norden.
München liegt nicht im Norden.

1. Wir besuchen unsere Freunde.
2. Herr und Frau Krause fahren morgen in Urlaub.
3. Ich kenne die Schweiz gut.
4. Das ist Herr Unger.
5. Im Süden wird es jetzt wärmer.

Zum Beispiel: Ich habe einen Koffer.
Ich habe keinen Koffer.

1. Daniel, warum trinkst du Bier?
2. Wir haben Ferien.
3. Bruno kauft Fahrkarten.
4. Das ist ein Tourist.
5. Ich habe ein Fahrrad.

Zum Beispiel: Liegt Berlin im Süden?   Lernen Sie nicht Deutsch?
Nein, Berlin liegt nicht im Süden.   Doch, ich lerne Deutsch.

1. Liegt Frankreich östlich von Deutschland?
2. Liegt Italien nicht südlich von Deutschland?
3. Besuchen nicht viele Deutsche Österreich?
4. Sind Sie keine Studenten?
5. Fliegt Lufthansa nicht nach Deutschland?

B. **Bilden Sie Fragen mit *nicht wahr*!** Reformulate the following false statements as questions using **nicht wahr?** A classmate should answer each question with **nein**, **nicht** (or **kein**), and the conjunction **sondern**.

Zum Beispiel: Dresden liegt in Westdeutschland.
Dresden liegt in Westdeutschland, nicht wahr? Nein, es liegt nicht in Westdeutschland, sondern in Ostdeutschland.

1. Der Eiffelturm steht in Bonn.
2. Die Alpen sind im Norden.
3. Beim Oktoberfest trinkt man viel Milch.
4. Österreich liegt westlich von Deutschland.
5. Die Fahrkarten kaufen wir im Restaurant.

C. **Übersetzen Sie die folgenden Sätze!**

1. I don't have a ticket.
2. Isn't Gabi going to Switzerland?
3. That is not a travel agency, but, on the contrary, a bank.
4. That is not our luggage. Yes (it is)!
5. It is not getting cold today.
6. Salzburg is in Austria, isn't it?

D. **Sie werden von Johnny Carson interviewt!** You have become a celebrity over-night and are invited to appear on *The Tonight Show*. The host asks you many questions, but since you are now a celebrity and don't feel like being cooperative, you answer in the negative.

Zum Beispiel: Fahren Sie oft ins Ausland?
Nein, ich fahre nicht oft ins Ausland.

1. Reisen Sie oft in Amerika?
2. Sie sind wohl kein Amerikaner (keine Amerikanerin), nicht wahr?
3. Haben Sie viele interessante Freunde?
4. Werden Sie gern interviewt?
5. Haben Sie einen guten Rat für die Leute im Studio?
6. Sind Sie immer so negativ?

Rückblick

Zur Wiederholung (Review). **Übersetzen Sie die folgenden Sätze!**

1. Rita, why don't you have any luggage?
2. Ursula and Thomas, answer Miss Preller.
3. Mr. Schirmer, let's not change the plan.
4. Does it rain often in Hamburg?
5. Max, you sleep too long. Don't sleep so long!
6. Does Miss Sperber work in a (**in einem**) travel agency or does she work in a (**in einem**) hotel?
7. Karin is staying home because she is waiting for (**auf**) Sigi.
8. We have been hiking for three hours.
9. Joachim says Brigitte does not come from (**aus**) Trier.
10. Max, let's take the bus!

2
In historischer Sicht

Das Rolandstandbild, Symbol der freien Stadt Bremen

Tenses Denoting Past Time: Weak Verbs

Tenses Denoting Past Time: Strong Verbs

The Auxiliary *sein*

The Past Perfect Tense

Wortschatz

die **Burg** (-en) fortress

die **Epoche** (-n) epoch

die **Geschichte** (-n) story; history

der **Kaiser** (-), die **Kaiserin** (-nen) emperor, empress

der **König** (-e), die **Königin** (-nen) king, queen

der **Krieg** (-e) war

das **Märchen** (-) fairy tale

das **Mittelalter** Middle Ages

das **Reich** (-e) kingdom, empire, realm

der **Ritter** (-) knight

die **Ruine** (-n) ruin

das **Schloß** (¨sser) castle

der **Thron** (-e) throne

das **Zeitalter** (-) age

---

bauen to build

dauern to last

enden to end

entdecken to discover

erkennen to recognize

errichten to erect, build

erzählen to tell

geschehen to happen

gewinnen to win

gründen to found

kämpfen to fight

zerstören to destroy

---

bekannt well-known

beliebt popular

berühmt famous

sehenswert worth seeing

---

bisher until now

damals then, at that time

eine Rolle spielen to play a role

inzwischen in the meantime

lange for a long time

zu Ende gehen to come to an end

A. *Match each noun with a verb that you would logically associate with it.*

1. Burg
2. Reich
3. Märchen
4. Preis
5. Filmstar

a. erkennen
b. erzählen
c. gründen
d. bauen
e. gewinnen

B. *Substitute another word with a similar meaning for the one in italics in the following sentences.*

1. Friedrich der Große war König von Preußen; er is heute noch sehr *berühmt*. *bekannt*
2. Der *König* ist beliebt im Land. *Kaiser*
3. *Das Schloß* steht am Rhein. *Die Burg*
4. Der Ritter *errichtet* eine Burg in den Alpen. *baut*
5. Kolumbus *findet* Amerika. *entdeckt*
6. *Das Zeitalter* des Computers ist hier. *Reich*
7. Die Party *geht* um Mitternacht *zu Ende*. *ist* *endet*

C. *Match each question or statement on the left with the most logical response on the right.*

h 1. Jetzt gehen wir noch auf die Burgruine, Kinder!

e 2. Prinzessin Diana ist eine gute Freundin von mir.

d 3. Was haben die Ritter denn den ganzen Tag gemacht, Vati?

g 4. Wie lange dauerte der Dreißigjährige Krieg?

b 5. Haben Sie inzwischen entdeckt, warum die Königin immer so traurig ist, Frau Doktor?

c 6. Wie konnte das geschehen? Sagen Sie mir das, Müller!

a. Das waren damals die Probleme des Mittelalters.

b. Nein, bisher leider nocht nicht.

c. Das ist eine lange Geschichte, Herr Major.

d. Die saßen auf der Burg oder kämpften für den König.

e. Erzähl' mir doch keine Märchen, Inge.

f. Ja, der ist sehr sehenswert.

g. Mann, das weiß ich auch nicht.

h. Um Gottes willen, uns tun ja jetzt schon die Füße weh.

D. *Complete the sentences.*

1. Die Kaiserin ist sehr wichtig; sie *baute* eine wichtige *Burg*.

2. Normale Menschen sitzen auf einem Stuhl, aber ein König sitzt auf einem *Thron*.

3. Der Tornado *zerstört* viele Häuser.

4. Niemand hat den König gern, aber die Königin ist sehr _beliebt_.

5. Meine Damen und Herren, wir sind hier im Land des Märchens, im _Zeitalter_ der Fantasie.

6. Ich weiß nur sehr wenig über das Mittelalter. Leider habe ich nie _darüber_ studiert.

Tenses Denoting Past Time: Weak Verbs*

There are three basic tenses denoting past time in German: the past tense, the present perfect tense, and the past perfect tense.

Past:	Die Königin liebte den König.
Present Perfect:	Die Königin hat den König geliebt.
Past Perfect:	Die Königin hatte den König geliebt.

The most common of the three tenses in conversational German is the present perfect; the most common in formal German (speeches and all writing except personal letters) is the past tense. The past perfect will be discussed in the last section of this chapter.

The Principal Parts of the Verb

In German as in English there are three principal parts to all verbs: the infinitive, the past stem, and the past participle. They are called principal parts because all other verb forms are based on them. The present tense is formed from the stem of the infinitive, as you saw in Chapter 1. The past tense is formed from the second principal part, the past stem. The third principal part, the past participle, is used in combination with auxiliary verbs to form other tenses denoting past time. The principal parts of the weak verb **lieben**, for example, are:

Infinitive	*Past Stem*	*Past Participle*
lieben	liebte	geliebt

The Past Tense of Weak Verbs

The past stem of weak verbs is formed by adding **-te** to the stem of the infinitive.

---

*There are three classes of verbs in German: weak, strong, and modal. Modal verbs are discussed in Chapter 5.

---

dauern	to last	dauerte	
suchen	to look for	suchte	
bemerken	to notice	bemerkte	
studieren	to study	studierte	
zerstören	to destroy	zerstörte	

The conjugation of the verb **lieben** illustrates the past-tense endings of weak verbs:

lieben

ich liebte	wir liebten
du liebtest	ihr liebtet
er ⎫	sie ⎫
sie ⎬ liebte	Sie ⎬ liebten
es ⎭	

Notice that the first- and third-person singular lack endings and are identical. If the stem ends in **-d** or **-t** (**gründen**, **errichten**) or **-m** or **-n** preceded by a consonant (**atmen**, **regnen**), **-ete** rather than **-te** is added to form the past stem. The **e** facilitates pronunciation.

Infinitive		*Past Stem*
gründen	to found	gründete
errichten	to erect	errichtete
atmen	to breathe	atmete
regnen	to rain	regnete

This rule does not apply to stems ending in **-m** or **-n** preceded by **l** or **r**:

filmen	to film	filmte
lernen	to learn	lernte

A few weak verbs (so-called "irregular weak" or "mixed" verbs) show a change of stem vowel from **e** (or **i**) in the infinitive to **a** in the past stem:

brennen	to burn	brannte
kennen	to know	kannte
nennen	to name	nannte
rennen	to run, to race	rannte
senden	to send	sandte
wenden	to turn	wandte

Two of these verbs show more extensive changes in the stem:*

bringen	to bring	brachte
denken	to think	dachte

Haben has an irregular past stem: **hatte**.

---

*The irregular weak verb **wissen** (past stem **wußte**) is discussed in Chapter 5.

The Past Participle of Weak Verbs

The past participle of weak verbs is formed by adding **-t** (or **-et** to facilitate pronunciation) to the infinitive stem. If the first vowel is accented, the prefix **ge-** is added; otherwise, it is not.

First Vowel of Stem Is Accented		First Vowel of Stem Is Not Accented	
Infinitive	*Past Participle*	*Infinitive*	*Past Participle*
átmen	geatmet	erríchten	errichtet
dáuern	gedauert	reparíeren	repariert
grúnden	gegründet	studíeren	studiert
lérnen	gelernt	zerstóren	zerstört

The following types of verbs lack the **ge-** prefix in the past participle (since the accent is not on the first syllable):

1. verbs that end in **-ieren** (**studieren**, for example)

2. verbs with inseparable prefixes (**be-**, **ent-**, **er-**, **ge-**, **miß-**, **ver-**, **zer-**: **errichten** or **zerstören**, for example)

The verbs **bringen**, **denken**, and those like **brennen** have the same stem changes in the past stem and the past participle.

Infinitive	*Past Stem*	*Past Participle*
bringen	brachte	gebracht
denken	dachte	gedacht
erkennen	erkannte	erkannt

The Present Perfect Tense of Weak Verbs

The present perfect tense of most weak verbs is formed with the present tense of the auxiliary verb **haben** together with the past participle. (Verbs that form their perfect tenses with **sein** are discussed on pages 47–49 of this chapter).

bauen
to build

ich habe gebaut	wir haben gebaut
du hast gebaut	ihr habt gebaut
er ⎫	sie ⎫
sie ⎬ hat gebaut	Sie ⎬ haben gebaut
es ⎭	

Word Order with the Past Tense and the Present Perfect Tense

As you saw in Chapter 1, the finite verb is the second element in normal and inverted word order.* Notice how the rule applies to the past and the present perfect tenses:

Normal Word Order

	Subject (1)	Finite Verb (2)	Other Element (3)	Past Participle (4)
Past	Die Königin	liebte	den König.	
Present Perfect	Die Königin	hat	den König	geliebt.

Inverted Word Order

	Other Element (1)	Finite Verb (2)	Subject (3)	Past Participle (4)
Past	Den König	liebte	die Königin.	
Present Perfect	Den König	hat	die Königin	geliebt.

Notice that the past participle is the last element in normal and inverted word order.

Transposed Word Order

Just as in the present tense, the finite verb is the last element in transposed word order (word order in subordinate clauses):

Main Clause	Subordinate Clause			
	Subordinating Conjunction		Past Participle	Finite Verb
Man sagt,	daß	die Königin den König		liebte. (past)
	daß	die Königin den König	geliebt	hat. (present perfect)

Notice that the past participle directly precedes the finite verb in transposed word order.

---

*Remember that the finite verb is the form of the verb that changes to indicate person: **wir liebten, du liebtest**.

Word Order in Questions

Just as in the present tense, the finite verb precedes the subject in questions:

	Question Word	Finite Verb	Subject
Past		Liebte	die Königin den König?
	Warum	liebte	die Königin den König?
Present Perfect		Hat	die Königin den König geliebt?
	Warum	hat	die Königin den König geliebt?

Use of the Past Tense and the Present Perfect Tense

The German past tense and the present perfect tense have basically the same meaning. They describe any action or situation completely finished in the past.

Man baute ein Schloß. *(past)*
Man hat ein Schloß gebaut. *(present perfect)*

They built a castle
They were building a castle.
They did build a castle.

However, the present perfect tense in German is generally used to translate the present perfect in English.

Man hat das Schloß schon gebaut.
They have already built the castle.

The past tense is the tense most frequently encountered in literature. It is the narrative or "story-telling" tense.

Als die Historikerin nach zehn Jahren in ihre Heimat zurückkehrte, begegnete sie ihrem alten Lehrer auf der Straße.* Der Alte *erkannte* sie aber nicht mehr.
When the historian returned to her homeland after ten years, she met her old teacher on the street. However, the elderly man didn't recognize her anymore.

The present perfect tense is the tense most frequently used in conversation or in personal letters to express past time.

Was *hast* du gestern *gekauft?*—Ich *habe* mir eine neue Schallplatte *gekauft*.
What did you buy yesterday?—I bought a new record.

---

*Notice the difference between **als** (*when*) and **wenn** (*when, whenever*) used to begin subordinate clauses in the past tense. **Als** is the more common form; **wenn** is used only for repeated events. **Als ich letztes Jahr in Deutschland war, besuchte ich meine Freunde.** *When I was in Germany last year, I visited my friends.* **Jedesmal, wenn ich in Deutschland war, besuchte ich meine Freunde.** *Every time I was in Germany I visited my friends.*

Modal verbs (such as **konnte, wollte, mußte**) and the strong verb **sein** (discussed in the next section) are more commonly used in the past tense in both conversation *and* literature.

> Was hast du gestern gemacht?—Ich *wollte* ins Kino gehen, aber ich habe kein Geld gehabt.
>
> What did you do yesterday?—I wanted to go to the movies, but I didn't have any money.

> Wo *warst* du heute morgen?—Ich *mußte* zu Hause bleiben, weil ich krank *war*.
>
> Where were you this morning?—I had to stay at home because I was sick.

Übungen

°A. **Ersetzen Sie die Pronomen!** Replace the pronouns in italics with the pronouns in parentheses and change the verbs accordingly.

Zum Beispiel: *Sie spielten* im Mittelalter eine große Rolle. (es)
Es spielte im Mittelalter eine große Rolle.

1. Hattest *du* heute früh keinen Hunger? (sie *sing.*, ihr, Sie)
2. *Er* liebte den Kaiser. (ihr, ich, wir)
3. Warum brachte *sie* die Ritter nicht auf die Burg? (du, ihr, er)
4. *Ich* öffnete alle Fenster im Haus. (wir, sie *sing.*, sie *pl.*)
5. Wann gründete *er* das Reich? (sie *pl.*, ihr, man)
6. Damals bauten *sie* ein Schloß für den Kaiser. (ich, wir, man)

°B. **Geben Sie die folgenden Sätze im Perfekt!** Change the following sentences from the present to the present perfect tense. Remember to place the past participle at the end of the clause.

Zum Beispiel: Das dauert aber lange!
Das hat aber lange gedauert!

1. Man errichtet eine Burg auf diesem Berg.
2. Regnet es hier wirklich jeden Tag im Winter?
3. Warum ändert Herr Schmeling den Plan nicht?
4. Wann endet dieser Krieg endlich?
5. Ingrid hört solche Geschichten gern.

C. **Geben Sie die folgenden Sätze im Perfekt!** Change the following sentences from the past to the present perfect tense. Remember to place the past participle in its proper position.

Zum Beispiel: Wir erkannten das alte Dorf.
Wir haben das alte Dorf erkannt.

1. Warum antwortete Monika Walter nicht?
2. Warum beantwortetest du die Frage nicht?
3. Wer baute diese alte Burg?

4. Cornelia dachte an ihre Freundinnen. *Cornelia hat ... gedacht.*
5. Erzählte der Vater immer solche Märchen? *Hat der ... erzählt.*
6. Weißt du, wann man den Eiffelturm errichtete?
hast du gewußt ...... errichtet hatte.

D. **Verbinden Sie die beiden Sätze mit der gegebenen Konjunktion!** Join the two sentences with the indicated conjunction and change the position of the verb if necessary.

    Zum Beispiel: Der Professor sagt. Die Ritter hatten kein leichtes Leben. (daß)
        Der Professor sagt, daß die Ritter kein leichtes Leben hatten.

1. Man kämpfte viel. Die Ritter lebten auf den Burgen. (als)
2. Dieter fragte. Das Leben des Volkes war im Mittelalter sehr hart. (warum)
3. Die Touristen reisten in sieben Tagen durch Europa. Sie hatten nicht viel Zeit. (weil)
4. Wir fragten den Professor. Das Volk hatte im Mittelalter genug zu essen. (ob)
5. Friedrich der Große hatte ein bekanntes Schloß. König Ludwig von Bayern hatte ein berühmtes Schloß. (aber)
6. Barbara fragte den Professor. Diese Epoche hat geendet. (wann)
7. Hat es gestern geregnet? Hat es geschneit? (oder)

E. **Bilden Sie Sätze zuerst im Imperfekt und dann im Perfekt!** Compose sentences first in the past tense, then in the present perfect tense, using the following words and phrases.

    Zum Beispiel: ich / erzählen / ein bekanntes Märchen
        Ich erzählte ein bekanntes Märchen.
        Ich habe ein bekanntes Märchen erzählt.

1. Petra / studieren / Geschichte
2. ich glaube, daß / es / viel regnen / im Winter
3. erkennen / ihr / die Ruine dort?
4. bringen / Klaus / den Gast nach Hause?
5. die Studenten fragten, ob / die Ritter / eine große Rolle spielen / im Mittelalter
6. denken / du / an deine alten Freunde?

F. **Übersetzen Sie die folgenden Sätze!** Translate each sentence first in the past tense and then in the present perfect.

1. Where did Jürgen study history?
2. Claudia, did you recognize the queen?
3. That king didn't live long.
4. How long did the Middle Ages last?
5. Our parents told us many fairy tales.
6. I believe that the Romans (**Römer**) erected this fortress.
7. The knights destroyed that castle.

G. **In meiner Kindheit . . .** Write a paragraph about your own past, mentioning things you liked to do or often did as a child. You might want to use some of the following expressions:

etwas mit Bausteinen bauen   *to building something with blocks*

Sandburgen am Strand bauen (zerstören) *to build (destroy) sand castles at the beach*

meine Freunde (Freundinnen) besuchen *to visit my friends*

mit Buntstiften (an die Wand) malen *to color with crayons (on the wall)*

mit einem Teddybären (einem Puppenhaus, mit Puppen, mit einer Spielzeugeisenbahn, mit Spielzeugautos, mit Legespielen) spielen *to play with a teddy bear (a doll house, dolls, a toy train, toy cars, puzzles)*

Insekten (Schmetterlinge, Ameisen, Bienen) suchen *to look for insects (butterflies, ants, bees)*

die Eltern früh morgens wecken *to wake up my parents early in the morning*

Zum Beispiel: In meiner Kindheit spielte ich gern mit Spielzeugautos.

H. **Was hast du als Kind gemacht?** Interview another student in class about what he or she did or liked to do as a child. Use the present perfect tense for both questions and answers.

Zum Beispiel: Hast du gern Ball gespielt?
Nein, aber ich habe gern mit Puppen gespielt.

Schloß Gymnich, Westfalen

Tenses Denoting Past Time: Strong Verbs

The Past Tense

Strong verbs are verbs that form the past stem by a change in stem vowel; the suffix **-te** is not added. Although strong verbs are among the most commonly used verbs in German, their number is very limited. Here are examples of strong verbs:

Infinitive		Past Stem
beginnen	*to begin*	begann
erfahren	*to experience; to learn*	erfuhr
schlagen	*to hit*	schlug
singen	*to sing*	sang
sprechen	*to speak*	sprach
vergeben	*to forgive*	vergab
vergessen	*to forget*	vergaß

The conjugation of the verb **singen** illustrates the past-tense endings of strong verbs:

singen

ich sang	wir sangen
du sangst	ihr sangt
er	sie
sie } sang	Sie } sangen
es	

Notice that the first- and third-persons singular lack endings and are identical. If the past stem ends in **-d, -t** or an / s / sound, the endings **-est** and **-et** rather than **-st** and **-t** are added to the stem:

Infinitive	Past Stem	Second-person Familiar
finden	fand	du fand**est**
lesen	las	du las**est**; ihr las**et**

The past stem of **werden**, *to become,* ends in **-e**: **wurde**. This final **-e** remains throughout the past tense:

werden

ich wurde	wir wurden
du wurdest	ihr wurdet
er	sie
sie } wurde	Sie } wurden
es	

The Past Participle

The past participle of strong verbs is formed by: (1) adding the suffix **-en** to the stem of the infinitive (which usually shows a change in vowel) and (2) adding the prefix **ge-** *if the first vowel is accented.*

First Vowel of Stem Is Accented		First Vowel of Stem Is Not Accented	
Infinitive	*Past Participle*	*Infinitive*	*Past Participle*
schlágen	geschlagen	begínnen	begonnen
síngen	gesungen	erfáhren	erfahren
spréchen	gesprochen	vergében	vergeben

Strong Verb Classes

Strong verbs are classified according to common vowel-change patterns in the principal parts. The following are the most common strong verbs; a complete alphabetical listing is in the appendix.*

Class 1

Infinitive **ei**	*Past Stem* **i(e)**	*Past Participle* **i(e)**
beißen *to bite*	bīß[†]	gebissen
bleiben *to remain*	blieb	(ist) geblieben
leiden *to suffer*	litt	gelitten
schneiden *to cut*	schnitt	geschnitten
schreiben *to write*	schrieb	geschrieben
steigen *to climb*	stieg	(ist) gestiegen
treiben *to drive (cattle, e.g.)*	trieb	getrieben

Class 2

Infinitive **ie**	*Past Stem* **o**	*Past Participle* **o**
bieten *to offer*	bot	geboten
fliegen *to fly*	flog	(ist) geflogen
schließen *to shut*	schlōß	geschlossen
verlieren *to lose*	verlor	verloren
ziehen *to pull*	**zog**	gezogen

---

*Repeating these verbs in a rhythmic pattern may be helpful in learning them.

[†]In these lists the length of the vowel has been indicated in cases where it cannot be determined from the spelling—for example, **bīß** from **beißen**. Other irregularities have been indicated by use of boldface type. If the verb uses the auxiliary **sein** in the perfect tenses, the form **ist** is included with the past participle; this is discussed in the next section.

Class 3

Infinitive **i**	Past Stem **a**	Past Participle **u** or **o**
beginnen *to begin*	begann	begonnen
finden *to find*	fand	gefunden
gewinnen *to win*	gewann	gewonnen
schwimmen *to swim*	schwamm	(ist) geschwommen
singen *to sing*	sang	gesungen
trinken *to drink*	trank	getrunken
verschwinden *to disappear*	verschwand	(ist) verschwunden

Class 4

Infinitive **e**	Past Stem **a**	Past Participle **o**
brěchen *to break*	bräch	gebröchen
empfehlen *to recommend*	empfahl	empfohlen
helfen *to help*	half	geholfen
kommen *to come*	ka**m**	(ist) gekommen
nehmen *to take*	nahm	geno**mm**en
sprěchen *to speak*	spräch	gesprǒchen
sterben *to die*	starb	(ist) gestorben
treffen *to meet; to hit*	traf	getroffen
werden *to become*	wur**de**	(ist) geworden

Class 5

Infinitive **e**	Past Stem **a**	Past Participle **e**
bitten *to request*	bat	gebeten
essen *to eat*	äß	gegessen
geben *to give*	gab	gegeben
geschehen *to happen*	geschah	(ist) geschehen
lesen *to read*	las	gelesen
liegen *to lie, recline*	lag	gelegen
sehen *to see*	sah	gesehen
sein *to be*	war	(ist) gewesen
sitzen *to sit*	säß	gesessen
vergessen *to forget*	vergäß	vergessen

Class 6

| Infinitive | Past Stem | Past Participle |
a	u	a
einladen *to invite*	lud . . . ein	eingeladen
fahren *to drive, ride*	fuhr	(ist) gefahren
schlagen *to strike*	schlug	geschlagen
tragen *to carry*	trug	getragen

*Class 7**

| Infinitive | Past Stem | Past Participle |
-	i (e)	-
fallen *to fall*	fiel	(ist) gefallen
gehen *to go*	ging	(ist) gegangen
halten *to hold*	hielt	gehalten
lassen *to let*	ließ	gelassen
laufen *to run*	lief	(ist) gelaufen
raten *to advise*	riet	geraten
rufen *to call*	rief	gerufen
schlafen *to sleep*	schlief	geschlafen

Other

Infinitive	Past Stem	Past Participle
stehen *to stand*	stand	gestanden
tun *to do*	tat	getan

past perfect

The Present Perfect Tense

The present perfect tense of most strong verbs is formed with the present tense of **haben** together with the past participle:[†]

singen

ich habe gesungen	wir haben gesungen
du hast gesungen	ihr habt gesungen
er ⎱	sie ⎱
sie ⎬ hat gesungen	Sie ⎰ haben gesungen
es ⎰	

---

*Class 7 verbs always have the vowel **i** or **ie** in the past stem. But the vowel of the past participle is the same as that of the infinitive.

[†]The use of the auxiliary **sein** in the perfect tenses is discussed in the next section.

Verbs That Have Similar Forms

The following pairs of verbs have similar forms, but very different meanings! These verbs have to be studied carefully:

1. bieten / bot / geboten   *to offer*
   bitten / bat / gebeten   *to request*

2. danken / dankte / gedankt   *to thank*
   denken / dachte / gedacht   *to think*

3. brechen / brach / gebrochen   *to break*
   bringen / brachte / gebracht   *to bring*

4. kennen / kannte / gekannt   *to know, be familiar with*
   können / konnte / gekonnt   *to be able, can*

5. legen / legte / gelegt   *to lay*
   liegen / lag / gelegen   *to lie, recline*

6. setzen / setzte / gesetzt   *to set*
   sitzen / saß / gesessen   *to sit*

7. lassen / ließ / gelassen   *to let; to leave (something behind)*
   lesen / las / gelesen   *to read*

8. fahren / fuhr / ist gefahren   *to drive*
   führen / führte / geführt   *to lead*

9. lernen / lernte / gelernt   *to learn*
   lehren / lehrte / gelehrt   *to teach*

10. ziehen / zog / gezogen   *to pull*
    zeigen / zeigte / gezeigt   *to show*

Ein Schritt weiter _____

There are many pairs of verbs like **sitzen** (*to sit*) and **setzen** (*to set*) or **liegen** (*to lie*) and **legen** (*to lay*):

Das Kind *sitzt* auf dem Stuhl.
Ich *setze* das Kind auf den Stuhl.

Das Kind *liegt* auf dem Bett.
Ich *lege* das Kind auf das Bett.

The first verb of these pairs is strong and intransitive—it cannot take a direct object. The second is weak and transitive—it requires a direct object. The weak verbs in such pairs are called "causatives."

Übungen

°A. **Ersetzen Sie die Pronomen!** Replace the italicized pronouns and change the verbs accordingly.

1. *Ich* sang für die Königin. (er, sie *pl.*, du)
2. Sah *er* die Gutenberg-Bibel? (du, ihr, Sie)
3. *Er* verlor den Krieg. (wir, ihr, sie *pl.*)
4. *Sie* trank ein Glas Bier. (ich, sie *pl.*, man)
5. Sprachst *du* über das Mittelalter? (er, ihr, Sie)
6. Wann bat *er* den Ritter um Hilfe? (ihr, du, Sie)
7. Fand *sie* die Ruine interessant? (du, ihr, Sie)
8. Lange stand *er* vor dem Schloß. (ich, ihr, sie *pl.*)

°B. **Geben Sie die folgenden Sätze im Perfekt** (*present perfect tense*)!

Zum Beispiel: Der Kaiser verlor den Krieg.
Der Kaiser hat den Krieg verloren.

1. Wohin zog das Pferd den Wagen?
2. Hermann trank ein Glas Wein.
3. Sprach Roberta nicht Deutsch?
4. Ich weiß nicht, warum der Kaiser uns um Hilfe bat.
5. Axel und Klara, schlosset ihr die Fenster im Haus?
6. Inzwischen fand man die Ruine.
7. Ich traf Julia, Bernadette und Ludwig auf der Burg.

°C. **Geben Sie die folgenden Sätze zuerst im Imperfekt** (*past tense*) **und dann im Perfekt** (*present perfect tense*)!

Zum Beispiel: Tom spricht nicht Deutsch.
Tom sprach nicht Deutsch.
Tom hat nicht Deutsch gesprochen.

1. Ich liege lange im Bett.
2. Lotte, schneidest du das Brot?
3. Wir verlieren viel Zeit.
4. Gewinnt ihr das Spiel?
5. Heidi singt viele Volkslieder.
6. Wir trinken gern Wein.
7. Nimmt Kurt immer den Bus?

D. **Bilden Sie Sätze!** Compose sentences first in the past tense, then in the present perfect tense, using the following words and phrases.

1. wann / dieser Film / beginnen?
2. Martin und Michael / sitzen / in diesem Restaurant
3. ich glaube, daß Hildegard und Peter / treffen / Marie und Karl im Schloß
4. Helmut / tragen / einen Hut, weil es / regnen / stark
5. leider / ich / lassen / meine Jacke zu Hause
6. du / schlafen / je in einem Schloß?

E. **Ein Märchen aus alten Zeiten.** Complete this fairy tale with the proper past-tense forms of the verbs in parentheses.

Eines Tages _gingen_ (gehen) ein junges Mädchen mit ihrem kleinen Bruder spazieren. Am Mittag _saßen_ (sitzen) sie auf dem Gras und _aßen_ (essen) alles, was die Mutter für sie eingepackt hatte. Das Mädchen _sang_ (singen) ein Lied, während ihr kleiner Bruder hinter ihr _spielte_ (spielen). Auf einmal (*suddenly*) _bemerkte_ (bemerken) die Schwester, daß ihr Brüderchen nicht mehr hinter ihr _____ (sein). Da _____ (rufen) die Schwester ihren Bruder. Als sie seine Antwort _____ (hören), _____ (laufen) sie zu ihm. Doch nun _____ (finden) die armen Kinder den Weg zurück nicht mehr. Der kleine Junge _____ (beginnen) bitterlich zu weinen. Da _____ (sehen) die armen Kinder etwas zu ihren Füßen: da _____ (sitzen) eine hungrige Maus. Das Mädchen _____ (nehmen) etwas Brot aus der Tasche und _____ (geben) es der Maus zu fressen. Bald _____ (kommen) die Nacht, und die müden Kinder _____ (schlafen) schnell ein. Auf einmal _____ (sehen) sie einen Ritter vor sich auf einem Pferd. Er _____ (sprechen) zu ihnen: „Kommt mit mir! Ich bringe euch nach Hause." Der Ritter _____ (tragen) die glücklichen Kinder zurück zu ihrem Haus, wo die Eltern sie schon _____ (suchen). Da _____

(rennen) die Kinder zu Vater und Mutter. Die Kinder _____ (erzählen) den

Eltern von dem Ritter, und die Eltern wollten ihm danken. Aber er _____ (sein)

nicht mehr da. Statt des Ritters _____ (finden) sie nur eine kleine Maus, die

im Gebüsch _____ (verschwinden).

F. **Übersetzen Sie die folgenden Sätze!**

1. In the meantime the knight found the children. (past tense)
2. When did you recognize the girl? (past tense)
3. Did the queen lose the castle? (present perfect)
4. He became emperor. (past tense)
5. They won the war. (present perfect)

G. **Ein berühmter Ort.** Tell about a place you have visited that is of historical interest or importance, in this country or abroad. You may want to include answers to some of the following questions.

1. Wann haben Sie diesen historischen Ort zum ersten Mal gesehen?
2. Haben Sie ihn interessant gefunden?
3. Haben Sie dort ein Souvenir gekauft?
4. Haben Sie etwas über diesen Ort gelesen oder in der Schule gehört?
5. Warum ist der Ort bekannt? Was hat man dort gemacht?

The Auxiliary *sein*

We have seen that most verbs—weak and strong—take the auxiliary **haben** in the present perfect tense. However, some verbs take the auxiliary **sein.** Verbs that take the auxiliary **sein** have two characteristics:

1. they are intransitive (they do not take a direct accusative object)

2. they express either a change of place (for example, **gehen**, *to go*) or a change of condition (for example, **sterben**, *to die*)

   Elke *ist* in das Schloß gegangen.
   Elke went into the castle.

   Der König *ist* gestern gestorben.
   The king died yesterday.

The verbs **bleiben** and **sein** are exceptions to the rule; although they do not express a change of place or condition, they take the auxiliary verb **sein.**

Werner *ist* zu Hause geblieben.
Werner stayed home.

Helena *ist* nie in einem Schloß gewesen.
Helena has never been in a castle.

Students of German often mistakenly use the auxiliary **sein** with the verbs **liegen**, **sitzen**, and **stehen**. But since these verbs do not express a change of place, they require the auxiliary **haben** in standard German.

Irmgard *hat* lange wegen ihrer Krankheit im Bett gelegen.
Irmgard lay in bed for a long time because of her illness.

Wir *haben* neben unseren Freunden gesessen.
We were sitting by our friends.

Der Ritter *hat* lange vor dem Thron gestanden.
The knight stood for a long time before the throne.

But:

Wir *sind* um neun Uhr aufgestanden.
We got up at nine o'clock.

The verbs **folgen** and **begegnen** take the auxiliary **sein** because these verbs take dative objects, not accusative objects.

Die Kinder *sind* dem Ritter gefolgt. (dative object)
The children followed the knight.

Hans *ist* seiner Freundin in der Stadt begegnet. (dative object)
Hans met his girlfriend downtown.

Some verbs expressing a change of place or condition can be used with or without a direct object. With an object, they take **haben** in the perfect tenses, but without an object they take **sein**. These verbs include:

brechen   *to break*
fahren   *to drive*
laufen   *to walk; to run*

trocknen   *to dry*
verderben   *to ruin*
zerbrechen   *to smash, to break*

With Direct Object	*Without Direct Object*
Der Junge *hat* den Arm gebrochen.	Sein Arm *ist* beim Turnen gebrochen.
The boy broke his arm.	His arm broke during gymnastics exercises.
Rolf *hat* das Auto gefahren.	Rolf *ist* nach München gefahren.
Rolf drove the car.	Rolf drove to Munich
Wolf *hat* die Meile in fünf Minuten gelaufen.	Yvonne *ist* sehr schnell gelaufen.
Wolf ran the mile in five minutes.	Yvonne ran very quickly.

Ulrich *hat* seine Wäsche getrocknet.	Die Wäsche *ist* draußen getrocknet.
Ulrich dried his wash.	The wash dried outside.
Die Hitze *hat* das Essen verdorben.	Das Essen *ist* bei der Hitze verdorben.
The heat ruined the food.	The food spoiled in the heat.
Das Kind *hat* den Teller zerbrochen.	Der Teller *ist* bei der Party zerbrochen.
The child broke the plate.	The plate broke during the party.

The verb **ziehen** means *to pull* when used with a direct object but *to move* when used without a direct object:

Die Pferde *haben* den Wagen gezogen.	Veronika *ist* nach Berlin gezogen.
The horses pulled the wagon.	Veronika moved to Berlin.

Study hint: The rules just given are useful in determining whether to use **haben** or **sein** in the perfect tenses; however, a more practical approach is to memorize **ist** together with the past participles of those verbs that require the auxiliary verb **sein: gehen, ging,** *ist* **gegangen.** Sometimes the addition of a prefix causes a change in auxiliary: **hat gestanden, ist aufgestanden; hat geschlafen** (*slept*), **ist eingeschlafen** (*fell asleep*).

Übungen

°A. **Ersetzen Sie die Pronomen!** Replace the italicized pronouns with the pronouns in parentheses and change the verbs accordingly.

1. *Wir* sind drei Tage in Gelsenkirchen geblieben. (ich, er, sie *pl.*)
2. *Wir* sind nach Bonn geflogen. (er, sie *sing.*, sie *pl.*)
3. Ist *sie* je im Ozean geschwommen? (du, ihr, Sie)
4. *Sie* ist gestern krank geworden. (wir, ich, sie *pl.*)
5. Sind *Sie* je auf einer Burg gewesen? (du, ihr, sie *sing.*)
6. Wann sind *Sie* nach Dortmund gefahren? (du, er, ihr)
7. Gestern bin *ich* zur Königin gegangen. (wir, er, sie *pl.*)
8. Bist *du* Frank zur Ruine gefolgt? (ihr, er, Sie)
9. Wann ist *er* nach Lemgo gereist? (du, ihr, Sie)
10. Jeden Tag sind *wir* im Park gelaufen. (ich, er, sie *pl.*)

B. **Ergänzen Sie die Sätze mit der richtigen Form von *haben* oder *sein*!** Complete the sentences with the proper form of the auxiliaries **haben** or **sein**.

1. Herr Neumann ＿＿＿＿＿＿ an einer schweren Krankheit gelitten.
2. Marie ＿＿＿＿＿＿ in der Burg verschwunden.
3. Der Prinz ＿＿＿＿＿＿ König geworden.

4. Wir _____ Egon in Köln getroffen.

5. Wann_____ Ludwig II gestorben?

6. _____ du den Zug nach Hamburg genommen?

7. Markus, wann _____ du aufgestanden?

8. Wer _____ diesen Film schon gesehen?

9. Was _____ gestern geschehen?

10. _____ ihr je in München gewesen?

11. Das Kind _____ vom Stuhl gefallen.

12. Wir _____ lange am Fenster gesessen.

13. Ich _____ nie nach Aachen gefahren.

14. _____ du Karlas neuen Wagen gefahren?

15. Wer _____ das Glas zerbrochen?

16. Das Glas _____ bei der Party zerbrochen.

17. Das Wetter _____ uns das Oktoberfest verdorben.

18. Die Pflanze _____ jetzt leider durch den Regen verdorben.

°C. **Geben Sie die folgenden Sätze im Perfekt!** Place the following sentences in the present perfect tense. Make sure to use the proper auxiliary, **haben** or **sein**.

Zum Beispiel: Andreas trifft seinen Vater auf der Uni.
Andreas *hat* seinen Vater auf der Uni getroffen.

Die Kinder verschwinden im Schloß.
Die Kinder sind im Schloß verschwunden.

1. Frau Sauerbruch leidet an einer Krankheit.
2. Spielst du Fußball?
3. Wir reisen nach Gummersbach.
4. Der Ritter gewinnt das Spiel.
5. Petra und Rolf schwimmen im See hinter der Burg.
6. Wohin ziehen die Pferde den großen Wagen?
7. Nora begegnet ihrem Freund heute in Linz.
8. Rainer schläft immer lange.

D. **Schreiben Sie Sätze im Perfekt!** Compose sentences in the present perfect tense, using the following words and phrases.

Zum Beispiel: Rainer / nehmen / den Bus
Rainer hat den Bus genommen.

1. das Wetter / werden / im Sommer warm
2. der Prinz / folgen / dem König
3. der Kaiser / sitzen / auf dem Thron

4. die Königin / sein / sehr beliebt
5. essen / du / schon?
6. liegen / Martin / auf dem Sofa?
7. die Touristen / fliegen / nach Stuttgart
8. das / geschehen / vor zwei Jahren

E. **Übersetzen Sie die folgenden Sätze!** Use the present perfect tense.

1. I asked for (**um**) coffee.
2. We flew to Munich.
3. Hansdieter and Karla, have you ever been (**je**) to the (**im**) castle?
4. The emperor got up and stood before the (**vor dem**) throne.
5. Klara and Paul, why did you stay home (**zu Hause**)?
6. Nora, did you drive the car yet? —Yes, I drove to (**nach**) Stuttgart.

F. **Eine Woche in Ihrem Tagebuch.** Compose two sentences that you could put in your diary for each day of the past week. Use the present perfect tense.

Zum Beispiel: Sontag: **Ich habe Sonja getroffen, und wir sind ins Kino gegangen. Ich habe meine Uhr verloren.**

Montag: **Ich habe ein Tennisspiel gewonnen. Ich bin im Park gelaufen.**

The Past Perfect Tense

There is another tense that denotes past time in German, the past perfect, formed with the past tense of **haben** or **sein** together with the past participle.

sprechen

ich hatte gesprochen	wir hatten gesprochen
du hattest gesprochen	ihr hattet gesprochen
er	sie
sie } hatte gesprochen	Sie } hatten gesprochen
es	

gehen

ich war gegangen	wir waren gegangen
du warst gegangen	ihr wart gegangen
er	sie
sie } war gegangen	Sie } waren gegangen
es	

The past perfect tense, like the past tense, occurs mainly in literature and is used to indicate that one action or event *had happened* before another past action or event.

Er *hatte* schon *gegessen,* bevor ich nach Hause kam.
He had already eaten before I came home.

Nachdem ich *gefrühstückt hatte,* fuhr ich zur Universität.
After I had eaten breakfast, I drove to the university.

Notice the use of tenses with **bevor** and **nachdem** in the preceding examples:

Main Clause	Subordinate Clause
past perfect tense	**bevor** + past tense
past tense	**nachdem** + past perfect tense

Word order in the past perfect is identical to word order in the present perfect; the finite verb (a form of **haben** or **sein**) is the second element in normal or inverted word order (see pages 35–36 of this chapter).

Übungen

°A. **Geben Sie das Plusquamperfekt!** Change the sentences from the present to the past perfect.

Zum Beispiel: Sie errichten eine Burg.
Sie hatten eine Burg errichtet.

Der Kaiser bleibt in Berlin.
Der Kaiser war in Berlin geblieben.

1. Diese Epoche dauert lange.
2. Er fährt zum Schloß.
3. Ingrid schreibt einen Brief.
4. Dieter gewinnt das Spiel.
5. Der Krieg geht zu Ende.

°B. **In der Vergangenheit!** Change the tenses of the verbs in each sentence.

Zum Beispiel: Die Studenten sprechen über das Mittelalter, bevor die Geschichtsklasse beginnt.

Die Studenten hatten über das Mittelalter gesprochen, bevor die Geschichtsklasse begann.

1. Max und Rita schreiben Briefe, bevor sie ins Museum gehen.
2. Die Touristinnen gehen in den Schloßgarten, bevor es regnet.
3. Wir trinken Coca-Cola, bevor der Film beginnt.
4. Ich fahre nach Berlin, bevor du nach Hause kommst.

C. **Nachdem . . . .** Add **nachdem** and change the tense of the verbs in each sentence, following the model.

Zum Beispiel: Ich sehe den alten Film. Ich gehe ins Bett.
Nachdem ich den alten Film gesehen hatte, ging ich ins Bett.

1. Der König stirbt. Die Königin entdeckt die Wahrheit.
2. Heidi fliegt nach Frankfurt. Sie besucht noch Freunde in Düsseldorf.
3. Die Arbeiter zerstören die alte Brücke. Man baut eine neue Brücke.
4. Die Touristen kaufen viele Souvenirs. Sie kommen zurück ins Hotel.

D. **Zeitmaschine.** A time machine takes you back into history during the following years. Tell what had just happened when you arrived; use the following time line for reference.

Zum Beispiel: 1518
Als ich ankam, hatte Martin Luther die Reformation begonnen.

1517 Martin Luther beginnt die Reformation.

1786 Friedrich der Große stirbt.

1850 Die Brüder Grimm sammeln *Kinder- und Hausmärchen.*

1888 Wilhelm II wird Kaiser.

1918 Der Erste Weltkrieg geht zu Ende.

1924 Adolf Hitler schreibt *Mein Kampf.*

1. 1889 _____

2. 1787 _____

3. 1851 _____

4. 1925 _____

5. 1919 _____

Wilhelm und Jacob Grimm

Martin Luther

A. **Zur Wiederholung. Übersetzen Sie die folgenden Sätze!** Use the present perfect tense to express past time unless otherwise indicated.

1. Yesterday I visited the castle.
2. Lorenz believes that Bruno and Gisela saw the film on the (**über das**) empire.
3. At that time the emperor lived in Berlin.
4. Why did they (**man**) destroy the castle?
5. When (**wann**) did the last (**letzte**) empress die?
6. Why did the children follow the knight?
7. The king had fought for a long time before he won the war.
8. We went to the museum after we had driven to the (**zum**) castle.

B. **Zur Gesamtwiederholung** (*general review*). **Übersetzen Sie die folgenden Sätze!**

1. The knight has been standing for two hours before the (**vor dem**) throne.
2. Next week Brigitte will visit the ruins in Cologne (**Köln**). (present tense)
3. Kai, don't talk so much about the (**über den**) war.
4. Frank and Marina, come with us to the (**ins**) museum.
5. Did the king go to France or did he remain in Germany? (present perfect)
6. The knights didn't love the king, but on the contrary they fought with him (**ihm**). (past tense)
7. Gerd didn't visit the queen. —Yes (he did)! (present perfect)

3
Landschaft

Die Kirche Ramsau bei Berchtesgaden

The Nominative and Accusative Cases; Definite and Indefinite Articles in the Nominative and Accusative

The Dative and Genitive Cases; Definite and Indefinite Articles in the Dative and Genitive

Uses of Definite and Indefinite Articles

Wortschatz

der Bach (⸚e) creek, stream

der Bauer (-n) farmer

die Bäuerin (-nen) female farmer

der Bauernhof (⸚e) farm

der Baum (⸚e) tree

der Berg (-e) mountain

die Blume (-n) flower

das Dorf (⸚er) village

der Fisch (-e) fish

der Fluß (⸚sse) river

der Frühling spring

der Garten (⸚) garden

der Herbst autumn

die Landschaft (-en) landscape

der See (-n) lake

die See (-n) ocean

der Sommer (-) summer

die Sonne (-n) sun

der Stein (-e) stone

das Tal (⸚er) valley

das Tier (-e) animal

der Vogel (⸚) bird

der Wald (⸚er) forest

der Winter (-) winter

es gibt* . . . there is . . . , there are . . .

fließen* to flow, to run

fotografieren to take photographs

gefallen* *(dat.)* to please; **. . . gefällt mir** I like . . .

scheinen* to shine

einen Spaziergang machen to take a walk

wachsen* to grow

heiß hot

hoch high

kalt cold

kühl cool

niedrig low

warm warm

---

*The verbs marked with asterisks are strong verbs; see the appendix for principal parts of strong verbs.

A. *Find the word that does not belong.*

1. Bach, Fluß, (der) See, Berg
2. Frühling, Sonne, Herbst, Winter
3. Bauernhof, Feld, (die) See, Bauer
4. Vogel, Katze, Fisch, Stein

B. *Complete the sentences.*

1. Jeden Sonntag macht die Familie einen _____ im Wald.
2. _____ _____ in Deutschland viele kleine Bauernhöfe.
3. Der Tourist _____ die Landschaft.
4. Sylvie liebt _____; sie hat einen Hund und eine Katze.
5. Alle Bauernhöfe haben Blumen in den _____ (*pl.*).
6. Die _____ in Bayern ist besonders schön; es gibt viele Seen, Flüsse, Berge und Täler.
7. Sind drei _____ schon ein Wald?

C. *Match the nouns with the verbs you associate with them.*

1. Bach
2. Sonne
3. Pflanze
4. Wanderer
5. Fisch

a. wachsen
b. wandern
c. schwimmen
d. scheinen
e. fließen

D. *Give the opposite of each word.*

1. heiß
2. kühl
3. niedrig
4. Berg

The Nominative and Accusative Cases; Definite and Indefinite Articles in the Nominative and Accusative

Definite and indefinite articles in German are either masculine, feminine, or neuter, in agreement with the gender of the nouns they modify. They are also in one of four cases: (1) nominative, (2) accusative, (3) dative, or (4) genitive. In this section, the nominative and accusative cases are discussed.

The Nominative Case

The basic function of the nominative case is to indicate the subject of the sentence. The subject usually performs the action of the verb. (In English, the subject is usually the first noun or pronoun in the sentence.) The gender of singular nouns in the nominative case is indicated by the definite articles **der** (masculine), **das** (neuter), or **die** (feminine), and the indefinite articles **ein** (masculine and neuter) and **eine** (feminine).

Masculine	*Neuter*	*Feminine*
Der Mann ⎫ Ein Mann ⎭ wohnt da.	Das Kind ⎫ Ein Kind ⎭ wohnt da.	Die Frau ⎫ Eine Frau ⎭ wohnt da.

The definite article is **die** in the nominative plural for all three genders; **ein** has no plural.

> Die Männer (Kinder, Frauen) wohnen da.

Like the subject of the sentence, nouns following a few verbs like **sein** and **werden** are in the nominative case; these are called predicate nouns. In normal word order, these verbs are flanked left and right by nouns in the nominative case:

> *Das* Kind wird *ein* guter Wanderer.
> The child is becoming a good hiker.

> *Der* Professor ist *ein* berühmter Schriftsteller.*
> The professor is a famous writer.

The Accusative Case

The basic function of the accusative case is to indicate the direct object of the verb. (In English, the direct object is usually the noun or pronoun that directly follows the verb.) The gender of singular nouns in the accusative case is indicated by the definite articles **den** (masculine), **das** (neuter), and **eine** (feminine), and by the indefinite articles **einen** (masculine), **ein** (neuter), and **eine** (feminine).

Masculine	*Neuter*
Ich sehe ⎰ *den* Mann. ⎱ *einen* Mann.	Ich sehe ⎰ *das* Kind. ⎱ *ein* Kind.

Feminine

Ich sehe ⎰ *die* Frau.
⎱ *eine* Frau.

---

*Be careful to use the nominative case after **ist**, since **ißt** (*eats*) has the same pronunciation but requires the accusative case. **Der Professor ist (*ißt*) einen berühmten Schriftsteller** would bring smiles from your German friends.

The definite article is **die** in the accusative plural:

Ich sehe *die* Männer (Kinder, Frauen).

The direct object of a sentence usually answers the question "Whom?" or "What?"

Andrea fotografiert die Landschaft. Was fotografiert Andrea? (Die Landschaft: direct object)
Andrea is photographing the landscape. What is Andrea photographing?

Gabriele kennt den Wanderer. Wen kennt Gabriele? (Den Wanderer: direct object)
Gabriela knows the hiker. Whom does Gabriele know?

The use of the accusative in prepositional phrases will be discussed in Chapter 11, and its use in certain adverbial expressions will be discussed in Chapter 14.

Ein Schritt weiter

A predicate complement is a word or phrase that completes the meaning of the verb and usually occurs at the end of the predicate. The predicate complements and the verbs they modify in the following sentences are in italics.

Marie *spricht* gut *Deutsch.*
Marie speaks German well.

Frau Schmidt *gibt* jeden Tag in diesem Zimmer *Unterricht.*
Frau Schmidt holds class in this room every day.

Herr Bürger kann gut *Auto fahren.*
Mr. Bürger knows how to drive well.

Compare the position of direct object nouns and complement nouns, which usually go at the end of the clause:

Wir *singen* oft *Lieder* im Klassenzimmer. (direct object noun)
We often sing songs in class.

Frau Schmidt *gibt* jeden Tag in diesem Zimmer *Unterricht.* (complement noun)
Frau Schmidt holds class in this room every day.

Complements are usually negated by placing **nicht** directly before them; however, **kein** is sometimes used instead.

Marie spricht nicht Deutsch.

Herr Bürger kann nicht Auto fahren.

Frau Schmidt gibt heute keinen Unterricht.

You will gradually develop a sense of which nouns are direct objects and which are complements.

Übungen

°A. **Verwenden Sie die Nomen in Klammern als Objekte!** Use the nouns in parentheses as direct objects; be sure to use the appropriate form of the definite article.

Zum Beispiel: Ich sehe das Tier. (Vogel)
Ich sehe den Vogel.

Ich sehe den Vogel. (Wälder)
Ich sehe die Wälder.

1. Gabi, kennst du den Berg? (Bäuerin, Bauernhof)
2. Ich schreibe das Buch. (Brief, Geschichte)
3. Haben Sie den Ball verloren? (Fisch, Bücher)
4. Wir haben das Dorf gefunden. (Bach, Wald)
5. Sonja fotografiert die Universität. (Landschaft, Gasthäuser)
6. Sie beobachten das Tier. (Meer, Fluß)

°B. **Ersetzen Sie den bestimmten Artikel mit dem unbestimmten Artikel!** Replace the definite article with the indefinite article in Exercise A. Remember that the indefinite article has no plural form.

Zum Beispiel: Ich sehe das Tier.
Ich sehe ein Tier. (Vogel)
Ich sehe einen Vogel. (Wälder)
Ich sehe Wälder.

C. **Ergänzen Sie die folgenden Sätze!** Complete the following sentences with the correct article in parentheses.

1. Wer hat _____ neuen Vogel gefangen? (der, den)

2. Wie heißt _____ Fluß? (der, den)

3. Heinrich wird _____ guter Fußballspieler. (ein, einen)

4. Margot hat _____ Bleistift gekauft. (ein, einen)

5. Das ist _____ Wald. (der, den)

6. Was für _____ Wagen ist das? (ein, einen)

7. Was für _____ Wagen haben Sie, Herr Fröhlich? (ein, einen)

°D. **Bilden Sie Sätze!** Compose sentences using the following words and definite articles.

Zum Beispiel: das / sein / Student   ich / fotografieren / Berg
               Das ist der Student.   **Ich fotografiere den Berg.**

1. Bach / fließen / im Wald
2. kennen / du / Wald?
3. Flüße / sein / sehr kalt

4. wo / wachsen / Baum?
5. das / sein / See (*lake*)?
6. im Sommer / Sonne / scheinen / jeden Tag

E. **Bilden Sie Sätze!** Compose sentences using the following words and indefinite articles.

Zum Beispiel: das / sein / Student
Das ist ein Student.

1. neben dem Fluß / stehen / Wald
2. sein / das / Fluß / oder / Bach?
3. es gibt / Berg / im Wald
4. gibt es / See (*lake*) / im Tal?
5. wir / machen / Spaziergang

F. **Übersetzen Sie die folgenden Sätze!**

1. Did Reinhard photograph the mountain?
2. Brigitte saw five animals.
3. Yesterday we visited a village on the (**am**) river.
4. Mr. Freiberg, do you (**Ihnen**) like the forest?
5. Is a tree growing in the (**im**) garden?
6. Andrea, did you see a tree or a bird?
7. Claudia and Werner, do you hear the river?

G. **Im schönen, grünen Wald.** Describe this scene:

The Dative and Genitive Cases; Definite and Indefinite Articles in the Dative and Genitive

The Dative Case

The basic function of the dative case is to indicate the indirect object of a sentence. The singular forms of the articles in the dative case are:

Masculine

Ich gebe es $\begin{cases} dem \text{ Mann.} \\ einem \text{ Mann.} \end{cases}$

Neuter

Ich gebe es $\begin{cases} dem \text{ Kind.} \\ einem \text{ Kind.} \end{cases}$

Feminine

Ich gebe es $\begin{cases} der \text{ Frau.} \\ einer \text{ Frau.} \end{cases}$

The plural form of the definite article in the dative is **den**:

Ich gebe es *den* Männern (Frauen, Kindern).

Notice that an **-n** is added to nouns in the dative plural.*

To determine the indirect (dative) object of most sentences, you can ask "To or for whom?"

Er hat *der* Frau die Blumen verkauft.
He sold the woman the flowers. (He sold the flowers *to* the woman. To whom . . . ?)

Wir haben *dem* Kind den Wasserfall gezeigt.
We showed the child the waterfall. (We showed the waterfall *to* the child. To whom . . . ?)

Sie hat *den* Kindern einen Rucksack gekauft.
She bought the children a backpack. (She bought a backpack *for* the children. For whom . . . ?)

---

*If the noun already ends in **-n** , **n** is not added: **Ich gebe es *den* Mädchen.** Nouns of foreign origin with plurals ending in **-s** do not take the dative ending **-n** either: **in den Restaurants, in den Autos**. Note also that the ending **-e** is occasionally added to the dative singular of masculine and neuter nouns of one syllable: **auf dem Lande** in the country; **nach Hause** home.

The preposition **zu** is not used in German to introduce the indirect object.

Order of Noun and Pronoun Objects

In German, indirect objects precede direct objects unless the direct object is a personal pronoun.

Wir zeigen *dem Lehrer das Buch.* (indirect before direct)
We are showing the teacher the book.

Wir zeigen *ihm das.* (indirect before direct)
We are showing him that.

Wir zeigen *es dem Lehrer.* (direct object is a personal pronoun)
We are showing it to the teacher.

Wir zeigen *es ihm.* (direct object is a personal pronoun)
We are showing it to him.

Uses of the Dative Case

1. Besides its use to express indirect objects, the dative case is used with many verbs, including the following:

antworten to answer	folgen to follow	helfen to help	~~stehlen~~ to steal
ausmachen to matter	gefallen to please	~~nehmen~~ to take	~~vergeben~~ to forgive
begegnen to meet	gehören to belong to	passieren to happen	~~versprechen~~ to promise
danken to thank	glauben to believe	schaden to harm, damage	weh tun to hurt, ache
erlauben to permit			

Regina antwortet *dem Professor.*
Regina is answering the professor.

Das macht *dem Gast* nichts aus.
That doesn't matter to the guest.

Fritz dankt *der Lehrerin.*
Fritz is thanking the teacher.

Warum folgt der Hund *dem Kind?*
Why is the dog following the child?

Gefällt dieser Roman *den Studenten* nicht?
Don't the students like this novel?

Wahrscheinlich gehört dieser Rucksack *den* Wanderern.
This backpack probably belongs to the hikers.

Gewöhnlich hilft Dieter *dem* Bruder bei der Arbeit.
Dieter usually helps his brother with the work.

Der Zahn tut *dem* Kind weh.
This tooth hurts the child.

The dative object used with the verbs **nehmen** or **stehlen** does not express the relationship *to* or *for someone* but *from someone*:

Der Dieb hat dem Bauern das Pferd genommen (gestohlen).
The thief took (stole) the horse from the farmer.

Study hint: Learn these verbs by repeating them in short sentences with the dative pronoun **mir**: **Diese Landschaft gefällt mir. Dieses Tier gehört mir.***

2. The dative case is used to indicate possession of parts of the body or articles of clothing.

Christa hat *der* Frau die Haare geschnitten.
Christa cut the woman's hair.

Zieh *dem* Kind die Jacke aus!
Take off the child's jacket.

3. The dative is also used with many adjectives, such as the following:

ähnlich   *similar*
angenehm   *pleasant*
nützlich   *useful*
peinlich   *embarrassing*

David sieht *der* Mutter ähnlich.
David looks like his mother.

Dieser Rat ist *den* Reisenden sehr nützlich.
This advice is very useful for travelers.

Die Frage war *dem* Jungen peinlich.
The question was embarrassing to the boy.

Notice that these adjectives follow the nouns to which they refer and that their English equivalents are usually used with the preposition *to* or *for*. The use of the dative in prepositional phrases will be discussed in Chapter 11, and its use in certain adverbial expressions will be discussed in Chapter 14.

---

*Other common verbs that require dative objects are **befehlen** (*to order, command*), **beistimmen** (*to agree with*), **drohen** (*to threaten*), **entsprechen** (*to correspond to*), **entgegeneilen** (*to hurry to meet*), **nachlaufen** (*to run after*), **passen** (*to fit*), **geschehen** (*to happen*), **scheinen** (*to appear*), **(ver)trauen** (*to trust*), **verbieten** (*to forbid*), and **zuhören** (*to listen to*). These verbs will not be practiced in this chapter.

The Genitive Case

The basic function of the genitive case is to indicate possession. The singular forms of the articles in the genitive case are:

Masculine

Das sind die Schuhe $\begin{cases} \textbf{des} \text{ Mannes.} \\ \textbf{eines} \text{ Mannes.} \end{cases}$

Neuter

Das sind die Schuhe $\begin{cases} \textbf{des} \text{ Kindes.} \\ \textbf{eines} \text{ Kindes.} \end{cases}$

Feminine

Das sind die Schuhe $\begin{cases} \textbf{der} \text{ Frau.} \\ \textbf{einer} \text{ Frau.} \end{cases}$

The plural definite article in the genitive is **der**.

Das sind die Schuhe **der** Männer (Kinder, Frauen).

The masculine and neuter forms of the article end in **-es**; the feminine and plural forms end in **-er**. Most masculine and neuter nouns of one syllable require the ending **-es** in the genitive singular; those of more than one syllable require the ending **-s**:*

der Name des Mannes (des Kindes)
the man's name, the name of the man (the child's name, the name of the child)

der Name der Frau
the woman's name, the name of the woman

die Namen der Männer
the men's names, the names of the men

Notice the use of the preposition *of* in the English translations.

In conversational German, the preposition **von** followed by the dative is often used in place of the genitive:

Die Eltern von *dem* Professor kommen aus Belgien. (Formal: Die Eltern des Professors)
The professor's parents come from Belgium.

The genitive of proper names and of nouns referring to family members is formed as in English but without an apostrophe:[†]

Petras Bruder	Mutters Wagen	Deutschlands Wälder
Petra's brother	Mother's car	Germany's forests

---

*Not all masculine nouns end in **-(e)s** in the genitive. This is discussed in Chapter 4.
[†]There are two other ways of forming the genitive of proper names: with **von** or by placing the name after the noun possessed: **die Wälder von Deutschland, die Wälder Deutschlands.**

Declension of Articles: Synopsis

The endings of the definite and indefinite articles (their declensions) are very similar:

	Masculine	Neuter	Feminine	Plural
Nominative	der	das	die	die
	ein	ein	eine	
Accusative	den	das	die	die
	einen	ein	eine	
Dative	dem	dem	der	den
	einem	einem	einer	
Genitive	des	des	der	der
	eines	eines	einer	

Notice that:

1. the nominative and accusative forms are the same except in the masculine singular

2. the feminine singular forms of the dative and genitive and the genitive plural are the same (**-er**)

3. the masculine and neuter singular forms of the dative are the same (**-em**)

4. the masculine and neuter singular forms of the genitive are the same (**-es**)

Übungen

°A. **Ersetzen Sie die Nomen!** Substitute the nouns in parentheses for the nouns in italics.

Zum Beispiel: Ich habe *dem Professor* ein Buch gegeben. (Frau)
Ich habe der Frau ein Buch gegeben.

1. Carla hat *dem Mann* die Blumen verkauft. (Mädchen *sing.*, Frau)
2. Wir hören *dem Sänger* gern zu. (Sängerin, Vogel)
3. Die Eltern haben *dem Sohn* einen Hund gekauft. (Tochter, Kinder)
4. Heidi antwortet *dem Kind.* (Freundin, Lehrer *sing.*)
5. Klaus hat *dem Gast* geglaubt. (Mädchen *sing.*, Brüder)
6. Wir sollen *dem Lehrer* danken. (Ärztin, Eltern)
7. München gefällt *den Lehrerinnen* sehr. (Deutsche, *pl.*, Mädchen *sing.*)
8. Rudi sieht *dem Vater* ähnlich. (Onkel *sing.*, Schwester)

°B. **Ersetzen Sie den bestimmten Artikel!** Replace the definite article in italics with the indefinite article.

Zum Beispiel: Der Beamte erlaubt *der* Touristin, ein Foto zu machen.
Der Beamte erlaubt einer Touristin, ein Foto zu machen.

1. Der Professor zeigt *dem* Amerikaner eine Landkarte von Süddeutschland.
2. Der Friseur hat *dem* Mädchen die Haare geschnitten.
3. Der Ober hat *der* Französin Kaffee gebracht.
4. Inge ist *dem* Hund gefolgt.
5. Gehört der Rucksack *dem* Gast?

°C. **Ersetzen Sie die Nomen!** Substitute the nouns in parentheses for the nouns in italics. (Remember to add -(e)s to the singular of masculine and neuter nouns.)

Zum Beispiel: Das Haus *des Amerikaners* steht in der Schillerstraße.
(Französin)
Das Haus der Französin steht in der Schillerstraße.

1. Die Rosen *der Blumenfrau* waren sehr schön. (Garten)
2. Der Preis *der Jacke* war zu hoch. (Fahrkarte)
3. Ich kenne die Eltern *des Mädchens*. (Studentinnen)
4. Wir haben das Haus *des Filmstars* gekauft. (Arzt)
5. Das Kind *des Lehrers* heißt Pamela. (Gäste)

Bauernhof bei Detmold

D. **Ergänzen Sie die Sätze!** Complete the following sentences with the appropriate definite article, genitive or dative.

1. Wer hilft _____ Bäuerinnen bei der Arbeit?

2. Der Wagen _____ Frau ist rot.

3. Der Rücken (*back*) tut _____ Wanderer weh.

4. Wer hat _____ Kind den Ball genommen?

5. Der Preis _____ Buches war nicht hoch.

6. Ich habe _____ Lehrerin ein Buch versprochen.

7. Die Blumen _____ Engländerin sind sehr schön.

E. **Schreiben Sie Sätze!** Compose sentences containing the following words and phrases. Each sentence should express interaction between at least two people.

Zum Beispiel: verkaufen
Heidi hat dem Freund einen Wagen verkauft.

1. geben
2. antworten
3. zeigen
4. danken

5. die Haare schneiden
6. gefallen
7. erlauben
8. folgen

F. **Übersetzen Sie die folgenden Sätze!**

1. Ruth is showing the guests the landscape.
2. What happened to the farmer?
3. The question was embarrassing to the teacher.
4. The house belongs to the woman.
5. Martin's car is very useful to the Americans.
6. Today I am helping my parents.
7. Where are Sabrina's photos?
8. We forgave the man.
9. The children's parents speak German.
10. The husband of the American (woman) works in Munich.

G. **Beantworten Sie die folgenden Fragen!**

Zum Beispiel: Wem helfen Sie bei den Hausaufgaben?
Ich helfe einem Freund (einer Freundin, einigen Freunden, einigen Freundinnen) bei den Hausaufgaben.

1. Wem schreiben Sie oft einen Brief?
2. Haben Sie einen Wagen? Wem erlauben Sie, den Wagen zu fahren?
3. Wem glauben Sie fast immer?
4. Wem haben Sie kürzlich (*recently*) etwas versprochen?
5. Wem möchten Sie nicht begegnen?
6. Wem möchten Sie gefallen?
7. Welchem Politiker glauben Sie?

Uses of Definite and Indefinite Articles

The Definite Article

The definite article is used similarly in German and English. Contrary to English, however, the definite article in German is also used:

1. to indicate abstract concepts (in the singular)

    Das Leben ist kurz; *die* Kunst ist lang.
    Life is short; art is long.

    Der Mensch ist sterblich.
    Man is mortal.

    Die Natur ist schön.
    Nature is beautiful.

2. with names of months, seasons, parts of the day, and meals

    Der Mai ist gekommen.
    May has come.

    Der Frühling ist endlich da.
    Spring is finally here.

    Ingrid arbeitet immer spät in *der* Nacht.
    Ingrid always works late at night.

    Das Abendessen war heute besonders gut.
    Dinner was especially good today.

3. with names of streets and with countries that are feminine*

    Wie komme ich in *die* Schillerstraße?
    How do I get to Schiller Street?

    Die Schweiz und *die* Tschechoslowakei liegen in Europa, aber *die* Türkei liegt in Kleinasien.
    Switzerland and Czechoslovakia are in Europe, but Turkey is in Asia Minor.

4. with units of measurement, to mean *per*

    Diese Eier kosten zwei Mark *das* Dutzend.
    These eggs cost two marks per dozen.

    Fritz fährt oft hundert Kilometer *die* Stunde.
    Fritz often drives one hundred kilometers an (per) hour.

---

*First names are occasionally used with the definite article even if they are not modified by an adjective: **Der Ludwig war gestern krank.** *Ludwig was sick yesterday.*

5. with parts of the body or articles of clothing instead of possessive adjectives

Karla steckt *die* Hand in *die* Handtasche und zieht fünf Mark heraus.
Karla sticks her hand in her purse and pulls out five marks.

Ich nehme *den* Pullover mit.
I'm bringing my pullover.

6. with proper names if they are modified by an adjective*

Die kleine Cornelia spielt gut Klavier.
Little Cornelia plays the piano well.

Das schöne Köln liegt am Rhein.
Beautiful Cologne is on the Rhine.

7. with each noun in a series

Das Gebirge und *die* Seen in Bayern sind sehr schön.
The mountains and lakes in Bavaria are very beautiful.

8. in certain idioms, especially with the preposition **zu**

zum Beispiel	zum Schluß	in der Regel
for example	in conclusion	as a rule
zum Nachtisch	mit dem Zug	in der Schule (Kirche)
for dessert	by train	in school (church)
im Bett	die meisten (Deutschen, etc.)	die beiden (Jungen, etc.)
in bed	most (Germans, etc.)	both (boys, etc.)

The Indefinite Article

The indefinite article is used similarly in English and in German. In German, however, it is not used:

1. with an *unmodified* noun denoting nationality, occupation, or social status after the verbs **sein** or **werden**

Robert ist Amerikaner.
Robert is an American.

Irene ist Studentin.
Irene is a student.

Daniela wird Krankenschwester.
Daniela is becoming a nurse.

Herr Braun ist Witwer.
Mr. Braun is a widower.

But:

Irene ist *eine fleißige* Studentin.
Irene is a diligent student.

Herr Braun ist *ein junger* Witwer.
Mr. Braun is a young widower.

---

*Most countries are neuter.

2. with the numbers **hundert** and **tausend**

Hamburg liegt über hundert Kilometer von Hannover.
Hamburg is over a hundred kilometers from Hanover.

Marie hat tausend Dollar geerbt.
Marie inherited a thousand dollars.

3. with idioms with **-weh**

Ich habe Kopfweh.   Kai hat Zahnweh.
I have a headache.   Kai has a toothache.

Übungen

°A. **Übersetzen Sie die folgenden Sätze!** Translate these sentences and explain the function of the definite articles in italics.

1. In *der* Regel fahre ich mit *dem* Zug.
2. *Der* große Albert hilft uns bei der Arbeit.
3. *Am* Tag arbeite ich schwer, und in *der* Nacht schlafe ich gut.
4. *Im* Herbst gehen *die* meisten Bayern zum Oktoberfest.
5. *Die* beiden Freunde wohnen in *der* Bismarckstraße.
6. Diese Äpfel kosten eine Mark *das* Pfund.
7. *Im* Winter stecke ich immer *die* Hände in *die* Taschen.
8. *Die* Tschechoslowakei liegt zwischen Deutschland und Rußland.
9. *Die* Liebe ist wunderbar.

°B. **Was ist der Unterschied?** Explain why the indefinite article is used in one of each of the following pairs of sentences but omitted in the other.

1. Klaus ist noch ein Junge. / Elke ist Musikerin.
2. Regina ist Ärztin. / Heinrich ist ein guter Physiker.
3. Eberhard wird Geologe. / Irmgard wird eine berühmte Schriftstellerin.
4. Dieses Buch über europäische Vögel hat über hundert Mark gekostet. / München hat über eine Million Einwohner (*inhabitants*).
5. Ich habe einen schlechten Zahn. / Ich habe Zahnweh.

C. **Übersetzen Sie die folgenden Sätze!** Use the dative case after prepositions unless otherwise directed.

1. As a rule we take a walk in the afternoon.
2. The child put his hand in (*accusative*) his pocket.
3. August is warmer than (**wärmer als**) December. Most Americans love August.
4. Little Uschi lives on (**in**) Ludwig Street.
5. Switzerland lies south of (**südlich von**) Germany.
6. Coffee costs over ten marks a pound (**das Pfund**).
7. Nicole is becoming a doctor.
8. Hans is a good teacher.
9. In conclusion, nature is beautiful.
10. Marie is bringing her hat.

D. **Beantworten Sie die folgenden Fragen!**

1. Welche Länder wollen Sie besuchen?
2. Sind Sie spät in der Nacht noch wach?
3. In welcher Straße wohnen Sie?
4. Welches deutschsprachige Land liegt in den Alpen?
5. In welchen Ländern spricht man Tschechisch und Türkisch?
6. Was machen die meisten amerikanischen Studenten im Sommer?
7. Was tun Sie in der Regel am Samstag abend?

Rückblick

A. **Zur Wiederholung. Übersetzen Sie die folgenden Sätze!**

1. Veronika is the professor's friend.
2. I gave the teacher the photo.
3. Wolfgang, did you show your parents the postcard?
4. I cut the child's hair.
5. Gabi and Lutz, did you thank the guest?
6. I believe that I have the hiker's backpack.
7. The children's father is a farmer.
8. We went by bus.
9. Switzerland is beautiful in the summer.

B. **Zur Gesamtwiederholung. Übersetzen Sie die folgenden Sätze!** Use the dative case after prepositions unless otherwise indicated.

1. Sylvia, give the animals water from the (**vom**) river, please. (Chapter 1)
2. Renate and Jost, answer the (female) teacher.
3. Roberta, let's help the children. (Translate in two ways.)
4. Karl and Eva, let's buy our parents a picture of the lake next to the (**neben dem**) mountain. (Translate in two ways.)
5. How long has Mrs. Unger lived in this village?
6. Josef, did you follow the animal into the (**in den**) forest? (Chapter 2)
7. I didn't believe the professor when he told me that.
8. The tourists liked the landscape. (The landscape pleased the tourists.)

4
In der Stadt

Römisches Tor in Aachen

der-Words

ein-Words

The Gender of Nouns

The Plural of Nouns; Noun Declensions

Wortschatz ━━━━━━━━━━━━━━━━━━━━━━━━━

die Apotheke (-n) pharmacy

der Bahnhof (̈e) train station

die Bank (-en) bank; **auf die Bank gehen*** to go to the bank

der Bürgermeister (-) mayor

das Café (-s) coffee shop, café

die Ecke (-n) corner

das Gasthaus (̈ er) restaurant, inn

das Gebäude (-) building

das Geschäft (-e) store

die Haltestelle (-n) (bus, streetcar) stop

die Haupstadt (̈ e) capital

die Hauptstraße (-n) main street

das Kaufhaus (̈ er) department store

die Kirche (-n) church

die Konditorei (-en) pastry shop

der Markt (̈ e) market; **auf den Markt gehen** to go to the market

der Park (-s) park

die Post post office; **auf die Post gehen** to go to the post office

das Rathaus (̈ er) town hall

das Schaufenster (-) shop window; **einen Schaufensterbummel machen** go window-shopping

das Schild (-er) sign

die Straße (-n) street

die Straßenbahn (-en) streetcar, tram

der Verkehr traffic

die Wohnung (-en) apartment

aus · steigen* to get off; **aus dem Bus aussteigen** to get off the bus

ein · kaufen to shop

ein · steigen* to get on; **in die Straßenbahn einsteigen** to get on the tram

überqueren to cross

zu Fuß gehen* to walk, to go on foot

---

*Verbs marked with an asterisk are strong verbs; see the appendix for principal parts of strong verbs.

A. Give the name of the place where you would go to get each of the following items.

1. Aspirin
2. Blumen
3. Briefmarken
4. Geld
5. Fahrkarten
6. Möbel
7. Kuchen

a. Konditorei
b. Kaufhaus
c. Bank
d. Post
e. Apotheke
f. Markt
g. Bahnhof

B. Choose from the list on the right the place that you associate with each of the activities on the left.

1. schlafen
2. Bier trinken
3. spazierengehen
4. heiraten (to marry)
5. mit dem Bürgermeister sprechen
6. auf den Bus warten

a. Haltestelle
b. Gasthaus
c. Park
d. Wohnung
e. Kirche
f. Rathaus

C. Match each question on the left with the most logical response on the right.

d 1. Warum bist du zu Fuß gegangen?
e 2. Warum willst du denn jetzt die Straße überqueren?
b 3. Willst du heute einkaufen gehen?
9 4. Kommst du mit ins Café Leitwanger, Susi?
a 5. Warum hast du grade nicht an der Ecke gehalten?
6. Wollen alle diese Leute in unseren Bus einsteigen?
7. Ist Bürgermeister Ocker da?

a. Ich habe das Halteschild zu spät gesehen.
b. Nein, ich mache nur einen Schaufensterbummel.
c. Tut mir leid, er ist noch beim Mittagessen im Gasthaus.
d. Mein Auto ist kaputt.
e. Meine Wohnung liegt auf der anderen Straßenseite.
f. Es sieht so aus. Ich hoffe, ein paar Leute steigen auch aus.
g. Ich habe leider im Augenblick keine Zeit. Ich muß noch zur Konditorei und auf die Bank gehen.

D. Complete the sentences.

1. Die Hauptstadt der Bundesrepublik ist Bonn.

2. Ich habe heute ein schönes Kleid im Schaufenster vom Kaufhaus Kofler gesehen, Mutti. Darf ich mir das kaufen?

3. Ich bin zu spät ins Büro gekommen, weil es so viel _Verkehr_ auf der Hauptstraße gab.

4. Werner fährt natürlich mit der _Straßenbahn_ in die Stadtmitte.

5. Diese Blumen hier sind auf dem Markt nicht so teuer wie im _Kaufhaus_.

6. Das Rathaus, die Kirche, die Post und der Bahnhof sind die größsten _Gebäude_ hier in der Stadt.

der-Words

The following adjectives take endings similar to those of the definite article (**der, das, die**) and are called "**der**-words":

1. dieser   *this, that, these, those*

   Dieses Gasthaus heißt „Zum Weißen Roß".
   This (that) tavern is called „Zum Weißen Roß" ("At the White Steed").

   Diese Schaufenster sind schön dekoriert.*
   These shop windows are nicely decorated.

   Dieser is used to point out a person or object regardless of the distance from the speaker. If the distance between the object and the speaker is important, the combination **dieser. . . . hier** with **der . . . dort** is used.

   Dieser Wagen *hier* ist teuer, aber *der dort* ist billig.
   This car is expensive, but that one over there is cheap.

   Diese Frau *hier* geht einkaufen, aber *die dort* macht nur einen Schaufensterbummel.
   This woman is going shopping, but that one over there is only window-shopping.

2. jener   *that, those*

   Jene Kirche ist der Kölner Dom.
   That church is the Cologne Cathedral.

---

*Das ist (das sind)** is the equivalent of English *this* or *that is* (*these* or *those are*): **Das ist ein interessantes Gebäude.** *This (that) is an interesting building.* **Das sind interessante Gebäude.** *These (those) are interesting buildings.*

Jener is avoided in conversational German, where the last example would simply appear as: **Diese Kirche ist der Kölner Dom.** In formal German **jener** is often used to mean *the former* in combination with **dieser** which, in this context, means *the latter*.

Münster ist eine Stadt in Deutschland, und Heidelberg ist auch eine Stadt in Deutschland. *Diese* ist bekannt für ihr Schloß, und *jene* ist bekannt für ihren Dom. *latter*   *former*
Münster is a city in Germany, and Heidelberg is also a city in Germany. The latter is known for its castle and the former is known for its cathedral.

Dieser refers to the item last mentioned, while **jener** refers to the item first mentioned.

3. jeder   *each, every* (plural: alle)

Nicht *jede* Hausfrau geht gerne einkaufen.
Not every housewife likes to go shopping.

Nicht *alle* Hausfrauen gehen gerne einkaufen.
Not all housewives like to go shopping.

The stem **all** is generally used without endings when it precedes other **der**-words or **ein**-words (**ein** and the possessive adjectives **mein, dein,** etc.).

All diese Busse fahren nach Berlin.
All meine Freunde wollen nach Deutschland reisen.
All die Studentinnen sprechen gut Deutsch.

4. mancher   *some, quite a few*

Manche is commonly used to refer to a sizeable group.

Manche Kaufhäuser führen Stereoanlagen.
Some department stores carry stereo sets.

Manche Leute lernen es nie.
Some people never learn.

5. solcher   *such, like that*

Solcher is rarely used in the singular; instead the stem **solch** followed by **ein** is used.

Solch eine Stadt hat natürlich einen Bahnhof.*
Such a city (a city like that) has a train station, of course.

In conversational German **solch ein** is reduced to **so ein: So eine Stadt hat natürlich einen Bahnhof.**

---

*Solch may also be preceded by ein, in which case it takes der-word endings: Eine solche Stadt hat natürlich einen Bahnhof. Solche is used in the plural and with abstract nouns: solche Geschäfte, solche Schönheit.

6. welcher *which*

Welche Straßenbahn fährt in die Stadtmitte?
Which streetcar goes to the center of town?

The stem **welch** followed by **ein** is sometimes used in exclamations.

Welch ein schönes Rathaus!
What a beautiful town hall!

Welch may also be used in this way before any adjective.

Welch schönes Wetter!

Declension of *der*-Words

The definite article provides the pattern for the declension of **der** words.

	Masculine	Neuter	Feminine	Plural
Nominative	der	das	die	die
	dieser	dieses	diese	diese
Accusative	den	das	die	die
	diesen	dieses	diese	diese
Dative	dem	dem	der	den
	diesem	diesem	dieser	diesen
Genitive	des	des	der	der
	dieses	dieses	dieser	dieser

Dieser Mann (*dieses* Kind, *diese* Frau) wohnt hier.   (nominative singular)

Diese Männer (Kinder, Frauen) wohnen hier.   (nominative plural)

Ich sehe *diesen* Mann (*dieses* Kind, *diese* Frau).   (accusative singular)

Ich sehe *diese* Männer (Kinder, Frauen).   (accusative plural)

Ich gebe es *diesem* Mann (*diesem* Kind, *dieser* Frau).   (dative singular)

Ich gebe as *diesen* Männern (Kindern, Frauen).   (dative plural)

Das sind die Schuhe *dieses* Mannes (*dieses* Kindes, *dieser* Frau).   (genitive singular)

Das sind die Schuhe *dieser* Männer (Kinder, Frauen).   (genitive plural)

Übungen

°A. **Ersetzen Sie den bestimmten Artikel!** Replace the definite article in italics with the proper form of the **der**-words in parentheses.

1. Steht *das* Rathaus in der Stadtmitte? (dieser, jeder)
2. *Die* Schaufenster in den Geschäften sind schön dekoriert. (mancher, alle)
3. Der Bürgermeister spricht gern mit *den* Touristen. (alle, dieser)
4. An *der* Haltestelle findest du viele Schilder. (mancher, solcher)
5. Die Eltern *des* Professors kommen aus der Hauptstadt. (dieser, jener)

°B. **Vergleichen Sie die zwei Nomen!** Use the correct form of **dieser ... hier** and **der ... dort**.

Zum Beispiel: Das Gasthaus ist neu. (alt)
   Dieses Gasthaus hier ist neu, aber das dort ist alt.

1. Der Apotheker ist freundlich. (unfreundlich)
2. Der Wagen läuft gut. (überhaupt nicht)
3. Die Touristinnen kommen aus England. (aus Spanien)
4. Der Zug fährt nach Hamburg. (nach Ulm)
5. Die Bank ist offen. (geschlossen)

°C. **Ersetzen Sie das der-Wort *solcher!*** Replace the definite article with the proper form of **solch ein** and then with the proper form of **so ein**.

Zum Beispiel: Die Wohnung ist sehr teuer.
   Solch eine Wohnung ist sehr teuer.
   So eine Wohnung ist sehr teuer.

1. Ich möchte in das Café gehen. *Ich möchte in solch ein Café gehen*
2. Die Stereoanlage spielt immer zu laut. *Solch eine Stereoanlage spielt immer zu laut*
3. Manfred will den Film nicht anschauen. *Manfred will solch einen Film*
4. Ich habe das Schild nicht gesehen. *Ich habe solch ein Schild ...*

°D. **Bilden Sie Ausrufe!** Form exclamations with the proper form of **welcher**.

Zum Beispiel: Das ist starker Verkehr.   Das ist ein schönes Gebäude.
   Welch starker Verkehr! Welch ein schönes Gebäude!

1. Das ist ein gemütliches Gasthaus. *Welch ein gemütliches ...*
2. Das ist schönes Wetter. *Welch schönes Wetter!*
3. Das ist schwacher Kaffee. *Welch schwacher Kaffee!*
4. Das ist eine interessante Hauptstraße. *Welch eine interessante*
5. Das ist eine gute Konditorei. *Welch eine gute Konditorei!*

E. **Übersetzen Sie die folgenden Sätze!**

1. Martha, which bus did you take? *Welches bus hast du genom*
2. Not all these people are going to the (**auf den**) railroad station. *Nicht alle Leute ging auf den Bahnhof*
3. Mr. Strubecker, where did you see that café? *Mr. Strubecker, wo hast du das Café gesehen*

4. These tourists want to visit the **Hofbräuhaus** in Munich.
5. I have seen such a cathedral in Münster. *Ich hab solche Kirche*
6. Bach and Goethe are both (**beide**) famous. The latter was a writer (**Schrift-steller**), but the former was a composer (**Komponist**).
7. Many (**viele**) Americans learn French, but some are also learning German.

F. **Gäste aus Amerika.** Regina is taking her American friends on a tour of Berlin. Complete their dialogue with the appropriate **der**-words. Use the dative case after all prepositions.

TOM: *dieses ist* ein interessantes Gebäude! Was für ein Gebäude

ist das?

REGINA: *Diese* Gebäude hier ist ein Museum und *das*

dort ist ein Kaufhaus.

CAROL: *D* Bus nimmt man, wenn man zum Charlottenburger

Schloß fahren will?

REGINA: Man nimmt Linie 10. Aber nicht _____ Deutschen nehmen

den Bus. _____ Deutschen gehen dorthin zu Fuß, denn

das Schloß ist nicht so weit weg von hier.

TOM: Auf diesem Schild hier steht „Linie 10". Hat _____

Haltestelle _____ Schild?

REGINA: Ja, fast _____ Haltestellen haben _____ Schilder.

Carol, warum wollt ihr _____ Museum—ich meine das

Museum in dem Charlottenburger Schloß—besuchen?

CAROL: Wir wollen die berühmte Galerie in *d* Museum

besuchen.

REGINA: _____ Bilder in _____ Galerie möchtet ihr sehen?

TOM: Das wissen wir noch nicht. Wir wollen dorthin, weil unsere deutschen

Freunde uns _____ Galerie empfohlen haben.

REGINA: Gibt es _____ Galerien auch in Amerika?

CAROL: Natürlich, aber nicht _____ Stadt in Amerika hat

_____ Galerie.

REGINA: Schon gut. Wir gehen zu _____ Galerie in dem Schloß.

Aber laßt uns danach in eine Konditorei gehen!

G. **Vergleichen Sie die folgenden Bilder!**

Zum Beispiel: Dieses Gebäude hier ist niedrig, aber das dort ist hoch.

1.
2.
3.
4.
5.

---

ein-Words

The possessive adjectives and **kein** all take the same endings as the indefinite article **ein** and are called "**ein**-words":

1. kein *no, not any*

   Wir haben noch *keine* Wohnung gefunden.
   We haven't found an apartment yet.

2. mein *my*

   Meine Großmutter kann Jiddisch.
   My grandmother knows Yiddish.

3. **dein** *your (familiar singular)*

Helmut, wo sind *deine* Bücher?
Helmut, where are your books?

4. **sein** *his; its*

Dieter sieht *seinem* Onkel ähnlich.   Das Kind hat *sein* Geld verloren.
Dieter looks like his uncle.   The child lost its money.

5. **ihr** *her*

Berta hat *ihren* Wagen verkauft.
Berta sold her car.

6. **unser** *our*

Unser Bürgermeister hat ein Büro im Rathaus.
Our mayor has an office in the town hall.

7. **euer** *your (familiar plural)*

Lotte und Egon, sind das *eu(e)re* Räder?
Lotte and Egon, are those your bikes?

8. **ihr** *their*

Vicki und Karl besuchen *ihren* Onkel.
Vicki and Karl are visiting their uncle.

Auf dem Weg zur Arbeit

9. Ihr   *your (polite)**

Herr Biermann, wo liegt *Ihre* Heimatstadt?
Mr. Biermann, where is your home town?

Frau Springer und Fräulein Leonhard, wann fährt *Ihr* Zug ab?
Mrs. Springer and Miss Leonhard, when does your train leave?

Declension of *ein*-Words

Notice that the declension of the possessive adjectives follows the declension of the indefinite article **ein** in the singular and the declension of the **der**-words in the plural:

	Masculine	Neuter	Feminine	Plural
Nominative	ein	ein	eine	diese
	mein	mein	meine	meine
Accusative	einen	ein	eine	diese
	meinen	mein	meine	meine
Dative	einem	einem	einer	diesen
	meinem	meinem	meiner	meinen
Genitive	eines	eines	einer	dieser
	meines	meines	meiner	meiner

Mein Freund (*mein* Kind, *meine* Freundin) wohnt dort.   (nominative singular)

Meine Freunde (Kinder, Freundinnen) wohnen dort.   (nominative plural)

Ich sehe *meinen* Freund (*mein* Kind, *meine* Freundin).   (accusative singular)

Ich sehe *meine* Freunde (Kinder, Freundinnen).   (accusative plural)

Ich gebe es *meinem* Freund (*meinem* Kind, *meiner* Freundin).   (dative singular)

Ich gebe es *meinen* Freunden (Kindern, Freundinnen.   (dative plural)

Das sind die Schuhe *meines* Freundes (*meines* Kindes, *meiner* Freundin).   (genitive singular)

Das sind die Schuhe *meiner* Freunde (Kinder, Freundinnen).   (genitive plural)

****Ihr** (polite) is always capitalized; **dein** and **euer** are capitalized in letters: **Liebe Mutti! Ich habe Deinen Brief gestern erhalten. . . . Deine Uschi.** *Dear Mom, I received your letter yesterday . . . (Your) Uschi.*

Use of *ein*-Words

1. The **-er** of **unser** and **euer** is often reduced to **-r** when an ending is added.

   Uns(e)re Wohnung ist gleich um die Ecke.   Wo ist eu(e)re Wohnung?
   Our apartment is right around the corner.   Where is your apartment?

2. When **ein**-words are not followed by another adjective or a noun they become pronouns and gain the endings **-er** and **-es** in the nominative singular masculine and nominative and accusative singular neuter.

   Mein Wagen ist alt. *Meiner* ist alt.   (masculine nominative)
   My car is old. Mine is old.

   Dein Auto is neu. *Dein(e)s* ist neu.   (neuter nominative)
   Your car is new. Yours is new.

   Bitte, geben Sie mir ein Buch. Geben Sie mir *ein(e)s*.   (neuter accusative)
   Please give me a book. Give me one.

   When **kein** is used as a masculine pronoun (**keiner**) it is equivalent to English *no one*.

   Keiner hat mich im Kaufhaus bedient.
   No one waited on me in the department store.

Study hint: Remember that in the singular, possessive adjectives always take the same ending as **ein** would if it occurred in the same position.

   Monika hat *ihrem* Bruder im Kaufhaus eine Krawatte gekauft.   (einem Bruder)
   Monika bought her brother a tie in the department store.

   Otto holt *seine* Freundin morgen vom Bahnhof ab.   (eine Freundin)
   Otto will pick up his girlfriend from the railroad station tomorrow.

In the plural, the possessives always take the same ending as a **der**-word in the same position.

   Regina hat *ihren* Brüdern das Rathaus gezeigt.   (diesen Brüdern)
   Regina showed her brothers the town hall.

Übungen

°A. **Ersetzen Sie den bestimmten Artikel!** Use the proper form of the **ein**-words in parentheses.

   1. Ist das der Arzt?   (ein, dein, sein, euer)
   2. Ich sehe *den* Wagen an der Ecke.   (Ihr, kein, unser)
   3. Wir haben *das* Fahrrad gefunden.   (mein, sein, ihr, ein)

4. Der Freund *der* Tochter arbeitet bei der Post.   (ein, sein, mein, unser)
5. Hast du *die* Schlüssel gefunden?   (dein, ihr, sein, kein)

B. **Ergänzen Sie die Sätze!** Complete each sentence with the proper form of the **ein**-word in parentheses.

1. Mein Großvater kommt aus Norwegen. Woher kommt _____ (dein)?

2. Ich wollte ein Taxi zum Bahnhof nehmen. Leider konnte ich _____

   (kein) finden.

3. Ich habe einige Äpfel gekauft. _____ (ein) ist noch übrig (*left*).

   Möchtest du ihn?

4. Ich kaufe meiner Schwester einen neuen Plattenspieler. _____ (ihr)

   ist kaputt.

5. Meine Freunde wollten mit uns den alten Dom zusammen besuchen. Aber

   _____ (kein) hatte heute Zeit.

6. Man sagt, daß das Wetter hier oft schlecht ist. _____ (unser) ist

   auch oft schlecht.

7. Wir machen jeden Samstag einen Schaufensterbummel. Aber heute machen

   wir _____ (kein).

8. Meine Straßenbahn kommt in fünf Minuten. Wann kommt denn

   _____ (euer)?

C. **Übersetzen Sie die folgenden Sätze!** Be careful to notice when **ein**-words are used as pronouns.

1. Walter and his sister went to the post office.
2. I'm looking for a taxi. Do you see one, Heidi?
3. Which car did you see? One is at the (**an der**) corner.
4. Today no tourists are visiting the town hall.
5. Virginia, is your brother's car new?
6. Yes, his is new but mine is old.
7. I am not going to the (**in die**) pharmacy because I do not have any money (I have no money).
8. Thomas showed his friends our house.
9. Our mayor reads *Der Spiegel*. What does yours read?

D. **Einen Brief an einen deutschen Freund (eine deutsche Freundin).** You are writing a short letter of about two paragraphs to a close friend in Germany who knows your family well. Relate news about members of your family using as many **ein**-words as you can in a meaningful manner. Begin with **Lieber** (*masculine*) or **Liebe** (*feminine*) . . . and close with **Dein(e)** and your name.

The Gender of Nouns

Although the gender of German nouns is largely unpredictable, there are some general rules that apply to large groups of nouns.

Masculine Nouns

The following nouns are masculine:

1. almost all nouns referring to male persons or animals

der Mann	der Junge	der Löwe	der Bürgermeister
man	boy	lion	mayor

2. days of the week, months of the year, seasons, points of the compass, and most phenomena of weather

(der) Montag	der Mai	der Sommer	der Osten
Monday	May	summer	East
der Regen	der Schnee	der Donner	der Wind
rain	snow	thunder	wind

3. nouns ending in **-er** derived from verbs

der Schwimmer	der Lehrer	der Plattenspieler	der Wecker
swimmer	teacher	record player	alarm clock

4. most nouns ending in **-el, -en,** or **-m**

der Mantel	der Flügel	der Boden	der Kasten
coat	wing	floor	box, case
der Baum	der Lärm	der Sturm	der Dom
tree	noise	storm	cathedral

5. nouns derived from past participles of strong verbs

der Bund	der Fall	der Fang
(gebunden)	(gefallen)	(gefangen)
alliance	fall	catch
der Gang	der Griff	der Hang
(gegangen)*	(gegriffen)	(gehangen)
motion	grip	slope
der Lauf	der Pfiff	der Rat
(gelaufen)	(gepfiffen)	(geraten)
run	whistle	advice

---

*Other nouns can be formed from these by the addition of prefixes: for example, **der Ausgang** *exit,* **der Eingang** *entrance,* **der Vorgang** *process,* **der Zugang** *access.*

der Schlaf	der Schlag	der Schnitt
(geschlafen)	(geschlagen)	(geschnitten)
sleep	blow	cut

der Stand
(gestanden)
position, condition

If the past participle contains the vowel **o**, the noun formed from it usually contains the vowel **u**:

der Bruch	der Flug	der Fluß
(gebrochen)	(geflogen)	(geflossen)
break	flight	river
der Genuß	der Wurf	der Zug
(genossen)	(geworfen)	(gezogen)
enjoyment	throw	train

The following nouns, although masculine in gender, are also used for females:

der Doktor*	der Gast	der Liebling
doctor	guest	darling
der Mensch	der Professor*	der Teenager
human	professor	teenager

Feminine Nouns

The following nouns are feminine:

1. almost all nouns referring to female persons or animals[†]

die Frau	die Tante	die Kuh
woman	aunt	cow

2. all nouns ending in the suffix **-in**[‡]

die Freundin	die Lehrerin	die Löwin
friend	teacher	lioness

---

*In direct address, **Herr** or **Frau** must precede a title such as **Doktor** or **Professor: Frau Doktor (Pohlmann), wie viele Tabletten sollte ich nehmen?** *Doctor (Pohlmann), how many pills should I take?* **Herr Professor (Schmidt), könnten Sie etwas erklären, bitte?** *Professor (Schmidt), could you please explain something?*

[†]An exception is **das Weib** (*female*). **Das Mädchen** and **das Fräulein** are neuter because they are diminutives.

[‡]The feminine forms ending in **-in** sometimes take umlauts that are not found in their masculine counterparts: **Arzt, Ärztin; Franzose, Französin.**

3. nouns ending in the suffix **-schaft** (usually abstract or collective nouns formed from concrete nouns)

die Freundschaft	die Landschaft	die Nachbarschaft
(der Freund)	(das Land)	(der Nachbar)
friendship	landscape	neighborhood

4. nouns ending in the suffix **-ung** (formed from verbs)

die Erklärung (erklären)	die Lieferung (liefern)
explanation	delivery
die Übung (üben)	die Wohnung (wohnen)
exercise	apartment

5. nouns ending in the suffixes **-heit** or **-keit** (usually formed from adjectives; if the adjective ends in **-ig** or **-lich**, the suffix **keit** is used)

die Dummheit (dumm)	die Klugheit (klug)	die Schönheit (schön)
stupidity	intelligence	beauty

die Freundlichkeit (freundlich)	die Gutmütigkeit (gutmütig)
friendliness	good nature, good-naturedness

6. nouns ending in the suffixes **-ei** or **-tion**

die Konditorei	die Konjunktion
pastry shop	conjunction
die Nation	die Partei
nation	(political) party

7. most nouns ending in **-e***

die Apotheke	die Ecke	die Haltestelle
pharmacy	corner	bus stop
die Kirche	die Stadtmitte	die Straße
church	city center	street

Neuter Nouns

The following nouns are neuter:

1. nouns with the diminutive suffixes **-chen** or **-lein** (an umlaut is added to the stem vowel in the formation of these nouns)

das Brüderlein (der Bruder)	das Fräulein (die Frau)
little brother	young lady, miss

---

*Exceptions: nouns referring to males (**der Junge, der Löwe**), the noun **das Auge** (eye), and nouns formed with the prefix **ge-**, discussed in the next section, on neuter nouns.

das Stühlchen (der Stuhl)
little chair, stool

das Städtchen (die Stadt)
little city

2. names of most cities, countries, and continents (exceptions: die Schweiz, die Tschechoslowakei, and die Türkei)

das alte Köln
old Cologne

das geheimnisvolle Asien
mysterious Asia

das sonnige Spanien
sunny Spain

3. infinitives used as nouns

das Essen
food

das Leben
life

The definite article is often omitted:

Irren ist menschlich.
To err is human.

4. nouns formed with the prefix **ge-** (many of these end in **-e**)

das Gebäude	das Gebirge	das Gefieder	das Geflügel
building	mountain range	plumage	poultry
das Gehör	das Gelände	das Gemälde	das Gerede
sense of hearing	tract of land	painting	talk, gossip

Gender of Compound Nouns

In general, compound nouns have the same gender as the last element:

das Gasthaus   (der Gast, das Haus)
inn

die Haltestelle   (halten, die Stelle)
bus stop

der Handschuh   (die Hand, der Schuh)
glove

das Schaufenster   (schauen, das Fenster)
display window

Ein Schritt weiter

Some nouns have different meanings depending upon their gender:

der Band / das Band / die (Jazz) Band
book, volume / ribbon / (jazz) band

der See / die See
lake / sea

Übungen

°A. **Erklären Sie das Geschlecht** (*gender*)! Translate and account for the gender of the following nouns.

Zum Beispiel: die Schwester
"sister," feminine because it refers to a female

der Ausgang
"exit," masculine because it is derived from the past participle *gegangen*

1. der Arm
2. der Westen
3. die Tante
4. die Mutter
5. der Fernseher
6. das Kätzchen
7. die Umgebung
8. die Mäßigkeit
9. der Spruch
10. die Religion
11. das bezaubernde Wien

12. der Sonnenschein
13. die Tageszeitung
14. das Büchlein
15. das Gefilde
16. der Läufer
17. die Landschaft
18. die Freundin
19. das Rathaus
20. der Mantel
21. die Bluse
22. der Schaum

°B. **Was ist der Artikel?** Provide the definite article for each of the following nouns, translate the noun, and account for your choice.

1. Farbfilm
2. Kuh
3. Schreiber
4. Einheit
5. Vetter
6. Stamm
7. Wurm
8. Flüssigkeit
9. Komponistin
10. Tochter

11. Biologin
12. Stückchen
13. Raum
14. Anfang
15. Version
16. Gehämmer
17. Wirtschaft
18. Bäckerei
19. Wiese
20. Getränk

21. Gastarbeiter
22. Schuß
23. Erscheinung
24. Herbst
25. Äuglein
26. Kindheit
27. Tankstelle
28. Lärm
29. Mannschaft
30. Musikkenner

C. **Bilden Sie Nomen!** Form both masculine and feminine nouns from these verbs; then translate them, using the end vocabulary of this text as a reference.

Zum Beispiel: schwimmen
der Schwimmer, die Schwimmerin: "swimmer"

anfangen
der Anfänger, die Anfängerin: "beginner"

1. arbeiten
2. tanzen (add an umlaut)
3. richten
4. laufen (add an umlaut)
5. entdecken
6. backen (add an umlaut)
7. nähen
8. herausgeben

D. **Bilden Sie Nomen!** Form abstract nouns from the following adjectives and verbs and translate them. (Check the end vocabulary of this text if in doubt about the translation.)

Zum Beispiel: verkleinern **die Verkleinerung: "reduction"**

klug **die Klugheit: "intelligence"**

freigiebig **die Freigebigkeit: "generosity"**

1. gleich *heit = equality*
2. freundlich *keit = friendliness*
3. reizen *der Reiz*
4. ausbeuten *Ausbeutung (ung)*
5. zerstören
6. pünktlich *keit*
7. gesund *heit health*
8. erklären *ung - explanation*
9. wild *heit - wildness*
10. ganz *lich = fully entirely*
11. abkürzen *ung - abbreviation*
12. ergänzen *ung - completing activity*
13. tätig *keit*
14. gemütlich *keit*
15. dumm *heit*

E. **Bilden Sie Verkleinerungen!** Form diminutives from the following nouns and translate them. Use both the suffixes **-chen** and **-lein** for each diminutive and add an umlaut to the root syllable when possible.

Zum Beispiel: Bruder
das Brüderchen, Brüderlein: "little brother"

1. Mutter
2. Kuß
3. Stern
4. Stock
5. Hut
6. Tier
7. Wurst
8. Garten (drop **en**)
9. Haus
10. Blume (drop **e**)

F. **Ergänzen Sie die folgenden Sätze!** Complete the following statements with the nouns given in parentheses and add two more similar nouns of your own choice. Make sure to use the correct form of the definite article.

1. Mein Lieblingsinstrument ist (Geige, Klavier, Trompete, . . .).
2. Ich fahre oft mit (*dative case* Bus, Wagen, Straßenbahn, . . .).
3. Meine Eltern gehen sonntags in (*accusative case* Kirche, Kino, Stadt, . . .).
4. (Musik, Rockkonzert, Schallplatte, . . .) gefällt (gefallen) mir sehr.

G. **Übersetzen Sie die folgenden Sätze!**

1. I like the sun, but I don't like the rain.
2. Mrs. Schäfer grows (**zieht**) little flowers in her (**ihrem**) little garden.
3. Wolfgang, please bring me a little sausage.
4. Anna is a seamstress (from **schneiden**).
5. Toni's intelligence and good-naturedness impressed (**imponieren**) us.

H. **Beschreiben Sie die Stadt, in der Sie leben!** Describe your home town, including the answers to the following questions.

1. Ist es eine Großstadt oder eine Kleinstadt?
2. Sind die Gebäude modern oder alt?
3. Gibt es viel Lärm? Verkehr? Smog? einen Park?

4. Gibt es dort viele Kirchen, Schulen, Museen?
5. Gibt es einen Marktplatz? einen Dom?
6. Gibt es eine Straßenbahn?
7. Findet man dort vielleicht ein deutsches Restaurant?
8. Was gefällt Ihnen am besten in dieser Stadt?
9. Was ist dort besonders wichtig oder interessant?
10. Wohnen Sie gern in solch einer Stadt? Warum? Warum nicht?

The Plural of Nouns; Noun Declensions

The Plural of Nouns

Masculine Nouns

The plural of most masculine nouns is formed with the suffix **-e** and often with an umlaut; nouns ending in **-m** and those derived from past participles almost always take an umlaut.

der Fuß → die Füße   der Hund → die Hunde

der Tag → die Tage   der Zug → die Züge

der Baum → die Bäume   der Eingang → die Eingänge (entrances)

Masculine nouns ending in **-el, -en,** or **-er** have the same forms in the plural as in the singular; some take an umlaut.

der Mantel → die Mäntel (coats)   der Bruder → die Brüder

der Wagen → die Wagen

Feminine Nouns

The plural of most feminine nouns is formed by adding **-n** or **-en**.

die Frau → die Frauen   die Tante → die Tanten (aunts)

If the noun ends in **-in, -nen** is added to form the plural.

die Freundin → die Freundinnen
die Amerikanerin → die Amerikanerinnen

The plural of a small group of monosyllabic feminine nouns is formed with umlaut and **e**.

die Hand → die Hände   die Kuh → die Kühe (cows)

die Maus → die Mäuse (mice)   die Nuß → die Nüsse (nuts)

die Wand → die Wände (walls)

Neuter Nouns

The plural of most neuter nouns is formed with the suffix **-er** and an umlaut.

    das Buch → die Bücher   das Haus → die Häuser

The plural of neuter nouns that end in **-chen** or **-lein** is the same as the singular.

    das Mädchen → die Mädchen   das Fräulein → die Fräulein

The plural of neuter nouns that begin with **ge-** is usually formed by adding **-e** unless the singular already ends in **-e**.

    das Gebiet → die Gebiete (*territories*)

    das Gebäude → die Gebäude

Noun Declensions

You have seen that most masculine and neuter nouns require the ending **-s** or **-es** in the genitive and that most nouns in the dative plural take an **-en** (Chapter 3). There are, however, a few nouns that require special endings.

(e)n-Masculines

A number of masculine nouns take no ending in the nominative singular but take the ending **-(e)n** everywhere else. These are called **(e)n**-masculines (or weak nouns).

	Singular	Plural	Singular	Plural
Nominative	der Student	die Studenten	der Nachbar	die Nachbarn
Accusative	den Studenten	die Studenten	den Nachbarn	die Nachbarn
Dative	dem Studenten	den Studenten	dem Nachbarn	den Nachbarn
Genitive	des Studenten	der Studenten	des Nachbarn	der Nachbarn

(E)n-masculines can usually be identified by the following characteristics:

1. They almost always refer to males; the female counterparts take the suffix **-in**.

    der Student (die Studentin)   der Nachbar (die Nachbarin)

2. Some of these nouns consist of two syllables and end in **-e**.

der Junge	der Löwe	der Hase	der Bote
boy	lion	rabbit	messenger

3. Most **(e)n**-masculines are of foreign origin, are stressed on the final syllable, and resemble their English equivalents.

der Student	der Astronaut	der Komponist	der Polizist
der Präsident	der Biologe	der Geologe	der Soldat

Most dictionaries identify **(e)n**-masculines by giving the genitive singular and plural: **der Student, -en, -en.**

The noun **Herr** takes an **-n** in all cases of the singular except the nominative. In the plural it takes **-en.**

Das ist Herr Braun.   (nominative)
Kennst du Herrn Braun?   (accusative)
Ich habe mit Herrn Braun gesprochen.   (dative)
Das ist Herrn Brauns Buch   (das Buch Herrn Brauns).   (genitive)
Kennst du diese Herren?   (accusative plural)

Irregular Masculines

A small group of masculine nouns take an **-ns** in the genitive singular and an **-n** in all other singular and plural forms:

der Buchstabe	der Gedanke	der Glaube	der Name
letter of alphabet	thought	belief, faith	name

Nominative	der Gedanke	der Glaube
Accusative	den Gedanken	den Glauben
Dative	dem Gedanken	dem Glauben
Genitive	des Gedankens	des Glaubens
Plural	Gedanken	Glauben

Mein *Vorname* ist Sandra.   (nominative)
My first name is Sandra.

Das Kind kann seinen eigenen *Namen* noch nicht schreiben.
   (accusative)
The child cannot write its name yet.

Otto, kennst du die neue Studentin mit *Vornamen*?   (dative)
Otto, do you know the new student by her first name?

Ein Mann *namens* Bernstein hat dich angerufen.   (genitive used
   adverbially)
A man by the name of Bernstein called you.

Der *Glaube* versetzt Berge.   (nominative)
Faith moves mountains.

Er hat seinen *Glauben* verteidigt.   (accusative)
He defended his faith (belief).

Monika hat das in gutem *Glauben* getan.   (dative)
Monika did that in good faith.

Das Herz (*heart*) is also irregular.

Nominative	das Herz
Accusative	das Herz
Dative	dem Herzen
Genitive	des Herzens
Plural	die Herzen

Martins *Herz* ist stark.   (nominative)
Martin's heart is strong.

Hand aufs *Herz*!   (accusative)
Honest to God! (Put hand on heart.)

Die Alte verabschiedete sich mit schwerem *Herzen*.   (dative)
The old woman said farewell with a heavy heart.

Im Grunde seines *Herzens* glaubt Kurt das nicht.   (genitive)
At the bottom of his heart Kurt does not believe that.

Study hint: **Der Gedanke** and other such nouns are declined like the noun **der Wagen** except that the nominative singular does not end in **-(e)n**; **das Herz** is declined like **das Mädchen** except that the nominative and accusative singular do not end in **-en**.

Ein Schritt weiter

Fewer than ten common masculine nouns form the plural with **-er** and an umlaut (when possible). Besides the noun **der Ski (Schi)** and its plural **die Skier (Schier)**, the others are contained in this sentence:

Der *Geist Gottes* ist nicht nur im *Leib des Mannes*, sondern auch im *Wurm* im *Strauch* am *Rand des Waldes*.
The spirit of God is not only in the body of man but also in the worm in the shrub at the edge of the forest.

A small number of neuter nouns, especially those of one syllable ending in **r**, form the plural with **-e** and without an umlaut.

das Haar	das Jahr	das Meer	das Tor	das Rohr
hair	year	sea	gate	reed, cane

Übungen

°A. **Was ist der Plural?** Account for the plural form of each of the following nouns and translate the singular form.

Zum Beispiel: der Turm → die Türme
masculine nouns ending in -*m* take umlaut and -e in the plural; "tower"

1. der Sturm → die Stürme
2. der Schatten → die Schatten
3. das Loch → die Löcher
4. der Ausgang → die Ausgänge
5. die Kunst → die Künste
6. das Heftchen → die Heftchen
7. die Tür → die Türen
8. die Ärztin → die Ärztinnen
9. der Lehrer → die Lehrer
10. das Fach → die Fächer
11. die Tafel → die Tafeln
12. die Blume → die Blumen
13. das Gebäude → die Gebäude
14. der Kasten → die Kasten
15. das Licht → die Lichter
16. der Garten → die Garten
17. das Blümchen → die Blümchen
18. die Schwester → die Schwestern

°B. **Bilden Sie den Plural!** Form the plural of the following nouns and translate them. Then check your answers in the end vocabulary.

1. die Feder
2. die Näherin
3. das Land
4. der Gastgeber
5. der Einfluß
6. der Finger
7. die Landkarte
8. der Gipfel
9. das Gelände
10. der Traum
11. das Häuschen
12. die Gabel
13. der Berg
14. das Röslein
15. das Huhn

°C. **Welche Nomen sind schwach?** Indicate which of the following nouns are **(e)n**-masculine (weak) nouns without consulting the end vocabulary, then translate them. The stress has been indicated as a hint.

1. Künstler
2. Proféssor
3. Schréiber
4. Bürgermeister
5. Astronóm (n)
6. Prophét (n)
7. Präsidént (n)
8. Músiker
9. Patiént (n)
10. Elefánt (n)
11. Juríst
12. Kommandánt (n)
13. Arzt
14. Phýsiker
15. Dóktor

D. **Bilden Sie weibliche Nomen!** Form feminine nouns from the **(e)n**-masculine nouns in Exercise C.

Zum Beispiel: der Student
die Studentin

E. **Ergänzen Sie die folgenden Sätze!** Complete the blanks with the appropriate endings where needed.

1. Kurt, kennst du diesen Student _____?

2. Herr _____ Schöning kommt aus Braunschweig.

3. Herr _____ Schönings Frau ist Anthropologin.

4. Wie heißen die Berater des neuen Präsident _____?

5. Ein guter Nam _____ ist besser als Silber und Gold.

6. Der junge Soldat _____ ist seinem Glaub _____

   treu geblieben.

7. Die letzten Gedank _____ sind die besten.

F. **Übersetzen Sie die folgenden Sätze!**

1. I did not see the sign.
2. Mrs. Bieberbach, do you have an alarm clock?
3. Silvia, do you know that boy?
4. Oskar, do you know the name of the professor?
5. Mr. Päsler's daughter works at the (**bei der**) post office.
6. In the Middle Ages (**im Mittelalter**) life was difficult.
7. Jochen, did you see my little brother (**Brüderchen**).
8. That is the mayor's office.

G. **Ergänzen Sie die folgenden Sätze!** Use the nouns in parentheses in the singular or the plural and an appropriate numeral (or **keine**).

Zum Beispiel: Ich habe . . . (Kind, Arzt, Onkel).
   Ich habe keine Kinder. (*or*)
   Ich habe einen Onkel.

1. Ich habe . . . studiert.   (Fremdsprache, Kapitel)
2. . . . haben (hat) mich diese Woche besucht.   (Freund, Freundin)
3. Letzten Monat habe ich . . . gelesen.   (Buch, Zeitung, Roman)
4. Letzte Woche habe ich . . . gesehen.   (Film, Drama)
5. Gestern habe ich . . . gegessen.   (Apfel, Orange, Ei, Brötchen, Wurst)

H. **Beschreiben Sie die Dinge, die Sie am liebsten haben!** Describe your favorite possessions and those of at least five of your friends or relatives. All the possessions should be in the plural.

Zum Beispiel: Mein Bruder hat drei Schallplatten von Elvis Presley.

Rückblick

A. **Zur Wiederholung. Übersetzen Sie die folgenden Sätze!**

1. Miss Bernstein, do you know this (male) student?
2. Kurt, which bus does one take to the (**zum**) town hall?
3. What a cathedral!
4. In America we have busses like that (such busses).
5. This building is new, but that one is old.
6. I know her brother, but I don't know her parents.
7. Their house is large, but ours is small.
8. Mr. Döring, did you visit the mayor's parents?

B. **Zur Gesamtwiederholung. Übersetzen Sie die folgenden Sätze!**

1. Dieter, don't take that bus.   (Chapter 1)
2. Monika, let's visit the cathedral.   (Translate in two ways.)
3. I have been working for three weeks in the (**in dem**) department store.
4. I believe that Elsa went to the market.   (Chapter 2)
5. I had gone to the post office before I did the homework.
6. Hans, why did you follow Mr. Brown and that (male) student?
7. Marie, is your father a doctor?   (Chapter 3)
8. What is the capital of Switzerland?

5
Über die Grenze

„Paßkontrolle!"

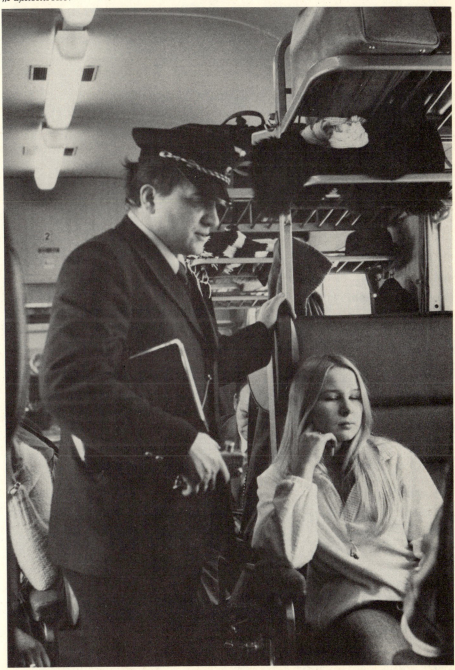

The Future Tense

The Future Perfect Tense

Modal Verbs: Present Tense and Past Tense

Modal Verbs: Future and Perfect Tenses

Verbs of Perception; the Verb *lassen*

The Use of the Preposition *zu* with the Infinitive

The Verbs *wissen*, *kennen*, and *können*

Wortschatz

die **Abfahrt (-en)** departure

das **Abteil (-e)** compartment

die **Ankunft ("e)** arrival

der **Ausweis (-e)** identification

die **Autobahn (-en)** freeway, expressway

der **Beamte (-n)** official, civil servant, government employee

die **Fahrkarte (-n)** ticket

der **Fahrkartenschalter (-)** ticket counter

der **Flüchtling (-e)** refugee

der **Flughafen (-)** airport

das **Flugzeug (-e)** airplane

der **Führerschein (-e)** driver's license

die **Grenze (-n)** border

der **Hafen (-)** harbor

der **paß ("sse)** passport

der **Schaffner (-)** train conductor

das **Schiff (-e)** ship

die **Tankstelle (-n)** gas station

die **Waren** *pl.* goods

der **Zoll** customs, duty

die **Zollkontrolle** customs inspection

ab · **fahren*** to depart

ab · **holen** to pick up, to go to meet

an · **halten*** to stop

an · **kommen*** to arrive

bewachen to watch over, to guard

durchsuchen to search (through), to examine

fliehen* to flee

---

*Verbs marked with an asterisk are strong verbs; see the appendix for the principal parts of strong verbs.

kontrollieren to inspect, to check	**vergleichen*** to compare
packen to pack	**verlangen** to demand
schmuggeln to smuggle	**verstecken** to hide
tanken to buy gasoline	**verzollen** to pay duty on
voll · tanken to fill up (a vehicle) with gasoline	**vor · zeigen** to show

A. *You are taking a trip by train. Arrange the following items in the order in which you would see them, starting with packing your suitcase and ending with sitting in your compartment and showing your ticket to the conductor.*

1. Fahrkartenschalter
2. Sitzplatz
3. Zug

4. Koffer
5. Schaffner
6. Abteil

B. *Find the person on the right that you associate with each of the activities on the left.*

1. die Ausweise vorzeigen
2. die Fahrkarten kontrollieren
3. Preise (*prices*) vergleichen
4. die Waren verzollen
5. die Pässe verlangen
6. die Autobahn benutzen
7. das Auto volltanken
8. verbotene Waren verstecken
9. an der Grenze arbeiten
10. die Koffer packen
11. das Gepäck durchsuchen
12. den Führerschein im Auto haben
13. Angst haben vor der Zollkontrolle

a. Tourist(in)
b. Schaffner(in)
c. Zollbeamte (Zollbeamtin)
d. Fahrer(in)
e. Schmuggler(in)

C. *Complete the sentences.*

1. Auf dem Fahrplan stehen die Zeiten für _____ und _____

    des Zuges aus Paris.

2. Der Zug wird um sieben Uhr _____ und dann um acht Uhr

    wieder _____.

3. Wir werden dich bestimmt am Flughafen _____.

4. In die USA kommen _____ aus vielen Ländern, um ein neues

    Leben anzufangen.

5. Ich habe keinen Zoll für diesen Whisky bezahlt; den habe ich einfach über

    die Grenze _____, Heinz.

6. Die Volkspolizei _____ die Grenze zwischen der DDR und der

    Bundesrepublik. Es ist nicht leicht, über diese Grenze zu _____.

7. Der Zug wird an der Grenze für die Zollkontrolle _____.

D. *Give the means of transportation which are associated with the following places.*

1. Flughafen
2. Bahnhof
3. Tankstelle
4. Hafen

The Future Tense

Formation

The future tense is formed from the present tense of the verb **werden** in combination with the infinitive of the main verb.

sprechen

ich werde sprechen	wir werden sprechen
du wirst sprechen	ihr werdet sprechen
er sie wird sprechen es	sie Sie werden sprechen

Er wird darüber sprechen.
He will talk about it. (He is going to talk about it.)

Wir werden an der Grenze halten.
We will stop at the border. (We are going to stop at the border.)

Word Order

As you saw in Chapter 1, the finite verb is the second element in normal and inverted word order in the present tense. Notice how the rule applies to the future tense:

	(1)	Finite Verb (2)	(3)	Dependent Infinitive (4)
Normal Word Order	Paul	wird	darüber	sprechen.
Inverted Word Order	Darüber	wird	Paul	sprechen.

Notice that the dependent infinitive is the last element.

Just as in the present tense, the finite verb is the last element in transposed word order (word order in subordinate clauses):

	Dependent Infinitive	Finite Verb
Transposed Word Order	Ich glaube, daß Paul darüber *sprechen*	*wird.*

Word Order in Questions:

Just as in the present tense, the finite verb precedes the subject in questions.

Question Word	Finite Verb	Subject		
	Wird	Paul	darüber	sprechen?
Wann	wird	Paul	darüber	sprechen?

Use

1. The future tense is used for actions or events that have not yet taken place, that *will* take place in the future.

   Ich werde zu Hause bleiben.
   I'll stay home.

   Marie wird mit dir sprechen.
   Marie will talk to you.

   However, if the context makes it clear that the action or event will occur in the future, the present tense is normally used in German. Compare these German sentences with their English equivalents.

   Wir *fahren* nächste Woche nach Ostdeutschland.
   We *will* drive to East Germany next week.

Ingrid *geht* morgen zur Berliner Mauer.
Ingrid *will* go to the Berlin Wall tomorrow.

Ich *hole* dich ab, wenn du ankommst.
I *will* pick you up when you arrive.

Since the phrases **nächste Woche**, **morgen**, and **wenn du ankommst** make it clear that the action will take place in the future, the present tense is used.

2. The future tense may be used to express probability. The adverb **wohl** is often used for emphasis.

Wer is denn das?—O das wird (wohl) der Zollbeamte sein.
Who's that, I wonder?—Oh, that's probably the customs official.

Es wird (wohl) fünf Uhr sein.
It is probably five o'clock.

Of course, probability can also be expressed by the adverb **wahrscheinlich** (*probably*) used with the present tense as in English: **O das ist wahrscheinlich der Zollbeamte. Es ist wahrscheinlich fünf Uhr.**

Übungen

°A. **Ersetzen Sie die Pronomen!** Replace the pronouns in italics with the pronouns in parentheses and change the verbs accordingly.

1. *Er* wird nicht in den Osten reisen.   (Sie, ihr, wir, ich)
2. *Ich* werde den Paß vorzeigen.   (sie *sing.*, wir, er, du)
3. Wo wird *er* den Koffer abholen?   (wir, du, ihr, Sie)

B. **Ändern Sie die Verben vom Präsens zum Futur!** In each of the following pairs of sentences, one sentence indicates future time through context, while the other indicates present time. Change the sentence that indicates present time to the future tense.

Zum Beispiel: a.   Ich studiere nächstes Jahr in Deutschland.
         b.   Ich studiere in Deutschland.
         Ich werde in Deutschland studieren. (b)

1. a.   Renate besucht nächsten Freitag ihre Freunde in Leipzig.
   b.   Renate besucht ihre Freunde in Leipzig.

2. a.   Oskar wohnt bei den Eltern.
   b.   Oskar wohnt bei den Eltern, wenn er nach Frankfurt kommt.

3. a.   Ingrid schreibt einen Brief an Wolfgang.
   b.   Wann schreibt Ingrid einen Brief an Wolfgang?

4. a.   Morgen reist Gottfried nach Dresden.
   b.   Gottfried reist nach Dresden.

5. a. Nach der Oper ißt Sabine sicher in der Stadt.
   b. Sicher ißt Sabine in der Stadt.

6. a. Jost fliegt am Ende des Schuljahrs nach Frankfurt.
   b. Jost fliegt nach Frankfurt.

°C. **Ändern Sie die Verben vom Präsens zum Futur!** Put the verbs in the future tense. Pay special attention to word order.

1. Edith besucht Freunde in der D.D.R.
2. Er wartet am Flughafen auf uns.
3. In dieser Stadt wohnt meine Freundin Elisabeth.
4. Die Zollbeamten sind heute nicht sehr höflich.
5. Wohin fährst du?
6. Warum durchsucht der Beamte diesen Koffer?
7. Wir kaufen die Fahrkarten am Fahrkartenschalter.
8. Ich packe schon heute alle Koffer.

D. **Was tun sie wohl?** Create sentences expressing what your friends are probably doing right now.

   Zum Beispiel: Ingrid / in der Klasse / sein
   Ingrid wird wohl in der Klasse sein.

1. Alex / zum Flughafen / mit Lisa / fahren
2. Karl / seine Eltern / abholen
3. Anna und Peter / Grenze nach Holland / überqueren
4. du / Karten / schreiben
5. Margot / ihre Koffer / packen

E. **Übersetzen Sie die folgenden Sätze!**

1. We'll stay overnight in Leipzig.
2. I won't forget my passport.
3. It is probably three o'clock.
4. The professor probably comes from (**aus**) Dresden.
5. Andrea and Sebastian are probably paying duty on these goods.
6. Marianne, will you stay at the (**an der**) border?
7. Horst is probably flying to (**nach**) Paris.
8. Mr. Schneider, the customs official will ask for your passport.

F. **Was machen Sie während der Ferien?** Make plans now for your next vacation. Compose five to ten sentences using the future tense. You might want to use some of the following expressions:

nach Berlin (mit einem Charterflug) fliegen
nach New York (mit dem Schiff, Bus, Zug, Auto, Fahrrad,
    Motorrad [*motorcycle*] fahren
an die Küste (*coast*) (an den Strand, aufs Land, ins Gebirge) fahren
alte Freunde besuchen
zu Hause bleiben
Skilaufen gehen

The Future Perfect Tense

Formation

The future perfect tense is formed from (1) the present tense of the verb **werden**, (2) the infinitive of the auxiliary **haben** or **sein**, and (3) the past participle of the main verb.

sprechen

ich werde gesprochen haben   wir werden gesprochen haben
du wirst gesprochen haben   ihr werdet gesprochen haben
er ⎫   sie ⎫
sie ⎬ wird gesprochen haben   Sie ⎬ werden gesprochen haben
es ⎭   ⎭

gehen

ich werde gegangen sein   wir werden gegangen sein
du wirst gegangen sein   ihr werdet gegangen sein
er ⎫   sie ⎫
sie ⎬ wird gegangen sein   Sie ⎬ werden gegangen sein
es ⎭   ⎭

Word Order

The infinitive—**haben** or **sein**—is always the final element in main clauses in the future perfect tense.* The past participle immediately precedes **haben** or **sein**.

Ich werde darüber *gesprochen haben.*
I will have spoken about it.

Sie werden nach Hause *gegangen sein.*
They will have gone home.

Use

1. The future perfect, which is rarely used in German, can express the completion of a future action, indicating that it *will have occurred* at some point of time in the future—in other words, that one future action will have occurred before another future action.

---

*The future perfect tense rarely occurs in subordinate clauses. When it does, the finite verb—a form of *werden*—immediately follows the past participle of the main verb and the infinitive of **haben** or **sein** in that order: **Petra sagt, daß Paul darüber gesprochen haben wird.** Petra says that Paul will have spoken about it.

Monika wird schon gegessen haben, wenn wir sie abholen.
Monika will already have eaten when we pick her up.

Sie werden schon durch den Zoll gegangen sein, wenn wir am
Flughafen ankommen.
They will already have gone through customs when we arrive at the airport.

In such sentences it is more common to use the present tense or the
future tense (as in English) instead of the future perfect:

Monika ißt schon, bevor wir sie abholen.
Sie werden schon durch den Zoll gehen, bevor wir am Flughafen
ankommen.

2. However, the future perfect is generally used to express probability in
the past. The adverb **wohl** is often used for emphasis.

Wo war dein Bruder gestern? —Er wird (wohl) bei der Arbeit
gewesen sein.
Where was your brother yesterday? —He was probably at work.

Es wird (wohl) sehr kalt gewesen sein.
It was probably very cold.

It is also possible to use the past tense (as in English) with **wahrscheinlich** (*probably*).

Er war wahrscheinlich bei der Arbeit.
Es war wahrscheinlich sehr kalt.

Auf dem Hamburger Hauptbahnhof

Übungen

°A. **Ersetzen Sie die Pronomen!** Replace the pronouns in italics with the pronouns in parentheses and change the verbs accordingly.

1. *Er* wird schon gegessen haben. (ich, sie *sing.*, wir)
2. *Sie* werden schon lange in Rostock gewesen sein. (du, ihr, Sie)

°B. **Ändern Sie die folgenden Verben vom Präsens zum zweiten Futur!** Change the sentences to the future perfect.

Zum Beispiel: Klara fährt nach Potsdam.
Klara wird nach Potsdam gefahren sein.

1. Wir gehen nicht zum Bahnhof.
2. Der Beamte verlangt den Paß.
3. Einige Touristen schmuggeln verbotene Waren.
4. Fliegt ihr nach Hannover?
5. Wir tanken nicht auf der Autobahn.
6. Cornelias Mutter kontrolliert ihre Hausaufgaben.
7. Es wird spät.
8. Die Flüchtlinge fliehen in den Westen.

C. **Übersetzen Sie die folgenden Sätze!** Use the future perfect tense to express probability referring to the past.

Zum Beispiel: Stefan was probably in Erfurt.
Stefan wird wohl in Erfurt gewesen sein.

1. Mr. Schlüter probably came from the (**aus der**) D.D.R.
2. Yesterday Suzanne was probably in (**in der**) school.
3. It was probably six o'clock.
4. Matthias probably paid duty on these goods.
5. Karl probably worked at the (**an der**) gas station.
6. They (**man**) probably examined Martin's suitcase.

D. **Sie sind Herr Clouseau aus Frankreich.** You have just come upon the scene of a crime. Through your keen deductive powers you are able to draw many amazing conclusions (most of which turn out to be false). Express these conclusions with the future or future perfect tenses and the adverb **wohl**.

Zum Beispiel: **Herr Dankwart wird wohl der Mörder sein.**
Er wird wohl Frau Friedland erschossen haben.

You may want to use some of the following vocabulary:

der Mörder (die Mörderin) sein*   *to be the murderer (murderess)*
das Gewehr   *the gun*

---

*This is a strong verb. See the appendix for the principal parts.

Herrn Schmidt (Frau . . . , Fräulein . . .) (im Wohnzimmer, Schlafzimmer, Büro, in der Küche) erschießen* *to shoot Mr. Schmidt (Mrs. . . . , Miss . . .) to death, (in the living room, bedroom, office, kitchen)*

mit einem Messer erstechen* *to stab with a knife*

erwürgen *to strangle*

Geld (wichtige Dokumente) stehlen* *to steal money (important documents)*

ins Ausland fliehen* *to flee to a foreign country*

böse auf Herrn . . . (Frau . . . , Fräulein . . .) sein* *to be angry with Mr. . . . (Mrs. . . . Miss . . .)*

Rache wegen einer Liebesenttäuschung nehmen* *to take revenge on account of disappointment in love.*

Modal Verbs: Present Tense and Past Tense

In the sentences **Wir müssen arbeiten** and **Wir wollen arbeiten,** the conjugated verbs **müssen** and **wollen** are called modal verbs; they express the attitude or "disposition" of the subject toward the action expressed by the dependent infinitive **arbeiten**. There are six modal verbs in German:

dürfen *to be permitted or allowed to; may*
können *to be able to; can*
mögen *to like*
müssen *to have to; must*
sollen *to be supposed to or obliged to; should*
wollen *to want to; to intend to; to claim to*

Present Tense of Modal Verbs

dürfen

ich darf	wir dürfen
du darfst	ihr dürft
er ⎫	sie ⎫
sie ⎬ darf	Sie ⎬ dürfen
es ⎭	

können

ich kann	wir können
du kannst	ihr könnt
er ⎫	sie ⎫
sie ⎬ kann	Sie ⎬ können
es ⎭	

mögen

ich mag	wir mögen
du magst	ihr mögt
er ⎫	sie ⎫
sie ⎬ mag	Sie ⎬ mögen
es ⎭	

müssen

ich muß	wir müssen
du mußt	ihr müßt
er ⎫	sie ⎫
sie ⎬ muß	Sie ⎬ müssen
es ⎭	

sollen

ich soll	wir sollen
du sollst	ihr sollt
er ⎫	sie ⎫
sie ⎬ soll	Sie ⎬ sollen
es ⎭	

wollen

ich will	wir wollen
du willst	ihr wollt
er ⎫	sie ⎫
sie ⎬ will	Sie ⎬ wollen
es ⎭	

Notice in these forms that: (1) the first- and third-persons singular have no endings and are identical, and (2) the singular forms have the same vowel, different from the vowel of the plural forms. **Sollen** is an exception in that the same vowel occurs in the singular and plural.

Dürfen wir hier rauchen?
May we smoke here? (Are we allowed to smoke here?)

Nein, Sie dürfen hier nicht rauchen.
No, you may (must) not smoke here.

Marie kann gut singen.
Marie can (is able to) sing well.

Edith mag keinen Fisch (essen).*
Edith doesn't like (to eat) fish.

Ich muß morgen arbeiten.†
I must (have to) work tomorrow.

Du sollst das nicht tun, Kurt.
You shouldn't do that, Kurt.

Toni soll sehr klug sein.
Toni is supposed to be very intelligent.

Rolf will Schaffner werden.
Rolf wants to become a train conductor.

Die Touristen wollen nach Bern fahren.
The tourists want to (intend to) travel to Bern.

***Mögen** occurs frequently in the subjunctive form **möchte** (Chapter 8), but less frequently otherwise, except to express dislike of foods.

†The negative of **müssen** is expressed by **nicht brauchen zu: Ich brauche morgen nicht zu arbeiten.** *I don't have to work tomorrow.*

Past Tense of Modal Verbs

The past tense of modal verbs is formed by dropping the umlaut from the stem of the infinitive, then adding to it the past-stem ending **-te** and the past-tense endings.

dürfen

ich durf**te**	wir durf**ten**
du durf**test**	ihr durf**tet**
er ⎫ sie ⎬durf**te** es ⎭	sie ⎫ Sie ⎬durf**ten**

können	ich, er / sie / es konnte
mögen	ich, er / sie / es mochte — *use wollte instead*
müssen	ich, er / sie / es mußte
sollen	ich, er / sie / es sollte
wollen	ich, er / sie / es wollte

Notice that the verb **mögen** shows a stem change form **mög-** to **moch-**.

Word Order with Modal Verbs

As you saw in Chapter 1, the finite verb is the second element in normal and inverted order. Notice how the rule applies to the present and past tenses of the modals:

	(1)	Finite Verb (2)	(3)	Dependent Infinitive (4)
Normal Word Order	Anna	will	nach Bern	fahren.
	Anna	wollte	nach Bern	fahren.
Inverted Word Order	Nach Bern	will	Anna	fahren.
	Nach Bern	wollte	Anna	fahren.

Notice that the dependent infinitive is the last element.

The modal verbs, just like other finite verbs, are the last elements in transposed word order (word order in subordinate clauses).

				Dependent Infinitive	Finite Verb
Transposed Word Order	Ich glaube, daß	Anna	nach Bern	fahren	will.
	Ich glaube, daß	Anna	nach Bern	fahren	wollte.

Notice that the dependent infinitive directly precedes the verb.

The modal verbs, just like other finite verbs, precede the subject in questions:

	Question Word	Finite Verb	Subject		
Word Order in Questions		Will	Anna	nach Bern	fahren?
	Wann	will	Anna	nach Bern	fahren?
		Wollte	Anna	nach Bern	fahren?
	Wann	wollte	Anna	nach Bern	fahren?

Verbs of motion (**fahren, gehen, reisen, fliegen**, etc.) and the verbs **machen** and **tun** are often omitted as infinitives dependent on modal verbs:

Anna will nach Bern.
Anna wants to go to Bern.

Ich muß zum Zahnarzt.
I have to go to the dentist.

Sabrina hat das gewollt.
Sabrina wanted to do that.

Übungen

°A. **Ersetzen Sie die Pronomen!** Replace the pronouns in italics with the pronouns in parentheses and change the verbs accordingly.

1. *Er* darf diese Waren nicht über die Grenze mitnehmen.   (Sie, ihr, wir, ich)
2. *Man* muß hier einen Führerschein haben.   (sie *sing.*, wir, Sie, er)
3. Nora meint, *wir* sollen jetzt tanken.   (ich, du, ihr, er)
4. Mögen *Sie* keinen Fisch?   (er, du, ihr, sie)
5. *Wir* wollen mit dem Schiff fahren.   (ich, er, sie *pl.*, sie *sing.*)

°B. **In der Vergangenheit.** Change the following sentences from the present tense to the past tense.

Zum Beispiel: Wir dürfen nicht rauchen.
Wir durften nicht rauchen.

1. Ich muß noch meine Fahrkarte kaufen. *mußte*
2. Sie mag die Intercity Züge. *wollte mochte*
3. Warum soll sie nicht in diesem Abteil sitzen? *sollten*
4. Ich kann das Fenster nicht öffnen. *konnte*
5. Sie will den Schaffner fragen. *wollten wollte*

C. **Bilden Sie Sätze!** Rearrange the words to form sentences. Use the proper form of the modal verb: past tense if the word **gestern** appears, present tense otherwise.

Zum Beispiel: ich weiß, daß du / mögen / keine Tomaten
Ich weiß, daß du keine Tomaten magst.

gestern / ich / müssen / schreiben / einen Bericht
Gestern mußte ich einen Bericht schreiben.

1. Hartmut meint, daß Inge / können / singen / nicht gut
2. Sabine / wollen / fahren / nach Bad Kreuznach / nächsten Samstag

3. Lorenz blieb gestern zu Hause, weil Diana / wollen / kommen / zu Besuch
4. leider / ihr / dürfen / spielen / nicht im Garten
5. Margot behauptet (*claims*), daß wir / gestern / sollen / schreiben / einen Bericht über die Berliner Mauer
6. hoffentlich / Kurt / dürfen / gehen / mit uns ins Kino
7. gestern / wir / können / nicht schwimmen gehen / wegen (*on account of*) schlechten Wetters.
8. gestern / Marianne / wollen / fahren / nach Rostock

D. **Bilden Sie Fragen!** Rearrange the words to form questions. Use the proper form of the modal verb: past tense if the word **gestern** appears, present tense otherwise.

Zum Beispiel: du / können / gehen / mit uns ins Kino?
Kannst du mit uns ins Kino gehen?

wann / ihr / wollen / essen / gestern zu Abend?
Wann wolltet ihr gestern zu Abend essen?

1. Sie / können / empfehlen / mir ein gutes Restaurant?
2. bis wann / ihr / müssen / einreichen (*turn in*) / den Bericht?
3. warum / du / können / finden / gestern / die Tankstelle nicht?
4. wir / sollen / kaufen / etwas für die Party?
5. was / du / wollen / machen / morgen?
6. warum / Sonja / müssen / bleiben / gestern zu Hause?
7. welchen Bus / wir / sollen / nehmen / zur Berliner Mauer?
8. ich / mögen / keinen Fisch

E. **Übersetzen Sie die folgenden Sätze!**

1. Yesterday I wanted to stay home (**zu Hause**).
2. Which bus are we supposed to take to the (**zum**) train station?
3. Are we supposed to write a report on (**über**) Berlin?
4. Georg could not understand the customs officials.
5. Gerd, did you have to stop for the customs inspection?
6. Rudi does not like tomatoes.
7. I wanted to fly to (**nach**) Bonn.
8. Gerd and Uschi, can you recommend a restaurant?
9. Klaus, do you want to play tennis?
10. Sigi and Lotte, when do you have to show your passports?

F. **In meiner Kindheit . . .** Create five sentences contrasting some aspect of your childhood with the present time; use the following modal verbs: **dürfen, können, mögen, sollen,** and **wollen.**

Zum Beispiel: Ich durfte (sollte) nicht allein ins Kino gehen, aber jetzt darf ich das allein.

Ich konnte nicht Auto fahren, aber jetzt kann ich das gut.

Ich mochte keine Tomaten, aber jetzt mag ich Tomaten gern.

Ich wollte immer mit meinen Spielzeugen spielen, aber jetzt will ich immer meine Freunde (Freundinnen) besuchen.

Modal Verbs: Future and Perfect Tenses

The Future Tense

The future tense of modal verbs is formed with the present tense of **werden** and a combination of a dependent infinitive and the infinitive of the modal verb. This combination occurs at the end of the clause and is called a "double infinitive."*

	Double Infinitive	
	Dependent Infinitive	Modal Infinitive
Hans wird gut	schwimmen	können.
Hans will be able to swim well.		
Eva and Peter werden Karten	spielen	wollen.
Eva and Peter will want to play cards.		

The Perfect Tenses

You have seen that the perfect tenses are formed with an auxiliary (**haben** or **sein**) and a past participle. All modal verbs use the auxiliary **haben**. Their past participles show changes similar to those of the past stem:

Infinitive	Past Stem	Past Participle
dürfen	durfte	gedurft
können	konnte	gekonnt
mögen	mochte	gemocht
müssen	mußte	gemußt
sollen	sollte	gesollt
wollen	wollte	gewollt

Gisela hat das gewollt. (present perfect)
Gisela wanted (to do) that.

Gisela hatte das gewollt. (past perfect)
Gisela had wanted (to do) that.

Das haben sie gekonnt. (present perfect)
They were able to do that.

Das hatten sie gekonnt. (past perfect)
They had been able to do that.

---

*In transposed word order (word order in subordinate clauses), the finite verb (**werden**) occurs after the double infinitive: **Gertrud sagt, daß Hans gut schwimmen können *wird*.**

However, if the modal has a dependent infinitive, the dependent infinitive and the modal form a double infinitive and are placed at the end of the clause, just as in the future tense:

	Double Infinitive		
	Dependent Infinitive	Modal Infinitive	
Hat Gisela	tanzen	wollen?	(not **gewollt**)
Did Gisela want to dance?			
Erich und ich haben nach Bonn	fahren	müssen.	(not **gemußt**)
Erik and I had to go to Bonn.			
Ich habe meinen Paß nicht	finden	können.	(not **gekonnt**)
I was not able to find my passport.			

You have seen that in subordinate clauses with the perfect tenses, the auxiliary is the final element of the clause: **Ich glaube, daß Gisela gestern abend bei der Party getanzt *hat*.** However, when there is a double infinitive in a subordinate clause, the auxiliary (a form of **haben**) always precedes the double infinitive:

Ich glaube, daß Gisela gestern abend bei der Party *hat* tanzen wollen.
I think that Gisela wanted to dance yesterday at the party.

Eberhard behauptet, daß er als Kind sehr gut *hat* schwimmen können.
Eberhard maintains that he was able to swim very well as a child.

In conversational German, the double infinitive is generally avoided by the use of the past tense:

Ich glaube, daß Gisela gestern abend bei der Party tanzen *wollte*.

Eberhard behauptet, daß er als Kind sehr gut schwimmen *konnte*.

Übungen

°A. **Setzen Sie die folgenden Sätze ins Futur!**

Zum Beispiel: Hans kann gut schwimmen.
Hans wird gut schwimmen können.

1. Erich muß nach Bonn fahren.
2. Man darf nicht lange an der Grenze halten.
3. Gisela und Wolfgang wollen nach Cochem reisen.
4. Wann dürfen wir ins Kino gehen?
5. Joseph will Freunde in Ostberlin besuchen.
6. Könnt ihr dem Flüchtling helfen?
7. Wie lange mußt du an der Grenze warten?

B. **Setzen Sie die folgenden Sätze ins Perfekt!** Place the following sentences in the present perfect and translate.

Zum Beispiel: Ich konnte das nicht.
Ich habe das nicht gekonnt.
I wasn't able to do that.

Ich konnte den Zollbeamten nicht verstehen.
Ich habe den Zollbeamten nicht verstehen können.
I wasn't able to understand the customs official.

1. Günther wollte das nicht.
2. Wann konnten Reinhold und Edith nach Zell reisen?
3. Warum mußtest du gestern deinen Paß vorzeigen?
4. Leider durfte ich das nicht.
5. Pamela und Klara sollten letztes Mal diese Kleider verzollen.

C. **Setzen Sie die folgenden Sätze ins Perfekt!** Place the following sentences in the present perfect being careful to place the auxiliary **haben** in the correct position.

Zum Beispiel: Monika konnte ihre Eltern nicht über die Grenze bringen.
Monika hat ihre Eltern nicht über die Grenze bringen können.

Ich glaube, daß Monika ihre Eltern nicht über die Grenze
bringen konnte.
**Ich glaube, daß Monika ihre Eltern nicht über die Grenze hat
bringen können.**

1. Julia und Bernadette durften nach Leipzig reisen.
2. Wir wollen wissen, ob Julia und Bernadette nach Leipzig reisen durften.
3. Ich bin gestern zu Hause geblieben, weil ich einen Bericht schreiben mußte.
4. Mußtet ihr die Pässe mitbringen?
5. Der Beamte meint, daß wir diese Waren mitbringen durften.
6. Ich glaube, daß Marie einen neuen Koffer kaufen wollte.

D. **Übersetzen Sie die folgenden Sätze!**

1. I'll have to write that report by (**bis**) tomorrow.
2. Traude, did you want to talk to me (**mit mir**)? (past and present perfect)
3. At the (**an der**) border the customs officials will want to search through our suitcases.
4. Therese and Wolf, were you permitted to drive the car? (past and present perfect)
5. I believe that Wilhelm wanted to see that film. (past and present perfect)
6. Yesterday we were supposed to show our passports. (past and present perfect)
7. Yes, but we didn't want (to do) that. (past and present perfect)
8. Miss Kuhn, didn't you like fish as a (**als**) child?

E. **Sie werden interviewt.** You are interviewed about your childhood. Choose one of the expressions in the parentheses on which to base your answer. Your answers should be in the present perfect tense following the model.

Zum Beispiel: Was hast du als Kind tun wollen? (mit einer Eisenbahn spielen *to play with a train*); Sandburgen am Strand bauen *to build sand castles at the beach*).

Ich habe oft Sandburgen am Strand bauen wollen.

1. Was hast du als Kind tun müssen? (mein Zimmer aufräumen *to clean up my room;* mir die Hände vor dem Essen waschen* *to wash my hands before eating*)

2. Was hast du als Kind nicht gedurft? (auf der Straße spielen *to play in the street;* Hunde ins Haus bringen *to bring dogs into the house*)

3. Was hast du als Kind tun wollen? (mit dem Bruder oder der Schwester streiten* *to fight with my brother or sister*; mit Buntstiften an die Wand malen *to color the walls with crayons*

4. Was hast du als Kind gut gekonnt? (etwas mit Bausteinen bauen *to build something with blocks*; mit Buntstiften an die Wand malen)

5. Was hast du als Kind tun sollen? (brav sein *to be well-behaved*; ruhig sein *to be quiet*)

Verbs of Perception; the Verb *lassen*

Like the modal verbs, verbs of perception—such as **fühlen** (*to feel*), **hören** (*to hear*), and **sehen** (*to see*)—are used with dependent infinitives without the preposition **zu**.

Wir sahen Petra Klavier spielen.
We saw Petra play(ing) the piano.

Wir hörten Petra Klavier spielen.
We heard Petra play(ing) the piano.

Dieter fühlte sein Herz schlagen.
Dieter felt his heart beat(ing).

The verb **lassen** is used with dependent infinitives without **zu** to mean *to let* (*allow*) or *to have (something) done*.[†]

---

*This is a strong verb; see the appendix for principal parts of strong verbs.

[†]**Lassen** is also used to form the first-person plural imperative (*Let's* . . .), as discussed in Chapter 1.

Ediths Chef ließ sie nach Amerika fahren.
Edith's boss let her go to America.

Wir lassen das Haus streichen.
We're having the house painted.

Cornelia läßt ihren Wagen reparieren.
Cornelia is having her car repaired.

Egon ließ sich die Haare kurz schneiden.
Egon had his hair cut short.

Ich ließ den Arzt rufen.
I had the doctor called. (I had someone call the doctor.)

Like modal verbs the verbs **hören**, **sehen**, and **lassen** form a double infinitive in their perfect tenses.

Ich habe Paul gestern singen hören. (not *gehört*)
I heard Paul sing(ing) yesterday.

Martins Vater hat ihn nicht mitkommen lassen. (not *gelassen*)
Martin's father didn't let him come along.

Wir haben unsere Mannschaft Fußball spielen sehen. (not *gesehen*)
We watched our team play(ing) soccer.

Übungen

A. **Bilden Sie Sätze!** Rearrange the words to form sentences. Use the indicated tense of the italicized verb.

Zum Beispiel: ich / *sehen* / Ruth / springen ins Wasser   (past)
 Ich sah Ruth ins Wasser springen.

1. wir / *hören* / gestern / singen / Richard   (past)
2. jeden Tag / Rainer / *sehen* / die Jungen / spielen / Fußball   (present)
3. Marina / *sehen* / spazieren / die Frau im Garten   (past)
4. Regina / *hören* gern / unser Orchester / spielen / die Neunte Symphonie   (present)

B. **Beim Oktoberfest.** Relate what you and your friends saw and heard at the Oktoberfest, following the model.

Zum Beispiel: ich / hören / eine Kapelle spielen
 Ich habe eine Kapelle spielen hören.

1. Gertrud / sehen / Leute tanzen
2. Peter / hören / eine Frau Klavier spielen
3. ich / sehen / eine Tanztruppe auf der Bühne (*stage*) tanzen
4. Otto und Horst / hören / eine Sängerin deutsche Volkslieder singen
5. du / sehen / Kinder heiße Würste essen
6. ich / hören / ein Mädchen mit einem Touristen flirten

C. **Bilden Sie Sätze!** Rearrange the words to form sentences. Use the indicated tense of the verb **lassen** and translate the sentence.

Zum Beispiel: der Professor / lassen / schreiben / uns immer viele
Berichte (present)
Der Professor läßt uns immer viele Berichte schreiben.
The professor always has us write a lot of reports.

ich / lassen / durchsuchen / die Beamten meinen Wagen (past)
Ich ließ die Beamten meinen Wagen durchsuchen.
I let the officials examine my car.

1. Manfred / lassen / bauen / ein neues Haus für seine Familie (past)
2. lassen / du / schneiden / dir die Haare immer kurz? (present)
3. Gudrun und Dietrich / lassen / waschen / nie ihren Wagen (present)
4. ich / lassen / gestern die Ärztin / rufen (past)
5. ich weiß, daß Gisela / lassen / abholen / ihren Koffer vom Bahnhof (present)
6. warum / Sie / lassen / gehen / Ihr Kind nicht ins Kino? (past)
7. ich glaube, daß Heinrich / lassen / machen / einen neuen Paß (present)

D. **Ändern Sie die Sätze von Übung C zum Perfekt!** Change the sentences in Exercise C to the present perfect tense.

Zum Beispiel: Der Professor läßt uns immer viele Berichte schreiben.
Der Professor hat uns immer viele Berichte schreiben lassen.

Ich ließ die Beamten meinen Wagen durchsuchen.
Ich habe die Beamten meinen Wagen durchsuchen lassen.

E. **Übersetzen Sie die folgenden Sätze!**

1. Gerd, did you hear Gisela sing yesterday? (present perfect)
2. I saw Heinz and Rita play tennis. (past)
3. Ute, why did you have your hair (**dir die Haare**) cut short? (present perfect)
4. Cornelia says that she heard the orchestra (**das Orchester**) playing jazz (**Jazz**). (present perfect)
5. Walter and Gerd, when did you have your house painted? (present perfect)
6. Did you see Edith going to the show with Rainer? (present perfect)
7. Mrs. Richter, why did you have the doctor called? (present perfect)

F. **Was wollen Sie machen lassen?** What are some of the things you need or want to have done? Write five sentences, following the model. You may want to use some of the following expressions:

mein Klavier stimmen (*tune*)
meine Schuhe, (Uhr, meinen Plattenspieler, Fotoapparat, Wagen) reparieren
mein Haus (Schlafzimmer, Wohnzimmer, Büro, meine Wohnung, Küche) streichen
mir die Haare schneiden
meine Kleider chemisch reinigen (*dry-clean my clothes*)

Zum Beispiel: Ich muß (will) meine Wohnung streichen lassen.

The Use of the Preposition *zu* with the Infinitive

You have seen in this chapter that the infinitive without the preposition **zu** is used with modal verbs, verbs of perception, and the verb **lassen**.

Eva darf (kann, muß) kommen.
Eva may (can, must) come.

Eva soll (will) kommen.
Eva is supposed to (wants to) come.

Ich sah Hans einen Brief schreiben.
I saw Hans write a letter.

Sie ließen ihn warten.
They had him wait.

The verbs **gehen** and **kommen** are also used without the preposition **zu** when they have dependent infinitives expressing physical activities.

Wir *gehen* jetzt *spazieren*.*
We are going for a walk.

Gehst du heute *schwimmen*?
Are you going swimming today?

Bist du gestern *schwimmen gegangen*?
Did you go swimming yesterday?

Fritz *kommt* mit uns Fußball *spielen*.
Fritz is coming with us to play soccer.

The verbs **helfen** and **lernen** are normally used without **zu** when they have a dependent infinitive.

Fritz hilft dem Vater das Auto reparieren.
Fritz is helping his father repair the car.

Annegret lernt gut schwimmen.
Annegret is learning to swim well.

After almost all verbs not already discussed in this section, **zu** should be used with the infinitive.

Sie beginnt zu lesen.
She begins to read.

Es ist nicht schwer, Deutsch zu lernen.
It's not hard to learn German.

***Spazieren** acts as a separable prefix and is written as one word with **gehen** when **spazieren** directly precedes **gehen**: **Wir sind gestern spazierengegangen.**

Du brauchst das nicht zu tun.
You don't have (need) to do that.

Der Beamte hat mir befohlen, meinen Paß vorzuzeigen.*
The official ordered me to show my passport.

Bernadette wünscht, in die Stadt zu fahren.
Bernadette wishes to drive downtown.

Notice that a comma separates the finite verb from the infinitive with its modifiers.

Zu is also used with the dependent infinitive in three prepositional constructions.

1. **um . . . zu**

   Rebekka studiert fleißig, um gute Noten zu bekommen.
   Rebekka is studying hard in order to get good grades.

   Philip fährt nach München, um am Oktoberfest teilzunehmen.
   Philip is going to Munich (in order) to participate in the Oktoberfest.

2. **ohne . . . zu**

   Peter fährt immer viel mit dem Auto, ohne an die Energiekrise zu denken.
   Peter drives a lot, without thinking about the energy crisis.

3. **(an)statt . . . zu**

   Hans spielt oft Tennis, statt seine Hausarbeit zu machen.
   Hans often plays tennis instead of doing his homework.

Übungen

°A. **Mit wem . . . ?** Ask questions using **Mit wem . . . ?** and a form of the verb **gehen**.

   Zum Beispiel: Petra schwimmt Montag nachmittags.
   Mit wem geht Petra Montag nachmittags schwimmen?

   1. Wir spielen morgen Fußball.
   2. Dietrich fischt am Wochenende.
   3. Monika tanzt am Freitag.
   4. Ihr trinkt morgen nach dem Unterricht Bier.
   5. Der Professor spielt nachmittags Tennis.

°B. **Wer . . . ?** Now ask questions using **Wer . . . ?** and a form of the verb **kommen**, using the items from Exercise A.

   Zum Beispiel: Petra schwimmt Montag nachmittags.
   Wer kommt mit Petra Montag nachmittags schwimmen?

---

*If the infinitive has a separable prefix, **zu** is placed between the prefix and the verb: **Vorzuzeigen**. Separable prefixes are discussed in Chapter 6.

C. **Bilden Sie Sätze mit *brauchen, helfen* und *lernen*!** Complete the sentences, following the models.

Zum Beispiel: Heidi und Egon schreiben den Bericht nicht. Heidi und Egon brauchen . . .
Heidi und Egon brauchen den Bericht nicht zu schreiben.

Philip wäscht seinen Wagen. Ich helfe . . .
Ich helfe Philip seinen Wagen waschen.

1. Marie macht etwas zu essen. Wir helfen . . .
2. Bettina spielt Baseball. Bettina lernt . . .
3. Rolf kontrolliert die Pässe. Helmut hilft . . .
4. Yvette fährt Fahrrad. Yvette lernt . . .
5. Walter packt seinen Koffer nicht. Walter braucht . . .

D. **„Morgen, morgen, nur nicht heute . . . !"*** Hans is a procrastinator and thinks nothing needs to be done until tomorrow. Make statements with **nicht brauchen**, following the model.

Zum Beispiel: Wir müssen den Bericht schreiben.
Wir brauchen den Bericht nicht heute zu schreiben.

1. Wir müssen die Koffer packen.
2. Der Lehrer muß die Berichte lesen.
3. Sie müssen das schreiben.
4. Wolf muß nach Berlin reisen.
5. Wir müssen das Auto tanken.

E. **Bilden Sie Sätze!** Form sentences with **um . . . zu**, **ohne . . . zu** or **(an)statt . . . zu**, following the models.

Zum Beispiel: Karoline geht in die Stadt. Sie will ein Geschenk (*present*) für Egon kaufen.
Karoline geht in die Stadt, um ein Geschenk für Egon zu kaufen.

David ist nach Frankfurt gereist. Er hat nicht auf uns gewartet.
David ist nach Frankfurt gereist, ohne auf uns zu warten.

Klara geht ins Kino. Sie lernt nicht Englisch.
Klara geht ins Kino, anstatt Englisch zu lernen.

1. Dieter arbeitet nach der Schule. Er will etwas Geld verdienen (*earn*).
2. Gertrud bleibt in Saarbrücken. Sie fährt nicht nach St. Wendel.
3. Christina hat über Potsdam gesprochen. Sie hat Schloß Sans Souci nicht erwähnt (*mentioned*).
4. Heinz geht zum Rockkonzert und macht die Hausaufgaben nicht.
5. Julia ist in die Stadt gegangen. Sie hat nicht mit Klaus gesprochen.
6. Rolf muß auf die Bank. Er will etwas Geld holen.
7. Frank und Katja studieren Medizin. Sie wollen Ärzte werden.
8. Sandra hat eine Rheinfahrt gemacht. Sie hat aber die Lorelei[†] nicht gesehen.
9. Nach dem Unterricht spielen wir Basketball. Wir gehen nicht gleich nach Hause.

---

*„**Morgen, morgen, nur nicht heute,**" **sagen alle faulen Leute** is a German saying.
[†] The **Lorelei** is a famous promontory on the Rhine River.

The Verbs *wissen,* *kennen,* and *können*

Forms

Although the present tense of **kennen** is perfectly regular, the verb **wissen** shares the irregularities of the present tense of the modals (including **können**), discussed earlier in this chapter:

1. The first- and third-persons singular have no endings and are identical.

2. The singular forms have a stem vowel different from that of the plural forms.

wissen
to know

ich weiß	wir wissen
du weißt	ihr wißt
er	sie
sie ⎬weiß	Sie ⎬wissen
es	

Kennen, können, and **wissen** form the past stem with the weak ending **-te;** they also show a vowel change. The same vowel change occurs in the formation of the past participle.

Infinitive	Past Stem	Past Participle
kennen	kannte	gekannt
können	konnte	gekonnt
wissen	wußte	gewußt

Uses

Wissen, kennen, and **können** can all mean *to know.* **Kennen** is used with direct objects that can be heard, seen, or touched; it means *to be familiar with (someone or something).*

Kennst du *die Neunte Symphonie* von Beethoven?
Are you familiar with Beethoven's *Ninth Symphony?*

Ich kenne Fräulein Lieder nicht.
I don't know Miss Lieder.

Wissen is used for facts, concepts, or information. Unlike **kennen,** it is usually used with clauses.

Wissen Sie, wo die Post ist?
Do you know where the post office is?

Nein, das weiß ich nicht.
No, I don't know.

Weißt du, wo Irmgard wohnt?
Do you know where Irmgard lives?

Weißt du die Antwort?
Do you know the answer?

The modal verb **können** is used to mean *to know* in the sense of *to be able to (do something), to know how to.* It is used with languages, things memorized (poems or songs, for instance), and activities.

Kannst du dieses Lied?
Do you know (how to sing) this song?

Helga kann gut Englisch.
Helga knows English well.

Unser Lehrer kann gut schwimmen.
Our teacher knows how to swim well.

Übungen

A. **Ergänzen Sie die Sätze!** Use the present tense of **kennen** or **wissen**, as appropriate.

1. _____ du Bachs *Chromatische Fantasie?*

2. _____ Sie, wo Darmstadt liegt?

3. Ich _____ Edith und Konrad gut.

4. _____ du, wann wir unsere Pässe vorzeigen müssen?

5. _____ Sie die Stadt Magdeburg?

6. _____ ihr die Antwort?

7. _____ ihr den Professor gut?

8. _____ Günther, wie lange dieser Film läuft?

9. Ihr _____ diese Musik schon, nicht wahr?

10. _____ du die Universität Bonn?

B. **Verwenden Sie das Verb *können*!** Use the present tense of **können** and translate each sentence.

1. _____ Elke Plattdeutsch?

2. Wir _____ alle gut schwimmen.

3. _____ ihr das Volkslied „Muß i' denn"?

4. Fräulein Furtwängler, _____ Sie auch Klavier spielen?

5. Joseph _____ Italienisch, Französich, Griechisch, Deutsch, und sogar Hebräisch.

C. **Ergänzen Sie die folgenden Sätze!** Use the proper form of **wissen**, **kennen**, or **können** as appropriate.

1. _____ du, wie man mit dem Bus in die Stadt kommt? (present)

2. Ich _____ Hartmut und Lotte schon lange. (present)

3. Eva _____ gut Deutsch. (present)

4. Klaus _____ als Kind Geige spielen. (past)

5. _____ du das Gedicht "Der Fischer" von Goethe?*

6. Wir _____ als Kinder viele Volkslieder. Leider haben wir sie alle verlernt (*forgotten*). (past)

7. _____ ihr, wie der neue Professor heißt? (present)

8. Gisela _____ immer die richtige Antwort. (present)

9. Ich _____ nicht, daß Gabi nach Limburg gefahren ist. (past)

10. _____ Traude und Werner als Kinder Tennis spielen? (past)

D. **Übersetzen Sie die folgenden Sätze!**

1. Sara, do you know where Oskar lives now?
2. Mrs. Zimmermann knows English but not Russian.
3. Ronald and Georg, do you know Edith Bieberbach?
4. Mr. Haack, did you know that Ruth comes from (**aus**) Stuttgart? (present perfect)
5. No, I didn't know that. (present perfect)

E. **Sind Sie klug? Sind Sie begabt?** Are you knowledgeable and talented? List ten things you know or can do using the verbs **kennen**, **können**, and **wissen**. You might want to use some of the following expressions:

Beethovens *Fünfte Symphonie*
Russisch
das Drama *Faust*
wie der Professor heißt
wer der deutsche Kanzler (*chancellor*) ist

Zum Beispiel: Ich kenne die *Mona Lisa*.
Ich kann Deutsch.
Ich weiß, wo Berlin liegt.

---

*There are two possible answers. What is the difference in meaning?

Rückblick

A. Zur Wiederholung. Übersetzen Sie die folgenden Sätze!

1. I'll do the homework at home (**zu Hause**).
2. Tomorrow we'll visit Anneliese.
3. They (**man**) probably packed the suitcases yesterday. (Translate in two ways.)
4. Miss Huber, you may sit here.
5. Helmut and Eva, did you have to show your passports? (past tense)
6. —No, we didn't have to do that. (present perfect)
7. I believe that Erika wanted to go to (**nach**) Berlin. (present perfect)
8. I heard Erika singing yesterday. (past and present perfect)
9. Mrs. Wendt, did you have the doctor called? (present perfect)
10. Heinz is letting us go in his (**mit seinem**) car.
11. Rosemarie and Sigi, did you go swimming yesterday? (present perfect)
12. Bruno is learning to drive.
13. Diana, do you know Hermann Behn? Do you know where he lives?
14. Paul and Julia went to the travel agency in order to buy the tickets.

B. Zur Gesamtwiederholung. Übersetzen Sie die folgenden Sätze!

1. Wolf and Ute, don't hide those goods in (*accusative*) your suitcases. (Chapter 1)
2. Roland, watch these books, please.
3. Mr. and Mrs. Küchler, how long have you been living in Berlin?
4. I had spoken to Mrs. Lerner before she went to Berlin to see Kurt. (Chapter 2)
5. We wanted to visit Horst but we did not have any time.
6. As a rule one may not smoke in (*dative*) the post office.
7. Which car does Sandra like? This car or that one? (Use **gefallen**. Chapter 4)
8. Not all students need to study a lot.

6
Kommunikation

Interview vor der Gedächtniskirche in Berlin

Verbal Prefixes: Verbs with Inseparable Prefixes

Verbal Prefixes: Verbs with Separable Prefixes

The Prefixes *durch, über, um, unter, wider,* and *wieder*

Wortschatz

der Aufsatz (¨e) essay
das Dia (-s) (photographic) slide
das Fernsehen television
der Fernseher (-) television set
die Nachrichten news
der Satz (¨e) sentence

die Schreibmaschine (-n) typewriter
die Sendung (-en) (t.v., radio) show, program
die Übertragung (-en) broadcast
die Zeitschrift (-en) magazine
die Zeitung (-en) newspaper

ab · schalten to turn off
an · rufen* to call, telephone
aus · drücken to express
aus · sprechen* to pronounce
beeinflussen to influence
beschreiben* to describe
besprechen* to discuss
ein · schalten to turn on

empfehlen* to recommend
erklären to explain
fern · sehen* to watch television
nach · schlagen* to look up (as in a book)
übersetzen to translate
vor · schlagen* to suggest
widersprechen* to contradict
zu · hören (*dat.*) to listen to

A. *Find the one thing that a newspaper article cannot do.*

Ein Zeitungsartikel kann . . .

1. viele Leute beeinflussen
2. den Fernseher einschalten
3. ein Restaurant empfehlen
4. ein Problem erklären
5. dem Präsidenten widersprechen
6. die Ideen des Autors ausdrücken

---

*Verbs marked with asterisks are strong verbs; see the appendix for the principal parts of strong verbs.

B. *Tell which of the following reactions you could not have to a newspaper article.*

Ich will den Zeitungsartikel. . . .

1. weiterlesen
2. widersprechen
3. meiner Schwester empfehlen
4. morgen anrufen
5. ins Spanische übersetzen

C. *Find the verb that does not apply. For each noun on the left, find the one thing that you could not do with it on the right.*

1. Aufsatz   besprechen, fernsehen, empfehlen, übersetzen
2. Schreibmaschine   beschreiben, vorschlagen, besprechen, nachschlagen
3. Fernseher   einschalten, widersprechen, zuhören, abschalten

D. *Complete the sentences.*

1. Ich muß einen Aufsatz über das Fernsehen in Deutschland schreiben, aber bis jetzt habe ich noch keinen einzigen _____ geschrieben. Hilfe!

2. Im Fernsehen gibt es viele _____, die mir überhaupt nicht gefallen.

3. Ich habe in meinem Urlaub sehr viele _____ gemacht. Wollt ihr die mal sehen?

4. Heute gibt es im Fernsehen eine Live-_____ des Fußballspiels Deutschland gegen England. Siehst du dir das an?

Verbal Prefixes: Verbs with Inseparable Prefixes

Verbal prefixes are generally one- or two-syllable elements attached to verbs. Sometimes they change the meaning of the verb in a predictable manner, as in these examples:

stehen	aufstehen	beistehen
to stand	to get up	to assist ("to stand by")

Sometimes, however, the change in meaning is quite radical:

stehen	verstehen	bestehen
to stand	to understand	to pass (a test)

These examples represent two types of verbal prefixes, separable and inseparable. The basic differences between these two types of prefixes are:

Inseparable Prefixes	Separable Prefixes
1. never separated from verb	1. sometimes separated from verb
Edda *versteht* den Aufsatz nicht.	Alex *steht* früh *auf.*
2. never stressed	2. always stressed
Edda verstéht den Aufsatz nicht. (verstéhen)	Alex steht früh áuf. (áufstehen)
3. past participles do not have **ge-** prefix	3. past participles have **ge-** prefix
verstanden	aufgestanden
4. usually change meaning of verb unpredictably	4. often change meaning of verb predictably
fallen *to fall;* gefallen *to please*	fallen *to fall;* hinfallen *to fall down*
hören *to hear;* gehören *to belong to*	hören *to hear;* zuhören *to listen to*
5. usually contain the vowel **e**	5. usually resemble prepositions
besprechen, bestehen, verstehen	*auf*stehen, *bei*stehen, *mit*bringen

In this section, inseparable prefixes are reviewed.

Inseparable Prefixes

The most common inseparable prefixes are:

Prefix	Examples
be-*	beschreiben *to describe* (schreiben *to write*)
	besprechen *to discuss* (sprechen *to speak*)
ent- (often connotes separation)	entdecken *to discover* (decken *to cover*)
	enthüllen *to reveal* (hüllen *to wrap*)
er-	erklären *to explain* (klären *to clear up*)
	erzählen *to tell, relate* (zählen *to count*)

---

*Verbs prefixed with **be-** usually have an accusative object or clause: **Cynthia bespricht das Problem. Kurt beantwortet die Frage. Sie behauptet, daß ...**

ge-*	gehören *to belong to* (hören *to hear*)
	gefallen *to please* (fallen *to fall*)
miß-[†] (often has a negative connotation)	mißbilligen *to disapprove of* (billigen *to approve of*)
	mißverstehen *to misunderstand* (verstehen *to understand*)
ver-[‡] (often connotes transition or destruction)	verbringen *to spend, as time* (bringen *to bring*)
	vergehen *to pass away* (gehen *to go*)
zer- (often connotes separation into pieces)	zerbrechen *to break in pieces* (brechen *to break*)
	zerreißen *to tear up* (reißen *to tear*)

Übungen

°A. **Suchen Sie die Präfixe!** Identify the verbal prefixes in the following sentences; indicate which are separable prefixes and which are inseparable. Then translate the sentences.

Zum Beispiel: Rudi hat versprochen, einige Dias mitzubringen.
ver-sprechen (*inseparable*) mit-zubringen (*separable*)
Rudi promised to bring along some slides.

1. Können Sie mir den Film beschreiben?
2. Matthias ruft dich morgen an.
3. Wer hat das Glas zerbrochen?
4. Wir wollen den Fernseher einschalten.
5. Wann bist du aufgestanden?
6. Wird der Professor uns seine Theorie erklären?
7. Paul und Sara, habt ihr die Nachrichten besprochen?

B. **Ergänzen Sie die folgenden Sätze!** Choose the appropriate verb form given in parentheses.

1. Hast du die letzte Prüfung _____? (bestanden, entstanden, gestanden)

2. Kolumbus hat Amerika _____. (bedeckt, entdeckt)

3. _____ dir diese Fernsehsendung? (zerfällt, gefällt, entfällt)

---

*The past participle of these verb pairs (**gehören** / **hören** for example) is the same. The sentence **Der Hund hat mich nicht gehört** means *The dog didn't hear me.* **Der Hund hat mir nicht gehört** means *The dog didn't belong to me.*

[†]In the verb **mißverstehen, miß** is stressed.

[‡]**Ver-** used with reflexive pronouns can imply error: **sich verfahren,** *to lose one's way;* **sich vertun,** *to make a mistake.*

4. Wir haben unsere Ferien in Österreich _____. (vollbracht, *complete*
verbracht, gebracht) *spend bring*

5. Erika hat mir _____, ihre Eltern mitzubringen. (besprochen, *discuss*
entsprochen, versprochen) *promised*

6. Wer hat das Fenster _____? (erbrochen, verbrochen, zerbrochen) *throw-up committing break*

°C. **Schreiben Sie die folgenden Sätze im Perfekt und übersetzen Sie sie ins Englische!**

Zum Beispiel: Die Propaganda beinflußte das Volk.
Die Propaganda hat das Volk beeinflußt.
The propaganda influenced the people.

1. Sebastian mißverstand den Touristen.
2. Veronika empfing die Gäste sehr freundlich.
3. Rita verbrachte viel Zeit vor dem Fernseher.
4. Diese Zeitung gehörte einem Ausländer.
5. Frau Heimberger erzählte uns die Geschichte.
6. Dieter mißbilligte die Taten der Terroristen.
7. Die Zeit verging zu langsam.

D. **Übersetzen Sie die folgenden Sätze!**

1. This newspaper has influenced many Americans.
2. Miss Schneider, does this magazine belong to you (**Ihnen**)?
3. The professor recommended this book.
4. Anna, why did you tear up that letter?
5. It is difficult to tell that story.
6. They discussed the film.

E. **Eine Rede.** Describe a speech that you have either heard or given. Use as many of the following verbs as possible: **beeinflussen, bemerken** (to notice), **beschreiben,* besprechen,* beweisen*** (to prove), **empfehlen,* erklären, erzählen.**

Zum Beispiel: In meiner Rede:
habe ich bewiesen, daß Amerikaner zuviel essen. Ich habe auch erklärt, warum Rauchen der Gesundheit schadet. Ich habe empfohlen, weniger Zucker zu essen.

---

*Verbs marked with an asterisk are strong verbs; see the appendix for principal parts of strong verbs.

Verbal Prefixes: Verbs with Separable Prefixes

The common separable prefixes and their typical English equivalents are:

Prefix	Examples
ab off, down	abschreiben to copy
	abschalten to turn off
an at, on	anreden to address (someone)
	anrufen to telephone
auf up, upon; open	aufmachen to open
	aufstehen to get up
aus out	aussprechen to pronounce
	ausreden to talk (someone) out of (doing something)
bei* by, with	beistehen to assist
	beitreten to join
ein in, into	einsteigen to get on, to step in
	einschalten to turn on
entgegen toward, against	entgegenkommen to come to meet
	entgegenlaufen to run to meet
fort away, on(ward)	fortfahren to continue; to go on
	fortdauern to continue; to last
heim home	heimgehen to go home
	heimkommen to come home
her here, hither	herbringen to bring here
	herkommen to come here
hin there, thither	hinfallen to fall down
	hingehen to go there
los loose, free	loskaufen to ransom, to redeem
	loslassen to release
mit with, along	mitbringen to bring along
	mitkommen to come along
nach[†] after	nacheilen to hurry after
	nachschlagen to look (something) up

---

*The objects of verbs with the prefix **bei** are usually in the dative case: **Ich trete *dem* Klub bei.**

[†]Personal objects of verbs with the prefix **nach** are usually in the dative case: **Ich muß *dem* Kind nacheilen.**

Prefix	Examples
nieder *down*	niederbrennen *to burn down* niederschießen *to shoot down*
vor *before, in front*	vorhaben *to plan to do* vorschlagen *to suggest*
weg* *away*	weggehen *to walk away, leave* wegmachen *to remove*
weiter *(connotes continuation)*	weiterlesen *to continue reading* weitersprechen *to continue speaking*
zu[†] *to, closed*	zuhören *to listen to* zuschließen *to lock up*
zurück *back*	zurückbleiben *to stay behind* zurückkehren *to return*
zusammen *together*	zusammenbringen *to bring together* zusammenfallen *to collapse*

Word Order with Separable Prefixes

In normal or inverted word order the separable prefix takes the following position in the sentence, using the verb **mitkommen** as an example:

Alex kommt Sonntag mit.   (present)
Alex kam Sonntag mit.   (past)
Alex wird Sonntag mitkommen.   (future)
Alex ist Sonntag mitgekommen.   (present perfect)
Alex war Sonntag mitgekommen.   (past perfect)
Alex wird Sonntag mitgekommen sein.   (future perfect)
Alex, komm Sonntag mit!   (imperative, **du** form)
Alex und Marie, kommt Sonntag mit!   (imperative, **ihr** form)
Frau Braun, kommen Sie Sonntag mit!   (imperative, **Sie** form)

From these sentences you can see that the prefix **mit** is separated from the finite verb in normal and inverted word order. You can also see that **mit** always occurs at the end of the clause in which it is contained. If the verb to which it belongs follows it, the two are combined into one word. This combination can occur:

1. in past participles

    Alex ist mitgekommen.

2. in subordinate clauses (transposed word order)

    Ich glaube, daß Alex morgen mitkommt.

---

*The prefix **weg** is pronounced as if it were written *weck*.
[†]When the prefix **zu** means *to*, the verb usually requires a dative object: **Eva hört dem Professor zu.**

3. in infinitives

Wir bitten Sie, mitzukommen.

Notice that if the infinitive is accompanied by **zu, zu** is placed between the separable prefix and verb: **mitzukommen.**

The Verbal Prefixes *hin* and *her*

The separable prefix **her** denotes motion toward the speaker:

Gabi und Gert, bringt die Schreibmaschine her!
Gabi and Gert, bring the typewriter here.

The separable prefix **hin** denotes motion away from the speaker.

Gabi und Gert, geht nicht hin.
Gabi and Gert, don't go there.

Hin and **her** are often attached to other prefixes:

Gert kommt in das Haus herein.
Gert is coming in the house.

Gert geht aus dem Haus hinaus.
Gert is going out of the house.

In colloquial German, the prefix **her** is used for both **hin** and **her** and is usually reduced to **'r** when it is attached to other prefixes.

'Raus!
Get out!

Ein Schritt weiter _____

1. Separable prefixes often appear in sentences containing the prepositions from which the prefixes are derived.

Sie kommt morgen *mit* uns mit.   (mitkommen)
She's coming along with us tomorrow.

Das Kind läuft *um* das Haus herum.   (herumlaufen)
The child is running around the house.

2. The past participles of verbs beginning with a combination of inseparable and separable prefixes do not have a **ge-** prefix:

Separable-Inseparable: Die Mutter hat das Essen *vorbereitet.*
The mother prepared the meal.

Inseparable-Separable: Hans hat sich mit Helga *verabredet.*
Hans made a date with Helga.

Übungen

A. **Ergänzen Sie die folgenden Sätze!** Complete the following sentences with the appropriate separable prefix in parentheses and translate the sentence.

Zum Beispiel: Bring mir das Buch _____! (hin, her, an, zusammen)
Bring mir das Buch her!
Bring me the book.

1. Nach dem Abendessen will ich den Fernseher

   _____schalten. (bei, ein, entgegen, fort, weg)

2. Die Lehrerin sagte: „Bitte, machen Sie Ihre Bücher _____!" (ein,

   bei, ab, auf)

3. Ingrid findet Englisch schwer _____zusprechen. (ab, bei, zu,

   aus, los)

4. Ich bin heute dem Tennisklub _____bei_____getreten. (bei, zu, an, mit,

   zurück)

5. Die Kinder sind der Mutter _____gelaufen. (ab, an, aus, entgegen)

6. Die Polizei hat den Verbrecher _____gelassen. (fort, los, zu, vor)

7. Philip versprach uns, Edith und Berta _____zubringen. (vor,

   mit, nieder, nach)

8. Das Feuer brannte die Stadt _____. (nieder, mit, ein)

9. Bitte, schließen Sie die Tür _____. (nach, mit, zusammen, zu)

10. Kurt sagt, daß Rita morgen _____kehrt. (los, nach, an, zurück, vor)

11. Das alte Gebäude ist endlich _____gefallen. (mit, los, zusammen,

    bei, auf)

12. Josef hat seinen Bericht einfach aus einer Zeitschrift_____geschrieben.

    (über, an, ab, weg)

°B. **Ich glaube. . . .** Answer in the affirmative, with **Ich glaube. . . .**

Zum Beispiel: Spricht man dieses Wort so aus?
Ich glaube, daß man dieses Wort so ausspricht.

1. Sehen amerikanische Kinder zu oft fern?
2. Schlägt Herr Neumann das vor?
3. Kommen die Studenten jetzt herein?
4. Gehört uns diese Schreibmaschine?
5. Drückt Anneliese ihre Ideen immer so klar aus?

°C. **Schreiben Sie Sätze im Präsens!** Change the following sentences from the future tense to the present tense and translate each sentence.

Zum Beispiel: Die Schriftstellerin wird ihre Ideen gut ausdrücken.
Die Schriftstellerin drückt ihre Ideen gut aus.
The writer expresses her ideas well.

Der Professor wird diesen Satz erklären.
Der Professor erklärt diesen Satz.
The professor is explaining this sentence.

1. Brigitte wird uns nach der Debatte anrufen.
2. Wir werden dem Reporter zuhören.
3. Frau Unger wird diese Schreibmaschine empfehlen.
4. Uschi, wann wirst du diesen Bericht weiterlesen?
5. Ich werde jetzt das Radio abschalten.
6. Wir werden ein bißchen fernsehen.

°D. **Bilden Sie den Imperativ!** Drop the modal verb **sollen** and place these sentences in the imperative. Translate each sentence.

Zum Beispiel: Helmut, du solltest den Fernseher abschalten.
Helmut, schalte den Fernseher ab!
Helmut, turn off the television set.

Sabrina und Kurt, ihr solltet der Lehrerin zuhören.
Sabrina und Kurt, hört der Lehrerin zu!
Sabrina and Kurt, listen to the teacher.

Herr Franck, Sie sollten dieses Restaurant nicht empfehlen.
Herr Franck, empfehlen Sie dieses Restaurant nicht!
Herr Franck, don't recommend that restaurant.

1. Veronika, du solltest nicht solange fernsehen.
2. Fräulein Krull, Sie sollten den Kindern ein Märchen erzählen.
3. Otto und Sabine, ihr solltet diese Wörter im Lexikon nachschlagen.
4. Sara und Wolfgang, ihr solltet diese Ratschläge befolgen.
5. Frau Preller, Sie sollten nicht so früh aufstehen.

°E. **Ergänzen Sie die folgenden Sätze!** Form complete sentences by attaching the prefixes **her** or **hin** to the indicated separable prefixes.

Zum Beispiel: Oskar stieg den Berg⎯⎯⎯⎯⎯. (auf)
Oskar stieg den Berg hinauf.

1. Harold kam zu mir ⎯⎯⎯⎯⎯. (ein)

2. Pamela ist ins Theater ⎯⎯⎯⎯⎯gegangen. (ein)

3. Gehen wir jetzt ⎯⎯⎯⎯⎯! (aus)

4. Frau Schmidt, Sie müssen diese Straße ⎯⎯⎯⎯⎯gehen. (unter)

5. Wir sind den Berg endlich ⎯⎯⎯⎯⎯gestiegen. (ab)

Gute Nachrichten? Schlechte Nachrichten?

F. **Bilden Sie Sätze!** Rearrange the words to form sentences; make sure to place the separable prefix in the proper position.

Zum Beispiel: morgen / Dieter / nach Stuttgart / zurückkehren (*present*)
Morgen kehrt Dieter nach Stuttgart zurück.

1. Cornelia fand es schwer, / ihrem Bruder das / zu / ausreden
2. Frau Niese, / Sie / beistehen / mir / bitte!
3. Michael hat / Renate / mitbringen / zur Party
4. Gabriele / zuhören / dem Professor   (*past*)
5. was / du / morgen / vorhaben?
6. es war kalt im Zimmer, / weil / aufmachen / jemand alle Fenster / hat
7. darf / abschreiben / ich diesen Aufsatz?
8. statt / zurückbleiben / zu / im Schwarzwald / fuhr Sonja nach Passau
9. nach dem Mittagessen / ich / weiterlesen / habe
10. warum / du mir / bist / nachlaufen?

G. **Schreiben Sie Sätze!** Use the separable verbs and adverbial phrases listed.

1. herauskommen / aus dem Fernsehstudio
2. heraufsteigen / auf den Berg
3. hereinkommen / zu mir
4. hinuntergehen / diese Straße

H. **Übersetzen Sie die folgenden Sätze!**

1. Claudia, did you lock the door?
2. I believe that Marie will call soon.
3. Is German hard to pronounce?

4. Franz never listens to his parents.
5. We stayed behind.
6. When does Erika want to return?
7. Hans, open the door.
8. Mr. Kreisler, please copy this letter.
9. I stayed home (**zu Hause**) because I wanted to get up early.

I. **Übersetzen Sie die folgenden Sätze!** Use **hin** or **her** in each sentence.

1. We climbed up the mountain.
2. Renate, please bring the slides here.
3. Richard is going into the house.
4. Mrs. Vollmer, please come in.
5. Children, go outside!

J. **Interview.**

1. Rufen Sie Ihre besten Freunde oft an?
2. Sehen Sie oft fern? Was sind Ihre Lieblingsprogramme?
3. Schalten Sie den Fernsehapparat an oder hören Sie Radio, wenn Sie Ihre Hausaufgaben machen?
4. Stehen Sie früh auf? Lesen Sie morgens die Zeitung? Schalten Sie das Radio ein, damit Sie die Nachrichten beim Frühstück hören können?
5. Kaufen Sie regelmäßig (*regularly*) Zeitschriften? Welche können Sie empfehlen? Verbringen Sie viel Zeit mit dem Lesen von Zeitungen und Zeitschriften?
6. Bekommen Sie viele Briefe? Schreiben Sie gleich zurück? Machen Sie Ihre Briefe immer sofort auf? Haben Sie schon einmal einen fremden Brief aufgemacht?

The Prefixes *durch, über, um, unter, wider,* and *wieder*

The prefixes **durch** (*through*), **über** (*over*), **um** (*around*), **unter** (*under*), **wider** (*against*), and **wieder** (*again, back*) can be separable or inseparable. As separable prefixes, they normally preserve the original (literal) meaning of the verb; as inseparable prefixes, they tend to give the verb a figurative meaning. Compare these examples of prepositions and inseparable prefixes in English:

John went under the bridge.   (literal meaning of *went*)
John underwent an operation.   (figurative meaning of *went*)

Julia looked over the table.   (literal meaning of *looked*)
Julia overlooked the mistake.   (figurative meaning of *looked*)

Now compare these examples in German:

Separable Prefix (Literal Meaning)	Inseparable Prefix (Figurative Meaning)
Die Soldaten *drangen* bis zur Stadtmitte *durch.* Die Soldaten sind bis in die Stadtmitte *durchgedrungen.* The soldiers penetrated the center of the city.	Der Lärm *durchdrang* die Wände. Der Lärm hat die Wände *durchdrungen.* The noise penetrated (could be heard through) the walls.
Er *setzte* uns mit seinem Boot *über.* Er hat uns mit seinem Boot *übergesetzt.* He transported us with his boat.	Er *übersetzte* den Satz. Er hat den Satz *übersetzt.* He translated the sentence.
Helga *kleidete* sich *um.** Helga hat sich *umgekleidet.* Helga changed her clothes.	Helga *umarmte* Alex. Helga hat Alex *umarmt.* Helga embraced Alex.
Kurt *ließ* die Jalousie *herunter.* Kurt hat die Jalousie *heruntergelassen.* Kurt let the venetian blind down.	Kurt *unterließ* oft die Bezahlung der Rechnung. Kurt hat oft die Bezahlung der Rechnung *unterlassen.* Kurt often neglected to pay the bill.
Die Sonne *spiegelte* sich im Wasser *wider.* Die Sonne hat sich im Wasser *widergespiegelt.* The sun was reflected in the water.	Fritz *widersprach* den Eltern nie. Fritz hat den Eltern nie *widersprochen.* Fritz never contradicted his parents.
Der Hund *holte* den Ball *wieder.*† Der Hund hat den Ball *wiedergeholt.* The dog retrieved the ball.	Jürgen *wiederholte* das Wort. Jürgen hat das Wort *wiederholt.* Jürgen repeated the word.

Notice from the examples that when these prefixes are separable, they are stressed and require the prefix **ge-** in the past participle. When used as inseparable prefixes, they are not stressed and do not require the prefix **ge-** in the past participle.

---

*When **um** is used separably it is often the equivalent of the English prefix *trans* and means to do in a different manner; for example, **umsteigen** to *transfer*, **umschreiben** to *rewrite.*

†The prefix **wieder** is almost always separable. The verb **wiederholen**, to repeat, is one of the few exceptions. In either usage **wieder** is usually equivalent to the English prefix *re-.*

Übungen

°A. **Suchen Sie die Präfixe!** Identify the verbal prefixes in the following sentences; indicate which are separable and which are inseparable. Then translate the sentences.

Zum Beispiel: Roswitha widersprach dem Professor.
wider-sprechen (*inseparable*)
Roswitha contradicted the professor.

1. Das Brot ist durchgebacken. (durchbacken *to bake thoroughly*)
2. Dieser Reporter hat das Publikum überzeugt. (überzeugen *to convince*)
3. Die Milch ist übergelaufen. (überlaufen *to run over, overflow*)
4. Jetzt mußt du deinen Aufsatz umschreiben. (umschreiben *to rewrite*)
4. Die Schmetterlinge umflatterten die Rosen. (umflattern *to flutter around*)
6. Der Kapitän meint, daß viele Schiffe oft im Sturm untergehen werden. (untergehen *to go down, sink*)
7. Es ist nicht höflich, andere zu unterbrechen. (unterbrechen *to interrupt*)
8. Wann hat man die Nachrichten übertragen? (übertragen *to broadcast*)
9. Sein Ruf hallte in den Gebirgen wider. (widerhallen *to echo*)
10. Gestern ist mir etwas Komisches widerfahren. (widerfahren *to befall*)
11. Ich glaube, daß Silvia ihren Hund wiederbekommen hat.
    (wiederbekommen *to retrieve, get back*)

B. **Bilden Sie Sätze!** Rearrange the words to make sentences; conjugate the prefixed verbs.

Zum Beispiel: hoffentlich / Frau Franck / wiederkommen / morgen
Hoffentlich kommt Frau Franck morgen wieder.

heute / übertragen / das Fußballspiel / der Süddeutsche Rund funk
Der Süddeutsche Rundfunk überträgt heute das Fußballspiel.

1. hat / überzeugen / der Professor / die Studenten
2. Klaus / wiederbekommen / morgen seinen Aufsatz
3. warum / Karla / hat / wiederholen / den ganzen Paragraphen?
4. Wolf / umschreiben / den Artikel für unsere Zeitung (*past tense*)
5. ist dir etwas Interessantes / widerfahren / gestern?
6. ich glaube, daß dieser Hund / wiederholen / den Ball nie / hat
7. es ist kompliziert / zu / umsteigen / in der Stadt
8. warum / du / hast / nicht übersetzen / diesen Satz?

C. **Übersetzen Sie die folgenden Sätze!**

1. Jost embraced his parents.
2. Is it difficult to translate this word?
3. They interrupted the broadcast.
4. Mr. Füger, please come again.
5. The ship went down in the (**im**) storm. (*past tense*)
6. Mr. Hartmann, please repeat that sentence.

D. **Ergänzen Sie diesen Bericht!** Complete the following report in the past tense, using the correct forms of the appropriate words listed below. Some blanks should remain empty.

umsteigen
wiederholen
unterbrechen
übersetzen
erklären

Gestern _____ ich vor dem Museum _____. Leider nahm ich den

falschen Bus. Der Schaffner versuchte, es mir zu_____, aber ich konnte ihn

nicht verstehen, denn mein Deutsch ist nicht besonders gut. Ich bat ihn, alles

noch einmal zu_____. Er sagte alles noch einmal, aber es half nichts.

Endlich _____ ein anderer Passagier unser Gespräch _____. Er sah ein,

daß ich den Schaffner nicht gut verstand, und er wollte alles für mich _____,

was der Schaffner sagte.

Rückblick

A. **Zur Wiederholung. Übersetzen Sie die folgenden Sätze!**

1. Mr. Jaspers, please explain this story.
2. Wolfgang described the film well (**gut**).
3. It is difficult to pronounce this word.
4. I usually listen to the radio (**Radio hören**), but today I'm watching television.
5. Ulrike, repeat those words.
6. Miss Teichmann, please come again.

B. **Zur Gesamtwiederholung. Übersetzen Sie die folgenden Sätze!**

1. Kurt, don't contradict your parents. (*Chapter 1*)
2. They (**man**) have been broadcasting this debate (**Debatte**) for two hours. (*Chapter 1*)
3. I had already looked up the word before Sara looked it up.
4. Hilde rewrote her brother's essays. (*Chapter 3*)
5. We suggested these plans to our friends.
6. Christine, which words did you translate? (*Chapter 4*)
7. Gabi and Udo, do you want to watch television now? (*Chapter 5*)
8. Mrs. Heissler, don't leave without locking the door.

7
Politik und Regierung

Protest gegen die Neutronbombe

Declension of Attributive Adjectives

Attributive Adjectives: Special Cases

Comparison of Adjectives and Adverbs

Adjectives Used as Nouns

Wortschatz

der Beamte (-n) die Beamtin (-nen) official, civil servant

der Bürger (-), die Bürgerin (-nen) citizen

der Bundeskanzler (-), die Bundeskanzlerin (-nen) chancellor (head of government)

der Bundestag West German parliament

die Demokratie democracy

die Freiheit freedom, liberty

der Frieden peace

das Gesetz (-e) law

der Kapitalismus capitalism

der Kommunismus communism

der Krieg (-e) war

die Lösung (-en) solution

die Macht (¨e) power

die Meinung (-en) opinion

das Mitglied (-er) member

der Nationalsozialismus national socialism

das Parlament (-e) parliament

die Partei (-en) party

die Politik politics

der Politiker (-), die Politikerin (-nen) politician

die Regierung (-en) government

der Sozialismus socialism

die Steuer (-n) tax

die Verantwortung (-en) responsibility

das Vorurteil (-e) prejudice

die Wahl (-en) election

regieren to govern, rule

verabschieden to pass (a law)

wählen *to vote*

aktiv active

aktuell current, of present importance

autoritär authoritarian

demokratisch democratic

ehrlich honest, truthful

friedlich peaceful

gerecht just, fair

idealistisch idealistic

kapitalistisch capitalist(ic)

kommunistisch communist

konservativ conservative

kriegerisch warlike, martial	**sozialistisch** socialistic
liberal liberal	**streng** strict
politisch political	**tolerant** tolerant
realistisch realistic	**unabhängig** independent

A. *Give the noun that corresponds to each of the following adjectives.*

1. verantwortlich	4. demokratisch	7. kriegerisch
2. friedlich	5. bürgerlich	8. politisch
3. parlamentarisch	6. mächtig	9. gesetzlich

B. *Complete the sentences.*

1. Die meisten Leute zahlen jedes Jahr _____.

2. Jürgen ist überhaupt nicht tolerant; leider hat er viele _____.

3. Früher gab es in Afrika viele Kolonien. Heute sind diese Länder _____.

4. Ich werde nie mehr lügen (*lie*). Ich will jetzt nur noch _____ sein.

5. Alle Leute sprechen über die Energiekrise. Dieses Problem ist heute

   sehr _____.

6. Sei neicht immer so idealistisch, Hans. Du mußt einfach mal ganz kühl

   und _____ denken.

7. Das Motto der französischen Revolution war: „_____, Gleichheit,

   Brüderlichkeit."

8. Mein Vater wollte nie eine andere _____ hören. Er war sehr

   autoritär und hat immer getan, was er wollte.

9. Man hat immer noch keine _____ für dieses Problem gefunden.

10. Normalerweise gibt es in der Bundesrepublik alle vier Jahre

    eine _____ für den Bundestag.

11. Das Parlament wird heute das Steuergesetz _____.

12. Die meisten Politiker sind _____ einer Partei.

C. *Give the adjective that corresponds to each of the following nouns.*

Zum Beispiel: Kommunismus
                 kommunistisch

1. Sozialismus	4. Nationalsozialismus
2. Kapitalismus	5. Liberalismus
3. Idealismus	6. Konservatismus

D. *Give the word that fits each of the following definitions.*

1. das deutsche Parlament
2. der deutsche Regierungschef
3. jemand, der für den Staat arbeitet (zum Beispiel bei der Post)
4. alle Minister und der Bundeskanzler zusammen
5. jemand, der sich zur Wahl stellt (*who runs for office*)

E. *Find the adjectives hidden in the following nouns and give their English equivalents.*

1. die Aktivität
2. die Gerechtigkeit
3. die Freiheit
4. die Unabhängigkeit
5. die Strenge

Declension of Attributive Adjectives

Predicate adjectives (adjectives not followed by a noun and appearing mainly after the verbs **sein** and **werden**) take no endings, but attributive adjectives (adjectives that modify a following noun) take endings determined by the number, gender, and case of the nouns they modify. Compare these examples:

Predicate Adjective	*Attributive Adjective*
Dieses Rathaus ist *alt.*	Ein *altes* Rathaus steht da.
This town hall is old.	An old town hall is standing there.
Diese Partei wird *stark.*	Eine *starke* Partei ist zur Macht gekommen.
This party is becoming strong.	A strong party has come to power.

Adjectives other than **ein-** or **der**-words* are declined according to two different sets of endings, strong and weak:

If the adjective is:	*The adjective follows:*
not preceded by a **der-** or **ein**-word with an ending	the strong declension
preceded by a **der-** or **ein**-word with an ending	the weak declension

---

*As discussed in Chapter 4, **ein**-words are **ein**, **kein**, and the possessive adjectives (**mein**, **dein**, **ihr**, etc); **der**-words are **der**, **dieser**, **jeder**, **alle**, **welcher**, **solcher**, **mancher**, and **jener**.

Strong Declension: Forms

	Masculine	Neuter	Feminine	Plural
Nominative	alter	altes	alte	alte
Accusative	alten	altes	alte	alte
Dative	altem	altem	alter	alten
Genitive	alten	alten	alter	alter

The strong endings are identical to the endings of **der**-words except for the masculine and neuter genitive ending **-en** (the ending is **-es** in **der**-words): **die Qualität alten Wein(e)s**. As the chart shows, there are five strong endings: **-er, -es, -e, -en**, and **-em**, which provide information about gender, case, and number. Here are examples of these forms in sentences.

1. Nominative

   Alter Wein ist teuer.   (masculine)

   Altes Brot ist trocken (*dry*).   (neuter).

   Alte Milch ist sauer.   (feminine)

   Alte Weine sind teuer.   (plural)

2. Accusative

   Ich kaufe *alten* Wein.   (masculine)

   Ich kaufe nie *altes* Brot.   (neuter)

   Ich kaufe nie *alte* Milch.   (feminine)

   Ich kaufe *alte* Weine.   (plural)

3. Dative

   Er kam mit *altem* Wein nach Hause.   (masculine)

   Er kam mit *altem* Brot nach Hause.   (neuter)

   Er kam mit *alter* Milch nach Hause.   (feminine)

   Er kam mit *alten* Weinen nach Hause.   (plural)

4. Genitive*

   Die Qualität *alten* Weins ist oft gut.   (masculine)

   Die Qualität *alten* Brotes ist oft schlecht.   (neuter)

   Die Qualität *alter* Milch ist oft schlecht.   (femine)

   Die Qualität *alter* Weine ist oft gut.   (plural)

---

*The dative and genitive endings of the strong declension occur infrequently in converstional German. Instead one finds, for example: **Er kam mit einem alten Wein nach Hause. Die Qualität von altem Wein ist oft gut.**

Strong Declension: Use

Adjectives take strong endings whenever there is no ending on a preceding **der**- or **ein**-word. This usually occurs when either: (1) no **der**- or **ein**-word precedes the adjective; (2) an **ein**-word without an ending precedes the adjective. The strong ending provides information about gender, case, and number that is otherwise not provided.

1. No **der**- or **ein**-word precedes

Starker Regen ist gestern in Bayern gefallen.
Strong rain fell in Bavaria yesterday.

Frisches Brot schmeckt gut.
Fresh bread tastes good.

In diesem Haus wohnen *viele* Studenten.
Many students live in this house.

Bei *gutem* Wind ist gut Segeln.
With a good wind there is good sailing.   (proverb)

Gestern habe ich *einige* Freunde besucht.
Yesterday I visited some friends.

Vier *deutsche* Politiker haben über dieses Problem debattiert.*
Four German politicians debated this problem.

Ich trinke *heiße* Schokolade gern.
I like to drink hot chocolate.

Letzten Montag haben wir *schönes* Wetter gehabt.
Last Monday we had nice weather.

Wir essen gern Brot mit *frischer* Butter.
We like to eat bread with fresh butter.

Verbotene Früchte schmecken süß.
Forbidden fruits taste sweet(er).

2. An **ein**-word without an ending precedes

As discussed in Chapter 3 there are three instances in which **ein**-words lack endings: in the masculine nominative, neuter nominative, and neuter accusative. Adjectives that follow these **ein**-words without endings take strong endings:

masculine nominative

Ist Herr Neumann *ein ehrlicher* Politiker?
Is Mr. Neumann an honest politician?

Unser neuer Bundeskanzler spricht fließend Englisch.
Our new chancellor speaks English fluently.

---

*Adjectives are generally not capitalized in German unless they are part of an official title or name **vier deutsche Politiker; das Deutsche Museum.**

Frau Mohr ist *ein aktives* Mitglied dieser Partei.
Frau Mohr is an active member of that party.

Mein *altes* Auto läuft gut.
My old car runs well.

neuter accusative

Dieses Jahr hat man *ein neues* Parlament gewählt.
This year a new parliament was elected.

Annette hat *ihr altes* Fahrrad verkauft.
Annette sold her old bicycle.

Weak Declension: Forms

	Masculine	Neuter	Feminine	Plural
Nominative	**alte**	**alte**	**alte**	alten
Accusative	alten	**alte**	**alte**	alten
Dative	alten	alten	alten	alten
Genitive	alten	alten	alten	alten

Notice that the ending **-en** is used throughout the declension except in the nominative singular and in the accusative neuter and feminine:

Der *alte* Plan war gut für unser Land.   (masculine nominative)
The old plan was good for our country.

Das *alte* Gesetz war gut für unser Land.   (neuter nominative)
The old law was good for our country.

Die *alte* Regierung war gut für unser Land.   (feminine nominative)
The old government was good for our country.

Wir sprechen über das *alte* Gesetz.   (neuter accusative)
We are discussing the old law.

Wir sprechen über die *alte* Regierung.   (feminine accusative)
We are discussing the old government.

Aside from these five instances, the ending **-en** is used for the weak declension. Since there are only two endings to express so many functions (case, gender, and number), the weak declension is not very distinctive.

Here are examples showing where the weak ending **-en** is used:

1. Nominative plural

    Die *alten* Pläne waren gut für unser Land.
    The old plans were good for our country.

2. Accusative plural

Wir sprechen über die *alten* Gesetze.
We are talking about the old laws.

3. Dative

Wir sind mit dem *alten* Wagen gefahren.   (masculine)
We took the old car.

Wir sind mit dem *alten* Taxi gefahren.   (neuter)

Wir sind mit der *alten* Straßenbahn gefahren.   (feminine)

Wir sind mit den *alten* Wagen gefahren.   (plural)

4. Genitive

Kennst du die Adresse des *alten* Ladens?   (masculine)
Do you know the address of the old shop?

Kennst du die Adresse des *alten* Rathauses?   (neuter)

Kennst du die Adresse der *alten* Schule?   (feminine)

Kennst du die Adressen der *alten* Läden?   (plural)

Weak Declension: Use

An adjective takes a weak ending when either a **der**-word or an **ein**-word with an ending precedes it. Information about gender, case, and number is provided by the **der**- or **ein**-word.

Wie heißt *der neue* Bundeskanzler?
What is the new chancellor's name?

Welche politischen Systeme hast du studiert?
Which political systems have you examined?

Der deutsche Tourist hat *dem amerikanischen* Studenten *das deutsche politische* System erklärt.
The German tourist explained the German political system to the American
    student.

Der deutsche Bürger darf mit 18 Jahren wählen.
The German citizen is allowed to vote at 18 years of age.

Alle gerechten Politiker *eines demokratischen* Landes sollten gegen Vorurteile kämpfen.
All just politicians of a democratic country should fight prejudice.

Manche deutschen Studenten studieren *das amerikanische* System.
A number of German students study the American system.

Parallel Endings

If several adjectives (other than **der**- or **ein**-words) occur in a series, they must all take the same ("parallel") endings.

Strong	*Weak*
Er ist ein *toleranter, gerechter* und *kompetenter* Politiker.	Dieser *tolerante, gerechte* und *kompetente* Politiker kommt aus Hamburg.
Ein *blonder junger* Mann kam aus dem Haus.	Der *blonde junge* Mann kam aus dem Haus.
Ich habe nicht genug Geld für ein *neues teures* Auto.	Ich habe nicht genug Geld für das *neue teure* Auto
Sie kam mit *altem, teurem* Wein nach Hause.	Sie kam mit einem *alten, teueren* Wein nach Hause.
Viele junge deutsche Studenten interessieren sich für Politik.	Diese *jungen deutschen* Studenten interessieren sich für Politik.

Study hint: The best way to learn adjective endings is to practice them in simple oral drills, such as those of Exercise A, which follows. Practice these on your own, changing the nouns, and you will develop what the Germans call a **Sprachgefühl**, a feeling for the language.

Übungen

°A **Ersetzen Sie die Adjektive!** Use weak or strong adjective endings, as indicated.

Zum Beispiel: Das ist eine *gute* Regierung. (demokratisch)
Das ist eine demokratische Regierung.

1. Das ist ein *altes* Gesetz. (gut, schlecht)
2. Er ist ein *konservativer* Politiker. (liberal, französisch)
3. Das sind *neue* Mitglieder. (jung, aktiv)
4. Wir besprechen eine *wichtige* Idee. (neu, interessant)
5. Ich suche mein *grünes* Buch. (gelb, rot)
6. Sie haben *konservative* Regierungen. (sozialistisch, unabhängig)
7. Sie fragten nach der *spanischen* Politikerin. (französisch, amerikanisch)
8. Das sind die Schlüssel des *jungen* Mannes. (alt, blond)

B. **Ergänzen Sie die folgenden Adjektive mit starken Endungen!** Insert the proper strong endings. Translate each sentence.

1. Ein friedlich＿＿＿＿＿＿＿ Mensch hat viele Freunde.

2. Der Preis gut＿＿＿＿＿＿ Weines ist oft hoch.

3. Ich glaube, daß das Parlament ein streng＿＿＿＿＿＿ Gesetz verabschieden wird.

4. Fünf jung＿＿＿＿＿＿ Mitglieder dieser Partei haben mit dem Minister gesprochen.

5. Sprichwort: „Wer kalt＿＿＿＿＿＿ Wasser trinken will, der muß zur Quelle (well) gehen."

6. Frau Lehmann, geht Ihr amerikanisch_____ Freund auf die

   Universität Bonn?

7. Sprichwort: „Still_____ Wasser sind tief."

8. Wir wollen nur aktuell_____ Probleme besprechen.

9. Gestern habe ich einig_____ Freunde in der Stadt getroffen.

10. Kalt_____, regnerisch_____ Wetter gefällt uns nicht.

°C. **Beantworten Sie die folgenden Fragen!**

Zum Beispiel: Was für ein Gesetz sollte man verabschieden? (autoritär /
demokratisch)
Man sollte ein demokratisches Gesetz verabschieden.

Was für Politiker sollten in der Regierung sein? (gerecht,
ungerecht)
Gerechte Politiker sollten in der Regierung sein.

1. Was für Kaffee trinkt man gern? (kalt / heiß)
2. Was für Bier trinken die meisten Amerikaner gern? (eiskalt / warm)
3. Mit was für Brot essen Sie gern Marmelade? (alt / frisch)
4. Was für einen Präsidenten haben die Amerikaner? (konservativ / liberal)
5. Was für Gesetze sollte man verabschieden? (gerecht / ungerecht)

D. **Ergänzen Sie die folgenden Adjektive mit schwachen Endungen!** Insert the
proper weak endings, **-e** or **-en**.

1. Jedes demokratisch_____ Volk soll tolerant sein.

2. Leider hat man einen autoritär_____ Politiker gewählt.

3. Unter einer faschistisch_____ oder kommunistisch_____

   Regierung hat der Mensch wenig Freiheit.

4. Eine neu_____, tolerant_____ Partei ist zur Macht gekommen.

5. In dem schön_____, grün_____ Wald stehen viele Bäume.

6. Wir haben mit dem klein_____ Sohn der Lehrerin gesprochen.

7. Das Parlament hat das streng_____, autoritär_____ Gesetz nicht

   verabschiedet.

8. Manche deutsch_____ Politiker wohnen in der neu_____ Hauptstadt.

9. Welcher deutsch_____ Bundeskanzler hat die USA neulich besucht?

10. Die eng_____ Straßen in den klein_____ Dörfern können gefährlich

    sein.

Beantworten Sie die folgenden Fragen!

Zum Beispiel: Welcher Mann sollte Politiker werden?   (ehrlich / unehrlich)
Der ehrliche Mann sollte Politiker werden.

Unter welcher Regierung wollen Sie leben?   (autoritär / tolerant)
Ich will unter der toleranten Regierung leben.

1. Welche Erklärung versteht man besser?   (lang / kurz)
2. Mit welcher Schreibmaschine tippen Sie gern?   (alt / neu)
3. Welche Zeitungen finden Sie schwer zu verstehen?   (arabisch / englisch)
4. Von welchem Film möchten Sie sprechen?   (langweilig / interessant)
5. Welchen Politiker hat man oft im Fernsehen gesehen?   (unbekannt / berühmt)
6. Welche Polizisten sollten für uns arbeiten?   (höflich / unfreundlich)
7. Welchen Politikern sollte man glauben?   (unehrlich / ehrlich)

F. **Ergänzen Sie die folgenden Adjektive mit passenden Endungen!** Insert the proper weak or strong endings.

1. Das deutsch_____ Parlament hat manche notwendig_____ Gesetze

    verabschiedet.

2. Alle gerecht_____ Mitglieder einer demokratisch_____ Organisation

    sollten gegen solche falsch_____ Vorurteile kämpfen.

3. Dieser blau_____ See hat klar_____ aber sehr kalt_____ Wasser.

4. Der klein_____, alt_____ Markt liegt am Ende einer eng_____,

    schön_____ Straße.

5. Sprichwort: „Ander_____ Länder, ander_____ Sitten (*customs*)."

G. **Übersetzen Sie die folgenden Sätze!** Use the dative case after all prepositions in this exercise.

1. The German parliament passed those strict laws.
2. Mrs. Herder spoke with our new chancellor.
3. The quality of German wine is often high.
4. No untruthful person (**Mensch**) should become a politician.
5. Gertrud Sehmsdorf is a very fair politician.
6. Karen, did your small children learn German in a German school?
7. American teenagers like to see such long horror films (**Gruselfilme**).
8. The new German chancellor is discussing current problems with the American president.
9. The parents of the young professor come from (**aus**) a big city in Germany.
10. My German (female) friend is studying capitalistic and socialistic governments.
11. In which German cities does one find such big churches?

H. **Es war einmal ein König. . . .** Complete the blanks with the proper adjective
ending. Some adjectives should remain without endings.

Es war einmal ein streng_____ König. Er war der König eines

klein_____ Landes namens Belturia. Seine Frau, die Königin, war aber sehr

mild_____ und tolerant_____. Das einfach_____ Volk dieses

friedlich_____ Landes liebte die Königin sehr. Es verstand den König aber

nicht, und er war nicht sehr beliebt_____. Der König wollte daß alle

jung_____ Männer Soldaten in der Armee von Belturia werden sollten, denn

er wollte einen lang_____ Frieden in seinem friedlich_____ Land. Eines

Tages kamen die Soldaten eines kriegerisch_____ Volkes nach Belturia,

um das klein_____ Land zu erobern. Aber Belturia gewann den Kampf und

blieb frei_____. Jetzt wußte das Volk von Belturia, daß sowohl die

hart_____ Strenge des Königs als auch die freundlich_____ Milde der

Königin wichtig_____ für das Land waren.

Attributive Adjectives: Special Cases

The Adjectives *andere, einige, mehrere, viele, wenige,* and *alle*

The attributive adjectives **andere** (*other*), **einige** (*some*), **mehrere** (*several*),
viele (*many*), and **wenige** (*few*) often introduce one or more adjectives.
Since they are neither **ein-** nor **der**-words, all adjectives following them use
the same (parallel) endings as these attributive adjectives.

Strong:

Wir haben *andere wichtige politische* Probleme besprochen.
We discussed other important political problems.

Einige deutsche Politiker sind gegen den Sozialismus, aber *andere
deutsche* Politiker sind dafür.
Some German politicians are against socialism, but other German politicians are
for it.

Mehrere politische Fragen haben wir noch nicht diskutiert.
We haven't discussed several political questions yet.

Das Parlament hat *viele neue* Gesetze verabschiedet.
The parliament passed several new laws.

Wenige junge amerikanische Studenten verstehen die deutsche Politik.
Few young American students understand German politics.

When preceded by **ein-** or **der-**words, these attributive adjectives and the adjectives following them take weak endings.

Weak:

Wir haben die *anderen wichtigen politischen* Probleme besprochen.
We discussed the other important political problems.

Since **alle** (the plural of **jeder**) is a **der-**word, adjectives that follow it take weak endings.

Alle gerechten, ehrlichen Politiker sollten gegen Vorurteile kämpfen.
All just, honest politicians should fight against prejudice(s).

However, **alle** has no effect on the declension of following **ein-** or **der-**words.

Diese Häuser sind neu. *Alle diese* Häuser sind neu.
Unsere Freunde sind interessant. *Alle unsere* Freunde sind interessant.

The Adjectives *mancher, solcher,* and *welcher*

These three **der-**words may be used with or without endings in the nominative masculine or the nominative or accusative neuter. When they are used with endings, the following adjectives take weak endings; when used without endings, the following adjectives take strong endings, since the strong endings are needed to provide information.

Mancher deutsche Student studiert Literatur.   (masculine nominative)
Manch deutscher Student studiert Literatur.
Many a German student studies literature.

Welches blaue Wasser!   (neuter nominative)
Welch blaues Wasser!
What blue water!

Solches schöne Wetter haben wir immer.   (neuter accusative)
Solch schönes Wetter haben wir immer.
We always have such beautiful weather.

Adjectives Derived from Names of Cities

Adjectives derived from names of cities are formed by adding **-er** with no further endings. They are always capitalized.

Diese Politikerin liest immer gern die *Berliner* Zeitungen.
That politician always likes to read the Berlin newspapers.

Ich esse gern *Wiener* Schnitzel.
I like to eat Viennese cutlets.

Adjectives Ending in *-el*; the Adjective *hoch*

Adjectives ending in **-el** (and often those that end in **-er**) lose the **e** in these syllables when endings are attached. Similarly, the adjective **hoch** loses the **c** when endings are attached.

Das Zimmer ist dunkel. Das ist ein *dunkles* Zimmer.
The room is dark. This is a dark room.

Dieses Buch ist teuer. Das ist ein *teures* Buch.
This book is expensive. This is an expensive book.

Diese Berge sind hoch. Das sind *hohe* Berge.
Those mountains are high. Those are high mountains.

Übungen

A. **Ergänzen Sie die folgenden Adjektive mit passenden Endungen.** Insert the proper adjective ending and translate each sentence.

1. Einig_____ jung_____ deutsch_____ Touristen besuchten gestern die amerikanisch_____ Hauptstadt.

2. Wie viel_____ neu_____ Mitglieder hat das Parlament?

3. Wenig_____ amerikanisch_____ Touristen können Deutsch.

4. Nicht all_____ deutsch_____ Touristen können Englisch, aber alle mein_____ Freundinnen können Englisch und Deutsch.

5. Das Parlament hat mehrer_____ neu_____ Gesetze verabschiedet.

6. Die meist_____ französisch_____ und deutsch_____ Studenten glauben an die Demokratie.

7. Die ander_____ liberal_____ Politiker wollten kein_____ streng_____ Gesetze.

8. Wir haben all_____ deutsch_____ Beamten gedankt.

B. **Bilden Sie Sätze!** Make two sentences for each group of words.

   Zum Beispiel: manch / klein / Kind spielt Fußball.
   Manches kleine Kind spielt Fußball.
   Manch kleines Kind spielt Fußball.

   1. solch / klar / Wasser sieht man selten im Ozean
   2. welch / ehrlich / Politiker (*singular*)!
   3. manch / klug / Student studiert Deutsch und Französich

°C. **Bilden Sie Adjektive!** Form adjectives from the following place names, following the model.

   Zum Beispiel: Ich lese eine Zeitung. Sie kommt aus Bonn.
   Ich lese eine Bonner Zeitung.

   1. Wir haben gestern einen Politiker gesehen. Er kommt aus Berlin.
   2. Marie geht zum Oktoberfest. Es findet in München statt.
   3. Ich besuche gern das Rathaus in München.
   4. Die Touristen haben den Bürgermeister kennengelernt. Er lebt in Hamburg.

D. **Schreiben Sie Sätze mit Adjektiven!**

   Zum Beispiel: Wir haben ein _____ Wohnzimmer. (dunkel)
   Wir haben ein dunkles Wohnzimmer.

   Das Wohnzimmer war _____. (dunkel)
   Das Wohnzimmer war dunkel.

   1. Herr Ohm hat einen _____ Hut gekauft. (teuer)

   2. Helmut, trink diese _____ Milch nicht! (sauer)

   3. Die Zugspitze ist ein _____ Berg. (hoch)

   4. Mount Whitney ist sehr _____. (hoch)

   5. Diese Limonade ist zu _____. (sauer)

E. **Übersetzen Sie die folgenden Sätze!**

   1. Not all American students have visited Germany.
   2. Yesterday some German politicians discussed several important problems in the (**im**) new parliament.
   3. A few young members of this political party are against the (**gegen den**) new chancellor.
   4. Yesterday I bought a Frankfurt newspaper.
   5. Kurt says that Viennese cutlet (**Schnitzel**) is expensive here.
   6. The town hall has a high tower.
   7. That expensive book is interesting.
   8. Not all these students are Americans.

F. **In einem dunklen Wald. . .** Complete the blanks with the appropriate adjective endings.

Einig_____ amerikanisch_____ und kanadisch_____ Touristen

gingen in den dunkl_____ Schwarzwald. Dort sahen sie viel_____

hoh_____ Bäume und mehrer_____ klar_____ Bäche.

Dieser schön_____ Wald war nicht all_____ amerikanisch_____

Touristen bekannt. Mehrer_____ jung_____ Amerikanerinnen besuchten

Deutschland zum ersten Mal. All_____ jung_____ Ausländerinnen

fanden die viel_____ groß_____ Wälder bezaubernd (*enchanting*).

Comparison of Adjectives and Adverbs

In German as in English adjectives have three degrees of comparison:

Positive	*Comparative*	*Superlative*
Hans ist *stark*. Hans is strong.	Paul ist *stärker*. Paul is stronger.	Wolf ist der *stärkste*. Wolf is the strongest.
Ute ist *klug*. Ute is smart.	Ingrid ist *klüger*. Ingrid is smarter.	Karin ist die *klügste*. Karin is the smartest.

Formation

The comparative degree is formed from the positive by adding **-er**. The superlative is formed from the positive degree by adding **-st** (not **-est** as in English).

schön	schöner	schönst-
fleißig	fleißiger	fleißigst-
reich	reicher	reichst-

In German there is no way of forming the comparative with equivalents of *more* or *most*, as in English: **schöner** = more beautiful, lovelier; **schönst** = most beautiful, loveliest.

Forms with Umlauts

If the positive degree consists of only one syllable and can take an umlaut, the comparative and superlative forms usually have umlauts.

jung	jünger	jüngst-
klug	klüger	klügst-
lang	länger	längst-

Important exceptions: The adjectives **klar** (*clear*), **schlank** (*slender*), **voll** (*full*), and adjectives with the diphthong **au** (such as **laut** [loud] or **schlau** [*clever*]) do not take umlauts.

klar	klarer	klarst-
laut	lauter	lautest-

Superlative in *-est*

If the positive degree ends in **-d** or **-t** or an /s/ sound, the superlative is formed by adding **-est** rather than **-st**.

gesund	gesünder	gesündest-
kalt	kälter	kältest-
kurz	kürzer	kürzest-
heiß	heißer	heißest-

However, if the last syllable is unstressed, **-st** is added as with other adjectives. For example, participles used as adjectives or adverbs take **-st** in the superlative even though they end in **-d** or **-t**.*

Marie ist das *reizendste* Mädchen, das ich kenne.
Marie is the most charming girl I know.

Lincoln war einer der *hochgeachtetsten* Präsidenten.
Lincoln was one of the most respected presidents.

Irregular Comparison of Adjectives

groß	größer	größt-
gut	besser	best-
hoch	höher	höchst-
nah	näher	nächst-
viel	mehr	meist-

---

*The present participle rarely occurs except in formal German. It is usually formed by adding **-d** to the infinitive: **laufend** (*running*), **reizend** (*charming*), etc.

Attributive Adjectives in the Comparative and Superlative

When the comparative or superlative form of an adjective modifies a following noun (that is, when it is an attributive adjective), it takes the same weak or strong ending as the adjective in the positive degree would.

Der junge Professor schreibt ein Buch über den Kommunismus.
  (positive)
Der *jüngere (jüngste)* Professor schreibt ein Buch über den
  Kommunismus.
The younger (youngest) professor is writing a book about communism.

Ein junger Professor unterrichtet politische Wissenschaft.   (positive)
Ein *jüngerer* Professor unterrichtet politische Wissenschaft.
A younger professor is teaching political science.

Ich verstehe das neue Gesetz nicht.   (positive)
Ich verstehe das *neuere (neuste)* Gesetz nicht.
I don't understand the newer (newest) law.

Das Parlament hat ein neues Gesetz verabschiedet.   (positive)
Das Parlament hat ein *neueres* Gesetz verabschiedet.
The parliament passed a newer law.

Die aktiven Mitglieder sind alle jung.   (positive)
Die *aktiveren (aktivsten)* Mitglieder sind alle jung.
The more active (most active) members are all young.

Bundesbürger wählen

The Adjective *viel*

The adjective **viel** takes endings like any other adjective in the plural:

Das Parlament hat *viele* neue Gesetze verabschiedet.
The parliament passed many new laws

However, it usually takes no endings in the singular.

Jeden morgen trinke ich *viel* heißen Kaffee.
Every morning I drink a lot of hot coffee.

Mehr, the comparative degree of **viel**, never takes endings.

Mehr deutsche Studenten lernen Französisch als Russisch.
More German students learn French than Russian.

Meist-, the superlative degree of **viel**, is always preceded by the definite article and takes weak endings.

Die *meisten* deutschen Studenten lernen Englisch.
Most German students learn English.

Predicate Adjectives in the Comparative and Superlative

Just as in the positive degree, adjectives in the comparative degree do not require weak or strong endings when they are used as predicate adjectives.

Monika ist *klug.* (positive)
Toni ist *klüger.* (comparative)

Hier wird es *kalt.* (positive)
Dort wird es noch *kälter.* (comparative)

However, in the superlative degree, adjectives take one of the following two forms when used as predicate adjectives:

1. **der, das, die . . . -ste(n)**

   Die Ärztin ist intelligent, der Zahnarzt ist intelligenter, aber die Juristin ist die intelligenteste (Frau) in der Stadt.
   The doctor is intelligent, the dentist is more intelligent, but the lawyer is the most intelligent one (woman) in the town.

2. **am . . . -sten**

   Das Rathaus ist groß, das Theater ist größer, aber der Dom ist am größten.

The first method can be used only if the superlative refers to a specific noun (for example, **Frau**), while the second method can always be used.

Comparison of Adverbs

Adverbs modify verbs, adjectives, or other adverbs and answer such questions as *when?*, *where?*, or *how?* In English most adverbs are formed by adding *-ly* to adjectives: *beautiful* → *beautifully*. In German no ending is added to adjectives to form adverbs: **schön** is the equivalent of the adjective *beautiful* and the adverb *beautifully*. Similarly, **schöner** is the equivalent of the adjective *more beautiful* and the adverb *more beautifully*:

Adjective: Dieses Rathaus ist *schön* (*schöner*).
This town hall is beautiful (more beautiful).

Adverb: Toni singt *schön* (*schöner*).
Toni sings beautifully (more beautifully).

Here are more examples:

Joachim schwimmt *gut*, aber Andrea schwimmt *besser*.
Joachim swims well, but Andrea swims better.

Dieser Film gefällt mir (*gut*), aber der andere Film gefällt mir *besser*.
I like this movie, but I prefer the other movie.

Ich schwimme *gern*, aber ich spiele *lieber* Fußball.
I like to swim but I prefer to play soccer.

Gertrud hat Martin gern, aber sie hat Rudi *lieber*.
Gertrud likes Martin, but she prefers Rudi.

Dieser Politiker arbeitet *fleißig*, aber der da arbeitet noch *fleißiger*.
This politician works hard, but that one works even harder.

The superlative of adverbs is based on the form **am . . . -sten**.

Dieser Film von Wertmüller gefällt mir *am besten*.
I like this film by Wertmüller best.

Gertrud hat Michael *am liebsten*.
Gertrud likes Michael best.

Der Bundeskanzler arbeitet *am fleißigsten*.
The chancellor works hardest.

Als, nicht so . . . wie, immer, je . . . je

Comparisons can be expressed by using **als** with the comparative degree or **nicht so . . . wie** or **ebenso . . . wie** with the positive.

Inge ist *klüger als* Hans.
Inge is smarter than Hans.

Hans ist *nicht so klug wie* Inge.
Hans isn't as smart as Inge.

Hans ist *ebenso klug wie* Martin.
Hans is just as smart as Martin.

Immer (+ the comparative) is the equivalent of *more and more.*

> Diese Regierung wird *immer schwächer.*
> This government is becoming weaker and weaker.

> Kurt arbeitet *immer fleißiger.*
> Kurt is working harder and harder.

> Inge singt *immer besser.*
> Inge is singing better and better.

Je . . . je (desto) means *the more . . . the more.*

> *Je* früher *je* lieber.
> The earlier the better.

> *Je* öfter man die Tageszeitung liest, *desto* besser versteht man die
>   politische Lage.
> The more often one reads the daily paper, the better one understands the
>   political situation.

Notice that transposed word order is required in the first clause but that
inverted word order must be used in the second.

The Prefix *aller-*

The prefix **aller-** may be added to any superlative form to mean *of all.*

> In diesem Seminar ist Karoline die *allerklügste* Studentin.
> Karoline is the smartest student of all in this seminar.

> Daniel spielt Fußball am *allerbesten.*
> Daniel plays soccer best of all.

> Das ist das *allerfriedlichste* Land.
> This is the most peace-loving country of all.

The Absolute Superlative

The superlative can be used to express a very high degree without actually
expressing any comparison. It usually takes the form **aufs . . . -e.**

> Kurt hat gestern *aufs fleißigste* gearbeitet.
> Kurt really worked very hard yesterday.

> Inge hat gestern *aufs schönste* gesungen.
> Inge sang most beautifully yesterday.

Höchst or **äußerst** followed by the positive degree has basically the same
meaning.

> Inge hat gestern *äußerst* schön gesungen.

> Er hat mir eine *höchst interessante* Nachricht geschickt.
> He sent me a most interesting piece of news.

The Suffix -*ens*

The suffix **-ens** is added to a number of adjectives to create adverbs with specialized meanings.

Rauchen ist hier *strengstens* verboten.
Smoking is absolutely forbidden here.

Ab und zu trinke ich Bier, aber *meistens* trinke ich Wasser.
Once in a while I drink beer, but mostly I drink water.

Kurt ist nicht vorbeigekommen, aber *wenigstens* hat er uns angerufen.
Kurt didn't come by but at least he called us.

Lisette kann nicht Deutsch lesen. Sie versteht *höchstens* ein paar
Wörter.
Lisette cannot read German. At best she understands only a few words.

Übungen

°A. **Vergleichen Sie!** Make comparisons, following the model.

Zum Beispiel:　Berlin / groß / Regensburg
Berlin ist größer als Regensburg.

1. Rothenburg / klein / Berlin
2. die Demokratie / gut / die Diktatur
3. der Kölner Dom / hoch / die Frauenkirche in München
4. deine Antwort / klar / meine
5. das Wetter in Alaska / kalt / das Wetter in Mexiko
6. Pierre Trudeau / liberal / Ronald Reagan
7. ein Flugzeug / schnell / Wagen
8. dieser Politiker / ehrlich / der da

°B. **Nach Guinness.** Make superlatives, based on the following items from the Guinness *Book of World Records*.

Zum Beispiel:　Jericho ist eine alte Stadt.
Jericho ist die älteste Stadt.

1. Die Sowjetunion ist eine großes Land.
2. Venus ist wahrscheinlich ein heißer Planet.
3. Der brasilianische Fußballspieler Pelé hat viele Tore (*goals*) geschossen.
4. Die Engländerin Jan Todd ist eine starke Frau.
5. Der Österreicher Arnold Schwarzenegger ist ein muskulöser Mann.
6. Zwischen Kanada und der USA liegt eine lange ununterbrochene
   (*uninterrupted*) Grenze.
7. Die *Mona Lisa* ist ein teures Bild.
8. Pluto ist ein kalter Planet.
9. Venus ist ein naher Planet.

Bilden Sie Komparative und Superlative!

Zum Beispiel: Ich kenne Frau Behns *jungen* Sohn.
Ich kenne Frau Behns jüngeren Sohn.
Ich kenne Frau Behns jüngsten Sohn.

1. Ist das der *konservative* Politiker?
2. Wir haben die *aktuellen* Probleme besprochen.
3. Henriette lebt in der *kleinen* Stadt.
4. Wer hat die *gute* politische Lösung gefunden?
5. Ich habe Kurts *altes* Auto gekauft.

D. **Bilden Sie Komparative und Superlative!** Use two variations of the superlative whenever possible, following the model.

Zum Beispiel: Marie ist siebzehn Jahre alt. Tina ist achtzehn Jahre alt. Virginia ist zwanzig Jahre alt.   jung
Tina ist jünger als Virginia, aber Marie ist die jüngste (Marie ist am jüngsten).

1. Thomas kann 122 Kilogramm stemmen (*lift*). Erich kann 130 Kilogramm stemmen. Wolfgang kann 160 Kilogramm stemmen.   stark
2. Wilfried versteht wenig. Frank versteht viel. Irmgard versteht alles.   klug
3. Der Everest im Himalaja ist ungefähr 8 850 Meter hoch. Der Vulkan Cayambe in Ekuador ist ungefähr 5 880 Meter hoch. Der Mont Blanc in den Alpen ist ungefähr 4 810 Meter hoch.   hoch
4. Liechtenstein ist 161 Quadratkilometer (*square kilometers*) groß. Die Schweiz ist 40 122 Quadratkilometer groß. Österreich ist 83 851 Quadratkilometer groß.   groß
5. Die Donau ist 2 859 Kilometer lang. Der Rhein ist 1 320 Kilometer lang. Die Mosel ist 515 Kilometer lang.   lang

E. **Beantworten Sie die folgenden Fragen!** Answer, following the model.

Zum Beispiel: Arbeitet Rita jetzt fleißig?
Ja, Rita arbeitet immer fleißiger.

1. Spricht Caroline gut Deutsch?
2. Müssen die Studenten lange arbeiten?
3. Werden die Tage im Winter kurz?
4. Wird das Wetter im Sommer heiß?
5. Werden die Preise jetzt hoch?

F. **Beantworten Sie die folgenden Fragen!**

Zum Beispiel: Ist die BRD (Westdeutschland) größer als Kanada?
Nein, die BRD ist nicht so groß wie Kanada.

1. Sind die Alpen höher als der Everest?
2. Ist die Sowjetunion ebenso klein wie die Schweiz?
3. Ist Ronald Reagan liberaler als Ted Kennedy?
4. Ist John Smith ebenso berühmt wie Albert Einstein?

G. **Was haben Sie gern?** Answer, following the models.

Zum Beispiel: Was trinken Sie gern?
Ich trinke gern Coca-Cola, aber ich trinke lieber Milch, und ich trinke am liebsten Apfelsaft.

Welche Filme haben Ihnen gefallen?
Der Exorzist **hat mir gefallen, aber** *Startrek* **hat mir besser gefallen, und** *Der Krieg der Sterne* **hat mir am besten gefallen.**

1. Welche Fernsehsendung sehen Sie gern?
2. Welche Schauspielerin gefällt Ihnen?
3. Welche Rockgruppe gefällt Ihnen?
4. Welchen Politiker hören Sie gern?

H. **Beantworten Sie die folgenden Fragen!**

Zum Beispiel: Wie kann man besser Deutsch sprechen?
Je mehr man Deutsch übt, desto besser spricht man Deutsch.

1. Wie wird man dicker?
2. Wie wird man schlanker?
3. Wie kann man mehr Geld verdienen?
4. Wie kann man besser Deutsch verstehen?

I. **Übersetzen Sie die folgenden Sätze.**

1. Kurt is older than his sister.
2. Monday was the hottest day of this year.
3. Mount Everest is the highest mountain in the (**in der**) world.
4. We saw the longest river in Germany, the Rhein.
5. I like "The Grateful Dead" better than "The Rolling Stones." But I like "The Beatles" best of all.
6. Mary is smarter than Anna, but Renate is the smartest.
7. This church is just as tall (**hoch**) as the town hall, but the cathedral is the tallest of all.
8. The French speak faster than the Americans, but the Spanish speak the fastest.
9. Are American politicians becoming more and more conservative?
10. That king ruled most (very) justly.
11. During (**bei**) tests talking is strictly forbidden.

J. **Beschreiben Sie Ihre Freunde!** Describe six of your friends, using superlatives with **aller-**.

Zum Beispiel: Sandra ist die allerklügste meiner Freundinnen.

K. **Wenn man mich zum Senator wählt . . .** What would you do if you were elected senator of your state? Create some campaign promises. You might want to use some of the following vocabulary:

die Luft / rein (*clean*)　　　　　　die Gesetze / gerecht

die Steuern (die Preise) / niedrig　　die Welt / friedlich

die Bürger / glücklich (reich)　　　　die Freiheit / groß

Zum Beispiel:　Die Preise werden niedriger sein.
**　　　　　　　　Die Bürger werden glücklicher sein.**

Adjectives Used as Nouns

Omissions of *Mann, Frau, Leute*

The nouns **Mann**, **Frau**, and **Leute** are often omitted after adjectives. If the adjective is a descriptive adjective (indicating size, shape, and the like) it is usually capitalized, since it is then used as a noun.*

Ein Deutscher (~~Mann~~) hat mir den Plan des Kanzlers erklärt.
A German explained the chancellor's plan to me.

Diese Deutsche (~~Frau~~) trinkt gern Bier.
This German (woman) likes beer.

Man hat mehr Konservative (~~Leute~~) als Liberale (~~Leute~~) gewählt.
More conservatives than liberals were elected.

These adjectival nouns have a natural gender and can be used for males or females of any age.

Die *Kleine* hat ihre Mutter um ein Glas Milch gebeten.
The little girl asked her mother for a glass of milk.

Hast du den *Kleinen* gesehen? Sein Vater sucht ihn.
Have you seen the little boy? His father is looking for him.

Present and past participles are also often capitalized and used in this manner.

Ein *Reisender* hat uns über den Fahrplan gefragt.
A traveler asked us about the (train) schedule.

Ich habe einen Brief von einer *Verwandten* bekommen.
I received a letter from a (female) relative.

Hast du viele *Verwandte?*
Do you have many relatives?

---

*Nondescriptive adjectives are not capitalized: **Hat der Kanzler das gesagt? —Nein, ein *anderer* hat das gesagt.**

Der *Beamte* steht am Schalter.
The official is standing at the counter.

Ein *Beamter* arbeitet da.*
An official works there.

The noun **Junge** is a true noun, not an adjective used as a noun; it does not take adjective endings. Compare:

Ein Junge arbeitet da.
A boy works there.

Ein Beamter arbeitet da.
An official works there.

Neuter Adjectives used as Nouns

Adjectives declined with neuter endings (weak or strong as appropriate) can be used to refer to things or concepts and are usually capitalized.

Platon hat an *das Gute, das Schöne* und *das Wahre* geglaubt.
Plato believed in the good, the beautiful, and the true.

Das Interessante daran war die Tatsache, daß der Bundeskanzler fließend Englisch kann.
What was interesting about the situation was the fact that the chancellor speaks English fluently.

Das Geschriebene war schwer zu lesen.
What was written was hard to read. (It was difficult to read what was written.)

Past participles can be used in this manner, as the last example illustrates.

Omission of Repeated Nouns

In German, a modified noun is sometimes understood rather than restated after an adjective. In this case, the adjective is not capitalized:

Gib mir nicht den großen Teller. Ich will den *kleinen* (~~Teller~~).
Don't give me the big plate. I want the *small one.*

Gehören dir die schwarzen Schuhe oder die *braunen* (~~Schuhe~~)?
Do the black shoes or the *brown ones* belong to you?

Haben die Schweizer eine demokratische Regierung oder eine *sozialistische* (~~Regierung~~)?
Do the Swiss have a democratic government or a socialistic one?

In English, the omitted noun is usually replaced with the word *one* or *ones*.

---

*Beamtin, the feminine counterpart of **Beamter**, is not a declined adjective but an ordinary feminine noun: **Die Beamtin hat uns geholfen.**

Übungen

°A. Ersetzen Sie die Wörter **Amerikaner, Amerikanerin(nen)!** Replace the words **Amerikaner, Amerikanerin(nen)** with the appropriate form of **Deutsche-**.

Zum Beispiel: Eine Amerikanerin hat das Rathaus fotografiert.
Eine Deutsche hat das Rathaus fotografiert.

1. Richard ist ein junger *Amerikaner.*
2. Viele *Amerikaner* bezahlen hohe Steuern.
3. Fräulein Unger, kennen Sie diese *Amerikanerinnen?*
4. Wann fliegt das Flugzeug der Amerikaner ab?
5. Das Kind ist der *Amerikanerin* gefolgt.
6. Der Beamte hat den *Amerikanern* das Gesetz erklärt.
7. Der *Amerikaner* besuchte das Rathaus mit seiner Frau.
8. Wir haben die Eltern des *Amerikaners* kennengelernt.

°B. **Übersetzen Sie die folgenden Sätze!**

1. Das Schönste im Leben ist nicht immer das Teuerste.
2. Hier sind die alten Bücher, aber wo sind die neuen?
3. Die konservativen Senatoren waren gegen hohe Steuern, aber ich weiß nicht, ob die liberalen dafür oder dagegen waren.
4. Wir sollten nur das Wichtige besprechen.
5. Udo, hast du das neue Rathaus gesehen oder nur das alte?

C. **Was ist der Unterschied?** Answer the questions, following the model:

Zum Beispiel: Was für ein politisches System haben die BRD und die DDR?
Die BRD hat ein demokratisches System, aber die DDR hat ein kommunistisches.

1. Was für Wetter findet man in Spanien und in Schweden?
2. Was für Senatoren sind Ted Kennedy und Barry Goldwater?
3. Was für Politiker sollte man wählen? Welche sollte man nicht wählen?
4. Was für Gesetze sollte das Parlament (oder der Kongreß) verabschieden?

D. **Übersetzen Sie die folgenden Sätze!**

1. Many Germans visit America.
2. A considerable number of (**manche**) Germans speak English.
3. Our new guest is a German.
4. Peter, did you help your (female) relative?
5. That (male) German's daughter speaks English well.
6. Those old (people) are relatives of that politician.
7. Do conservatives prefer (like better) strong laws or weak ones?

E. **Es war einmal ein Beamter. . . .** Complete this story with the correct forms of **Deutsche-, Beamte-,** or **Verwandte-,** as appropriate.

Eine alte _____ ging an den Schalter in der Post und sagte dem _____:

„Ein _____ von mir in Amerika hat mir ein Paket geschickt, aber ich habe es noch nicht bekommen. Vielleicht ist dieses Paket von meinem

_____ verlorengegangen." Der _____ fragte die _____: „Wie wissen

Sie, daß Ihr _____ in Amerika dieses Paket schon geschickt hat?"

Die _____ antwortete: „Der _____ hat mir letzten Monat einen Brief

geschickt und hat geschrieben, daß ich bald ein Paket bekomme."

Der _____ sah sehr zufrieden aus und sagte der _____: „Sehen Sie, wir

haben doch etwas richtig gemacht. Sie haben ja den Brief bekommen!"

Rückblick━━━━━━━━━━━━━━━━━━━

A. **Zur Wiederholung. Übersetzen Sie die folgenden Sätze!**

1. They (**man**) built a new town hall because the old one was too small.
2. Good wine is more expensive than good beer.
3. Did the German parliament pass many strict laws?
4. Several young Germans asked about the American political system.
5. My German relatives do not understand our American laws.
6. Which German tourists visited these American cities?
7. Mrs. Scheer, do you always read Munich newspapers?
8. Eduard is stronger than his brother, but their father is the strongest. (Translate two ways.)
9. Which high mountain do you like best of all, Kurt?
10. Veronika, do you like to drink coffee or do you prefer (like better) to drink milk?
11. Most older Americans believe that America needs stronger laws.
12. Wolfgang's younger brother is smarter than he.
13. American students are studying longer and longer.
14. The more you (**man**) earn (**verdienen**), the higher the taxes become.
15. I like the German language best of all.
16. Many young people (**Jugendliche-**) like to hear rock music.

B. **Zur Gesamtwiederholung. Übersetzen Sie die folgenden Sätze!**

1. The old (man) had died before the young (female) doctor arrived.   (Chapter 2)
2. I wrote a long essay on the (**über den**) West German parliament after I read an interesting book on it (**darüber**).
3. Jost, did you answer the new (female) teacher?   (Chapter 3)
4. Where is the professor's youngest son?
5. Monika, do you know that young Frenchman?   (Chapter 4)
6. Martin's grandfather is old, but mine is older.
7. We have to write three long reports on the (**über das**) American political system.   (Chapter 5)
8. Inge, did you hear Rosemarie singing that beautiful Spanish song?
9. These long foreign words are hard to pronounce.   (Chapter 6)
10. Young Germans often talk about (**über die**) politics.

8
Familie und Gesellschaft

München: Spaziergang am Sonntagnachmittag

Introduction to the Subjunctive; Formation of the Subjunctive

Uses of the Subjunctive

Wortschatz

der Bruder (-) brother

die Ehe (-n) marriage, institution of marriage

die Einladung (-en) invitation

die Eltern *pl.* parents

das Enkelkind (-er) grandchild

die Frau (-en) woman, wife

der Freund (-e), die Freundin (-nen) friend; **mein Freund** my boyfriend; **meine Freundin** my girlfriend

der Geburtstag (-e) birthday

die Gesellschaft (-en) company, society

die Großeltern *pl.* grandparents

die Großmutter (-) grandmother

der Großvater (-) grandfather

die Hochzeit (-en) wedding

die Jugend youth

die Kusine (-n) female cousin

der Mann (-er) man, husband

die Mutter (-) mother

die Mutti mama

der Nachbar (-n), die Nachbarin (-nen) neighbor

die Oma (-s) grandma

der Onkel (-) uncle

der Opa (-s) grandpa

die Party (-s) party

die Schwester (-n) sister

der Sohn (-e) son

die Tante (-n) aunt

die Tochter (-) daughter

der Vater (-) father

der Vati papa

der Vetter (-n) male cousin

ein · laden* to invite

heiraten to get married; to marry

kennen · lernen to meet, make the acquaintance of

lieben to love; to like

vermissen to miss

versorgen to take care of, look after

zusammen · halten* to hold together

geboren born, née

geschieden divorced

verheiratet married

---

*Verbs marked with an asterisk are strong verbs; see the appendix for principal parts of strong verbs.

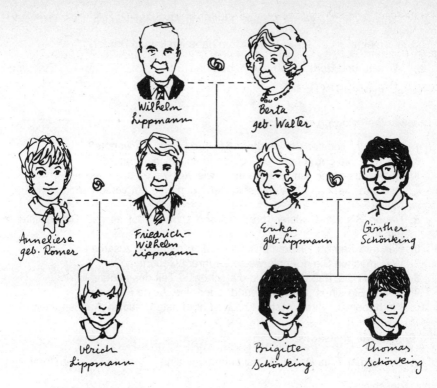

Wilhelm Lippmann — Berta geb. Walter

Anneliese geb. Römer — Friedrich-Wilhelm Lippmann — Erika geb. Lippmann — Günther Schönking

Ulrich Lippmann — Brigitte Schönking — Thomas Schönking

A. Eine deutsche Familie

1. Ulrich sagt: „Mein <u>Vater</u> heißt Friedrich-Wilhelm, und

   mein <u>Onkel</u> heißt Günther".

2. Brigitte sagt: „Meine <u>Großeltern</u> heißen mit Nachnamen Lippmann;

   meine <u>Großmutter</u> nenne ich immer ‚Oma‘, und

   meinen <u>Großvater</u> nenne ich einfach ‚Opa‘".

3. Erika Schönking hat eine _____ und einen _____.

   Friedrich-Wilhelm Lippmann ist ihr _____; sie nennt ihn meistens

   „Fritz".

4. Thomas fragt: „Kennst du eigentlich meine _____ Anneliese?"

5. Ulrich sagt zu Brigitte: „Ich bin dein _____, und du bist

   meine _____. Wir können nicht heiraten."

6. Thomas fragt seinen Vater: „Papa, Tante Anneliese ist doch mit Onkel Fritz

   verheiratet, nicht? Dann ist sie seine _____ und Onkel Fritz ist ihr

   _____, oder?"

7. Thomas sagt zu seiner Mutter: „Mutti, mit Brigitte spiele ich nicht. Die ist ja

nur meine _____. Warum habe ich keinen Bruder?"

8. Wilhelm und Berta Lippmann haben drei _____, zwei Jungen und

ein Mädchen.

B. *Answer the following questions.*

1. Wer ist Ihr liebster Verwandter oder Ihre liebste Verwandte?
2. Möchten Sie gerne heiraten? Wenn ja, in welchem Alter?
3. Hätten Sie gerne Kinder? Wenn ja, wie viele?
4. Glauben Sie, daß ein Vater sein Baby genauso gut versorgen kann wie eine Mutter?
5. Haben Sie Geschwister (*brothers and sisters*)? Ist es gut, Geschwister zu haben?
6. Hält Ihre Familie zusammen? Wer hält ihre Familie zusammen?
7. Was machen Sie normalerweise an Ihrem Geburtstag?
8. Glauben Sie, daß die Jugend die schönste Zeit des Lebens ist?
9. Haben Sie einen „besten Freund" oder eine „beste Freundin"?
10. Wo haben Sie Ihren besten Freund (Ihre beste Freundin) kennengelernt?

C. *Complete the sentences.*

1. Schau mal, Rita. Rolf und Susi haben uns eine _____ zu ihrer Party

geschickt.

2. Hast du schon gehört, daß Werner und Barbara diese Woche heiraten? Die

_____ ist am Samstag. Haben sie dich _____?

3. Mein _____ ist am Samstag. Ich werde zwanzig Jahre alt.

4. Jeden Mittwoch gehen die alten Damen zum Kaffeeklatsch und sprechen über

die jungen Leute: „Jaja, die _____ von heute!"

5. Bei uns nebenan wohnen jetzt sehr freundliche Leute. Ich bin wirklich froh,

daß wir jetzt so nette _____haben.

6. Meine Mutter liebt meinen Vater, und mein Vater liebt meine Mutter. Ihre

_____ist sehr gut. Sie sind seit zwanzig Jahren _____,

und unsere Familie _____ _____.

7. Christine, laß uns noch nicht nach Hause gehen. Wir sind hier in guter

_____.

8. Meine Eltern sind _____. Ich wohne bei meiner Mutter, und mein

Bruder wohnt bei meinem Vater.

Introduction to the Subjunctive; Formation of the Subjunctive

Introduction to the Subjunctive

So far in this text the indicative mood has been used—the mood that is used to state facts or ask questions. In this chapter we'll discuss the subjunctive mood, the mood used to express wishes, conjecture, doubt, or denial. Compare these sentences:

Meine Eltern *kommen* heute.   (indicative)
My parents are coming today.

Wenn meine Eltern heute *kämen, besprächen* wir die
    Hochzeit.   (subjunctive)
If my parents came today, we would discuss the wedding.

Wenn meine Eltern nur heute *kämen!*
If only my parents were coming today!

Ich *habe* genug Geld.   (indicative)
I have enough money.

Wenn ich genug Geld *hätte,* so *ginge* ich mit meiner Freundin ins
    Konzert.   (subjunctive)
If I had enough money, I'd go to the concert with my girlfriend.

Wenn ich nur eine Schwester *hätte!*   (subjunctive)
If only I had a sister!

As you can see, the sentences in the indicative express facts, but the sentences in the subjunctive do not; the speaker or writer using the subjunctive is expressing a conjecture or wish. The uses of the subjunctive will be presented in the next sections, but for now let's look at its formation.

Formation of the Present Subjunctive

The present subjunctive is formed from the past stem of the verb. To form the first- and third-persons singular, -e is added to the past stem if it does not already end in -e, then an umlaut is added if the stem vowel of the past is different from the stem vowel of the infinitive.

Infinitive	Past Stem	Present Subjunctive
geben	gab	gäbe
dürfen	durfte	dürfte
können	konnte	könnte
sein	war	wäre

Most weak verbs (verbs with past stems ending in **-te**) and the modals **sollen** and **wollen** have present subjunctive forms identical to their past forms since the past stem already ends in **-e** and has the *same stem vowel* as the infinitive.

Infinitive	*Past Stem*	*Present Subjunctive*
lernen	lernte	lernte
lieben	liebte	liebte
machen	machte	machte
sollen	sollte	sollte
wollen	wollte	wollte

Haben is irregular in the present subjunctive in that it requires an umlaut even though the stem vowel of the past stem (**hatte**) is the same as the stem vowel of the infinitive (**haben**): **hätte**.

The other persons of the present subjunctive are formed by adding the endings shown in bold in the following conjugations of **sein** and **geben**.

sein

ich wär**e**	wir wär**en**
du wär**est**	ihr wär**et**
er sie es } wär**e**	sie Sie } wär**en**

geben

ich gäb**e**	wir gäb**en**
du gäb**est**	ihr gäb**et**
er sie es } gäb**e**	sie Sie } gäb**en**

The present subjunctive has various English equivalents:

Wenn Onkel Rudi mir nur sein altes Auto *gäbe*!
If only Uncle Rudi *would give (gave, were to give)* me his old car!

Wenn Ulrike uns zur Party nur *einlüde*!
If only Ulrike *would invite (invited, were to invite)* us to the party!

Formation of the Past Subjunctive

The past subjunctive is formed by using the present subjunctive of the auxiliary verbs **haben** or **sein** together with the past participle of the main verb. Verbs that take **haben** in the perfect tenses take **haben** in the past subjunctive; verbs that take **sein** in the perfect tenses take **sein** in the past subjunctive:

Wenn ich nur nicht deine Kusine *geheiratet hätte*!
If only I had not married your cousin.

Wenn ich nur in meiner Heimatstadt *geblieben wäre*!
If only I had stayed in my home town!

Here is the complete conjugation of the past subjunctive of two verbs, one which takes **haben** and the other which takes **sein**:

sehen

ich hätte gesehen	wir hätten gesehen
du hättest gesehen	ihr hättet gesehen
er ⎫	sie ⎫
sie ⎬ hätte gesehen	Sie ⎬ hätten gesehen
es ⎭	

gehen

ich wäre gegangen	wir wären gegangen
du wärest gegangen	ihr wäret gegangen
er ⎫	sie ⎫
sie ⎬ wäre gegangen	Sie ⎬ wären gegangen
es ⎭	

Übungen

°A. **Wünsche.** Gretchen is always wishing that things were different; make sentences as she would, following the models.

Zum Beispiel: Mein Bruder stellte nicht so viele Fragen.
Wenn mein Bruder nur nicht so viele Fragen stellte!

1. Mein Schwester lernte Deutsch.
2. Gerd spielte mit uns Tennis.
3. Hermann wollte mit uns in die Oper gehen.
4. Wir besuchten die Verwandten.
5. Du wartetest auf uns.
6. Hans liebte mich.
7. Monika versorgte ihre Kinder.
8. Werner lernte meine Kusine kennen.
9. Inge heiratete meinen Bruder.

Zum Beispiel: Meine Freundin verstand gut Englisch.
Wenn meine Freundin nur gut Englisch verstände!

1. Ich wußte die Antwort.
2. Die Großeltern waren hier.
3. Der Vetter kam mit uns ins Kino.
4. Toni konnte den Eltern helfen.
5. Es gab mehr Geld.
6. Die Großmutter sprach schon wieder über die guten alten Zeiten.
7. Sandra las dieses Buch.
8. Meine Mutter sah das Leben so wie ich.

Zum Beispiel: Es ging Margarete besser.
Wenn es nur Margarete besser ginge!

1. Meine Tante schrieb mir einen Brief.
2. Die Sonne schien heute.
3. Meine Schwester blieb zu Hause.
4. Deine Kusine ging mit uns ins Kino.

B. **Die guten alten Zeiten** (*The Good Old Days*). Grandmother is reminiscing about the past and wishes things were still the way they were then. Make sentences as she would, following the models.

Zum Beispiel: Wir waren jung.
Wenn wir nur jung wären!

Es gab keine Atombomben.
Wenn es nur keine Atombomben gäbe!

1. Die jungen Leute waren höflich.
2. Wir hatten mehr Zeit.
3. Fleisch kostete weniger.
4. Die Jugend arbeitete fleißiger.
5. Die Familien hielten zusammen.
6. Wir brauchten kein Auto.
7. Die Luft war sauber.
8. Die Preise waren niedriger.

C. **Ersetzen Sie die Pronomen!** Replace the pronouns in italics with the pronouns in parentheses and change the verbs accordingly.

1. Wenn *du* nur die Gäste abgeholt hättest! (ich, ihr, Sie)
2. Wenn *wir* nur zum Großvater gefahren wären! (ich, du, sie *sing.*)
3. Wenn *du* nur nicht so krank gewesen wärest! (Sie, wir, ich)
4. Wenn *ihr* nur nicht diesen Wagen gekauft hättet! (wir, du, Sie)
5. Wenn *wir* nur geschieden wären! (du, ich, sie *pl.*)
6. Wenn *ich* nur dieses Mädchen kennengelernt hätte! (du, wir, er)
7. Wenn *wir* nur die Großeltern besser versorgt hätten! (sie *sing.*, man, du)

D. **Bilden Sie den Konjunktiv der Vergangenheit!** Form the past subjunctive from the present perfect indicative using the model given. Change affirmative sentences to negative ones, and vice versa.

Zum Beispiel: Ich habe den Film nicht gesehen.
Wenn ich nur den Film gesehen hätte!

1. Ulrich ist nicht mit uns gegangen.
2. Gisela ist bei ihrem Vetter gewesen.
3. Ich habe Edith nicht angerufen.
4. Die Nachbarn haben das nicht gewußt.
5. Wir haben Günter nicht geschrieben.
6. Du bist gestern krank geworden.
7. Man hat uns zur Hochzeit eingeladen.

E. **Wenn nur . . .!** Anneliese wishes she had done things differently. What does she say in the following situations?

Suggested verbs: *zu Hause bleiben, essen, fliegen, kaufen, lernen, studieren, vergessen.*

Zum Beispiel: Das Auto ist kaputt.
   Wenn ich nur dieses Auto nicht gekauft hätte!

1.   Pierre spricht Französich, und ich verstehe ihn nicht.
2.   Die Prüfung ist sehr schwer.
3.   Der Fernseher ist kaputt.
4.   Meine Kusine wollte mich besuchen, aber ich war im Konzert.
5.   Es regnet und ich habe keinen Regenschirm.
6.   Ich habe heute morgen nichts gegessen, und jetzt habe ich Hunger.
7.   Ich hatte eine Gelegenheit nach Berlin zu fliegen, aber ich bin mit dem Auto gefahren.

F. **Übersetzen Sie die folgenden Sätze!**

1. If only Marie loved me (**mich**)!
2. If only that student were not married!
3. Sara, if only you studied more!
4. If we only had more money!
5. If I had only understood the professor better!
6. If I only knew the answer!
7. If we only had grandchildren!
8. If only the neighbors had called us!
9. If only our family had held together!
10. If only I had met Richard before (**vor**) Wolf!

G. **Wenn ich nur . . .!** Every member of your family probably has a special wish. Many of these wishes refer to the future, but some also refer to missed opportunities in the past. Pretend that you can read their thoughts and write at least ten such wishes. Indicate the member of the family with each wish.

Zum Beispiel: die Mutter: **Wenn wir nur ein größeres Haus hätten!**
   der Onkel: **Wenn ich nur meine Haare nicht verloren hätte!**
   der Bruder: **Wenn ich nur diesen Wagen nicht gekauft hätte!**

Uses of the Subjunctive

The Subjunctive in Conditional Sentences

The Present Subjunctive

A conditional sentence is a sentence with a main clause and a subordinate clause, introduced by the conjunction **wenn** (*if*), that states a condition that must be fulfilled in order for the result expressed by the main clause to occur. The following are examples of conditional sentences that do *not* require the subjunctive:

> Wenn meine Tochter fleißig *lernt*, (so) *wird* sie bestimmt gute
>   Noten *bekommen*.
> If my daughter *studies* hard, she *will* definitely *get* good grades.

> Ich *hole* Gottfried, wenn ihn jemand *anruft*.
> I *will go get* Gottfried if someone *calls* him.

Ein Bummel auf dem Berliner Kurfürstendamm

In these sentences, the indicative mood is used in both English and German because there is a real possibility that the conditions will occur. The conditions are entirely within the realm of possibility or probability. But look at the following sentences, which also express a condition.

Wenn ich du *wäre*, (so) *ginge* ich nicht in dieses Restaurant.
If I *were* you, I *would* not *go* to that restaurant.

Wenn wir reich *wären*, (so) *kauften* wir uns einen neuen Mercedes.
If we *were* rich, we *would buy* a new Mercedes.

Wenn Regina nächste Woche zu Hause *bliebe*, (so) *besuchten* wir sie.
If Regina *would stay* home next week, we *would visit* her.

Wenn ich nach Hause *ginge*, (so) *könnte* ich mein Rad holen.
If I *were to go* home, I *could* get my bike (but I probably won't go home).

In all of these sentences the speaker or writer is expressing something that he or she sees as doubtful, untrue, or contrary to fact: I am not you, we are not rich, Regina is probably not going to stay home next week, and I'm not planning to go home to get my bike. The conditions stated in the **wenn**-clause are either impossible to fulfill or, in the speaker's or writer's mind, very unlikely to happen.

The present subjunctive is used in both the **wenn**-clause and the result clause in these sentences to express improbable or contrary-to-fact conditions in the present:

Wenn-*clause*	*Result-clause*
Wenn ich du wäre,	(so) schriebe ich den Brief sofort.
If I were you,	I would write the letter immediately.

Würde + Infinitive

The present subjunctive of most verbs is often avoided by using **würde** (**würdest, würdet, würden**) with the infinitive of the main verb.

Present Subjunctive	**Würde** + *Infinitive*
Wenn ich du wäre, *ginge* ich nicht in dieses Restaurant.	Wenn ich du wäre, *würde* ich nicht in dieses Restaurant *gehen*.
Wenn wir reich wären, *kauften* wir einen neuen Mercedes.	Wenn wir reich wären, *würden* wir einen neuen Mercedes *kaufen*.
Wenn ich genug Geld hätte, *ginge* ich ins Konzert.	Wenn ich genug Geld hätte, *würde* ich ins Konzert *gehen*.

In conversational German, a form of **würde** with the infinitive is generally used; the only other subjunctive forms besides **würde** commonly used in conversational German are:

1. the modals **dürfte** (*could, would be permitted*), **könnte** (*could*), **möchte** (*would like*), **müßte** (*would have to*), and **sollte** (*should*).

2. the auxiliary verbs **hätte** (*would have*) and **wäre** (*would be*)

Würde in combination with the infinitive is used in formal as well as in conversational German, but most careful writers avoid it in **wenn**-clauses in formal German:

> Wenn mein Sohn nur deine Tochter heiraten würde! (conversational German)
> Wenn mein Sohn nur deine Tochter heiratete! (formal German)

The Past Subjunctive

If the conditional sentence expresses a condition that is contrary to fact or, in the speaker's or writer's mind, unlikely to occur, and if the sentence refers to the present or to some future period, the present subjunctive is used, as we have seen. However, if the conditional sentence refers to the past, the past subjunctive is used. Compare:

Present Subjunctive	Past Subjunctive
Wenn ich mehr Geld *verdiente,* *so reiste* ich nach Deutschland. If I *earned* more money, I *would travel* to Germany.	Wenn ich mehr Geld *verdient hätte,* so *wäre* ich letztes Jahr nach Deutschland *gereist.* If I *had earned* more money, I *would have traveled* to Germany last year.
Wenn sie das *wüßte,* so *bliebe* sie hier. If she *knew* that, she *would stay* here.	Wenn sie das *gewußt hätte,* so *wäre* sie hier *geblieben.* If she *had known* that, she *would have stayed* here.
Wenn wir Zeit *hätten,* so *gingen* wir ins Konzert. If we *had* time, we *would go* to the concert. (today or tomorrow)	Wenn wir Zeit *gehabt hätten,* so *wären* wir ins Konzert *gegangen.* If we *had had* time, we *would have gone* to the concert. (yesterday or earlier)

Occasionally, the **wenn**-clause is in the past subjunctive, but the result clause is in the present subjunctive (rather than the past):

> Wenn ich gestern die Hausaufgaben *gemacht hätte, könnte* ich jetzt ins Kino gehen. (present subjunctive in result clause)
> If I *had done* the homework yesterday, I *could go* to the show now.

> Wenn Kurt Claudia nicht zu seiner Party eingeladen hätte, würde ich sie jetzt nicht kennen.
> If Kurt *hadn't invited* Claudia to his party, I *wouldn't know* her now.

Word Order

The main clause shows inverted word order if the **wenn**-clause (or any other subordinate clause) precedes it:

Wenn ich Kinder hätte, würde ich sie versorgen.

If the subordinate clause comes after the main clause, the word order of the main clause is unaffected.

Ich würde meine Kinder versorgen, wenn ich Kinder hätte.

Sometimes the conjunction **wenn** is omitted; in this case, the clause normally introduced by **wenn** must begin with the verb and must come first, and the main clause is usually introduced by **so** or **dann**.

Hätte ich genug Geld, so würde ich nach Deutschland fahren.
Had I enough money, I would go to Germany.

Könnte meine Schwester gut Tennis spielen, so ginge sie mit.
If my sister played tennis well, she'd go along.

Liebte ich Annegret, dann würde ich sie heiraten.
If I loved Annegret, then I'd marry her.

As you have seen, the **wenn**-clause can stand alone, without the result clause; in this case, the adverb **nur** is used.

Wenn Sonja nur mit ins Kino gekommen wäre!

Wenn wir nur mehr Zeit hätten!

The Subjunctive in Clauses Introduced by *als ob*

The subjunctive is used in clauses introduced by **als ob** (*as if*).

Diese amerikanische Studentin spricht Deutsch, als ob sie Deutsche wäre.
This American student speaks German as if she were a German.

Wolf tut, als ob er mich nicht vermißt hätte.
Wolf acts as if he had not missed me.

Notice that the present subjunctive is used after **als ob** if reference is made to present (or future) time: **als ob sie Deutsche wäre** *as if she were a German (now)*. The past subjunctive is used if reference is made to a past event or situation: **als ob er mich nicht vermißt hätte** *as if he had not missed me (while I was gone)*.

Als ob is sometimes shortened to **als**; in this case, the verb immediately follows **als**:

Diese amerikanische Studentin spricht Deutsch, als wäre sie Deutsche.

Wolf tut, als hätte er mich nicht vermißt.

The Subjunctive in Wishes, Polite Requests, and Conjectures

The subjunctive forms of the modals (**könnte**, **müßte**, etc.) and the auxiliary verbs (**wäre**, **hätte**, and **würde**) are often used in main clauses to express:

1. a wish or desire

   Ich wollte, ich hätte mir diesen Wagen nicht gekauft!
   I wish I hadn't bought this car!

   Ich wünschte, Sonja wäre mit ins Kino gegangen.
   I wish Sonja had gone along to the movies.

2. politeness

   Dürften wir Sie um ein Autogramm bitten?
   May we ask you for an autograph?

   Könnten Sie mir bitte sagen, wie spät es ist?
   Could you please tell me what time it is?

   Möchtest du ins Kino gehen? —Ja, das wäre nett.
   "Would you like to go to the show?" "Yes, that would be nice."

   Würdest du mir einen Gefallen tun, Papa?
   Would you do me a favor, Papa?

3. conjecture

   Das könnte wahr sein.
   That could be true.

   Meine Mutter würde vielleicht für unsere Party einen Kuchen backen.
   My mother might bake a cake for our party.

Occasionally other subjunctive forms are used in this manner:

   Wüßten Sie, wo das Deutsche Museum ist?
   Would you (happen to) know where the German Museum is?

Study Hint: Do not confuse the forms **könnte** and **konnte**. Although both can often be translated by *could*, they have very different meanings in German. **Könnte** is the present subjunctive and is the equivalent of English *would be able to.* **Konnte** is the past indicative and is the equivalent of English *was able to.* **Konnte** always refers to the past; **könnte** can only refer to the present or future:

   Ich konnte Vati *gestern* helfen.
   I *was able to* help Dad *yesterday.*

   Ich könnte Vati *morgen* helfen.
   I *could* help Dad *tomorrow.*

The form **sollte** is the equivalent of English *should* when it refers to the present or future; it is the equivalent of English *was supposed to* when it refers to the past:

Ich *sollte* gestern zu Hause bleiben.
I *was supposed to* stay home *yesterday.*

Ich *sollte* morgen zu Hause bleiben.
I *should* stay home *tomorrow.*

The Past Subjunctive of Modal Verbs

The past subjunctive of modal verbs is usually expressed by a double-infinitive construction (see Chapter 5 for more on the double infinitive). **Können** and **sollen** are the most commonly occurring modals in this construction:

Opa, du *hättest* gestern *mitgehen können.*
Grandpa, you *could have gone* along yesterday.

Opa, du *hättest* gestern *mitgehen sollen.*
Grandpa, you *should have gone* along yesterday.

Wir *hätten* diesen Mercedes sowieso nicht *kaufen können.*
We *couldn't have bought* that Mercedes anyway.

Wir *hätten* diesen Mercedes nicht *kaufen sollen.*
We *shouldn't have bought* that Mercedes.

Notice the difference between these two expressions:

Ralf *hätte* die Großeltern *besuchen können.*
Ralf could have visited his grandparents (he had the opportunity but didn't).

Ralf *könnte* die Großeltern *besucht haben.*
Ralf might have visited his grandparents (but speaker is not sure he did).

Übungen

°A. **Ersetzen Sie den Konjunktiv des Hauptverbs mit *würde*!** Replace the subjunctive in the result clause with the proper form of **würde** and the infinitive of the main verb.

Zum Beispiel: Wenn wir genug Geld hätten, reisten wir nach Deutschland.
Wenn wir genug Geld hätten, würden wir nach Deutschland reisen.

1. Wenn mein Vater nicht krank wäre, so käme er heute mit uns fischen.
2. Wenn wir eine Party gäben, so lüden wir dich ein.
3. Ich sagte dir die Antwort, wenn ich sie wüßte.
4. Wenn unsere Verwandten nicht kämen, spielte ich heute Fußball.
5. Wenn die Großmutter jünger wäre, so ginge sie öfter schwimmen.
6. Die Großeltern besuchten ihre Enkelkinder heute abend, wenn es nicht so spät wäre.
7. Ich läse diesen Roman, wenn ich mehr Zeit hätte.
8. Ich versorgte meine Eltern, wenn sie alt wären.

°B. **Wenn ich nur . . .!** Tell what the following people would do if they had more time or money.

Zum Beispiel: Wir gehen gern ins Kino.
Wenn wir genug Geld hätten, würden wir ins Kino gehen.

Jost sieht oft fern.
Wenn Jost genug Zeit hätte, würde er oft fernsehen.

1. Die Kinder gehen ins Marionettentheater.
2. Irmgard hilft gern ihren Großeltern.
3. Julia und Rolf kaufen gern viele Schallplatten.
4. Du sprichst gern mit deiner neuen Nachbarin.
5. Wir spielen gern nach dem Unterricht Fußball.

Now express the result clause without **würde**.

Zum Beispiel: Wir gehen gern ins Kino.
Wenn wir genug Geld hätten, gingen wir ins Kino.

Jost sieht oft gern fern.
Wenn Jost genug Zeit hätte, sähe er oft fern.

C. **Wenn ich du wäre, würde ich . . .!** Hilde and her brother Jürgen are having a friendly discussion; make sentences as they would, following the model.

Zum Beispiel: Du ißt zuviel Kuchen!
Wenn ich du wäre, würde ich nicht soviel Kuchen essen!

1. Du schläfst zu lange!
2. Du gehst zu oft aus!
3. Du sprichst zu laut!
4. Du rauchst zuviel!
5. Du siehst zu oft fern!

D. **Wenn nur . . .!** Mr. and Mrs. Neumann are talking about what the family did during the past year; make sentences following the model.

Zum Beispiel: HERR NEUMANN: Vicki hat keine guten Noten bekommen, weil sie nicht genug gearbeitet hat.

FRAU NEUMANN: **Wenn Vicki genug gearbeitet hätte, hätte sie gute Noten bekommen.**

HERR NEUMANN: Ich bin nicht in die Schweiz gefahren, weil ich keine Zeit gehabt habe.

FRAU NEUMANN: **Du wärest in die Schweiz gefahren, wenn du mehr Zeit gehabt hättest.**

1. Wir sind nicht nach Spanien gefahren, weil wir nicht genug Geld gehabt haben.
2. Wir haben nicht oft im Garten gesessen, weil es viel geregnet hat.
3. Uschi hat wenig Englisch gelernt, weil sie dieses Jahr keinen Englischunterricht gehabt hat.

4. Ich bin nicht nach Berlin gefahren, weil meine Kinder krank gewesen sind.
5. Du hast deine Geschwister nicht wiedergesehen, weil wir sie nicht besucht haben.

E. **Übersetzen Sie den folgenden Dialog!** Translate the following dialogue making sure to use the present or past subjunctive to translate the italicized forms.

HERBERT: I *should* read this book now.

FRANZ: You *should have* read it yesterday. Now we can't play soccer!

HERBERT: Yes. I *could have* read it yesterday. I *wish(ed)* I *had* already read it!

FRANZ: I *would* read it tonight if I *were* you. It *could* be important for our exam (**unsere Prüfung**).

F. **Wünschen.** Write five sentences telling what you would do if you were rich and five sentences telling what you would do if you had more time.

G. **Ein bißchen Fantasie.** Complete the sentences using your imagination.

1. Mein Vater kocht, als ob . . .
2. Mein Bruder (meine Schwester) spricht, als ob . . .
3. Linda Ronstadt singt, als ob . . .
4. Bjorn Borg spielt Tennis, als ob . . .
5. Mona Lisa lächelt, als ob . . .

Eine Familie am Mittagstisch

Rückblick

A. **Zur Wiederholung. Übersetzen Sie die folgenden Sätze!**

1. If I have time tomorrow I will visit my uncle and my aunt.
2. If we had enough money we would fly to (**nach**) Europe.
3. Veronika, I would tell you (**dir**) if I knew the answer.
4. If Ursula had worked last (**letzten**) summer, she could now go with us to Germany.
5. If only my grandparents had stayed here!
6. My (female) cousin speaks German as if she were a German.
7. I wish I had seen that film.
8. Hans, you should meet my (female) cousin.
9. Marie was not able to find that book yesterday.
10. Rita, could you help us?
11. John could have bought that Mercedes, but he did not want it (**ihn**).
12. Toni, you should have invited Richard.

B. **Zur Gesamtwiederholung. Übersetzen Sie die folgenden Sätze!**

1. I wouldn't have gone to (**nach**) Canada if I hadn't bought a car.   (Chapter 1)
2. If we went by bus to school it would cost less.   (Chapter 3)
3. If only I could become a doctor!
4. Brigitte, could you help this American tourist?   (Chapter 4)
5. Carlos, if our weather were only as warm as yours!
6. If Gisela knew the answer she would tell us.   (Chapter 5)
7. If they only hadn't reelected that dishonest politician!   (Chapters 6 and 7)
8. The parliament should not have passed those new, strict laws.

9
Guten Appetit!

„Hm, das sieht lecker aus!"

Indirect Discourse: Introduction, the Tenses of the Subjunctive, the Alternate Subjunctive

Use of the Subjunctive in Indirect Discourse

Questions and Commands in Indirect Discourse, Indirect Discourse in Conversational German, the Subjunctive in Wishes and Directions

Wortschatz

das Abendbrot (-e) evening meal

das Bonbon (-s) hard candy

der Durst thirst; **Durst haben** to be thirsty

das Eis (die Eiskrem) ice cream

die Erdbeere (-n) strawberry

die Flasche (-n) Wein bottle of wine

das Fleisch meat

die Gabel (-n) fork

der Gastwirt (-e) innkeeper

das Gemüse (-) vegetable

das Gericht (-e) dish

der Hunger hunger; **Hunger haben** to be hungry

die Kartoffel (-n) potato

der Kartoffelsalat potato salad

der Kellner (-) waiter

die Kellnerin (-nen) waitress

der Kuchen (-) cake; **das Stück Kuchen** piece of cake

das Lebensmittel (-) food, provisions

das Lebensmittelgeschäft (-e) grocery store

der Löffel (-) spoon

das Messer (-) knife

der Nachtisch dessert

der Ober (-) (head) waiter; **Herr Ober!** Waiter!

das Obst fruit

der Pfeffer pepper

das Reformhaus (¨er) health-food store

die Reformkost health food

das Rezept (-e) recipe

die Tasse Kaffee (Tee) cup of coffee (tea); **Zwei Tassen Kaffee, bitte!** Two cups of coffee, please.

der Saft (¨e) juice

das Salz salt

die Schokolade (-n) chocolate; **eine Tafel Schokolade** chocolate bar

die Speisekarte (-n) menu

die Suppe (-n) soup

die Süßigkeiten pl. candy, sweets

der Teller (-) plate

der Vegetarier (-) vegetarian

die Wurst (¨e) sausage

der Zucker sugar

ab·nehmen* to lose (weight), to take off

auf·geben* to give up

backen* to bake

bestellen to order

bezahlen: die Rechnung bezahlen to pay the bill

essen*: zu Abend (Mittag) essen to have dinner (lunch)

frühstücken to have breakfast

kochen to cook

rauchen to smoke

schmecken to taste

zu·nehmen* to gain (weight), to put on

dick fat; **das macht dick** that's fattening

frisch fresh

gesund healthy

lecker delicious

schlank slim

süß sweet

A. *Match each word on the left with a word that you associate with it on the right.*

1. Frühstück
2. Pfeffer
3. Kaffee
4. Messer
5. Hunger
6. Fleisch
7. Gemüse

a. Obst
b. Gabel
c. Durst
d. Abendbrot
e. Wurst
f. Salz
g. Tee

B. *Describe this scene.*

---

*Verbs marked with an asterisk are strong verbs; see the appendix for the principal parts of strong verbs.

C. *What utensils do you use to eat the following?*

1. Suppe
2. Fleisch
3. Kuchen
4. Kartoffelsalat
5. Eis

D. *Find the word that does not belong.*

1. Kaffee, Saft, Bier, Eis
2. Nachtisch, Bonbon, Wurst, Süßigkeiten
3. Löffel, Messer, Teller, Gabel
4. Ober, Lebensmittel, Speisekarte, Kellnerin

E. *Complete the following sentences.*

1. Könntest du mir bitte das _____ für deine leckere Erdbeertorte

    geben, Mutti?

2. Das Gasthaus gehört natürlich dem _____. Der _____ und

    die _____ bedienen nur die Gäste.

3. Ich muß heute unbedingt noch ins _____ gehen und Fleisch, Brot,

    Gemüse und eine _____ Wein für das Wochenende einkaufen.

4. Mein Vater hat früher vierzig Zigaretten am Tag _____, aber jetzt hat

    er das total _____.

5. Was? Du ißt schon wieder Schokolade? Das macht doch

    furchtbar _____!

6. _____ Erdbeeren schmecken mir gut.

7. Klemens ist sehr _____, weil er nur Reformkost ißt und viel Tennis

    spielt.

8. Wie _____ dir denn dieser Rotwein?

F. *Answer the following questions.*

1. Kochen und backen Sie gern?
2. Sind Sie Vegetarier oder essen Sie Fleisch?
3. Essen Sie gern süße Sachen?
4. Versuchen sie gerade, abzunehmen oder zuzunehmen?
5. Wieviel Geld geben Sie in der Woche für Essen und Lebensmittel aus?
6. Essen Sie gern italienische, chinesiche, japanische, französische oder
   deutsche Gerichte?
7. Kaufen Sie im Reformhaus ein? Oder essen Sie keine Reformkost?
8. Was ist ihr Lieblingsgericht?

Indirect Discourse: Introduction, the Tenses of the Subjunctive, the Alternate Subjunctive

Introduction

Direct discourse is used to report statements or questions exactly as they were first spoken or written. Quotation marks must be used:

> Herr Kümmel hat gesagt: „Meine Kinder essen zuviel Zucker."
> Mr. Kümmel said, "My children eat too much sugar."

Indirect discourse is used to report the same information without repeating the original words in their exact form. No quotation marks can be used:

> Herr Kümmel hat gesagt, daß seine Kinder zuviel Zucker essen.
> Mr. Kümmel said that his children eat too much sugar.

The present indicative form **essen** in this last sentence would only appear in conversational German. In formal German the subjunctive would normally be used and this last sentence would appear as:

> Herr Kümmel hat gesagt, daß seine Kinder zuviel Zucker
> äßen. (present subjunctive)

Im Lebensmittelgeschäft

The Tenses of the Subjunctive Used in Indirect Discourse

In Chapter 8 you saw how the present and past tenses of the subjunctive are formed. Both of these tenses are used in indirect discourse.

1. Present Subjunctive (**essen**)

   Herr Kümmel hat gesagt, daß ich zuviel Zucker *äße.*
   daß du zuviel Zucker *äßest.*

   daß $\begin{Bmatrix} \text{er} \\ \text{sie} \\ \text{es} \end{Bmatrix}$ zuviel Zucker *äße.*

   daß wir zuviel Zucker *äßen.*
   daß ihr zuviel Zucker *äßet.*

   daß $\begin{Bmatrix} \text{sie} \\ \text{Sie} \end{Bmatrix}$ zuviel Zucker *äßen.*

2. Past Subjunctive (**essen**)

   Herr Kümmel hat gesagt, daß ich zuviel Zucker *gegessen hätte.*
   daß du zuviel Zucker *gegessen hättest.*

   daß $\begin{Bmatrix} \text{er} \\ \text{sie} \\ \text{es} \end{Bmatrix}$ zuviel Zucker *gegessen hätte.*

   daß wir zuviel Zucker *gegessen hätten.*
   daß ihr zuviel Zucker *gegessen hättet.*

   daß $\begin{Bmatrix} \text{sie} \\ \text{Sie} \end{Bmatrix}$ zuviel Zucker *gegessen hätten.*

3. Future Subjunctive (**essen**)

   A third tense, the future subjunctive, is also used in indirect discourse. It is formed by using the present subjunctive of **werden** with the infinitive of the main verb.

   Herr Kümmel hat gesagt, daß ich zuviel Zucker *essen würde.*
   Mr. Kümmel said that I *would (will) eat* too much sugar.

   daß du zuviel Zucker *essen würdest.*

   daß $\begin{Bmatrix} \text{er} \\ \text{sie} \\ \text{es} \end{Bmatrix}$ zuviel Zucker *essen würde.*

   daß wir zuviel Zucker *essen würden.*
   daß ihr zuviel Zucker *essen würdet.*

   daß $\begin{Bmatrix} \text{sie} \\ \text{Sie} \end{Bmatrix}$ zuviel Zucker *essen würden.*

The Alternate Subjunctive in Indirect Discourse

In indirect discourse, an alternate form of the subjunctive often occurs in the third-person singular. The alternate subjunctive has the same meaning as the normal form but is considered more elegant. Here are examples of the three tenses of the subjunctive, which you have already learned, showing the alternate subjunctive forms:

1. Present Subjunctive (**essen**)

Herr Kümmel hat gesagt, daß $\begin{Bmatrix} \text{er} \\ \text{sie} \\ \text{es} \end{Bmatrix}$ zuviel Zucker *äße*.*   (normal form)

Herr Kümmel hat gesagt, daß $\begin{Bmatrix} \text{er} \\ \text{sie} \\ \text{es} \end{Bmatrix}$ zuviel Zucker *esse*.*   (alternate form)

2. Past Subjunctive (**essen**)

Herr Kümmel hat gesagt, daß $\begin{Bmatrix} \text{er} \\ \text{sie} \\ \text{es} \end{Bmatrix}$ zuviel Zucker *gegessen hätte*.* (normal form)

Herr Kümmel hat gesagt, daß $\begin{Bmatrix} \text{er} \\ \text{sie} \\ \text{es} \end{Bmatrix}$ zuviel Zucker *gegessen habe*.* (alternate subjunctive)

3. Future Subjunctive (**essen**)

Herr Kümmel hat gesagt, daß $\begin{Bmatrix} \text{er} \\ \text{sie} \\ \text{es} \end{Bmatrix}$ zuviel Zucker *essen würde*.* (normal form)

Herr Kümmel hat gesagt, daß $\begin{Bmatrix} \text{er} \\ \text{sie} \\ \text{es} \end{Bmatrix}$ zuviel Zucker *essen werde*.* (alternate form)

The alternate subjunctive is formed by replacing the ending **-(e)n** of the infinitive with **-e**:

Infinitive	Alternate subjunctive
Main Verb: ess*en*	$\begin{Bmatrix} \text{er} \\ \text{sie} \\ \text{es} \end{Bmatrix}$ esse
Perfect Auxiliary: hab*en*	$\begin{Bmatrix} \text{er} \\ \text{sie} \\ \text{es} \end{Bmatrix}$ habe
Future Auxiliary: werd*en*	$\begin{Bmatrix} \text{er} \\ \text{sie} \\ \text{es} \end{Bmatrix}$ werde

*The first vowel in **äße** is long; the first vowel in **esse** is short.

Here are more examples of the alternate subjunctive in the present tense:

Viele Leute behaupten, daß Toni sehr gut *koche*.   (infinitive: **kochen**)
Many people claim that Toni cooks very well.

Der Kranke sagt, daß er immer Kopfschmerzen *habe*.   (infinitive:
 haben)
The sick man says that he always has headaches.

Der Arzt meint, daß Frau Huber das Rauchen aufgeben
 müsse.   (infinitive: **müssen**)
The doctor thinks that Mrs. Huber must give up smoking.

Heidi schrieb mir, daß sie jetzt in einem kleinen Dorf
 wohne.   (infinitive: **wohnen**)
Heidi wrote me that she is living in a little village now.

Erich sagt, daß seine Schwester in den Alpen *wandere*.   (infinitive:
 wandern)
Erich says that his sister is hiking in the Alps.

Das Kind klagt, daß der Zahn ihm weh *tue*.   (infinitive: **tun**)
The child is complaining that his tooth hurts.

The Alternate Subjunctive of the Verb *sein*

The alternate subjunctive of the verb **sein** is formed by dropping **-n** of the
infinitive: **sei**. Unlike other alternate subjunctive forms, **sei** can be used as
the basis for forming the entire present subjunctive of **sein:**

Normal forms

ich wäre
du wärest
er ⎫
sie ⎬ wäre
es ⎭
wir wären
ihr wäret
sie ⎫ wären
Sie ⎭

Alternate forms

ich sei
du seiest
er ⎫
sie ⎬ sei
es ⎭
wir seien
ihr seiet
sie ⎫ seien
Sie ⎭

Der Arzt hat gesagt, daß ich gesund *wäre*.   (normal form)
Der Arzt hat gesagt, daß ich gesund *sei*.   *(alternate subjunctive)*
The doctor said that I am healthy.

Der Arzt hat gesagt, daß die Kinder gesund *wären*.   (normal form)
Der Arzt hat gesagt, daß die Kinder gesund *seien*. (alternate
 subjunctive)
The doctor said that the children are healthy.

Both forms of the present subjunctive of **sein** are used to form the past subjunctive of verbs that require the auxiliary **sein.** There is no difference in meaning. For example, the past subjunctive of **gehen** has these forms:

Normal forms

ich wäre gegangen
du wärest gegangen
er ⎫
sie ⎬ wäre gegangen
es ⎭
wir wären gegangen
ihr wäret gegangen
sie ⎫
Sie ⎭ wären gegangen

Alternate forms

ich sei gegangen
du seiest gegangen
er ⎫
sie ⎬ sei gegangen
es ⎭
wir seien gegangen
ihr seiet gegangen
sie ⎫
Sie ⎭ seien gegangen

Ein Schritt weiter

The normal forms of the subjunctive are often called "subjunctive two forms" because they are formed from the past stem which is the second principal part of the verb; the alternate forms of the subjunctive are often called "subjunctive one forms" because they are formed from the infinitive which is the first principal part of the verb. In earlier times the alternate subjunctive was more widely used. For example, in older books, instead of the normal form **du wüßtest,** you might find **du wissest** which is based on the alternate subjunctive **wisse: Der König sagt, daß du die Antwort schon *wissest.*** *The king says that you already know the answer.*

Übungen

°A. **Ersetzen Sie die Pronomen!** Replace the pronoun in italics with the pronouns in parentheses and change the verbs accordingly.

1. Der Arzt meint, daß *ich* ein bißchen abnehmen müßte. (er, wir, sie *pl.*)
2. Mein Bruder behauptet, daß *sie* bald nach Hause käme. (ihr, du, Sie)
3. Fräulein Eberhard sagte, daß *du* eine neue Wohnung gefunden hättest. (sie *sing.*, wir, Sie)
4. Herr Volker fragte, ob *wir* nach Berlin gefahren wären. (du, ich, sie *pl.*)
5. Reinhard sagte, daß *er* noch ein Stück von dem leckeren Kuchen bestellen würde. (du, sie *sing.*, ihr)
6. Toni fragte, ob *ihr* für sie eine Flasche Wein kaufen würdet. (du, Sie, wir)

B. **Schreiben Sie die folgenden Sätze um!** Restate the following sentences using the alternate subjunctive. Then translate each sentence.

Zum Beispiel: Heinz sagte, er tränke gern Orangensaft.
                  Heinz sagte, er trinke gern Orangensaft.
                  Heinz said that he likes (to drink) orange juice.

1. Richard sagte, er dürfte kein Salz mehr essen.
2. Der Arzt behauptet, ich wäre ganz gesund.
3. Meine Schwester sagte, der Kuchen schmeckte sehr gut.
4. Mein Freund sagte, er wollte zunehmen.
5. Sandra behauptete, sie frühstückte immer zu Hause.
6. Erich sagt, sein Vater könnte sogar chinesische Gerichte kochen.
7. Der Junge sagte dem Arzt, der Hals täte ihm weh.

Zum Beispiel: Marina sagte, ihre Großmutter hätte ihr eine Tafel Schokolade
                  gekauft.
                  Marina sagte, ihre Großmutter habe ihr eine Tafel Schokolade
                  gekauft.
                  Marina said that her grandmother had bought her a bar of
                  chocolate.

Drehorgelmann im Biergarten

Hermann sagte, seine Freunde wären letztes Jahr nach Berlin
geflogen.
**Hermann sagte, seine Freunde seien letztes Jahr nach Berlin
geflogen.**
Hermann said that his friends had flown to Berlin last year.

1. Meine Schwester sagte, sie hätte das Rauchen aufgegeben.
2. Heinrich und Roswitha sagten, sie wären noch nie in Österreich gewesen.
3. Käte schrieb, Toni hätte sie letzten Monat besucht.
4. Wolfgang sagte, er hätte Kartoffelsalat bestellt.
5. Wolf schrieb mir, du wärest Vegetarier geworden.
6. Sabine sagte, sie hätte ein bißchen abgenommen.

Zum Beispiel: Karsten sagte, er würde sich ein Auto mieten.
Karsten sagte, er werde sich ein Auto mieten.
Karsten said that he would rent a car.

1. Robert sagte Susanne, er würde zum Abendbrot zurückkommen.
2. Herr Diels sagte, er würde das neue Haus nicht kaufen.
3. Theresa sagte uns, sie würde die Rechnung bezahlen.
4. Rudi sagte uns, der Nachtisch würde gut schmecken.

C. **Übersetzen Sie die folgenden Sätze!**

1. John said that he ordered three sausages. (Translate two ways, using the past subjunctive)
2. Rebekka told us that he would lose weight. (future subjunctive)
3. Werner said that his aunt is a doctor. (Translate two ways, using the present subjunctive.)
4. Gerd wrote that he bought a health food store. (Translate two ways, using the past subjunctive.)
5. The dentist said that I eat too much candy. (present subjunctive)
6. Mrs. Schubel asked us if we were vegetarians. (present subjunctive)

Use of the Subjunctive in Indirect Discourse

The following is a fictitious article that might have been taken from the front page of an American newspaper:

Police claim that Jeanette Brown attempted
to bribe the mayor of Jonesville. . . . Brown,
according to these sources, handed Mayor
Finch an envelope with $5,000. *It is further
alleged* that Brown and her partner
embezzled $500,000 in funds from the firm
of Edgar, Edgar, and Smith.

The italicized phrases in this passage serve to place a certain distance between the reporter who wrote the article and the incriminating statements against the accused. Without such phrases it would appear that the reporter is personally accusing Brown of the crimes mentioned. Because of these qualifying phrases, the reporter's attitude toward the allegations can be described as neutral.

In German, the same effect of neutrality is achieved by use of the subjunctive mood (the mood, remember, of doubt and conjecture). By placing every allegation against Brown in the subjunctive mood the reporter implicitly refuses to take a position on the validity of the allegations against Brown. The reporter appears to be simply reporting what the authorities have stated:

> Die Polizei behauptet, Jeanette Brown habe
> versucht, den Bürgermeister von
> Jonesville . . . zu bestechen. Brown habe
> Bürgermeister Finch einen Umschlag mit
> $5 000 überreicht. Brown und ihr Partner
> hätten auch der Firma Edgar, Edgar und
> Smith $500 000 abgeschwindelt.

If the indicative had been used, the reporter would have been accusing Brown of the charges: **Brown hat versucht, den Bürgermeister zu bestechen. . . .**

The German version provides one advantage: the source of the allegations does not have to be repeated in sentences like *Police claim. . . , ... according to these sources . . . , It is further alleged. . . .* Only one reference to the source of the allegations need be made: **Die Polizei behauptet. . . .***

The present subjunctive is used in indirect discourse in German if the present indicative is used in the corresponding statement in direct discourse. Notice that the tense may shift in English, as the following pairs of sentences illustrate, but not in German. (The forms in parentheses are the alternate subjunctive forms.)

Direct Discourse:	*Indirect Discourse: Present Subjunctive*
Der Arzt: „Ihr Kind *hat* eine Erkältung."	Der Arzt sagte, mein Kind *hätte* (habe) eine Erkältung.
The doctor: "Your child *has* a cold."	The doctor said my child *had* a cold.
Karin: „Ich *kaufe* Eiskrem."	Karin sagte, sie *kaufte* (kaufe) Eiskrem.
Karin: "I'm *buying* ice cream."	Karin said she *was buying* ice cream.

---

*The conjunction **daß** is usually omitted, with the result that the verb is not transposed to the end of the dependent clause: **Die Polizei behauptete, daß Klaus Scheidt schuldig sei** or, more commonly, **Die Polizei behauptete, Klaus Scheidt sei schuldig.** *The police claimed that Klaus Scheidt is guilty.*

It is important to remember that the subjunctive has only one past tense, a compound past formed with an auxiliary verb and the past participle of the main verb:

Direct Discourse (Indicative)	Indirect Discourse Subjunctive
Karin: „Ich wurde sehr hungrig." (past)	
Karin: „Ich bin sehr hungrig geworden." (present perfect)	Karin sagte, sie wäre (sei) sehr hungrig geworden. (past)
Karin: „Ich war sehr hungrig geworden." (past perfect)	

As you can see, the three tenses of the indicative that denote past time are all represented by the past subjunctive in indirect discourse. This fact has special consequences for the modal verbs (**können, müssen, sollen,** and so forth), since they usually occur in the past indicative (a simple tense) rather than the present perfect (a compound tense):

Direct Discourse	Indirect Discourse
Marie: „Ich *konnte* als Kind gut Spanisch." Marie: "I knew Spanish well as a child."	Marie behauptete, sie *hätte* (*habe*) als Kind gut Spanisch *gekonnt*. Marie claimed that she knew Spanish well as a child.
Marie: „Ich *konnte* als Kind gut schwimmen." Marie: "I knew how to swim well as a child."	Marie behauptete, sie *hätte* (*habe*) als Kind gut *schwimmen können*. Marie claimed that she knew how to swim well as a child.

In the second example, the modal in direct discourse has a dependent infinitive (**konnte . . . schwimmen**), which appears as a double infinitive in indirect discourse. (Double infinitives are discussed in Chapter 5.)

There are other verbs that commonly occur in the past in direct discourse— for example, **war, hatte, wurde.** These verbs also need an auxiliary and past participle in the past subjunctive of indirect discourse.

Direct Discourse	Indirect Discourse
Fritz :„Ich *war* gestern krank." Fritz: "I was sick yesterday."	Fritz sagte, er *wäre (sei)* gestern krank *gewesen*. Fritz said that he was (had been) sick yesterday.
Inge: „Meine Mutter *hatte* ein Lebensmittelgeschäft." Inge: "My mother had a grocery store."	Inge sagte, ihre Mutter *hätte* (*habe*) ein Lebensmittel- geschäft gehabt. Inge said her mother had (had had) a grocery store.

Direct Discourse	Indirect Discourse
Heidi: „Mein Großvater *wurde* schon als junger Mann Vegetarier.“	Heidi behauptete, ihr Großvater *wäre (sei)* schon als junger Mann Vegetarier *geworden*.
Heidi: "My grandfather became a vegetarian when he was a young man."	Heidi remarked that her grandfather became (had become) a vegetarian when he was only a young man.

Study hint: To master the subjunctive of indirect discourse, begin with the original statement in direct discourse—for example:

Marie sagte: „Ich muß ein bißchen abnehmen.“
Marie said, "I have to lose a little weight."

To practice conversational German, place the statement in indirect discourse using the *same* tense as in the indicative mood:

Marie sagte, daß sie ein bißchen abnehmen muß.

Then replace the indicative with the corresponding tense of the subjunctive as used in formal German, the German you should use in all your essays:

Marie sagte, daß sie ein bißchen abnehmen *müßte (müsse)*.

Finally, drop the conjunction **daß** and use normal word order:

Marie sagte, sie müßte (müsse) ein bißchen abnehmen.

Übungen

A. **Schreiben Sie die folgenden Sätze in indirekter Rede!** Rewrite the following sentences as indirect statements. Give both the normal subjunctive and the alternate subjunctive where appropriate. Translate the indirect statement.

Zum Beispiel: Friedrich sagte: „Ich bin Verkäufer im Reformhaus.“
Friedrich sagte, er wäre Verkäufer im Reformhaus.
Friedrich sagte, er sei Verkäufer im Reformhaus.
Friedrich said (that) he is a salesperson in a health food store.

1. Meine Freunde sagten: „Wir werden nie wieder Schokolade essen.“
2. Irmgard und Heinrich antworteten ihrem Freund: „Wir haben uns die Speisekarte noch nicht angeschaut.“
3. Die Zeitung berichtete: „Fleisch und Wurst sind teurer geworden.“
4. Der Ober antwortete: „Eine Tasse Kaffee kostet drei Mark.“
5. Die Köchin sagte: „Diese Suppe wird bestimmt lecker.“
6. Helga antwortete mir: „Ich muß morgen zu Hause das Mittagessen kochen.“
7. Die Kellnerin behauptete: „Die Bayern essen sehr viele Weißwürste.“
8. Der Zahnarzt sagte der Mutter: „Ihre Kinder dürfen nicht soviel Zucker essen.“
9. Axel schrieb Susanne: „Dies Rezept wird dir bestimmt gefallen.“
10. Sabine sagte: „Ich habe noch nicht zu Abend gegessen.“

B. **Schreiben Sie die folgenden Sätze in indirekter Rede!** Rewrite the following sentences as indirect statements in the past subjunctive. Give both the normal subjunctive and the alternate subjunctive where appropriate. Translate the indirect statement.

Zum Beispiel: Sophia sagte: „Ich mußte gestern zum Zahnarzt gehen."
Sophia sagte, sie hätte gestern zum Zahnarzt gehen müssen.
Sophia sagte, sie habe gestern zum Zahnarzt gehen müssen.
Sophia said (that) she had to go to the dentist yesterday.

1. Die Mutter telefonierte und sagte: „Ich mußte gestern nach Hause zurückkehren. Der Großvater war sehr krank."
2. Herr Grünfeld erzählte uns: „Viele Deutsche mußten 1935 Deutschland verlassen."
3. Frau Behner behauptete: „Fritz Weimer war einer der berühmtesten Küchenchefs."
4. Gretchen sagte: „Ich wollte gestern vorbeikommen, aber ich hatte keine Zeit."
5. Doktor Simmel sagte: „Leider wurde Anna gestern sehr krank."

C. **Ein berühmtes Rezept. . . .** You are a reporter for a German newspaper and have been told to cover a case involving the theft of a famous recipe. After discussing the theft with the police, you file a report five to ten sentences in length beginning **Die Polizei behauptet. . . .** You might want to use some of the following vocabulary:

der Dieb   *thief*
dem Küchenchef ein Rezept stehlen*
ins Ausland fliehen*

You might also want to tell what kind of recipe was stolen and how the thief got it.

*These are strong verbs; see the appendix for principal parts of strong verbs.

D. **Übersetzen Sie die folgenden Sätze!** Use both the normal subjunctive and the alternate subjunctive where appropriate; remember to refer to the original statement to determine the tense of the subjunctive.

Zum Beispiel: Helga told us she was hungry. (Original statement: I am hungry.)
Helga sagte uns, sie hätte Hunger.
Helga sagte uns, sie habe Hunger.

1. Joseph told Karolina he (had) ordered vegetable soup.
2. The newspaper reported (**berichtete**) that many people are giving up smoking.
3. Elke answered that she wanted a knife and fork.
4. The chef told us he liked to read recipes.
5. Pamela claimed her father was a chef.
6. The girl answered that she had ordered a glass of wine.
7. My parents said Sigi and Elfi had gone to the (**ins**) grocery store.
8. Your relatives said they drank only tea with (**zum**) the evening meal.

Questions and Commands in Indirect Discourse, Indirect Discourse in Conversational German, the Alternate Subjunctive in Wishes and Directions

Questions in Indirect Discourse

The same principles that apply to statements in indirect discourse discussed in the previous section also apply to questions:

Direct Question (Indicative)	*Indirect Question (Subjunctive)*
Kurt fragte: „Habt ihr den Kartoffelsalat bestellt?"	Kurt fragte, ob wir den Kartoffelsalat *bestellt hätten.*
Kurt asked: "Have you ordered the potato salad?"	Kurt asked if we (had) ordered the potato salad.
Petra fragte: „*Ist* Maries Mutter Ärztin?"	Petra fragte, ob Maries Mutter Ärztin *sei (wäre).*
Petra asked: "Is Marie's mother a doctor?"	Petra asked whether Marie's mother is (was) a doctor.
Tina fragte: „Wann *kommst* du zu Besuch?"	Tina fragte mich, wann ich zu Besuch *käme.*
Tina asked: "When are you coming over?"	Tina asked me when I was coming over.

Notice that **ob** corresponds to *if* or *whether* in English.

Commands in Indirect Discourse

Again, the principles that apply to statements in indirect discourse apply to commands. However, the modal **sollen** must be used in indirect discourse to capture the force of the original command:

Direct Command (Imperative)	Indirect Command (Subjunctive)
Frau Schmidt: „Hans, geh zum Markt und hol mir fünf Kilo Kartoffeln."	Frau Schmidt sagte Hans, er *sollte (solle)* zum Markt gehen und fünf Kilo Kartoffeln holen.
Frau Schmidt: "Hans, go to the market and get me five kilos of potatoes."	Frau Schmidt told Hans that he should go to the market and get five kilos of potatoes.
Herr Heller: „Kinder, eßt eure Suppe!"	Herr Heller sagte den Kindern, sie *sollten* ihre Suppe essen.
Herr Heller: "Children, eat your soup."	Herr Heller told the children to eat their soup.

Notice that in English indirect commands are usually expressed with the infinitive of the main verb: Mrs. Schmidt told Hans *to go* to the market and *get* her five kilos of potatoes.*

Indirect Discourse in Conversational German

The subjunctive of indirect discourse is generally avoided in conversational German. Instead, the tense of the indicative that appeared in the original statement appears in indirect discourse.

Direct Discourse	Indirect Discourse
Margot: „Die Bonbons haben gut geschmeckt."	Margot sagte, daß die Bonbons gut geschmeckt haben.[†] (had)
Margot: "The candy tasted good."	Margot said that the candy (had) tasted good.
Philip: „Ich trinke gern Apfelsaft."	Philip sagte, daß er gern Apfelsaft trinkt.
Philip: "I like (to drink) apple juice."	Philip said that he liked (to drink) apple juice.
Marie fragte: „*Bleibst* du morgen hier?"	Marie fragte mich, ob ich morgen hier *bleibe*.
Marie asked: "Are you staying here tomorrow?"	Marie asked me if I was staying here tomorrow.

---

*This construction is only permitted in German with a few verbs such as **befehlen: Der General befahl den Soldaten aufzustehen.** *The general commanded the soldiers to stand up.*

[†]The conjunction **daß** is not omitted in indirect discourse if the indicative mood is used.

An exception to this rule is that indirect commands in conversational German are treated just as they are in formal German; however, the alternate subjunctive form **solle** is never used:

> Herr Schmidt sagte Paul, er *sollte (solle)* mehr Gemüse und Obst essen. (formal)
>
> Herr Schmidt sagte Paul, er *sollte* mehr Gemüse und Obst essen. (conversational)

The Alternate Subjunctive in Wishes and Directions

The alternate subjunctive occurs in main clauses in certain set phrases in formal German to express a wish:

> Es *lebe* die Freundschaft!
> Long live friendship!
>
> Sie *ruhe* in Frieden!
> May she rest in peace!
>
> Unser lieber Bürgemeister, er *lebe* hoch, hoch, hoch!
> Our dear mayor, let's give him three cheers!

The alternate subjunctive also occurs in directions appearing in manuals, cookbooks, or texts:

> Man *nehme* zwei Pfund Mehl, ein Pfund Zucker und drei Eier.
> Take two pounds of flour, one pound of sugar and three eggs.
>
> Die Figur A *sei*. . .
> Let Figure A be (represent). . .
>
> Der Leser *merke* diesen Unterschied.
> The reader should note (let the reader note) this difference.

The English equivalents of these wishes or directions often contain the verbs *should, let,* or *may.*

This use of the alternate subjunctive should not be confused with its use in indirect discourse. In indirect discourse the subjunctive forms are always accompanied by a statement or phrase of reporting such as **Die Polizei sagte, (daß). . . .**

Übungen

A. **Schreiben Sie indirekte Fragen!** Rewrite the following sentences as indirect questions. Give both the normal subjunctive and the alternate subjunctive where appropriate.

Zum Beispiel: Eduard fragte Anne: „Hast du Durst?"
Eduard fragte Anne, ob sie Durst hätte.
Eduard fragte Anne, ob sie Durst habe.

1. Hildegard fragte Sara: „Hast du schon bestellt?"
2. Rebekka fragte Toni: „Trinkst du ungern Wein?"
3. Das Kind fragte die Großmutter: „Mußtest du früher euer Brot selbst backen?"
5. Toni fragte Hans: „Bist du Vegetarier?"
6. Sie fragten ihre Freunde: „Gibt es hier eine gute Pizzeria?"
7. Thomas fragte Herrn Schneider: „Kaufen Sie immer im Reformhaus ein?"

Zum Beispiel: Kurt fragte seine Freundin: „Warum ißt du kein Fleisch?"
Kurt fragte seine Freundin, warum sie kein Fleisch äße.
Kurt fragte seine Freundin, warum sie kein Fleisch esse.

1. Der Tourist fragte mich: „Wo kann man hier gut essen?"
2. Marie fragte ihren Großvater: „Wann hast du denn Oma kennengelernt?"
3. Rolf fragte seine Mutter: „Welchen Nachtisch hast du denn heute gemacht?"
4. Peter fragte Frau Kofler: „Wie macht man denn Wiener Schnitzel?"
5. Ich fragte Herrn und Frau Herter: „Warum essen Sie eigentlich nur Reformkost?"
6. Meine Freundin fragte mich: „In welchem Kochbuch steht denn dieses Rezept?"
7. Rolf fragte seine Schwester: „Was gibt es denn heute zum Mittagessen?"

B. **Schreiben Sie indirekte Befehle!** Rewrite the following sentences as indirect commands. Give both the normal subjunctive and the alternate subjunctive where appropriate. Translate the indirect command.

Zum Beispiel: Inge sagte ihrem Freund: „Schreib mir bald!"
Inge sagte ihrem Freund, er sollte ihr bald schreiben.
Inge sagte ihrem Freund, er solle ihr bald schreiben.
Inge told her boyfriend to write her soon.

1. Der Vater sagte dem Jungen: „Gib deiner Schwester etwas von deiner Schokolade!"
2. Die Mutter befahl den Kindern: „Geht sofort aus der Küche!"
3. Mein Mann sagte mir: „Koch doch mal wieder eine gute Suppe mit Wurst."
4. Der Vater sagte seiner Tochter: „Iß nicht so schnell!"
5. Die Ärztin sagte Herrn Schneider: „Frühstücken Sie morgens wie ein König, essen Sie mittags wie ein Bürger, und fasten Sie abends wie ein Bettler (*beggar*)!"
6. Mutti sagte dir erst (*just*) gestern: „Nimm nicht soviel Nachtisch."
7. Die Kellnerin riet dem Gast: „Bestellen Sie die Erdbeertorte."
8. Der Mann sagte uns: „Trinkt nicht soviel Coca-Cola!"

C. **Schreiben Sie die folgenden Sätze in indirekter Rede!** Rewrite the following sentences in indirect discourse as they would appear in conversational German. Do not omit the conjunction **daß**.

Zum Beispiel: Friedrich sagte: „Ich suche eine Wohnung."
Friedrich sagte, daß er eine Wohnung sucht.

Eduard fragte die Kellnerin: „Kommen Sie aus Italien?"
Eduard fragte die Kellnerin, ob sie aus Italien kommt.

Inge sagte ihrem Freund: „Schreib mir bald!"
Inge sagte ihrem Freund, daß er ihr bald schreiben sollte.

1. Der Ober antwortete: „Die Erdbeertorte kostet drei Mark das Stück."
2. Sonja sagte: „Ich habe die Speisekarte noch nicht gesehen."
3. Manfred behauptete: „Schokolade macht dick."
4. Die alte Dame sagte: „Ich war noch nie in einem Reformhaus."
5. Wolfgang fragte die Kellnerin: „Können Sie mir ein Gericht empfehlen?"
6. Elisabeth fragte ihren Freund: „Warum nimmst du immer soviel Salz?"
7. Der Zahnarzt sagte den Kindern: „Eßt nicht soviel Süßigkeiten!"
8. Der Vater sagte seinem Sohn: „Bleib zu Hause und mach die Hausaufgaben!"

D. **Übersetzen Sie die folgenden Sätze ins Englische!**

1. Möge es nie wieder einen Krieg geben!
2. Der Leser merke das folgende. . .
3. Man nehme einen Liter Milch, ein halbes Pfund Zucker, und hundert Gramm Butter.
4. Die Figur X sei ein Rechteck (*rectangle*).

E. **Übersetzen Sie die folgenden Sätze!** In determining the tense of the subjunctive to use, refer to the original question. Use both the normal subjunctive and the alternate subjunctive where appropriate.

Zum Beispiel: Marina asked Rolf whether he spoke German well. (Original question: "Do you speak German well?"
Marina fragte Rolf, ob er gut Deutsch spräche.
Marina fragte Rolf, ob er gut Deutsch spreche.

1. The guest asked the innkeeper (**Wirt**) when he could eat breakfast.
2. Richard asked Christine where the knives and forks were.
3. The doctor asked Wolf whether he drank coffee.
4. Wilhelmina asked Ulrich if the potato salad was good.
5. The policeman asked Vicki whether she needed help.
6. Rosemarie asked Peter what he had ordered.
7. Ingrid asked Sylvia whether she was hungry.
8. Julia asked us where we had bought our groceries.

F. **Übersetzen Sie die folgenden Sätze!** Use both the normal subjunctive and the alternate subjunctive where appropriate.

Zum Beispiel: Hilde told Volker to speak German.
Hilde sagte Volker, er sollte Deutsch sprechen.
Hilde sagte Volker, er solle Deutsch sprechen.

1. My mother told us not to eat so much ice cream.
2. The doctor told Xavier not to smoke.
3. The dentist told Georg not to eat sweets.
4. We told Franz to bring a bottle of wine to the (**zur**) party.
5. They told the waiter to bring some coffee.

G. **Ein französisches Rezept. . . .** Translate this recipe for a wine sauce; you might want to try it over fresh strawberries or on a pudding. Hints: **Eßlöffel** *tablespoon*, **Dotter** *yolk*, **Topf** *pot*, **steigen** *to become fluffy*, **gießen** *to pour*.

Weinsauce

Man nehme drei Eßlöffel Weißwein, zwei Eßlöffel Zucker und das Dotter eines Eis. Man tue das alles in einen Topf und schlage das Ganze über heißem Wasser in einem zweiten Topf, bis es steigt. Man gieße die Sauce über frische Erdbeeren oder einen Pudding und serviere es gleich.

H. **Ein Reformkostfanatiker.** One of your friends is a health food fanatic; tell what advice he gives you, following the models.

Zum Beispiel: Trink nur Milch oder Saft!
Er sagte, daß ich nur Milch oder Saft trinken sollte.

1. Kauf nur im Reformhaus ein!
2. Koch nicht mit Salz!
3. Kauf kein Lebensmittel mit Konservierungsmitteln (*preservatives*)!
4. Nimm kein Aspirin!
5. Iß keine Eiskrem!

Now add three more statements he might have made to you: **Er sagte, daß ich. . .**

Rückblick ▬▬▬▬▬▬▬▬▬▬▬▬

A. **Zur Wiederholung. Übersetzen Sie die folgenden Sätze!** Omit the conjunction **daß** and use both the normal subjunctive and the alternate subjunctive where appropriate.

1. The doctor said that I must give up coffee.
2. Roswitha told us that she wanted to buy fruit and vegetables.
3. Albert claimed that he had been able to swim well as a child.
4. The guest asked the waitress how much the Wiener Schnitzel cost.
5. The waiter asked us whether we wanted salad.
6. Hilde told her friend to go to the (**ins**) grocery store.

B. **Zur Gesamtwiederholung. Übersetzen Sie die folgenden Sätze!** Omit the conjunction **daß** and use both the normal subjunctive and the alternate subjunctive where appropriate.

1. Wilhelmina said she did not use a recipe.   (Chapter 1)
2. The tourists said they had been in Germany for two weeks.
3. My sister said Mr. Simmel cooked a delicious vegetable soup yesterday.   (Chapter 2)
4. Rita asked me when I last (**zum letzten Mal**) was in Berlin.
5. The waiter said he had already brought the chef a cup of coffee.   (Chapter 4)
6. The woman asked where the mayor's office was.
7. Robert told us we could sit at his (**an seinem**) table.   (Chapter 5)
8. Tina asked her father if he had to give up salt.
9. The American tourists said German words are hard to pronounce.   (Chapter 6 and 7)
10. The German (woman) told her American girlfriend that she would bring her (**ihr**) hot coffee and fresh strawberries.   (Chapter 7)

10
Feste und Trachten

Büttnertanz (Barrel-makers' dance) vor der Burg in Nürnberg

Declension and Uses of Personal Pronouns

Reflexive Pronouns and Verbs

The Pronoun *einander*; the Intensive Pronouns *selbst* and *selber*

Es in Impersonal Expressions

Wortschatz

der Adventskranz (-̈e) Advent wreath; one candle on the wreath is lighted every week for four weeks before Christmas

der Anzug (-̈e) suit, clothing

der Bierwagen (-) horse-drawn beer wagon

die Bluse (-n) blouse

die Bowle (-n) punch, punchbowl

das Dirndl dirndl, Bavarian women's costume

der Fasching Carnival, Mardi Gras

das Fest (-e) holiday, festival

die Feier (-n) holiday, festival

die Handtasche (-n) purse

das Hemd (-en) shirt

die Hose (-n) pants

der Hut (-̈e) hat

die Jacke (-n) jacket

der Jägerhut (-̈e) hunting hat

der Karneval Carnival, Mardi Gras

die Kerze (-n) candle

das Kleid (-er) dress

das Kostüm (-e) costume, dress

das Kostümfest (-e) costume ball

die Krawatte (-n) tie

die Lederhose (-n) leather shorts

der Mantel (-̈) overcoat

die Maske (-n) mask

der Nikolaus Santa Claus

das Oktoberfest (-e) Bavarian autumn festival

das Picknick (-s) picnic

der Pullover (-) sweater, pullover

der Rock (-̈e) skirt

der Rosenmontag Monday before Lent

der Schuh (-e) shoe

der Silvesterabend New Year's Eve

die Socke (-n) sock

der Strumpf (-̈e) hose; **Kniestrümpfe** knee socks

die Tracht (-en) traditional costume, dress

der Umzug (-̈e) parade

das Volkslied (-er) folksong

die Weihnachten *pl.* Christmas; **etwas zu Weihnachten schenken** to give something for Christmas

der Weihnachtsbaum (-̈e) Christmas tree

die Weihnachtskarte (-n) Christmas card

das Weinfest (-e) wine festival

auf · räumen to clear away, straighten up

feiern to celebrate

passen to fit; to match, suit

statt · finden* to take place

tragen* to wear

altmodisch old-fashioned
blau blue
braun brown
bunt colorful; multicolored
grau gray

grün green
modern modern
rot red
schwarz black
weiß white

A. *Find the word that does not belong.*

1. Oktoberfest, Nikolaus, Bierwagen, Brezeln
2. Dirndl, Volkslied, Lederhose, Jägerhut
3. Silvesterabend, Karneval, Fasching, Rosenmontag
4. Bowle, Picknick, Wein, Bier
5. Fest, Feier, Party, Kerze
6. Weihnachten, Weinfest, Weihnachtsbaum, Weihnachtskarte

B. *Describe what Ferdl and Rosi are wearing.*

Ferdl trägt: Rosi trägt:

_____

*The verbs marked with asterisks are strong verbs; see the appendix for principal parts of strong verbs.

C. *Name the colors you associate with each of the following.*

1. Rose
2. Elefant
3. Himmel
4. Sonne
5. Schnee
6. Kaffee
7. Weihnachten
8. Frieden
9. Valentinstag
10. Frühling
11. Herbst
12. Langeweile

D. *Mr. and Mrs. Obermayer went shopping for new clothes. Name the items of clothing they bought.*

Frau Obermayer kaufte . . . . . .   Herr Obermayer kaufte . . . . . .

E. *Complete the sentences.*

1. Der Dezember ist mein liebster Monat. Am 6. Dezember kommt der

   _____ und bringt mir etwas; wir haben einen _____ mit vier

   roten Kerzen, und natürlich ist dann am 24. Dezember _____.

2. Das berühmteste Fest in Bayern ist das _____.

3. Dieses Jahr gehe ich im Karnevalszug als Clown mit. Ist das nicht ein gutes

   _____? Niemand wird mich erkennen.

4. Bei jeder Party muß man leider am nächsten Morgen _____.

5. Meine Mutter sagt, moderne Kleidung macht jung und _____

   Kleider machen alt. Findest du das auch?

6. Dieser Mantel _____ mir nicht; er ist viel zu eng.

7. Wir _____ heute Roberts Geburtstag. Kommst du auch?

8. Chanukkah findet im Dezember _____.

F. *Complete the following paragraph about* **Fasching**.

Zuerst muß man natürlich ein _____ haben. Man kann zum Beispiel als

Clown, Prinzessin oder Frankenstein gehen. Viele Leute veranstalten (*organize*)

_____, wo man tanzen, trinken und flirten kann. Im Karneval darf man

alle Leute küssen. Manche Leute wollen nicht, daß man sie erkennt (*recognize*),

und tragen deshalb eine _____. Man trinkt viel Bier oder Wein und singt

neue und alte Karnevalslieder. Am Rosenmontag schaut man sich den

_____ mit seinen vielen Festwagen an. Am Aschermittwoch (*Ash*

Wednesday) ist dann leider alles vorbei. Bis zum nächsten Jahr! Dann können wir

wieder Kostüme _____ und verrückt spielen.

Declension and Uses of Personal Pronouns

Declension of Personal Pronouns

Personal pronouns are declined as follows:

	First Person	Second Person*		Third Person		
		Familiar	Polite	Masculine	Feminine	Neuter
Singular						
Nominative	ich	du	Sie	er	sie	es
Accusative	mich	dich	Sie	ihn	sie	es
Dative	mir	dir	Ihnen	ihm	ihr	ihm
Plural						
Nominative	wir	ihr	Sie		sie	
Accusative	uns	euch	Sie		sie	
Dative	uns	euch	Ihnen		ihnen	

*Notice that the second-person polite forms, singular and plural, are all capitalized. The second-person familiar forms, singular and plural, are capitalized in letters: **Liebe Monika, ich habe von *Dir* lange nicht gehört.**

1. Nominative singular

   Zu Weihnachten schenke *ich* der Mutter eine schöne Bluse.
   For Christmas I'm giving my mother a beautiful blouse.

   Veronika, singst *du* Weihnachtslieder gern?
   Veronika, do you like to sing Christmas carols?

   Er (*sie, es*) ist beim Oktoberfest.
   He (she, it) is at the Oktoberfest.

2. Nominative plural

   Wann gehen *wir* (*sie, Sie*) zum Oktoberfest?
   When are we (they, you) going to the Oktoberfest?

   Heidi und Karl, habt *ihr* euren Adventskranz schon gemacht?
   Heidi and Karl, have you already made your Advent wreath?

3. Accusative singular

   Toni hat *mich* (*dich, ihn, sie, es*) zum Kostümfest gebracht.
   Toni took me (you, him, her, it) to the costume ball.

4. Accusative plural

   Marie hat *uns* (*euch, sie, Sie*) beim Karneval gesehen.
   Marie saw us (you, them, you) at the Carnival (Mardi Gras) festivities.

5. Dative singular

   Kurt hat *mir* (*dir, ihm, ihr*) seine neue Lederhose gezeigt.
   Kurt showed me (you, him, her) his new leather pants.

6. Dative plural

   Der Professor wird *uns* (*euch, ihnen, Ihnen*) von dem heidnischen Ursprung des Karnevals erzählen.
   The professor will tell us (you, them, you) about the pagan origin of the carnival.

Uses of the Personal Pronouns

1. Remember that there are three ways to say *you* in German: **du**, **ihr**, and **Sie**. **Du** is used to address a close relative, a child (under thirteen or fourteen), an animal, or a friend you know well enough to address by a nickname. It is also used in prayers. Groups of athletes, students, soldiers, and blue-collar workers commonly address each other as **du**, and among young people in general today the use of **du** is becoming more and more common. The plural of **du** is **ihr**.

   Anna, trägst *du* dein Dirndl beim Oktoberfest?
   Anna, are you wearing your *dirndl* (Bavarian dress) at the Oktoberfest?

Beim Oktoberfestumzug in München

Mutti, has du je die Bierwagen beim Oktoberfest gesehen?
Mom, have you ever seen the beer carts at the Oktoberfest?

Kinder, habt *ihr* schon die Schuhe vor die Tür gestellt? Sankt Nikolaus kommt heute!
Children, have you put your shoes in front of the door yet? Saint Nicholas is coming tonight!

The form **Sie** is used in all other situations—that is, with one or more persons you do not know well. When in doubt about whether to use **du** or **Sie**, it is better to use the polite form **Sie**.

Herr Professor, können *Sie* erklären, was der Ursprung der Weiberfastnacht* ist?
Professor, can you explain what the origin of the "women's carnival" is?

Fräulein Stark und Herr Schleicher, haben *Sie* Lust, zum Fasching zu gehen?
Miss Stark and Mr. Schleicher, do you feel like going to Fasching?

---

*The **Weiberfastnacht** takes place on the Thursday before Ash Wednesday (seven weeks before Easter) and opens the **Karneval**. On this Thursday women are by tradition in charge of the city. Originally, this was the only **Karneval** festivity women were allowed to attend.

2. Third-person pronouns must agree in gender and number with the nouns to which they refer.

Hast du den Festwagen gesehen? —Ja, *er* ist sehr bunt!
Did you see the float? —Yes, it's very colorful!

Ist die Bowle gut? —Ja, *sie* ist ausgezeichnet.
Is the punch good? —Yes, it's excellent.

Two exceptions: **das Fräulein** and **das Mädchen** are referred to by natural gender (**sie, ihr**) in conversational German: **—Kennst du dieses Mädchen (Fräulein)? —Nein, ich kenne sie nicht.** Neuter forms are used for **das Mädchen** in formal German: **—Nein, ich kenne es nicht.**

3. The suffix **-et** is attached to possessive adjectives (discussed in Chapter 4) to express personal pronouns when they are the objects of the prepositions **wegen, halben** (*on account of*), or **um . . . willen** (*for the sake of*); the pronoun and preposition are written as one word.

Sonja, ich bin *deinetwegen* (*deinethalben*) nicht zum Weinmarkt gegangen.*
Sonja, I didn't go to the *Weinmarkt* on account of you.

Andrea hat um *unsretwillen* mit dem Lehrer gesprochen.
Andrea spoke to the teacher for our sake.

4. The pronoun **es** is used in certain idiomatic expressions:

Ich bin *es*.   Wir sind *es*.
It's me.   It's us.

Word Order with Personal Pronouns

1. Personal pronouns generally precede nouns when the two occur adjacent to each other.

	Pronoun Object	*Noun Subject*
Schmeckt	dir	diese Bowle?

Does this punch taste good to you?

Here are other examples:

Uschi, gefällt *dir dieses Volkslied?*
Uschi, do you like this folksong?

Sag mir, ob *dir dieses Volkslied* gefällt.
Tell me if you like this folksong.

---

*The **Weinmarkt** (at Bad Dürkheim) is the biggest of the wine festivals that take place yearly in the wine-growing regions (mainly along the Rhine and in the South). In a recent year 50,000 gallons of wine were consumed at the **Weinmarkt**.

Max und Elke, wer hat *euch diese* Weihnachtsgeschenke gegeben?
Max and Elke, who gave you these Christmas presents?

2. Direct object pronouns always precede indirect object pronouns.

	Direct Object Pronoun	Indirect Object Pronoun	
Max und Elke, wer hat	sie	euch	gegeben?
Max and Elke, who gave	them	to you?	

Notice that this order is the exact opposite if both objects are nouns:

	Indirect Object Noun	Direct Object Noun
Wer hat	den Kindern	die Weihnachtsgeschenke gegeben?
Who gave	the children	the Christmas presents?

As the above examples illustrate, the preposition **zu** (*to*) is not used in German to introduce the indirect object.

Übungen

°A. **Ersetzen Sie die Pronomen!** Replace the italicized nouns with the proper forms of the pronouns in parentheses.

Zum Beispiel: Herr Dehn kennt *diese Frau* nicht. (ich)
Herr Dehn kennt mich nicht. (du)
Herr Dehn kennt dich nicht.

1. Der Professor hat *der Studentin* dieses Heft gegeben. (ich, er, wir)
2. Wir verstehen *die Touristen* nicht. (Sie, ihr, sie *plural*)
3. Die Touristen haben *dem Deutschen* gedankt. (ich, wir, er)
4. Frau Vasmer hat *den Arzt* am Silvesterabend gerufen.
5. Wer hat *dem Lehrer* dieses Restaurant empfohlen? (du, ihr, wir)

°B. **Ein Gespräch mit Fräulein Bahrdt.** You and Fräulein Bahrdt, an acquaintance, are having a chat; reply to her statements, following the models.

Zum Beispiel: Ich habe Sie gestern angerufen.
Warum haben Sie mich angerufen? (or)
Wann haben Sie mich angerufen?

1. Ich habe Ihnen einen Brief geschickt.
2. Ich wollte mit Ihnen über das Picknick sprechen.
3. Herr Zimmermann hat etwas gegen Sie gesagt.
4. Ich möchte etwas für Sie tun.
5. Fräulein Deimler hat nach Ihnen gefragt.

°C. **Noch eine Frage!** Your younger brother Ernst is always asking questions. Answer him in the affirmative with a pronoun, following the model.

Zum Beispiel: Kannst du mir dein Karnevalskostüm zeigen?
Ja, ich kann dir mein Karnevalskostüm zeigen.

1. Darf ich mit dir zum Rosenmontagszug gehen?
2. Muß ich mir die Jacke anziehen?
3. Hast du mir ein Geschenk gekauft?
4. Nimmst du mich zum Karneval mit?
5. Kann ich dich noch etwas fragen?
6. Gehe ich dir auf die Nerven?

°D. **Ein Gespräch mit zwei Freunden.** You are having a discussion with your friends Uschi and Rudi; answer their questions affirmatively, following the model.

Zum Beispiel: Gehst du mit uns ins Kino?
Ja, ich gehe mit euch ins Kino.

1. Hast du uns gestern beim Straßenfest gesehen?
2. Können wir dir bei der Party helfen?
3. Kannst du uns vielleicht morgen mitnehmen?
4. Möchtest du morgen abend mit uns zum Kostümfest gehen?
5. Haben wir dich schon zu unserem Picknick eingeladen?
6. Kommst du zu Weihnachten mit uns in die Kirche?

°E. **Ein Besuch in Düsseldorf.** You and your brother are visiting an old friend in Düsseldorf, Rita Fauser, during Karneval. Answer her questions affirmatively, following the model.

Zum Beispiel: Möchtet ihr in die Stadt mitfahren?
Ja, wir möchten in die Stadt mitfahren.

1. Habt ihr je den Rosenmontagszug gesehen?
2. Darf ich euch mein Kostüm zeigen?
3. Möchtet ihr mit mir zu einer Party gehen?
4. Könntet ihr mich am Abend in der Stadt abholen?

F. **Unsere Freunde.** Your sister is asking you about people you both know. Answer her questions affirmatively, following the model. (Use the dative with prepositions.)

Zum Beispiel: Kennst du Helmut Herder?
Ja, ich kenne ihn.

1. Hast du Klaus und Brigitte zur Adventsfeier eingeladen?
2. Hast du eine Einladung von Max bekommen?
3. Warst du gestern abend bei Margot?
4. Fährst du morgen zu Theodor und Heidi?
5. Findest du Regina und ihren Bruder sympathisch?

G. **In meiner Wohnung (meinem Zimmer) . . .** Answer these questions about things in your apartment or room.

Zum Beispiel: Gefällt Ihnen die Couch?
   Ja, sie ist sehr bequem.

1. Welche Farbe hat der Teppich?
2. War die Lampe teuer?
3. Funktioniert der Fernseher gut?
4. Wo steht der Tisch?
5. Ist der Plattenspieler neu?

H. **Bilden Sie Sätze!** Rearrange the words to form sentences. Pay careful attention to the order of object nouns and pronouns.

Zum Beispiel: ich habe / meinem Freund / es / gezeigt
   Ich habe es meinem Freund gezeigt.

   ich habe / den Kranz / Herrn Böhme / gegeben
   Ich habe Herrn Böhme den Kranz gegeben.

1. wir haben / einige Geschenke / unseren Freunden / gegeben
2. wir haben / ihnen / gegeben / sie
3. hast du / den Weihnachtsbaum / gezeigt / den Kindern?
4. hast du / gezeigt / ihn / ihnen?
5. zu Weihnachten / meine Eltern / haben / gegeben / mir / es
6. Heinz / uns / hat / geschickt / eine Weihnachtskarte

I. **Ersetzen Sie die kursiv gedruckten Wörter.** Replace the italicized words and phrases in the following passage with the appropriate personal pronouns.

Schon im Juli fragte Ferdl seine Freundin Rosi, ob *Rosi* zum Oktoberfest gehen wollte. *Rosi* antwortete: „Ja, gern", und fragt Ferdl, ob *Ferdl* auch dorthin gehen wollte. Ferdl nahm Rosi in den Arm, gab *Rosi* einen Kuß und sagte: „Aber ja, mein Schatz". Also war sicher, daß *Ferdl und Rosi* zum Oktoberfest gehen würden.

Im September fuhren die Beiden dann nach München und gingen auf die Theresienwiese, wo das Oktoberfest stattfindet. *Das Oktoberfest* war viel größer, als *die beiden* gedacht hatten. Es gab viele Leute, viel Bier und viel Musik. Ferdl und Rosi gingen zunächst ein bißchen auf der Wiese spazieren. *Die beiden* waren festlich angezogen. Ferdl trug seine schöne neue Lederhose. Ferdl hatte *die Lederhose* von seinen Eltern als Geburtstagsgeschenk bekommen. Rosi hatte ein wunderschönes bayrisches Dirndl an. Sie hatte *das Dirndl* speziell für das Oktoberfest gekauft, und *das Dirndl* sah sehr gut an ihr aus. Die beiden waren wirklich ein schönes Paar.

Sie kauften ein paar Brezeln und aßen *die Brezeln* sofort, weil sie großen Hunger hatten. Dann tranken sie Bier in einem Bierzelt und fuhren nach Hause zurück. Das ganze Fest gefiel *den beiden* sehr gut, und sie wollen nächstes Jahr wieder aufs Oktoberfest gehen.

Übersetzen Sie die folgenden Sätze!

1. My brother bought a Christmas tree. I like it very much.
2. Who is there? —It's us.
3. I gave her a blouse, but she never wears it.
4. Gerd and Lotte, come over tomorrow.
5. Jürgen, on account of you I stayed home. *wegen dir*
6. Mr. Barner, do you come from (**aus**) Vienna?
7. Mother (**Mutti**), did you give Marie my sweater? —No, I didn't give it to her.
8. This hat is very old and it is out of style.
9. Dieter, did Sonja give you this jacket? —Yes, she gave it to me.

K. **Wie sieht der gut angezogene Mensch aus?** How should the well-dressed man or woman look? Answer the following questions following the models.

Der Mann

Zum Beispiel: Welche Farbe hat seine Hose?
Sie ist grau.

1. Ist sein Hemd schwarz, weiß oder grün?
2. Sind seine Socken rot?
3. Ist sein Anzug altmodisch?
4. Welche Farbe haben seine Schuhe?
5. Ist seine Krawatte breit oder schmall?
6. Paßt sein Hemd zur Krawatte?

Die Frau

Zum Beispiel: Paßt ihre Handtasche zu ihren Schuhen?
Ja, sie paßt zu ihren Schuhen.

1. Ist ihr Rock kurz?
2. Ist ihr Hut modern?
3. Welche Farbe hat ihre Jacke?
4. Passen ihre Schuhe zum Kleid?
5. Ist ihre Bluse zu eng?
6. Sind ihre Kleider sehr bunt?

Reflexive Pronouns and Verbs

Reflexive Pronouns

Reflexive pronouns take their name from the fact that they "reflect back" (refer) to the subject: I hurt *myself*, he is enjoying *himself*. For example, in the sentence **Ich habe mich verletzt** (*I hurt myself*), the reflexive pronoun **mich** refers to the subject pronoun **ich**. In the following English sentences, notice that reflexive pronouns can be direct or indirect objects of the verb.

I hurt *myself*.   (direct object)
I taught *myself*.   (direct object)
I bought *myself* a new car.   (indirect object)
I gave *myself* the day off.   (indirect object)

Similarly, in German, reflexive pronouns can be direct objects (accusative case) or indirect objects (dative case).

Accusative	Dative
Ich habe *mich* verletzt.	Ich habe *mir* einen Wagen gekauft.
Du hast *dich* verletzt.	Du hast *dir* einen Wagen gekauft.
Er (sie, es) hat *sich* verletzt.	Er (sie, es) hat *sich* einen Wagen gekauft.
Wir haben *uns* verletzt.	Wir haben *uns* einen Wagen gekauft.
Ihr habt *euch* verletzt.	Ihr habt *euch* einen Wagen gekauft.
Sie (sie) haben *sich* verletzt.	Sie (sie) haben *sich* einen Wagen gekauft.

Notice from these examples that the reflexive pronouns are identical in form to the dative or accusative forms of the personal pronouns except in the third person. The reflexive pronoun **sich** is used with the subject pronouns **er, sie, es, Sie** (second-person formal), and **sie** (plural). Notice also that the accusative and dative forms of the reflexive pronouns are identical except for **ich** and **du**: **mich/mir** and **dich/dir**.

Reflexive Verbs that Take Accusative Objects

Reflexive verbs are verbs that generally take reflexive pronouns, accusative or dative. Most reflexive verbs take accusative reflexive pronouns:

sich anziehen to get dressed	sich entschließen to decide	sich freuen über to be happy about
sich ausruhen to rest	sich erinnern an to remember	sich fühlen to feel
sich ausziehen to undress, get undressed	sich erkälten to catch cold	sich fürchten vor* to be afraid of
sich beeilen to hurry	sich freuen auf to look forward to	sich gewöhnen an to get used to

---

*Notice that the preposition **vor** is the only one in this list that is followed by the dative case; all the other prepositions here take the accusative.

sich verlieben in	sich interessieren für	sich legen
to fall in love with	to be interested in	to lie down
sich waschen	sich kümmern um	sich setzen
to wash (oneself)	to trouble oneself about, look after	to sit down
sich wundern über		
to be surprised at		

Möchten Sie *sich ausruhen?*
Would you like to rest?

Die Studenten müssen *sich beeilen.*
The students have to hurry.

Ich *fühle mich* heute besser.
I feel better today.

Wir haben uns *entschlossen,* nach Müchen zu fahren.
We decided to drive to Munich.

Die kleine Cornelia *freut sich auf* den Nikolaustag.
Little Cornelia is looking forward to Saint Nicholas' Day (December 6).

Fürchtest du *dich vor* dieser Maske?
Are you afraid of this mask?

Edda *hat sich an* dieses Wetter *gewöhnt.*
Edda has gotten used to this weather.

Kümmerst du *dich um* die Getränke?
Are you looking after the drinks?

Herr Vollmer, *setzen Sie sich,* bitte!
Mr. Vollmer, sit down please.

Udo *hat sich in* das Mädchen *verliebt.*
Udo fell in love with the girl.

Some of these verbs can be used reflexively or nonreflexively. When used nonreflexively, they have objects that refer to persons other than the subject.

Reflexive	*Nonreflexive*
Kathrin zieht *sich* an.	Kathrin zieht *sie* (ihre Tochter) an.
Kathrin is getting dressed.	Kathrin is dressing her (her daughter).
Axel ärgert *sich* über seinen Bruder.	Was ärgert *dich?*
Axel is angry at his brother.	What is annoying you?
Wir bedienen *uns.*	Wir bedienen *sie* (die Gäste).
We're helping (serving) ourselves.	We're serving them (the guests).

Erinnern Sie *sich* an diesen Festwagen?	Ich erinnere *ihn* (Hans) an sein Versprechen.
Do you remember that float?	I am reminding him (Hans) of his promise.
Ich wasche *mich*.	Ich wasche *ihn* (den Wagen).
I'm washing (myself).	I'm washing it (the car).

From the preceding examples, you can see that the English equivalents of reflexive constructions in German often do not contain reflexive pronouns, although sometimes a reflexive construction is understood, as in the sentence **Kathrin zieht sich an.** *Kathrin is dressing (herself).*

Reflexive Verbs That Take Dative Objects

A dative object is required in sentences like **Ich kaufe mir einen neuen Hut** or **Du bestellst dir eine Tasse Tee**, when someone is buying, ordering, or acquiring something for himself, herself, etc. In these cases the dative reflexive pronoun does not change the basic meaning of the verb. There are a few other reflexive constructions that require dative objects, the most common of which are:

sich leisten	sich Sorgen machen um
to afford	to worry about, be anxious about
sich (etwas) vorstellen	sich weh tun
to imagine (something)	to hurt oneself

Ich *kann mir* keinen neuen Anzug *leisten.*
I can't afford a new suit.

Gerda, *mach dir* keine Sorgen um dein Kostüm.
Gerda, don't worry about your costume.

Ich *habe mir* so *etwas vorgestellt.*
I imagined something like this.

Erich, *hast du dir weh getan?*
Erich, have you hurt yourself?

Study hint: A good way to remember these verbs is to memorize them in short sentences with the dative pronouns **mir** and **dir**.

Dative reflexive pronouns are also used in sentences with parts of the body or articles of clothing, where possessive adjectives are normally used in English:

Ich wasche *mir* die Hände.	Zieh *dir* die Jacke aus!
I'm washing my hands.	Take off your jacket.

Reflexive Verbs in the Perfect Tenses

All reflexive verbs require the auxiliary **haben** in the perfect tenses. In normal word order, the reflexive pronoun follows the auxiliary in the perfect tenses, as you have seen in preceding examples (**ich habe mich verletzt; ich habe mir einen Wagen gekauft**).

Übungen

°A. **Ersetzen Sie die Pronomen!** Replace the subjects in italics with the subjects in parentheses and change the verbs and reflexive pronouns accordingly.

1. Ziehst *du* dich immer so schnell an?   (ihr, Sie, Heidi)
2. Wie fühlen *Sie* sich?   (du, ihr, er)
3. *Rolf* muß sich ausruhen.   (ich, du, wir)
4. *Ich* habe mich endlich an dieses Klima gewöhnt.   (Marion und Franz, Sonja, wir)
5. *Wir* müssen uns beeilen.   (du, ihr, Sie)
6. Hat sich *Lotte* erkältet?   (Sie, ihr, du)
7. Hat sich *Reinhard* an das Weihnachtslied erinnert?   (ihr, sie, du)
8. *Ich* kann mir keinen neuen Fernseher leisten.   (du, wir, er)
9. *Du* solltest dir die Jacke anziehen.   (er, ich, Sie)
10. Hat *Kurt* sich weh getan?   (du, ihr, sie *sing.*)

B. **Geben Sie Toni Ratschläge!** Give Toni advice using reflexive verbs from the column on the right.

Zum Beispiel: Ich bin verspätet.
　　　　　　　　Du solltest dich beeilen.

1. Mir ist sehr warm.
2. Ich bin von der Arbeit müde. So ein Streß!
3. Ich will zum Fasching nach München, aber ich will auch zum Karneval nach Köln. Ich weiß nicht, was ich tun soll.
4. Ach, laß mich doch noch etwas schlafen.
5. Ich stehe hier schon viel zulange. Die Beine tun mir weh.
6. Es geht mir alles viel zu schnell hier.
7. Ach du liebe Zeit! So spät ist es schon? Ich werde bestimmt den Zug verpassen (*miss*).

a. sich setzen
b. sich entschließen
c. sich waschen und sich anziehen
d. sich die Jacke ausziehen
e. sich an das Tempo hier gewöhnen
f. sich ausruhen
g. sich beeilen

C. **Wählen Sie das passende Verb!** Choose the appropriate reflexive verb from the column on the right to form a sentence describing each statement on the left.

Zum Beispiel: Elke sammelt Weihnachtskarten aus der Schweiz.
Elke interessiert sich für die Schweiz.

1. Ich bin schrecklich müde. Wo ist der nächste Stuhl?
2. Ferdinand und Greta haben genug Geld, um sich einen neuen Mercedes zu kaufen.
3. Herbert sieht heute viel besser aus.
4. Toni hustet (*is coughing*) viel.
5. Arnold hatte einen Unfall und liegt im Krankenhaus (*hospital*).
6. Gretchen versteht nicht, warum sie dieses teure Geschenk bekommen hat.
7. Renate ist sehr glücklich, denn sie macht eine Reise nach Köln.
8. Helmut bleibt bei seinen kranken Eltern und hilft ihnen jeden Tag.

a. sich leisten können
b. sich erkälten
c. sich wundern über
d. sich interessieren für
e. sich kümmern um
f. sich freuen auf
g. sich setzen wollen
h. sich fühlen
i. sich verletzen

D. **Übersetzen Sie die folgenden Sätze!**

1. Regina, did you hurt yourself?
2. We should rest now.
3. I'm worried about my grades (**Noten**).
4. Otto, can you afford this house?
5. Lotte, why did you put your **Dirndl** on?
6. Miss Sperber, did you buy yourself that costume?
7. Veronika and Michael, why are you hurrying?
8. I caught cold at the Oktoberfest.
9. Heinz got used to the weather here.
10. Mrs. Zietemann, are you interested in Austrian holidays?
11. Annegret, do you remember that Christmas card?
12. I've decided to go to the wine festival.
    Ich habe mich entschlossen, zum Weinfest zu gehen.

E. **Eine Party am Silvesterabend.** Choose the correct verb in parentheses to complete the sentences.

REINER: Ich habe _____, zur Party zu gehen (sich verletzen / sich

entschließen). Kommst du mit?

SONJA: Ich weiß noch nicht. Gestern abend habe ich _____ ein

bißchen _____ (sich erkälten / sich fühlen). Ich habe

_____ noch nicht _____ dieses Wetter

_____ (sich gewöhnen an / sich verlieben in).

REINER: Ich _____ dich (sich ärgern über / sich Sorgen machen

um). Du solltest _____ etwas Wärmeres _____

(sich ausziehen / sich anziehen). Hoffentlich _____ vor

der Party etwas besser (sich fühlen / sich waschen).

SONJA: Das hoffe ich auch, denn ich _____ diese Party (sich

freuen auf / sich kümmern um).

F. **Wählen Sie das passende Verb!** Choose the correct reflexive verb to use in a sentence describing each drawing.

Zum Beispiel: Das Kind freut sich über das Weihnachtsgeschenk.

a. sich wundern über
b. sich freuen auf
c. sich erkälten
d. sich den Jägerhut aufsetzen

e. sich weh tun
f. sich ein Dirndl kaufen
g. sich freuen über

1.

2.

3.

4.

5.

6.

The Pronoun *einander*; the Intensive Pronouns *selbst* and *selber*

The Pronoun *einander*

The plural form of the reflexive pronouns is often the equivalent of English *each other*. The meaning can also be expressed by the pronoun **einander**:

Wir sehen *uns* beim Fest.
Wir sehen *einander* beim Fest. } We'll see each other at the festival.

Kennt ihr *euch*?
Kennt ihr *einander*? } Do you know each other?

Diese drei Mädchen kennen *sich* schon.
Diese drei Mädchen kennen *einander* schon. } These three girls know each other already.

Einander sometimes occurs in combination with prepositions and is written together with them as one word:

Gisela und Ernst saßen *nebeneinander* auf dem Rummelplatz.
Gisela and Ernst sat next to each other at the amusement park.

Hartmut und Anna interessieren sich *füreinander*.
Hartmut and Anna are interested in each other.

Jürgen und Brigitte haben *miteinander* beim Maskenball getanzt.
Jürgen and Brigitte danced with each other at the masquerade ball.

The Intensive Pronouns *selbst* and *selber*

The intensive pronouns **selbst** and **selber** are used for emphasis (to "intensify" the meaning of a noun or pronoun).

Peter *selbst* (*selber*) hat diesen Kranz gemacht.} Peter made this wreath
Peter hat diesen Kranz *selbst* (*selber*) gemacht.} himself.

Annegret *selbst* (*selber*) hat es gesagt.} Annegret said it herself.
Annegret hat es *selbst* (*selber*) gesagt.}

As you can see from these sentences, the intensive pronoun emphasizes the fact that the subject (not someone else) performed the action of the verb.*

Selbst and **selber**, which do not change form, can also be used with reflexive pronouns:

Wer hat die kleine Cornelia gebadet? —Sie hat sich *selbst* gebadet.
Who gave little Cornelia a bath? —She gave herself a bath (no one else did it).

Übungen

°A. **Übersetzen Sie die folgenden Sätze!** Translate the following sentences and then replace the reflexive pronoun with the pronoun **einander**.

Zum Beispiel: Wir kennen uns schon.
We know each other already.
Wir kennen einander schon.

1. Wir sehen uns am Rosenmontag.
2. Sigi und Barbara, helft ihr euch immer bei den Hausaufgaben?
3. Fräulein Lotze und Herr Schäfer, kennen Sie sich schon?
4. Traude und Rudi haben sich auf dem Weihnachtsmarkt kennengelernt.

°B. **Beantworten Sie die folgenden Fragen mit dem Pronomen *einander*!**

Zum Beispiel: Neben wem sitzen Renate und Gudrun?
Sie sitzen nebeneinander.

Für wen kauft ihr diese Geschenke?
Wir kaufen diese Geschenke füreinander.

1. Mit wem gehen Heidi und Cornelia zum Maskenball?
2. An wen schreibt ihr?
3. In wen sind Edith und Lorenz verliebt?
4. Mit wem besprecht ihr dieses Problem?
5. Neben wem wohnen Herr Becker und Herr Behn?

---

*While the English translations of **selbst** and **selber** (*himself, herself*, etc.) have the same forms as reflexive pronouns, these sentences are not reflexive; the action of the verb does not "reflect back" to the subject as it does in sentences like *Peter hurt himself.*

C. **Übersetzen Sie die folgenden Sätze!**

1. Sonja and Sigi, do you know each other yet (*schon*)? (Translate in two ways.)
2. Miss Henglein and Mrs. Küchler live next to each other.
3. Kurt and Christine are in love with each other.
4. Rolf, did you make that wreath yourself?
5. Sara made the skirt herself.

D. **Eine Party am Silversterabend.** Brigitte is giving a party. Answer the questions following the model, using either **selbst** or **selber**.

Zum Beispiel: Wer hat Brigitte geholfen, alles aufzuräumen?
Brigitte hat alles selbst aufgeräumt.

Wer hat den Champagner für Brigitte gekauft?
Brigitte hat den Champagner selber gekauft.

1. Wer hat das Wohnzimmer für Brigitte geschmückt (*decorated*)?
2. Wer hat die Torten für Brigitte gebacken?
3. Wer hat Brigitte geholfen, den Tisch zu decken?
4. Wer hat die Bowle gemacht?
5. Wer hat die Gäste eingeladen?
6. Wer hat ihre amerikanischen Freunde vom Hotel abgeholt?

Es in Impersonal Expressions

The pronoun **es** is used as the subject of a sentence without an antecedent (a noun to which it refers) in many expressions:

1. with verbs designating natural phenomena

Es hat beim Weinfest den ganzen Tag geregnet.
It rained all day at the wine festival.

Es blitzt und donnert im Gebirge.
There is lightning and thunder in the mountains.

Es schneit oft zu Weihnachten.
It often snows at Christmas.

2. with verbs designating events whose agents are unknown

Es klopft an der Tür.
There is a knock at the door.

Es läutet vom Kirchturm.
It (the bells) are ringing from the church tower.

3. with verbs or verb phrases that express a feeling

Es graut dem Kind vor der Dunkelheit.
The child is terrified of the dark.

Es ist ihr kalt.
She is (feels) cold.

Er trank zuviel Bier, und es wurde ihm schlecht.
He drank too much beer and he became nauseated.

Graut es dir vor diesem Hund?
Are you afraid of that dog?

Gertrud sagt, daß ihr kalt ist.*
Gertrud says that she is cold.

4. with many sentences that have a true subject; this anticipatory **es** precedes the verb directly (the verb agrees with the true subject)

Es weiß hier niemand, ob Sankt Nikolaustag am sechsten oder am siebten Dezember ist. (subject: *niemand*)
No one here knows whether St. Nicholas' Day is on December sixth or seventh.

Es kommen viele Freunde zu uns auf Besuch. (subject: *viele Freunde*)
Many friends are coming to visit us.

5. in certain idomatic expressions, including **es gibt** and **es sind**

Wie geht es Ihnen?
How are you? (How goes it for you?)

Es gefällt mir sehr hier beim Fasching.
I like it here very much during Fasching.

Ist es dir gelungen, schöne Weihnachtskarten zu finden?
Did you succeed in finding beautiful Christmas cards?

Was gibt es Neues?
What's new?

Es gibt viele Bierzelte auf dem Oktoberfest.
There are many beer tents at the Oktoberfest.

Gibt es ein Oktoberfest in dieser Stadt?
Is there an Oktoberfest in this city?

Es ist ein großes Geschenk unter dem Baum.
There is a big present under the tree.

Es sind vier Kerzen auf dem Adventskranz.
There are four candles on the advent wreath.

Es gibt is general in meaning and usually refers to an indefinite number of items in a location that is not precisely specified. It is followed by a direct object. **Es ist (sind)** usually refers to a definite number of items in

---

*****Es** is dropped in these expressions if it does not immediately precede the verb: **Graut es dir vor diesem Hund? Gertrud sagt, daß es ihr kalt ist. Ihr ist es kalt.**

---

a specific location. It is followed by the true subject, with which the verb must agree. However, **es ist (sind)** are used much less often than *there is (are)* in English; it is more common to say, for instance, **Ein großes Geschenk liegt (ist) unter dem Baum** or **Vier Kerzen stehen (sind) auf dem Adventskranz.**

Übungen

A. **Wählen Sie den richtigen Satz!** Choose the logical response on the right for each statement on the left.

1. Es graut mir vor der Prüfung.
2. Ist dir hier auch so warm?
3. Mir ist kalt.
4. Uns wird schlecht.

a. Soll ich das Fenster aufmachen?
b. Hast du nicht genug gelernt?
c. Zieh dir einen Pullover an.
d. Haben Sie zu viele Bonbons gegessen?

B. **Übersetzen Sie die folgenden Sätze!** Use the dative case after the prepositions below.

1. Peter, why are you terrified of the mask?
2. Mr. Biehle, are you warm enough?
3. I feel nauseated.
4. There is a knock (someone is knocking).

C. **Beschreiben Sie die folgenden Bilder!** Describe the following pictures using an expression with **es** as the subject.

Zum Beispiel: Es regnet beim Picknick.

3.

4.

5.

Rückblick

A. Zur Wiederholung. Übersetzen Sie die folgenden Sätze!

1. Mrs. Nagel, I saw you yesterday at the costume ball.
2. Sigi, I want to show you my new suit. —It fits you well.
3. Heidi and Otto, did you go to the (**auf das**) **Oktoberfest**?
4. Regina, could you help me with the (**bei der**) party?
5. Greta, did you see Kurt's **Lederhose**?
6. Rolf bought himself a **Jägerhut**. It is green.
7. Sara, did you decide to buy a **Dirndl**?
8. Fritz, can you afford a new coat?
9. Hansdieter and Jost know each other. (Translate in two ways.)
10. Gertrud made the Advent wreath herself.
11. It always rains here in winter.
12. Are you too warm, Mr. Lietzmann?

B. Zur Gesamtwiederholung. Übersetzen Sie die folgenden Sätze!

1. Not all Germans go to the **Oktoberfest**. (Chapters 4 and 7)
2. The (female) German gave the American student a present at Christmas.
3. Anneliese probably bought herself some green stockings. (Chapters 5 and 7)
4. We would have gone to the wine festival if it hadn't rained so much. (Chapter 8)
5. Anneliese, would you like to visit some old German friends on New Year's Eve? (Chapters 7 and 8)

11
Schule und Beruf

Münchener Studenten genießen einen sonnigen Tag

Prepositions That Take Dative Objects

Prepositions That Take Accusative Objects

Prepositions That Take Either Dative or Accusative Objects;
Adverbs Indicating a Place

Prepositions in Time Expressions; Prepositions Used Figuratively

Prepositions That Take Genitive Objects; *da*-Compounds; Word
Order with Adverbs and Prepositional Phrases

Wortschatz

das Abitur final exam that entitles
you to go from a *Gymnasium* to a
university

**der Architekt (-en, -en), die
Architektin (-nen)** architect

der Beruf (-e) occupation,
profession

die Bibliothek (-en) library

der Bogen (-) sheet (of paper)

das Bücherregal (-e) bookshelf

die Buchhandlung (-en) bookstore

**der Computerwissenschaftler (-),
die Computerwissenschaftlerin
(-nen)** computer scientist

das Examen (-) comprehensive
exam at the end of a course of
study

das Fach (¨er) subject

die Fremdsprache (-n) foreign
language

die Grundschule (-n) elementary
school

der Hörsaal (-säle) lecture hall

**der Ingenieur (-e), die
Ingenieurin (-nen)** engineer

**der Journalist (-en, -en), die
Journalistin (-nen)** journalist

das Labor (-s) laboratory

**der Mathematiker (-), die
Mathematikerin (-nen)**
mathematician

die Mensa (-en) student restaurant

**der Physiker (-), die
Physikerin (-nen)** physicist

**der Politikwissenschaftler (-), die
Politikwissenschaftlerin (-nen)**
political scientist

**der Psychologe (-n, -n), die
Psychologin (-nen)** psychologist

**der Rechtsanwalt (¨e), die
Rechtsanwältin (-nen)** lawyer

der Schreibtisch (-e) desk

die Stellung (-en) job, position

das Studium postsecondary school
studies lasting about five years
(giving the equivalent of a master's
degree)

die Vorlesung (-en) lecture

bei · bringen* to teach; to show how to

bestehen* to pass

besuchen to attend; to visit

durch · fallen* to fail, flunk

lesen* (über) to lecture (about)

machen: eine Prüfung machen to take a test; **den Doktor machen** to get one's doctorate

pauken to cram

unterbrechen* to interrupt

unterrichten to teach (subject)

A. Complete the following sentences.

1. Geben Sie mir bitte einen _____ Papier.

2. Ich habe ein paar interessante Bücher über das deutsche Schulsystem in meinem _____.

3. Professor Vogelsang _____ heute über italienische Renaissance-Architektur.

4. Letztes Semester habe ich drei Vorlesungen _____. Das war zuviel!

5. Meine Mutter hat mir _____, wie man Apfelstrudel bäckt.

6. Herr Oerking ist unser Englischlehrer, aber er _____ auch Französich.

7. Frau Dr. Rosenberg sitzt im Büro immer an ihrem _____.

B. As a student, where would you go to do each of the following?

1. ein Buch kaufen
2. eine Vorlesung hören
3. essen
4. Experimente machen
5. Bücher, Zeitungen oder Dokumente lesen

C. Give the profession of the person who has studied each of the following.

Zum Beispiel: Psychologie
Psychologe (Psychologin)

1. Ingenieurwesen
2. Journalismus
3. Medizin
4. Physik
5. Politikwissenschaft

6. Architektur
7. Jura (law)
8. Mathematik
9. Computerwissenschaft

---

*The verbs marked with asterisks are strong verbs; see the appendix for principal parts of strong verbs.

D. *Complete the following paragraph about the German school system.*

Wenn man sechs Jahre alt ist, geht man zur _____ bis zum Alter von zehn

Jahren. Danach geht man zur Hauptschule (fünf Jahre lang), zur Realschule

(sechs Jahre lang) oder zum _____ (neun Jahre lang). Am Ende des

Gymnasiums macht man das _____. Wenn man will, kann man dann auf die

Universität gehen und studieren. Ein _____ dauert normalerweise fünf Jahre.

Am Ende dieser Zeit steht ein großes _____, für das man sehr viel lernen

muß. Manche Studenten studieren noch länger und machen dann

ihren _____.

E. *Answer the following questions.*

1. Gehen Sie in alle Ihre Vorlesungen?
2. Lernen Sie regelmäßig oder pauken Sie erst vor einer Prüfung?
3. Was war Ihre schlechteste Note? Und in welchem Fach? Haben Sie die Abschlußprüfung (*final exam*) bestanden oder sind Sie durchgefallen?
4. Was ist Ihr Lieblingsfach (*favorite subject*)?
5. Glauben Sie, jeder Student sollte eine Fremdsprache studieren?
6. Gehen Sie jede Woche ins Sprachlabor?
7. Glauben Sie, Sie werden eine Stellung in Ihrem Fach bekommen, oder werden Sie sich eine Stellung in einem anderen Fach suchen müssen?
8. Haben Sie Ihr Studium schon einmal unterbrochen, oder möchten Sie es unterbrechen? Warum?
9. Welche Sommerjobs haben Sie schon gehabt? Haben Sie im Augenblick einen Job?
10. Für welchen Beruf interessieren Sie sich?

Prepositions That Take Dative Objects

When using prepositions in German, two things must be taken into account: (1) the proper case to use with the object of the preposition and (2) the proper preposition to use in a given situation. The dative case is used in most prepositional phrases. The following prepositions always take the dative case:

1. aus   *out of; from (a place of origin); made of*

   Wann kommst du *aus der Bibliothek?*
   When will you leave the library?

   Dieser Schreibtisch ist *aus Eiche.*
   This desk is (made of) oak.

2. **außer**   *but, except; besides, in addition to*

Außer meinem Freund ist niemand in der Prüfung durchgefallen.
No one but (except) my friend flunked the test.

Außer ihr waren viele Studenten bei der Vorlesung.
Besides (in addition to) her, many students were at the lecture.

3. **bei**   *at (place of residence, work, functions); near (building or geographical location); while; with or on (one's person)*

Gerd wohnt *bei seiner Tante.*
Gerd lives at his aunt's.

Er arbeitet *bei einer Bank.*
He works at (for) a bank.

Wir lernen Deutsch *bei Professor Schmidt.*
We're learning German in Professor Schmidt's class.

Elisabeth ist *beim Rechtsanwalt.*
Elisabeth is at the lawyer's.

Warst du *bei der Party (der Vorlesung, dem Konzert, dem Picknick)?*
Were you at the party (lecture, concert, picnic)?

Die Cafeteria ist *beim Hörsaal 10.*
The cafeteria is near lecture hall 10.

Ich wohne *bei der Uni.*
I live near the university.

Bei welcher Stadt liegt das Dorf Füssen?
Near which city is the village Füssen situated?

Fritz raucht immer *beim Lesen.**
Fritz always smokes while reading.

Inge, hast du einen Kugelschreiber *bei dir?*
Inge, do you have a ballpoint pen with (on) you?

4. **gegenüber**   *across from*

Das Chemiegebäude steht *gegenüber der Bibliothek.*
The chemistry building is across from the library.

5. **mit**   *with; by (means of transportation)*

Marie geht *mit Reinhardt* zur Vorlesung.
Marie is going to the lecture with Reinhardt.

Ich schreibe immer *mit dem Kugelschreiber.*
I always write with a ballpoint pen.

Ich fahre *mit dem Zug* nach Wien.
I'm going to Vienna by train.

---

*In this use, **bei** is always contracted with the article to **beim**, and the infinitive is capitalized since it is used as a noun.

6. **nach** *after; according to; to (with geographic names, directions, home); about (with verbs of inquiry).*

Nach dem Unterricht spielen wir oft Fußball.
After class, we often play soccer.

Dem Professor nach lernen heute die meisten Deutschen wenigstens eine Fremdsprache.*
According to the professor, most Germans learn at least one foreign language today.

Wir fahren morgen nach Köln (Afrika, Oregon, Amerika).†
Tomorrow we're traveling to Cologne (Africa, Oregon, America).

Sie gehen nach links (oben, dem Osten, Hause).
They're going left (upstairs, east, home).

Er fragte nach dem Examen.
He asked about the exam.

Marie erkundigte sich nach ihren Noten.
Marie inquired about her grades.

7. **seit** *since; for (with a time period)*

Seit der letzten Party habe ich Kurt nicht gesehen.
I haven't seen Kurt since the last party.

Ich lerne (schon) seit drei Monaten Deutsch.‡
I've been studying German for three months.

Ich studiere (schon) seit fünf Jahren Politikwissenschaft.
I've been studying political science for five years.

Egon wohnt (schon) seit zehn Monaten in Stuttgart.
Egon has been living in Stuttgart for ten months.

8. **von** *by (an author, composer, agent in passive sentences); of (possessive); from*

Dieses Drama ist von Schiller.
This drama is by Schiller.

Viele schöne Symphonien wurden von Haydn komponiert.**
Many beautiful symphonies were composed by Haydn.

Zeigst du uns morgen deine Bilder von Deutschland?
Are you going to show us your pictures of Germany tomorrow?

---

*In this case, **nach** may either precede or follow its object: **nach dem Professor. . . .**
†The names of a few countries are feminine or plural. Movement to these countries is expressed by **in die: Wir fahren in die Schweiz (Tschechoslowakei, Turkei, U.S.A.).**
‡Remember that when **schon, seit,** or **schon seit** is used to introduce a period of time and the action or situation described is still in progress, the present tense is used (see Chapter 1).
**This sentence is in the passive voice, which is discussed in Chapter 13.

Erich hat dieses Buch *von seiner Tante* bekommen.
Erich received this book from his aunt.

Mein Vater ist gestern *von Hamburg* zurückgekommen.
My father returned from Hamburg yesterday.

Note: **aus** must be used to indicate one's place of origin: **Giselas Vater kommt aus Deutschland.** Notice also that the preposition **von** is not used in the following expressions:

a. with the names of cities, months, and dates

die Stadt München
the city of Munich

der 24. Dezember
the 24th of December

der Monat September
the month of September

b. with units of measure

ein Glas Wasser
a glass of water

ein Bogen Papier
a sheet of paper

eine Tasse Kaffee
a cup of coffee

9. zu   *at (home); to (person's residence or place of work, an event, geographic locations not mentioned by proper name)*

Ich habe leider heute meine Bücher *zu Hause* gelassen.
I unfortunately left my books at home today.

Annegret geht *zu Meyers.*
Annegret is going to the Meyers's (house).

Elisabeth geht heute *zum Zahnarzt.*
Elisabeth is going to the dentist today.

Wir gehen morgen *zu einer Vorlesung (einem Fest).*
We're going to a lecture (a celebration) tomorrow.

Wir gehen morgen *zum Bahnhof (zur Universität, zum Fußballspiel).*
We're going to the train station (university, soccer game) tomorrow.

Contractions	
an + dem → am	in + dem → im
an + das → ans	in + das → ins
auf + das → aufs	von + dem → vom
bei + dem → beim	zu + dem → zum
für + das → fürs	zu + der → zur

Übungen

A. **Ergänzen Sie die folgenden Sätze!** Complete each sentence with the proper form of the word in parentheses.

Zum Beispiel: Albert wohnt bei _____ Eltern. (sein)
Albert wohnt bei seinen Eltern. *lecture hall.*

1. Herr Ohm kommt aus _____ Hörsaal. (dieser)

2. Niemand außer _____ hat die Hausaufgaben gemacht. (er)

3. Bei _____ Professor studieren Sie Germanistik? (welcher)

4. Andrea und Erika waren gestern bei _____ Vorlesung. (die)

5. Das Physikgebäude steht gegenüber _____ Mensa. (die)

6. Wer geht mit _____ in die Bibliothek? (du)

7. Bei _____ Gebäude steht das Labor? (welcher)

8. Wir fahren gern mit _____ Zug. (dieser)

9. Wir gehen nach _____ Unterricht (*class, lesson*) zum Fußballspiel. (der)

10. _____ Lehrerin nach lernen viele deutsche Studenten Englisch. (die)

11. Wir fahren jetzt nach _____ Norden. (der)

12. Wer hat nach _____ gefragt? (ich)

13. Heinz besucht schon seit _____ Jahr die Universität. (ein)

14. Ich habe dieses Geschichtsbuch von _____ Freund bekommen. (mein)

15. Morgen fahren wir zu _____ Buchhandlung. (die)

B. **Ergänzen Sie die folgenden Sätze!** Complete each sentence with an appropriate preposition requiring the dative case. Sometimes an English equivalent has been included to help you in your choice.

Zum Beispiel: Hilde arbeitet nie _____ Hause.
Hilde abeitet nie zu Hause.

1. Anna studiert _____ letztem Dezember Mathematik.

2. Fährst du morgen nach Stuttgart?

3. Ich habe einen wissenschaftlichen Bericht von Einstein gelesen.

4. Morgen gehen wir zu dem Fest, nicht wahr?

5. Ist Herr Simmel Österreicher, oder kommt er aus der Schweiz?

6. Wer war gestern __*bei*__ der Vorlesung?

7. __*Außer*__ mir waren dreißig Studenten bei dem Konzert. (*besides*)

8. Meiner Lehrerin __*nach*__ ist Russisch schwerer als Englisch.

9. Das Labor steht _____ der Mensa.

10. Irene studiert Musik _____ Professor Jungbluth.

C. **Wählen Sie die passende Präposition!** Using a phrase from the following list, write a sentence to describe each picture.

Zum Beispiel: Das Gymnasium ist beim Park.

a. beim Park
b. aus der Schweiz
c. zur Vorlesung
d. beim Lesen
e. zu Hause

f. bei der Vorlesung
g. gegenüber der Buchhandlung
h. nach Hause
i. mit dem Zug
j. nach München

1.

2.

3.

4.

5.

6.

7.

8.

D. **Übersetzen Sie die folgenden Sätze!**

1. Rita, are you going home?
2. Nobody except my sister is interested in this subject.
3. Tonight we'll study (**arbeiten**) at my house.
4. Was Siegfried at the lecture?
5. Miss Altheim comes from Austria.
6. According to the professor, I'm going to get a good grade.
7. Roland has been studying music for five years.
8. Did you receive the report from your friend, Martha?
9. Mrs. Schäfer, would you like a piece of paper?
10. This is a book by Hermann Hesse.
11. Sabine, why are you staying home?
12. Tomorrow we are going to Bonn.
13. I always drink coffee while reading.
14. What stands across from the chemistry building?
15. Did you ask about the job, Hermann?

Prepositions That Take Accusative Objects

The following prepositions always take accusative objects:

1. **bis**   *until; by (time); as far as*

   Ich arbeitete *bis elf Uhr* in der Bibliothek.
   I studied until eleven o'clock in the library.

   Ich muß das Referat *bis nächsten Montag* fertig haben.
   I have to finish the paper by next Monday.

   Helga fuhr mit dem Zug *bis München*.   (Dann mußte sie umsteigen.)
   Helga took the train as far as Munich.   (Then she had to transfer.)

   If the prepositional object is preceded by the definite article, another preposition must be used with **bis**. The second preposition determines the case of the object without changing the meaning.

   Andrea fuhr mit dem Zug *bis in die Schweiz*.
   Andrea took the train as far as Switzerland.

   Die Schulpflicht gilt *bis zum achtzehnten Lebensjahr*.
   School attendance is compulsory up to the age of eighteen.

2. **durch**   *through; by, by means of (also an impersonal force in passive sentences)*

   Wir sind *durch die Mensa* gegangen.
   We went through the student restaurant.

   Die Vorlesung wurde *durch Lärm* gestört.
   The lecture was interrupted by noise.

   Durch viel Arbeit hat er sein Ziel erreicht.
   He reached his goal by working hard (by means of a lot of work).

3. **entlang**   *along*

   Die Kinder gingen *die Straße entlang*.*
   The children walked along the street.

4. **für**   *for*

   Ich muß heute abend *für die Prüfung* pauken.
   I have to cram for the exam tonight.

   Sie hat es *für uns* übersetzt.
   She translated it for us.

   Gretchen, interessierst du dich *für diesen Beruf*?
   Gretchen, are you interested in this profession?

   ---
   *__Entlang__ usually follows its object.

Im Chemielabor

5. **gegen** *against; into; around or about (time)*

Er ist *gegen das Notengeben.*
He is against giving grades.

Der Wagen fuhr *gegen einen Lastwagen.*
The car drove into (against) a truck.

Professor Steinacker liest *gegen zwei Uhr* in Hörsaal 20.
Professor Steinacker is lecturing in room 20 at around two o'clock.

6. **ohne** *without*

Traude is hilflos *ohne ihre Bücher.*
Traude is helpless without her books.

Altes Sprichwort: „*Ohne Fleiß* kein Preis."
An old proverb: "There is no reward without hard work."

7. **um** *around (place); at (time); for (acquisition of something)*

Der Professor ging um *seinen Schreibtisch herum.**
The professor walked around his desk.

---

*With verbs of motion **um** is often reinforced by the separable prefix **herum: Wir gehen (fliegen, reisen, fahren) um die Stadt herum.** We are going (flying, traveling, driving) around the city.

Man hat Blumen *um die Mensa* herum gepflanzt.
They planted flowers around the student restaurant.

In der Regel beginnt der Unterricht *um neun Uhr.*
As a rule, the class begins at nine o'clock.

Spielst du Karten *um Geld?*
Do you play cards for money?

Oskar bat *um drei Bogen Papier.*
Oskar asked for three sheets of paper.

Toni bewirbt sich *um diese Stellung.*
Toni is applying for this job.

8. wider   *against*

Er sprach *wider das Notengeben.*
He spoke against giving grades.*

Übungen

A. **Ergänzen Sie die folgenden Sätze!** Complete each sentence with the proper form of the word in parentheses. Translate each sentence.

Zum Beispiel: Helmut und Marianne sind gerade
durch _____ Hörsaal gegangen. (der)
**Helmut und Marianne sind gerade durch den Hörsaal
gegangen.**
Helmut and Marianne just went through the lecture hall.

1. Der Student lief _____ Haupstraße entlang. (die)

2. Uschi, interessierst du dich für _____ Universität? (diese)

3. Rudi hat mich um _____ Bogen Papier gebeten (ein)

4. Ich will nicht ohne _____ zur Party gehen. (du)

5. Franz hat gegen (wider) _____ Bericht gesprochen. (unser)

6. Wir liefen um _____ Park herum. (der)

7. Der Lastwagen ist gegen _____ Baum gefahren. (ein)

8. Oskar macht sich Sorgen um _____ Noten. (seine)

B. **Ergänzen Sie die folgenden Sätze!** Complete each sentence with an appropriate preposition requiring the accusative case. Sometimes an English equivalent has been included to aid you in your choice.

---

*Wider is only used in formal German; **gegen** is used in either formal or conversational German (see point 5).

Zum Beispiel: Ich warte _____ zehn Uhr auf dich.   (*until*)

Ich warte bis zehn Uhr auf dich.

1. Die Architekten sind _____ das Gebäude

   herumgegangen.   (*around*)

2. Wir müssen diesen Weg _____ laufen.   (*along*)

3. Dieses Bücherregal ist _____ dich.   (*for*)

4. Der Rechtsanwalt hat _____ unsere Pläne gesprochen.   (*against;*

   two possibilities)

5. _____ elf Uhr erwarten wir Professor Rohrbach.   (*around*)

6. Sophia und ihre Schwester sind _____ die Bibliothek

   gegangen.   (*through*)

7. Egon interessiert sich _____ Physik.

8. Kannst du dich _____ meine Pflanzen kümmern, während ich in

   Urlaub bin?

9. Der Wagen ist _____ eine Mauer gefahren.

C. **Wählen Sie die passende Präposition!** Using a phrase from the following list,
write a sentence to describe each picture.

    a.   um ein Buch über Psychologie
    b.   für mich
    c.   ohne meinen Regenschirm
    d.   gegen neun Uhr
    e.   durch das Labor
    f.   gegen einen Baum

1.

2.

3.

4.

5.

6.

D. **Übersetzen Sie die folgenden Sätze!**

1. Is this desk for me?
2. Albrecht is against giving grades.
3. Klara waited until ten o'clock.
4. Marianne is interested in mathematics.
5. At nine o'clock, we are going home.
6. We have to turn in this report by the tenth (**zehnten**) of September.
7. Konrad went without me to Hamburg.

Prepositions That Take Either Dative or Accusative Objects; Adverbs Indicating a Place

Prepositions That Take Either Dative or Accusative Objects

The prepositions **an, auf, hinter, in, neben, über, unter, vor,** and **zwischen** are generally used to express spatial relationships and take either dative or accusative objects. They take dative objects:

---

1. when location or position rather than movement is expressed

Jost und Paula sitzen *in der Mensa.*
Jost and Paula are sitting in the student restaurant.

Der Professor steht oft *an der Tafel.*
The professor often stands at the blackboard.

2. when movement or action within a limited space, with no destination or direction, is expressed

Die Studenten arbeiten heute *im Labor.*
The students are working in the laboratory today.

Professor Hagemeister liest immer nur *in diesem Hörsaal.*
Professor Hagemeister only lectures in this lecture room.

Die neuen Studenten sind den ganzen Tag *in der Bibliothek*
herumgegangen.
The new students walked around the library all day long.

They take accusative objects when movement with a destination or direction is expressed:

Die Studenten sind *ins Labor* gegangen.
The students went into the laboratory.

Professor Hagemeister ist *in diesen Hörsaal* gegangen.
Professor Hagemeister went into this lecture room.

Die neuen Studenten sind *in die Bibliothek* gegangen.
The new students went inside the library.

Der Professor hat sich *an die Tafel* gestellt.
The professor moved next to the blackboard.

The most common uses of these prepositions follow:

1. an   *at, to, on; proximity to objects in a room; contact with a vertical surface (such as a wall or blackboard) or a boundary or border*

Dative	Accusative
Berta sitzt *am Schreibtisch (Fenster).* Berta is sitting *at the desk (window).*	Berta geht *an den Schreibtisch (ans Fenster).* Berta is going to the desk (window).
Die Landkarte hängt *an der Wand.* The map is hanging on the wall.	Der Professor hängt die Landkarte *an die Wand.* The Professor is hanging the map on the wall.
Die Kinder spielen *am Strand.* The children are playing at the beach.	Wir fahren heute *an den Strand.* We're going to the beach today.

2. **auf** upon; on; contact with a horizontal surface (a table top, the floor); at, to; with certain buildings and places (**Bank, Universität, Post,** and a few others)

Dative	Accusative
Das Buch liegt *auf dem Schreibtisch.* The book is lying on the desk.	Otto legt das Buch *auf den Schreibtisch.* Otto is laying the book on the desk.
Wir spielen Fußball *auf dem Rasen.* We're playing soccer on the lawn.	Man darf hier nicht *auf den Rasen gehen.* One isn't allowed to go onto the lawn here.
Fritz ist heute *auf der Bank (Post).* Fritz is at the bank (post office) today.	Fritz geht heute *auf die Bank (Post).* Fritz is going to the bank (post office) today.

3. **hinter** behind; *to the back*

Dative	Accusative
Der Stuhl steht *hinter dem Tisch.* The chair is behind the table.	Monika stellt den Stuhl *hinter den Tisch.* Monika puts the chair behind the table.

4. **in** in; *to; into*

Dative	Accusative
Anna sitzt *im Hörsaal.* Anna is sitting in the lecture hall.	Anna geht jetzt *in den Hörsaal.* Anna is going into the lecture hall now.
Karoline schwamm lange *im Wasser.* Karoline was swimming in the water for a long time.	Karoline ist *ins Wasser* gesprungen. Karoline jumped into the water.

5. **neben** *next to*

Dative	Accusative
Der Mathematiker sitzt *neben dem Physiker.* The mathematician is sitting next to the physicist.	Der Mathematiker setzte sich *neben den Physiker.* The mathematician sat down next to the physicist.
Anneliese und Joachim sprechen miteinander *neben der Buchhandlung.* Anneliese and Joachim are talking to each other next to the bookstore.	

6. über   over; across

Dative

Eine Lampe hängt über dem Tisch.
A lamp is hanging over the table.

Der Hubschrauber flog den ganzen Tag über der Stadt.
The helicopter flew over the city all day.

Accusative

Herr Huber hängt eine Lampe über den Tisch.
Mr. Huber is hanging a lamp over the table.

Der Vogel flog über den See.
The bird flew across the lake.

7. unter   under; among

Dative

Cynthia ist unter dem Baum eingeschlafen.
Cynthia fell asleep under the tree.

Unter den Studenten ist keiner, der Russisch lernt.
No one among the students is learning Russian.

Accusative

Wir haben uns unter den Baum gesetzt.
We sat down under the tree.

Der Professor verteilte Aufsatzthemen unter die Studenten.
The professor distributed essay topics among the students.

8. vor   before; in front; to the front; up to

Dative

Dianas Wagen steht vor der Grundschule.
Diana's car is (standing) in front of the elementary school.

Jürgen und Cornelia treffen sich jeden Tag vor der Bibliothek.
Jürgen and Cornelia meet each other every day in front of the library.

Accusative

Diana fährt ihren Wagen vor die Grundschule.
Diana is driving her car up to the elementary school.

9. zwischen   between

Dative

Das Regal steht zwischen der Lampe und dem Sofa.
The bookcase is between the lamp and the sofa.

Wir liefen zwischen dem Labor und dem Hörsaal hin und her.
We ran back and forth between the lab and the lecture hall.

Accusative

Alex hat das Regal zwischen die Lampe und das Sofa gestellt.
Alex placed the bookcase between the lamp and the sofa.

Adverbs Indicating a Place

In German, the choice of an adverb to indicate a place (*here, there, where, inside,* etc.) depends on whether the adverb describes a location (or movement within a location) or movement toward a destination. This is the same concept that governs the use of the dative or accusative with objects of the prepositions discussed in the preceding section. Compare these examples:

Location	*Destination*
Wo steht die Grundschule? Where is the elementary school?	**Wohin** fahren Sie morgen? Where are you driving tomorrow?
Wo unterrichtet Professor Diel? Where does Professor Diel teach?	**Wohin** laufen die Kinder? Where are the children running?

Wilhelm steht *da* mit Rosemarie.
Wilhelm is standing there with
   Rosemarie.
	Die Rechtsanwältin fliegt Freitag
	   dahin.
	The lawyer is flying there Friday.

Die Mensa ist *da* drüben. The student restaurant is over there.	Ich fahre mit dem Fahrrad *dahin.* I'll go there by bike.
Wir bleiben heute *drinnen.* We're staying indoors today.	Wir gehen jetzt *hinein.* We're going indoors now.

Professor Schneider liest heute
   hier über Philosophie.
Professor Schneider is lecturing here
   on philosophy today.
	Udo, komm *her!* Komm *hierher!*
	Udo, come here. Come right here.

Der Journalist arbeitet heute *zu
   Hause.*
The journalist is working at home
   today.
	Der Journalist ist schon *nach
	   Hause* gefahren.
	The journalist has already gone home.

Xavier und Uschi spielen *draußen.* Xavier and Uschi are playing outside.	Gehen wir jetzt *hinaus.* Let's go outside now.
	Willst du jetzt *hinausgehen?* Do you want to go out(side) now?

	Yvette, komm *heraus* und spiel
	   Fußball mit uns!
	Yvette, come out and play soccer
	   with us.

The adverbs **oben** (*upstairs*), **unten** (*downstairs*), **rechts** (*to or on the right*), **links** (*to or on the left*), **vorne** (*in the front*), and **hinten** (*in the back*) are generally preceded by the preposition **nach** to express movement into a space.

Bruno ist *nach oben (unten)* gegangen.
Bruno went upstairs (downstairs).

Wir müssen jetzt *nach rechts (links)* fahren.
We have to drive to the right (left) now.

Der Professor geht jetzt *nach vorne (hinten)* im Klassenzimmer.
The professor is going to the front (back) of the classroom now.

Übungen

°A. **Ergänzen Sie die folgenden Sätze!** Complete each sentence with an appropriate preposition. Sometimes an English equivalent has been included to aid you in your choice.

1. Gisela, warum stehst du immer _____ dem Fenster? (*three possibilities*)

2. Petra arbeitet oft _____ der Bibliothek.

3. Ich sitze beim Schreiben immer _____ dem Tisch.

4 Fräulein Sommer, legen Sie diese Hefte _____ den Schreibtisch, bitte!

5. Ich muß heute _____ die Post, um einige Briefmarken (*stamps*) zu kaufen.

6. Jost, es klopft. Bitte, geh _____ die Tür!

7. Alex wohnt _____ Herrn Sehmsdorf. (*next to*)

8. Joachim hat den Ball _____ den Baum geworfen.

9. Die Bank steht _____ der Post und dem Bahnhof.

10. _____ meinen Freundinnen ist keine, die Tennis spielt.

11. Wann ist Brigitte _____ die Stadt gefahren?

°B. **Ergänzen Sie die folgenden Sätze!** Complete each sentence with the proper form of the word or words in parentheses.

1. Wir spielen gerne Volleyball an _____ Strand. (*dieser*)

2. Jetzt geht der Professor an _____ Tafel. (*die*)

3. Bitte, stellen Sie die Lampe auf _____. Schreibtisch. (mein)

4. Auf _____ Schreibtisch liegen deine Bücher? (welcher)

5. Mein Wagen steht hinter _____ Mensa. (die)

6. Warum ist Otto hinter _____ Labor gelaufen? (das)

7. Hildegard arbeitet gerne in _____ Bibliothek. (die)

8. Toni, kannst du mich in _____ Stadt bringen? (die)

9. Gerda hat die Lampe neben _____ Regal gestellt. (ihr)

10. Rita wohnt neben _____ Professor. (unser)

11. Dein Kugelschreiber liegt unter _____ Heft. (mein)

12. Stellen Sie bitte den Korb unter _____ Tisch. (dieser)

13. Unter _____ Touristen spricht keiner gut Deutsch. (die)

14. Der Architekt steht vor _____ Haus. (sein)

15. Der Turm steht zwischen _____ Schule

    und _____ Bibliothek. (unsere; die)

C. **Ergänzen Sie die folgenden Sätze!** Complete each sentence with an appropriate preposition and the appropriate form of the word or words in parentheses.

   Zum Beispiel: Ich arbeite _____
   _____ Buchhandlung. (die)
   Ich arbeite in der Buchhandlung.

   1. Paula liegt _____ _____ Sofa. (dieses)

   2. Der Dom steht _____ _____ Park
      und _____ Universität. (der, die)

   3. Inge geht oft _____ _____ Fenster, um
      hinauszuschauen. (das)

   4. _____ _____ Museum ist ein großer Wald. (dieses)

   5. Daniel, leg deine Jacke nicht _____
      _____ Schreibtisch! (mein)

   6. Wann fährst du heute _____ _____ Stadt? (die)

   7. _____ _____ Labor arbeitet Julia? (welches)

   8. Findet die Vorlesung _____ _____ Hörsaal
      statt? (dieses)

D. **Schreiben Sie Sätze!** Rewrite each sentence, replacing the italicized phrases with the appropriate form of the words in parentheses.

Zum Beispiel: Der Professor steht *vor der Tafel.* (da, dahin)
Der Professor steht *da.*

1. Professor Schmidt liest *in einem Hörsaal.* (drinnen, hinein)
2. Elsa und Gerd, kommt sofort *ins Labor!* (hier, hierher)
3. Ich habe meine Bücher *im Garten* gesucht. (draußen, hinaus)
4. Wir gehen heute abend *ins Kino.* (draußen, hinaus)
5. Ich lese oft *in meinem Zimmer.* (zu Hause, nach Hause)

E. **Übersetzen Sie die folgenden Sätze!**

1. Is Mainz on the Rhine?
2. On which wall is the picture?
3. Heidi, lay your jacket on the sofa.
4. Please come into the house, Mrs Unger.
5. Today I have to go to the bank.
6. Helmut is at the post office.
7. Regina, who lives next door to you?
8. The student restaurant is between the laboratory and the library.
9. Who is standing in front of the bookstore?
10. Among the students, there is no one from France.
11. A plane just (**eben**) flew over the lecture hall.
12. Does Otto work in the library?
13. I want to live on the North Sea coast (**Nordseeküste**).
14. Why did you stay home, Mrs. Becker?
15. In summer, I often sit outside in the evening.
16. The Oktoberfest is in Munich. Let's go there!
17. It is raining outside. Rolf, come inside.
18. It is getting late. I'm going home.

F. **Beschreiben Sie die Folgenden Bilder!**

1.　　　　　　　　　　2.

3.

1920 1960 2000

4.

BIBLIOTHEK

5.

6.

7.

8.

BIBLIOTHEK

G. **Schreiben Sie Fragen!** Rewrite your answers for Exercise F as questions using **wo** or **wohin** as appropriate.

Zum Beispiel: Wohin legt Anna das Buch?

Prepositions in Time Expressions; Prepositions Used Figuratively

Prepositions in Time Expressions

The prepositions **in, an,** and **vor** always take the dative in expressions of time.

Im Mai mache ich mein Abitur.
In May, I'll take my Abitur.

In einem Jahre mache ich den Doktor.
In one year, I'll receive my doctorate.

Am Donnerstag habe ich eine Prüfung.
On Thursday, I have a test.

In der Regel mache ich die Hausaufgaben *am Abend.*
As a rule, I do my homework in the evening.

Vor dem Abitur pauken alle Schüler.
All high school students cram before the Abitur.

Vor zwei Monaten habe ich diese Prüfung bestanden.*
Two months ago, I passed that test.

The preposition **über** is always used with the accusative in time expressions.

Edith war *über eine Woche* (lang) in Berlin.
Edith was in Berlin (for) over a week.

---

*Vor is the equivalent of *ago* in English; it should not be confused with **für** (*for*): **Ich fahre für** (or **auf**) **zwei Monate in die Schweiz.** *I'm going to Switzerland for two months.*

Prepositions Used Figuratively

The prepositons **an**, **auf**, **in**, and **über** usually take the accusative case when they are used figuratively.

Herr Jaspers denkt immer *an dieses Thema*.
Mr. Jaspers is always thinking about this topic.

Pamela schreibt oft *an ihre Eltern*.
Pamela often writes to her parents.

Ich warte *auf den Lehrer*.
I'm waiting for the teacher.

Cornelia fährt *auf drei Tage* nach Deutschland.
Cornelia is going to Germany for three days.

Wir freuen uns *auf die Deutschlandreise*.*
We're looking forward to the trip to Germany.

Heinrich ist *in dieses Mädchen* verliebt.
Heinrich is in love with this girl.

Rita schrieb einen Bericht *über das deutsche Schulwesen*.
Rita wrote a report about the German school system.

Übungen

°A. **Ergänzen Sie die folgenden Satze!** Complete each sentence with an appropriate preposition. Translate each sentence.

1. Was machen Sie _____ Sonntag? (im, am, für, auf)

2. Ich fahre _____ vier Tagen nach Berlin. (vor, auf, in, für)

3. _____ zwei Jahren hat er sein Abitur gemacht. (in, für, an, vor)

4. Wir wollen _____ einen Monat in Salzburg bleiben. (über, vor, in, an)

5. Elisabeth und Lotte fliegen _____ zwei Monate nach Wien. (auf, in, an, vor)

B. **Ergänzen Sie die folgenden Sätze!** Complete each sentence with one of the prepositons in parentheses. Compose a similar sentence using the same preposition. Translate both sentences.

Zum Beispiel: Kurt freut sich _____ den Film. (an, für, auf)
Kurt freut sich auf den Film.
Kurt is looking forward to the film.

Ich freue mich auf die Vorlesung.
I am looking forward to the lecture.

---

*Most figurative uses of **auf** express hope or expectation: **Auf Wiedersehen.** *Till we meet again.*

1. Wir müssen einen Bericht _____ dieses Thema schreiben.   (auf, in, an, über)
2. _____ wen warten Sie, Herr Keller?   (auf, über, an)
3. Liselotte ist _____ diesen jungen Mann verliebt.   (auf, für, mit, in)
4. Rainer hofft _____ eine gute Note von Professor Altheim.   (für, auf, in, an)
5. Gabi, du solltest _____ deine Eltern schreiben.   (zu, an, auf)

C. **Übersetzen Sie die folgenden Sätze!**

1. In the summer we always go to Baden Baden.
2. Egon, where are you going on Saturday?
3. Gabi is flying to France in two months.
4. Three years ago I took my Abitur.
5. We were in Berlin for over a month.
6. Pamela and Georg are flying to Freiburg for a week.
7. Did you write about that subject, Miss Pahlow?
8. We are looking forward to your lecture, Professor Grünfeld.
9. In four months, Miss Sperber will receive her doctorate.
10. Manfred and Regina are waiting for a friend in front of the student restaurant.

D. **Interview.** Use a time expression containing the indicated preposition.

1. Wann sind Sie geboren?   (im Jahre, am)
2. Wann haben Sie Ihren Führerschein (*driver's license*) gemacht?   (vor)
3. Wann möchten Sie nach Deutschland fahren?   (in)
4. Wie lange möchten Sie in Deutschland bleiben?   (über)
5. Wie viele Stunden schlafen Sie pro Tag?   (über, unter)
6. Wann haben Sie zuletzt gegessen?   (vor)

Prepositions That Take Genitive Objects; *da*-Compounds; Word Order with Adverbs and Prepositional Phrases

Prepositions That Take Genitive Objects

The following prepositions take genitive objects:

1. (an)statt   *instead of*

   Wir brauchen hier einen Rechtsanwalt *(an)statt eines Ingenieurs.*
   We need a lawyer here instead of an engineer.

2. trotz   *in spite of*

   Trotz seiner guten Noten hat Helmut sein Studium nicht beendet.
   In spite of his good grades, Helmut did not finish his studies.

3. um . . . willen   *for the sake of*

Um Gottes willen, du kannst doch dein Studium jetzt nicht aufgeben!
For heaven's sake, you can't give up your studies now!

Wenn du das nicht *um deinetwillen* machen willst, mach(e) es *um meinetwillen*!*
If you don't want to do it for your own sake, do it for mine!

4. während *during*

Während des Sommers haben wir Ferien.
During the summer, we have vacation.

5. wegen *on account of*

Wegen meines Berufs lerne ich viele Geschäftsleute kennen.
On account of my occupation, I meet a lot of business people.

*Deinetwegen** bin ich Ingenieur und nicht Musiker geworden.
On account of you, I became an engineer and not a musician.

Another group of prepositions, less commonly used, also requires genitive objects: **außerhalb** (*outside of, beyond*), **innerhalb** (*inside of, within*), **oberhalb** (*above, overlooking*), **unterhalb** (*below, at the base of*), **diesseits** (*on this side of*), and **jenseits** (*on the other side of*).

Der Philosophieprofessor wohnt *außerhalb der Stadt.*
The philosophy professor lives outside of town.

Oberhalb des Waldes steht ein altes Schloß.
Overlooking the woods there stands an old castle.

In meinem Bücherregal stehen die Bücher über Geologie *oberhalb der Bücher über Architektur.*
In my bookcase, the books about geology are above the books about architecture.

Unterhalb der Tafel ist nicht genug Platz für deinen Schreibtisch.
Below the blackboard there isn't enough room for your desk.

Salzburg liegt *diesseits (jenseits) des Gebirges.*
Salzburg lies on this side (on the other side) of the mountain range.

Ein Schritt weiter _____

The four common prepositions **während**, **wegen**, **trotz**, and **(an)statt** often take the dative case in conversational German—for example: **Während dem Sommer gehe ich nicht in die Schule.** The other prepositions that require the genitive in formal German are generally avoided in conversation or are used in conjunction with the preposition **von**, which takes the dative case: **Salzburg liegt diesseits vom Gebirge.**

---

*For more about **um meinetwillen (deinetwegen)**, see Chapter 10.

da-Compounds

Most prepositions that take accusative or dative objects can form compounds with **da-**. Here are the most common:

Ich lese beim Essen.
I read while eating.

Ich lese *dabei.**
I read while doing that.

Ich habe viel durch das
    Studium gelernt.
I learned a lot through my studies.

Ich habe viel *dadurch*
    gelernt.
I learned a lot through them.

Hans interessiert sich für
    Journalismus.
Hans is interested in journalism.

Er interessiert sich
    dafür.
He is interested in it.

Die Bank steht hinter der
    Buchhandlung.
The bank is behind the bookstore.

Die Bank steht *dahinter.*
The bank is behind it.

Udo fährt nie mit dem Bus.
Udo never takes the bus.

Udo fährt nie *damit.*
Udo never takes it.

Das Spiel beginnt nach dem
    Unterricht.
The game begins after (the) class.

Das Spiel beginnt *danach.*
The game begins after it.

Das Labor steht neben dem
    Physikgebäude.
The laboratory is next to the physics
    building.

Das Labor steht *daneben.*
The laboratory is next to it.

Vicki weiß nichts von der Stellung.
Vicki knows nothing about the job.

Vicki weiß nichts *davon.*
Vicki knows nothing about it.

Das Museum steht vor der
    Universität.
The museum is in front of the university.

Das Museum steht *davor.*
The museum is in front of it.

Die Bank steht zwischen der Post
    und dem Rathaus.
The bank is between the post office and
    the town hall.

Die Bank steht *dazwischen.*
The bank is between them.

A **da**-compound is usually used instead of a preposition followed by a pronoun object when the pronoun refers to something inanimate. **Da**-compounds are never used to refer to people. They can refer to several inanimate objects or to an abstraction or concept:

---

*Prepositions are usually stressed in **da**-compounds: **dabéi, dadúrch**.

Weißt du etwas von Computern? —Nein, ich weiß leider nichts
    davon.
Do you know anything about computers? —No, unfortunately I know nothing
    about them.

Warum kommst du nicht mit? —Meine Eltern sind *dagegen*.
Why don't you come along? —My parents are against it.

Das Abitur ist schwer. —*Darüber* kann man nicht streiten!
The Abitur is hard. —No one can argue about that!

If the preposition that forms the **da**-compound begins with a vowel, **dar-**
rather than **da-** is prefixed to it.

Eine Landkarte hängt an der Wand.   Eine Landkarte hängt *daran*.
A map is hanging on the wall.   A map is hanging on it.

Ich freue mich auf mein Studium.   Ich freue mich *darauf*.
I'm looking forward to my studies.   I'm looking forward to them.

Er hat ein Buch über deutsche   Er hat *darüber* geschrieben.
    Literatur geschrieben.   He wrote about it.
He wrote a book about German literature.

Ein Schritt weiter

Prepositions that require genitive objects do not form **da**-compounds; however, the
following adverbs are close equivalents to **da**-compounds:

deshalb, deswegen   trotzdem   währenddessen   stattdessen
for this reason   in spite of this during this time   instead of this

Da-compounds are often used to introduce an infinitive and its modifiers
as well as **daß**-clauses. Compare the following:

Ich freue mich *auf die*   Ich freue mich *darauf*, zur
    Vorlesung.   Vorlesung zu gehen.
I'm looking forward to the lecture.   I'm looking forward to going to the
                                          lecture.

Pamela interessiert sich *für*   *Pamela interessiert sich dafür*,
    Deutsch.   Deutsch zu studieren.
Pamela is interested in German.   Pamela is interested in studying German.

Ich freue mich *über* deine neue   Ich freue mich *darüber*, daß du eine
    Stellung.   neue Stellung hast.
I'm happy about your new job.   I'm happy that you have a new job.

Word Order with Adverbs and Prepositional Phrases

Adverbs

Adverbs indicating time may either precede or follow any direct or indirect object noun.

Adverb
of time   *I.O. noun*   *D.O. noun*

Die Studentin hat gestern dem Professor die Arbeit gegeben.
The student gave the professor the paper yesterday.

I.O. noun   *Adverb*
of time   *D.O. noun*

Die Studentin hat dem Professor gestern die Arbeit gegeben.

Adverbs of manner and place follow adverbs of time and object nouns in this order:

Object noun
Adverb of time   *Adverb of manner*   *Adverb of place*

Adverb   *Object*   *Adverb of*   *Adverb*
of time   *noun*   *manner*   *of place*

Wir beobachten abends die Mannschaft gewöhnlich dort.
We usually watch the team there in the evening.

Object   *Adverb*   *Adverb of*   *Adverb*
noun   *of time*   *manner*   *of place*

Wir beobachten die Mannschaft abends gewöhnlich dort.

Prepositional Phrases

Prepositional phrases generally follow adverbs. The order of prepositional phrases is the same as that of adverbs.

Adverb ————————————— *Prepositional phrases*
        Time   *Manner*   *Place*

Helga fuhr gestern nach dem Unterricht mit dem Bus nach Hause.
Helga went home by bus yesterday after class.

Study hint: The word TEMPO is a mnemonic device for remembering the order *time* + *manner* + *place*.

Übungen

A. **Ergänzen Sie die folgenden Sätze!** Complete each sentence with the appropriate preposition requiring the genitive case: **während, wegen, trotz, statt, jenseits, um . . . willen**.

1. _____ eines Volkswagens hat Cornelia einen Mercedes gekauft.

2. _____ meines kleinen Bruders muß ich heute abend zu Hause bleiben.

3. Wir haben _____ des Wochenendes wenig Zeit zum lernen.

4. Könnten Sie mit Professor Gehler _____ unsret _____ sprechen?

5. _____ dieses Parks ist das Hauptgebäude (*main building*) der Universität.

°B. **Ergänzen Sie die folgenden Sätze!** Complete each sentence with the proper form of the word in parentheses.

1. Während _____ Semesterferien arbeite ich nicht so oft in der Bibliothek.   (die)

2. Trotz _____ Schnees fahren wir zum Labor.   (dieser)

3. Ich habe mein Geschichtsbuch statt _____ Psychologiebuchs mitgebracht.   (mein)

4. Wir müssen wegen _____ Examens pauken.   (unser)

5. Außerhalb _____ Stadt liegt ein großer Park.   (die)

6. Jenseits _____ Rheins steht der Kölner Dom.   (der)

7. Diesseits _____ Universität stehen viele Häuser.   (die)

C. **Beantworten Sie die folgenden Fragen!** Use **da**-compounds or personal pronouns as appropriate.

Zum Beispiel: Schreibst du immer mit dem Kugelschreiber?
Ja, ich schreibe immer *damit*.

Hast du mit Gisela gesprochen?
Ja, ich habe *mit ihr* gesprochen.

1. Denkst du oft an die Prüfungen?
2. Hat sie durch seine Briefe viel über ihn erfahren?
3. Hat Berta einen Brief an Roswitha geschrieben?
4. Was macht ihr nach der Vorlesung?
5. Haben die Studenten über diese Themen gesprochen?
6. Liegt mein Bericht unter deinem Heft?
7. Hast du dieses Paket von deinen Eltern bekommen?
8. Freuen sich Hartmut und Günter auf unsere Party?
9. Steht die Bibliothek zwischen dem Labor und der Mensa?

D. **Bilden Sie Sätze!** Rearrange the words to form sentences.

Zum Beispiel: Heidi / in die Stadt / morgen / nicht / mit dem Bus / fährt
Heidi fährt morgen nicht mit dem Bus in die Stadt.

1. Heinrich / den Wagen / gestern / nicht / hat / gekauft
2. Ute / oft / geht / ins Kino / mit Udo
3. wir / nach dem Unterricht / oft / gehen / ins Gasthaus
4. ich / nicht / gehe / morgen / sondern übermorgen / zur Vorlesung
5. Peter / die Hausaufgaben / gemacht / hat / nicht
6. warum / nicht / Toni / mit dem Zug / fährt?

E. **Übersetzen Sie die folgenden Sätze!**
1. In spite of his parents, Jürgen is studying politics.
2. Why did you tell your sister instead of your brother, Michael?
3. Edith has to cram on account of her exam.
4. I often study in the library because I live next to it.
5. Mr. and Mrs. Jacobi, where are you going on vacation?
6. Wolfgang, as far as I'm concerned (**wegen**) you can stay home if you want.
7. On the other side of this university is (lies) a park.
8. Miss Lisband, please speak to the professor for our sake.
9. Salzburg lies on this side of the Alps.
10. Vicki, is my notebook on your books? —No, it is under them.
11. I take (**fahren mit**) the bus, but my sister never takes it.
12. When is the lecture? I'm waiting for it.
13. Mr. Herder, do you know Mrs. Niese? I received a letter from her.
14. Erika and Marie-Luise, do you know the bookstore? My car is behind it.
15. Dieter, did you read those books? —Yes, and I wrote a report about them.
16. Claudia, are you visiting your friends in Germany? —Yes, and I'm looking forward to it.
17. I am not going to the post office tomorrow.
18. Kai, didn't you see Marina yesterday?
19. We didn't eat in the student restaurant today.

F. **Beschreiben Sie Ihr Zimmer!** Describe your room in ten sentences using at least five **da**-compounds.

   Zum Beispiel: **In der Ecke steht die Stereoanlage.** *Daneben* **steht eine Lampe.**

   You may wish to use some of the following vocabulary in your paragraph (in addition to words you already know):

der Aschenbecher (-) ashtray	die Stereoanlage (-n) stereo set	der Teppich (-e) rug
der Papierkorb (¨e) wastebasket	die Vase (-n) vase	der Sessel (-) armchair

Rückblick

A. **Zur Wiederholung. Übersetzen Sie die folgenden Sätze!**

   1. Miss Weden, are you going to the lecture hall now?
   2. Albert and Uschi, were you at the lecture last night?
   3. The library is across from the physics building.

4. Rita, please don't go to the party tomorrow without me.
5. Does David work in the bookstore?
6. Why did Miss Böhm go to the bank by bus?
7. I went there at three o'clock.
8. The children are playing inside because of the rain.
9. We are flying to Munich for a week.
10. The class is supposed to write a report on this subject.
11. Where are you going in winter, Mr. and Mrs. Bieberbach?
12. Three years ago, I took the Abitur.
13. Heinz, are you waiting for the professor?
14. I am looking forward to my trip to Austria.
15. We stayed home on account of the weather.
16. Klara, why did you buy a pencil instead of a ballpoint pen (**Kugelschreiber**)?
17. We are going to a restaurant. After that, we are going to the show.
18. Frank, I gave you my pencil. What did you do with it?

B. **Zur Gesamtwiederholung. Übersetzen Sie die folgenden Sätze!**

1. Walter says that he will do his homework in the library.   (Chapter 5)
2. Gudrun, may I go with you to the bank?
3. We don't have to be at the lecture today.
4. Gertrud, why did you contradict the professor?   (Chapter 6)
5. Toni and Hans, turn out the lights in the library.
6. Mr. Eberhard, did you visit the new library next to the old physics building? (Chapter 7)
7. Many German students are interested in American films.
8. Miss Steinhauer, if I were you, I would not give up my studies.   (Chapter 8)
9. Vicki, you look tired. You shouldn't have crammed for the test last night.
10. The professor said that German literature is difficult to read.   (Chapter 9)
11. Mrs. Ritter claimed that all the students passed the exam.
12. Konrad, did you write that report yourself or did someone help you? (Chapter 10)
13. I'm worried about the German test (**Deutschprüfung**). I have to pass it.

12
Freizeit und Sport

Am Schwimmbad

Interrogative Pronouns; the Interrogatives *welcher* and *was für (ein)*

Relative Pronouns

Demonstrative Pronouns

Indefinite Pronouns and Adjectives

Wortschatz

das Autorennen (-) car race, car racing

der Ball (-̈e) ball

der Berufsspieler (-), die Berufsspielerin (-nen) professional player

die Eintrittskarte (-n) ticket

der Eisläufer (-), die Eisläuferin (-nen) ice skater

der Federball (-̈e)† badminton, birdie

der Fußballplatz (-̈e) soccer field

der Korbball (-̈e)† basketball

der Läufer (-), die Läuferin (-nen) runner

die Mannschaft (-en) team

das Netz (-e) net

das Pferderennen (-) horse race, horse racing

der Rekord (-e) sports record; **einen Rekord brechen** to break a record

das Rennen (-) race, racing

(das) Schach chess

der Schiedsrichter (-), die Schiedsrichterin (-nen) referee

der Schläger (-) racket

der Schuß (-̈sse) shot

das Schwimmbad (-̈er) swimming pool

die Skier *pl.* skis; **das Paar Skier** pair of skis

der Skiläufer (-), die Skiläuferin (-nen) skier

die Sportart (-en) type of sport

die Sporthalle (-n) gymnasium

der Sportler (-), die Sportlerin (-nen) athlete

die Sportveranstaltung (-en) sports event

das Stadion (-dien) stadium

der Tennisplatz (-̈e) tennis court

(das) Tischtennis table tennis

der Trainer (-), die Trainerin (-nen) coach

---

†When the article is used, **der Ball** refers to the ball itself. In referring to the game, no article is used: **Ich spiele Federball (Fußball, etc.).**

das Turnier (-e) tournament
der Verein (-e) club
der Volleyball (-̈e)† volleyball

der Wettkampf (-̈e) competition, meet
das Tor (-e) goal; **ein Tor schießen*** to score a goal

aus · spannen to relax
reiten* to ride (horses)
segeln to sail

ski · laufen* to ski
trainieren to train
üben to practice

A. *Find the word that does not belong.*

1. Wettkampf, Schwimmbad, Turnier, Rennen
2. Skier, Eisläufer, Sportler, Fußballspieler
3. Volleyball, Tennis, Segeln, Tischtennis
4. Schiedsrichter, Berufsspieler, Trainer, Schuß
5. Stadion, Tor, Sporthalle, Tennisplatz
6. Eintrittskarte, Klub, Verein, Mannschaft
7. Ball, Schläger, Federball, Schach
8. Autorennen, Pferderennen, Rekord, Marathonrennen
9. Paar Skier, Schläger, Netz, Läufer

B. *Complete the sentences.*

1. Ich _____ jedes Wochenende mit meinem Boot auf dem See.

2. Toni Sailer war einmal ein berühmter _____. Jetzt hat er eine

   Skischule und tritt manchmal im Fernsehen auf.

3. Ich gehe oft _____ mit meiner Freundin; sie hat ihr eigenes Pferd.

4. Wenn du an der Olympiade (*olympic games*) teilnehmen willst, mußt du

   jeden Tag zum Training kommen und fleißig _____, Angelika.

5. Immer dieser Streß! Ich wünschte, ich könnte einmal garnichts tun und

   richtig _____.

6. Die Eisläuferin _____ ihre Figuren immer und immer wieder, bis

   sie perfekt waren.

7. Thorsten hat ein Tor _____.

8. Man spielt Fußball auf einem _____.

9. Unsere Mannschaft hat beim _____ gewonnen; wir haben zehn

   Körbe geworfen.

---

*Verbs marked with an asterisk are strong verbs; see the appendix for principal parts of strong verbs.

C. *Answer the following questions.*

C. *Answer the following questions.*

1. Treiben Sie Sport? Welchen Sport oder welche Sportarten treiben Sie?
2. Glauben Sie, daß jeder Mensch Sport treiben sollte, um gesund zu bleiben?
3. Was halten Sie vom Berufssport? Glauben Sie, daß es gute Sportler gibt, die noch Amateure sind?
4. Wann waren Sie zuletzt auf einer Sportveranstaltung? Wo war diese Veranstaltung?
5. Gehören Sie zu einer Mannschaft oder zu einem Sportverein?
6. Gehen Sie manchmal zu einem Wettkampf oder einem Turnier?
7. Welchen Sport finden Sie langweilig? Welchen Sport finden Sie sehr spannend (*exciting*)?
8. In welchem Sport würden Sie gerne einen Rekord brechen, wenn Sie könnten?
9. Welche Sportart möchten Sie gerne einmal ausprobieren (*try*)?
10. Gehen Sie oft skilaufen?

Interrogative Pronouns; the Interrogatives *welcher* and *was für (ein)*

Interrogative Pronoun *wer*

The declension of **wer** is illustrated in the following examples:

Nominative: Wer hat ein Tor geschossen?
Who scored a goal?

Accusative: Wen has du zum Stadion gebracht?
Whom did you bring to the stadium?

Dative: Wem hast du deinen Schläger verkauft?
To whom did you sell your racket?

Genitive: Wessen Mannschaft übt jetzt in der Sporthalle?
Whose team is practicing in the gymnasium now?

If the interrogative pronoun **wer** is the object of a preposition, it must be in the appropriate case:

Für *wen* ist dieser Brief?   (accusative)
For whom is this letter? (Who is this letter for?)

Mit *wem* gehen Sie Skilaufen?   (dative)
With whom are you going skiing? (Who are you going skiing with?)

In conversational English a preposition governing an interrogative pronoun is usually moved to the end of the clause; this is not possible in German:

> **Für wen ist dieser Brief?**
> *Who* is this letter *for?*   (conversational English)
> *For whom* is this letter?   (formal English)

Interrogative Pronoun *was*

The form **was** is invariable and is used only in the nominative and accusative cases.*

> **Was ist mit dem Sportler geschehen?**   (nominative)
> What happened to the athlete?

> **Was hat der Schiedsrichter gesagt?**   (accusative)
> What did the referee (umpire) say?

When preceded by a preposition, **was** is usually reduced to the prefix **wo-** and is attached to the preposition.

> **Wodurch wird man eigentlich ein guter Sportler?   —Durch Talent und Training.**
> By what means does one become a good athlete?   —By means of talent and training.

> **Wofür brauchen Sie diesen Ball?   —Für das Korbballspiel.**
> What do you need that ball for?   —For the basketball game.

> **Wogegen ist der Volleyballspieler gelaufen?   —Gegen das Netz.**
> What did the volleyball player run into (against)?   —Into the net.

> **Wohinter ist der Federballplatz?   —Hinter dem Schwimmbad.**
> What is the badminton court behind?   —Behind the swimming pool.

> **Womit spielt Ilse Tennis?   —Mit einem Tennisschläger.**
> What is Ilse playing tennis with?   —With a tennis racket.

> **Wonach suchen Sie?   —Nach meiner Eintrittskarte.**
> What are you looking for?   For my ticket.

If the preposition begins with a vowel, the compound begins with **wor-**.

> **Woran denkst du?   —An das nächste Autorennen.**
> What are you thinking about?   —About the next auto race.

> **Worauf wartet ihr?   —Auf den Spielbeginn.**
> What are you waiting for?   —For the start of the game.

---

*The genitive form **wes** occurs only in combination with a few prepositions to form adverbs: **weshalb, weswegen** *why, for what purpose.*

Woraus ist dieser Schläger?   —Aus Holz.
What is this racket made of?   —Of wood.

Worüber sprechen die Sportlerinnen?   —Über Vitamine und Hormone.
What are the athletes talking about?   —About vitamins and hormones.

Worum bittet der neue Spieler?   —Um einen neuen Tischtennisball.
What is the new player asking for?   —For a new table-tennis ball.

In conversational German, these contractions are not always made: *Über was* sprechen die Sportlerinnen?

Wer and *was* Used with *sein*

In German as in English, **wer** and **was** used as subjects of a sentence take a singular verb.

Wer hier *spielt* Volleyball?
Who here plays volleyball?

Was ist das?
What is that?

With the verb **sein**, however, the verb can occur in the plural, just as it can with *to be* in English.

Wer *sind* diese Berufsspieler?
Who are these pros (professional players)?

Was sind die Dinge da?   —Das sind Schachfiguren.
What are those things?   —Those are chess pieces.

The Interrogatives *welcher* and *was für (ein)*

The interrogative adjective **welcher** must agree with the noun it modifies in gender, number, and case as does any other adjective. Because it is a **der**-word, all adjectives following it must take weak endings.

Welches neue Fahrrad gehört dir?   —Das rote da gehört mir.
Which new bike belongs to you?   —That red one belongs to me.

As an interrogative pronoun, **welcher** agrees with its antecedent in gender.

Wir haben verschiedene Schläger. *Welchen* möchten Sie gebrauchen?
We have various rackets. Which one would you like to use?

The phrase **was für (ein)** functions as an interrogative adjective. For this reason **für** does not function as a preposition and has no effect on the case of the following noun.

Was für ein Spielplatz ist das?   (subject)
What kind of a playing field (court) is that?

Was für einen Ball hast du gekauft?   (object)
What kind of a ball did you buy?

Both **welcher** and **was für** can be used in exclamations, although **was für** is much more common.

Was für ein herrlicher Schuß!
What a magnificent shot!

Welch ein schönes Tor! (Welch schönes Tor!)
What a beautiful goal!

Übungen

°A. **Bilden Sie Fragen über Leute!** Form questions by replacing the italicized words and phrases with the proper form of **wer**.

Zum Beispiel: *Mein Bruder* hat heute ein Autorennen gewonnen.
Wer hat heute ein Autorennen gewonnen?

Michael hat vorgestern *einige Freunde* zum Fußballspiel mitgenommen.
Wen hat Michael vorgestern zum Fußballspiel mitgenommen?

Herr Schneider hat gestern mit *Frau Berger* Tischtennis gespielt.
Mit wem hat Herr Schneider gestern Tischtennis gespielt?

Das ist *Annas* Eintrittskarte.
Wessen Eintrittskarte ist das?

1. Die jüngste Rekordbrecherin war *die Schwimmerin Gertrude Caroline Ederle*.
2. Ruth hat *den Sportlern* die Sporthalle gezeigt.
3. *Brasiliens* Mannschaft gewinnt sehr oft.
4. Gestern hat Jürgen *einen Berufsspieler* auf dem Tennisplatz kennengelernt.
5. Marie wartet auf *den neuen Schiedsrichter.*
6. Der junge Läufer denkt oft an *sein nächstes Marathonrennen*.
7. Diese Eisläuferin interessiert sich für *Dieter*.
8. Der Schiedsrichter hat *Karl* den Ball gegeben.

°B. **Bilden Sie Fragen über Dinge!** Form questions by replacing the italicized phrases with the proper **wo**-compound.

Zum Beispiel: Wir fahren *mit dem Bus* zum Stadion.
Womit fahren wir zum Stadion?

1. Anneliese hat lange *über das Schachspiel* gesprochen.
2. Ihr habt gestern *mit dem Ball* im Park gespielt.
3. Du mußt *auf den Spielbeginn* warten.

4. Richart läuft jeden Tag *durch den kleinen Park*.
5. Michael interessiert sich *für amerikanischen Fußball*.
6. Hans denkt immer *nur ans Segeln*.

°C. **Bilden Sie Fragen mit *welcher*!** Be sure to use the proper endings on following adjectives.

Zum Beispiel: Der neue Schläger gehört mir.
Welcher neue Schläger gehört dir?

Wir sprechen mit dem brasilianischen Fußballspieler.
Mit welchem brasilianischen Fußballspieler sprecht ihr?

1. Der alte Volleyball gehört Gabi.
2. Ich denke an das herrliche Tennisspiel.
3. Wir haben mit der jungen Eisläuferin gesprochen.
4. Wir interessieren uns für dieses neue Hobby.
5. Ich habe heute den deutschen Schiedsrichter gesehen.
6. Wir gehen jetzt in das neue Schwimmbad.

°D. **Bilden Sie Fragen mit *was für*!**

Zum Beispiel: Ein kaputter Schläger liegt auf dem Tennisplatz.
Was für ein Schläger liegt auf dem Tennisplatz?

Wir spielen mit neuen Tennisbällen.
Mit was für Tennisbällen spielt ihr?

1. Ich habe blaue Tennisschuhe gekauft.
2. Wir haben einen schönen Fußballplatz gefunden.
3. Wir haben einen interessanten Wettkampt gesehen.
4. Max hat einen teuren Fußball verloren.
5. Wir gehören einem kleinen Sportverein an.

°E. **Bilden Sie Ausrufe mit *welcher* und *was für*!**

Zum Beispiel: Das ist ein starker Sportler.
Welch ein starker Sportler!
Was für ein starker Sportler!

1. Sie ist eine herrliche Eisläuferin.
2. Er ist ein dummer Schiedsrichter.
3. Das ist ein langer Schuß.
4. Das ist ein großer Ball.
5. Das ist ein schwerer Schläger.
6. Das ist ein interessantes Hobby.
7. Das ist ein spannender Wettkampf.

F. **Übersetzen Sie die folgenden Sätze!**

1. Who did you play tennis with yesterday, Edith?
2. Miss Wendt, what did you talk about at the party?

3. Heinrich, who did you bring to the game? *wen hast du zum Spiel mitgebracht*
4. Tina and Kurt, what kind of rackets do you play with? *Mit welchen Schlägen*
5. Mr. Kropp, we have two tennis courts. Which one do you want?
6. What a small stadium! *das Stadion*

G. **Fragen über Sport!** Ask a classmate questions about sports, based on the following facts.

Zum Beispiel: Eine Fußballmannschaft besteht *aus elf Spielern.*
Woraus besteht eine Fußballmannschaft?

Skilaufen ist *ein Wintersport.*
Was für ein Sport ist Skilaufen?

Jeder Berufsspieler muß monatelang hart trainieren.
Wer muß monatelang hart trainieren?

1. Hockey spielt man meistens *auf dem Eis.*
2. Handball ist *ein Hallensport (indoor sport).*
3. Die meisten Schläger bestehen *aus Holz.*
4. Viele Spieler ärgern sich *(become angry) über den Schiedsrichter.*
5. Schlittschuhlaufen ist *ein Wintersport.*
6. Man spielt Schach *auf einem Schachbrett (chessboard).*
7. *Volleyball* spielt man oft am Strand.
8. Der Lieblingssport *der meisten Amerikaner* ist amerikanischer Fußball.
9. *Im Boxen* war Joe Louis ganz groß.
10. Segeln ist *ein Wassersport.*

Now ask a classmate questions about your own favorite sports.

Relative Pronouns

Der, das, die

In the sentences **Das ist der Rennwagen, den Hans gekauft hat** (*This is the race car that Hans bought*), **den** is a relative pronoun; it refers to **der Rennwagen** and relates the second clause to the first clause. Sentences with relative pronouns can be viewed as two independent sentences that have been combined:

Ich habe *das* Mädchen
kennengelernt. Sie sprechen }
von *dem* Mädchen.

Ich habe *das* Mädchen
kennengelernt, von *dem* Sie
sprechen.
I met the girl (that) you are talking about.

Wo wohnt *der* Trainer? Fritz hat ⎱
  dem Trainer geholfen. ⎰

Wo wohnt *der* Trainer, *dem* Fritz
  geholfen hat?
Where does the coach who Fritz
  helped live?

Das ist *der* Sportler. *Der* ⎱
  Sportler hat den Wettkampf ⎰
  gewonnen.

Das ist *der* Sportler, *der* den
  Wettkampf gewonnen hat.
That is the athlete who won the
  competition.

The clause that contains the relative pronoun (called a relative clause) is a subordinate clause: it cannot stand alone. For this reason it is set off by a comma, and the conjugated verb appears at the end. The relative clause closely follows its antecedent (the noun the relative pronoun replaces). The relative pronoun must agree with the noun it replaces in gender and number: if the noun is feminine singular, the relative pronoun must also be feminine singular; if the noun is plural, the relative pronoun must also be plural. The case of the relative pronoun is determined by its function in its clause (subject, accusative object, dative object, etc.) and not by the case of the noun to which it refers. Here is how the relative pronouns **der**, **das**, and **die** are declined:

	Masculine	Neuter	Feminine	Plural
Nominative	der	das	die	die
Accusative	den	das	die	die
Dative	dem	dem	der	denen
Genitive	dessen	dessen	deren	deren

1. Nominative

   Das ist der Sportler, *der* den Wettkampf gewonnen hat.   (masculine).
   Das ist das Mädchen, *das* den Wettkampf gewonnen hat.   (neuter)
   Das ist die Sportlerin, *die* den Wettkampf gewonnen hat.   (feminine)
   Das sind die Sportler, *die* den Wettkampf gewonnen haben.   (plural)

2. Accusative

   Das ist der Sportler, *den* ich gestern kennengelernt habe.   (masculine)
   Das ist das Mädchen, *das* ich gestern kennengelernt habe.   (neuter)
   Das ist die Sportlerin, *die* ich gestern kennengelernt habe.   (feminine)
   Das sind die Sportler, *die* ich gestern kennengelernt habe.   (plural)

3. Dative

   Das ist der Sportler, *dem* ich gestern geholfen habe.   (masculine)
   Das ist das Mädchen, *dem* ich gestern geholfen habe.   (neuter)

Das ist die Sportlerin, *der* ich gestern geholfen habe.   (feminine)
Das sind die Sportler, *denen* ich gestern geholfen habe.   (plural)

4. Genitive

Das ist der Sportler, *dessen* Sportverein den Wettkampf gewonnen
    hat.   (masculine)
Das ist das Mädchen, *dessen* Sportverein den Wettkampf gewonnen
    hat.   (neuter)
Das ist die Sportlerin, *deren* Sportverein den Wettkampf gewonnen
    hat.   (feminine)
Das sind die Sportler, *deren* Sportverein den Wettkampf gewonnen
    hat.   (plural)

Notice that the relative pronouns are declined similarly to the definite article (discussed in Chapter 3), except that the dative plural is **denen**, not **den**,
and that there are two genitive forms to express *whose*: **dessen** for masculine or neuter antecedents and **deren** for feminine or plural antecedents:

Antecedent	*Relative clause*
Der Mann,	*dessen* Skier ich gekauft habe, heißt Max Schmidt. (masculine)
The man	whose skis I bought is called Max Schmidt.
Das Mädchen,	*dessen* Tante hier arbeitet, ist Eisläuferin. (neuter)
The girl	whose aunt works here is an iceskater.
Die Frau,	*deren* Sohn Trainer wird, ist Journalistin. (feminine)
The woman	whose son is becoming a coach is a journalist.
Die Kinder,	*deren* Vater aus Mexiko kommt, sprechen gut Spanisch. (plural)
The children	whose father is from Mexico speak Spanish well.

In English, the relative pronoun is often omitted, but this is not possible in
German.

Hast du die Skier gesehen, *die* ich gekauft habe?
Have you seen the skis (that) I bought?

A preposition governing a relative pronoun often occurs at the end of the
clause in English, especially if the relative pronoun is omitted; this cannot
be done in German.

Hast du die Skier gesehen, über *die* wir gesprochen haben?
Did you see the skis we were talking *about*?

Wo-compounds are often substituted for a preposition and a following relative pronoun if the antecedent is a thing, not a person. The antecedent is usually indefinite.

Wo ist der rote Ball, mit dem wir gespielt haben?   (definite antecedent)
Where is the red ball with which we were playing?

Gibt es hier ein Spiel, *womit* (mit dem) ich spielen kann?   (indefinite antecedent)
Is there a game here I can play with?

Wer and *Was*

1. If there is no antecedent noun (or personal pronoun), the relative pronoun **wer** is used to refer to a person and **was** is used to refer to a thing or concept.

    Wer die meisten Spiele gewinnt, bekommt den Preis.
    Whoever wins the most games gets the prize.

    Wer (auch immer) den Rekord bricht, wird berühmt.*
    No matter who breaks the record, he will become famous.

    Alles, *was* Helga wollte, war zu teuer.
    Everything that Helga wanted was too expensive.

    Nichts, *was* Hans las, hat ihn interessiert.
    Nothing that Hans read interested him.

2. **Was** is also used to refer to an antecedent that is a superlative adjective used as a neuter noun.

    Das ist *das Schwerste, was* ich je gemacht habe.[†]
    That is the most difficult thing I have ever done.

    Das ist *das Interessanteste, was* ich je beim Wandern erlebt habe.
    That is the most interesting thing that I have ever experienced while hiking.

3. If the antecedent is an entire clause, **was** is used, meaning *which,* or *something which.*

    Meine Freunde kommen auch zum Fußballplatz, *was* mich sehr freut.
    My friends are coming to the soccer field, too, (something) which makes
      me happy.

    Diese Tennisspielerin interessiert sich auch für Mathematik,
      was ihren Eltern sehr gefällt.
    This tennis player is also interested in mathematics (something) which pleases
      her parents greatly.

---

*__Auch immer__ or **immer** are often added for emphasis.
[†]Such forms are often equivalent to phrases in English containing the word *thing.*

Ein Schiwettlauf in einem bayerischen Dorf

Übungen

°A. **Verbinden Sie die zwei Sätze!** Form relative clauses by joining the two sentences. Translate the new sentence.

Zum Beispiel: Ich habe *den Trainer* kennengelernt. *Der Trainer* arbeitet an unserer Universität.
Ich habe den Trainer kennengelernt, der an unserer Universität arbeitet.
I met the coach who works at our university.

Ist das *die Skiläuferin*? Du hast mit *der Skiläuferin* gesprochen.
Ist das die Skiläuferin, mit der du gesprochen hast?
Is that the skier you talked to (to whom you talked)?

Der Tennisplatz ist mitten im Park. Wir haben *auf dem Tennisplatz* gespielt.
Der Tennisplatz, auf dem wir gespielt haben, ist mitten im Park.
The tennis court we played on (on which we played) is in the middle of the park.

1. Kennst du den Eisläufer? Der Eisläufer kommt aus der Schweiz.
2. Ich habe gestern mit diesem Sportler gesprochen. Der Sportler will seinen Schläger verkaufen.
3. Sind das die Eintrittskarten? Du wolltest die Eintrittskarten haben.
4. Die Sporthalle gehört der Stadt Münster. Wir trainieren in der Sporthalle.
5. Heute ist der Schwimm-Wettkampf. Ich habe dir gestern etwas über den Schwimm-Wettkampf erzählt.

6. Trainiert der Volleyballspieler in dieser Sporthalle? Wir haben den Volleyballspieler gestern gesehen.
7. Das Fahrrad ist kaputt. Du wolltest mit dem Fahrrad fahren.
8. Ich gehe zu der Sportveranstaltung. Die Sportveranstaltung findet im Stadion statt.
9. Die Trainer sind abgefahren. Wir haben den Trainern gestern gedankt.

Die Trainer, denen wir gestern gedankt haben, sind abgefahren.

°B. **Verbinden Sie die zwei Sätze mit *dessen* oder *deren*!** Translate the new sentence.

Zum Beispiel: Der Schwimmer hat einen Rekord gebrochen. Ich kenne die Eltern des Schwimmers.
Der Schwimmer, dessen Eltern ich kenne, hat einen Rekord gebrochen.
The swimmer whose parents I know broke a record.

Hast du mit der Tennisspielerin gesprochen? Der Bruder der Tennisspielerin ist in deiner Klasse.
Hast du mit der Tennisspielerin gesprochen, deren Bruder in deiner Klasse ist?
Did you talk to the tennis player whose brother is in your class?

1. Was hat der Trainer gesagt? Die Mannschaft des Trainers hat sehr gut gespielt.
2. Ich habe das Mädchen kennengelernt. Die Mutter des Mädchens ist unsere Trainerin.
3. Woher kommen die Sportler? Der Trainer der Sportler spricht gut Spanisch.
4. Welchen Sport treibt der Junge? Die Schwester des Jungen ist Skiläuferin.
5. Wie heißt die Schwimmerin? Du hast das Fahrrad der Schwimmerin gekauft.
6. Ich habe den Mädchen gestern geholfen. Der Wagen der Mädchen war kaputt.

C. **Ergänzen Sie die folgenden Sätze!** Complete the sentences with the correct relative pronoun.

1. Die teuerste Sportart, _____die_____ man treiben kann, ist das Jachtrennen (*yacht racing*).

2. Vor viertausend Jahren gab es in China ein Spiel, _____ dem modernen Federballspiel sehr ähnlich ist.

3. Das moderne Federballspiel, für _____ viele junge Sportler sich heutzutage interessieren, haben die Engländer in Badminton Hall in Avon erfunden (*invented*).

4. Der kleinste Baseballberufsspieler, über _____den_____ man im *Guinness Book of World Records* berichtet, war Eddie Gaedel, _____der_____ nur 1,09 Meter groß war.

5. Das Schachspiel, _dessen_ Name von dem persischen Wort *Schah*

herkommt, hat man wahrscheinlich schon vor über 1800 Jahren gespielt.

D. **Ergänzen Sie die folgenden Sätze mit *wer* oder *was!***

1. Alles, _was_ der Schiedsrichter sagte, war richtig.

2. _Wer_ das Rennen gewinnen will, muß fleißig trainieren.

3. Das Teuerste, _was_ ich gekauft habe, war dieses Paar

Tennisschuhe.

4. Joachim, hast du alles verstanden, _was_ der Trainer dir gesagt

hat?

5. _Wer_ zu unserer Mannschaft gehören will, muß jeden Tag üben.

6. Das ist das Leichteste, _was_ ich je gemacht habe.

E. **Ergänzen Sie die folgenden Sätze mit *wer*, *was* oder dem Relativpronomen
der, *das*, *die!* Complete with *wer*, *was*, or the appropriate relative pronoun.**

1. Nichts, _was_ ich vorgeschlagen habe, hat Cornelia interessiert.

2. Wo ist das Volleyballnetz, _das_ ich gestern gekauft habe?

3. Der Spieler, _der_ aus Brasilien kommt, spielt sehr gut Fußball.

4. Ich habe nichts im Schaufenster des Sportgeschäfts gesehen,

was ich wirklich wollte.

5. „_Wer_ anderen eine Grube gräbt (*digs a ditch*), fällt selbst

hinein." (Sprichwort)

6. Wo steht das neue Stadion, über _das_ Herr Meyer

gesprochen hat?

7. Alle, _die_ zu der Sportveranstaltung mitkommen wollen, müssen

sich heute abend um sieben Uhr bei mir treffen.

F. **Übersetzen Sie die folgenden Sätze!**

1. The (female) ice skater whom I met yesterday comes from Switzerland.
2. I spoke to the coach whose team had won.
3. The little girl whose mother is an athlete is called Rita.
4. What did those players with whom the referee was speaking do?
5. Is that the racket with which you were playing, Kurt?
6. The most boring thing that I read was that report on golf.
7. Whoever wins this game gets the prize (**der Preis**).

G. **Was für ein Tennisspiel ist das?** Tell what is wrong with the following picture using relative clauses.

Zum Beispiel: Das Mädchen, das vor dem Netz steht, hat einen Volleyball in der Hand.

Der Mann, der mit dem Schiedsrichter spricht, sitzt auf einem Pferd.

Demonstrative Pronouns

Der, das, die

Der, das, and **die** can be used as demonstrative pronouns as well as relative pronouns.

Kennst du diese Schwimmerin? Nein, *die* kenne ich nicht.
Do you know that swimmer? No, I don't know that one (her).

Demonstrative pronouns are more emphatic than personal pronouns, are strongly stressed in speech, and usually precede the verb. The answer to the question **Kennst du diese Schwimmerin?** could have been, **Nein, ich kenne sie nicht,** but this would have been less emphatic. Demonstrative pronouns (**der, das, die**) have the same forms as relative pronouns (see the chart on page 278).

Ingrid, hast du den neuen Mercedes gesehen? —Mensch, der kostet viel! (nominative masculine)
Ingrid, have you seen the new Mercedes? —Man, that one costs a lot!

Wo ist dein neuer Schläger? —Den habe ich leider heute nicht mitgebracht. (accusative masculine)
Where is your new racket? —Unfortunately I didn't bring it (that one) with me today.

Hast du die neue Trainerin kennengelernt? —Ja, die ist freundlicher als ich dachte. (nominative feminine)
Have you met the new coach? —Yes, she (that one) is friendlier than I thought.

Wo ist denn Kurt heute? —Ach, dessen Schwester nimmt heute an einem Tennisturnier teil, und er wollte sich das ansehen. (genitive masculine)
Where is Kurt today? —Oh, his sister is taking part in a tennis tournament and he wanted to see it.

Ich habe heute leider das Autorennen verloren. Aber Petra hatte noch weniger Glück. Deren Auto wollte nicht starten. (genitive feminine)
Unfortunately I lost the auto race today. But Petra was even less lucky. Her car wouldn't start.

Welchen Spieler kennst du? —Den neben dem Tor. (accusative masculine)
Which player do you know? —The one next to the goal.

The neuter forms **das** or **dies** can be used with the verb **sein** to introduce a singular or plural predicate in any gender.

Das (dies) ist die neue Sporthalle.
That (this) is the new gymnasium.

Das (dies) sind meine Tennisschuhe.
Those (these) are my tennis shoes.

Das (dies) waren interessante Spiele.
Those (these) were interesting games.

The genitive plural has two forms: **deren** and **derer. Derer** is used if a relative clause immediately follows:

Kennst du die Namen *derer*, die Schach spielen wollen?
Do you know the names of those who want to play chess?

But:

Kennst du diese Studenten? —Ja, deren Lieblingssport ist Reiten.
Do you know these students? —Yes, their favorite sport is horseback riding.

Kauf noch einige Tennisbälle. *Deren* kann man nie zu viele haben.
Buy some more tennis balls. One can never have too many of them.

Derselbe vs. der gleiche

Both of these demonstratives mean *the same* and can be used as adjectives or pronouns. They are composed of a definite article followed by the adjectives **selb-** or **gleich-** and are declined accordingly. **Derselbe** is written as one word unless the first syllable—the definite article—is contracted with a preceding preposition: **dasselbe Haus**, but **im selben Haus. Derselbe** indicates identity between concrete objects, while **der gleiche** indicates similarity between concrete objects. Here are examples of their use as adjectives:

Eberhard fährt *dasselbe* Fahrrad wie Gisela.　(identify)
Eberhard rides the same bike as Gisela.

Eberhard hat *das gleiche* Fahrrad wie Gisela.　(similarity)
Eberhard has the same kind of bike as Gisela.

Either can be used for non-concrete entities:

Ludwig und Julia kamen *zur selben* (*gleichen*) Zeit in die Sporthalle.
Ludwig and Julia came to the gymnasium at the same time.

Here are examples of their use as pronouns:

Tina hat sich einen neuen Tischtennisschläger gekauft. Ich möchte *den gleichen.*
Tina bought a new table-tennis racket. I'd like the same thing.

Gabi hat schon wieder einen neuen Freund! Oder ist das *derselbe* wie letzte Woche?
Gabi has a new boyfriend again! Or is that the same one as last week?

Baden-Baden: ein Schachspiel im Park

1. If a demonstrative pronoun refers to inanimate objects or whole clauses and is used as the object of a preposition, it must be expressed by a **da**-compound with stress on the first syllable, **dá-**.

   Fährst du nach Europa? —Nein, *dafür* habe ich leider kein Geld.
   Are you going to Europe? No, unfortunately I don't have any money *for that*.

2. Definite articles can be given demonstrative force in speech by pronouncing them with heavy stress: **Kennst du dén Mann (da)?** *Do you know that man?*

Übungen

°A. **Beantworten Sie die Fragen mit *das*.** Answer using the demonstrative pronoun **das.**

   Zum Beispiel: Wer sitzt dort drüben? (die Schwimmerinnen aus Frankreich)
   Das sind die Schwimmerinnen aus Frankreich.

   Wer hat mit dir über das Volleyballspiel gesprochen? (der Trainer)
   Das war der Trainer.

   1. Wer hat Schach gespielt? (einige Freunde von mir)
   2. Wer ist das Mädchen, das so gut Tennis spielt? (meine Schwester)
   3. Welcher Professor geht jedes Wochenende Segeln?
      (der Geschichtsprofessor)
   4. Wer hat ein Tor geschossen? (der Spieler aus Berlin)

°B. **Beantworten Sie die Fragen mit Demonstrativpronomen!** Answer in the affir-mative with demonstrative pronouns. Remember that demonstrative pronouns are strongly stressed in speech.

   Zum Beispiel: Hast du schon mal mit Rudi und Ralf Volleyball gespielt?
      (jede Woche)
   Ja, mit denen spiele ich jede Woche.

   Kennst du die schwedische Eisläuferin? (schon lange)
   Ja, die kenne ich schon lange!

   1. Ist das die berühmte Schwimmerin? (sehr bekannt)
   2. Ist dieser Schiedsrichter gerecht? (sehr gerecht)
   3. Hast du mit dem Trainer gesprochen? (vor zwei Stunden)
   4. Hast du die Freundin deines Gegners (*opponent*) kennengelernt?
      (vor einer Woche)
   5. Hast du je mit diesen Spielern Fußball gespielt? (einmal)

C. Ergänzen Sie die Sätze mit *deren* oder *derer!*

1. Das ist der Trainer _____, die dieses Jahr das Turnier

   gewonnen haben.

2. Die amerikanischen Volleyballspieler sind noch nicht

   da. _____ Flugzeug hat sich verspätet.

3. Hast du eine Liste _____, mit denen wir segeln gehen wollen?

4. Sollte ich noch einige Tischtennisbälle kaufen? —Nein,

   _____ haben wir genug.

D. Ergänzen Sie die folgenden Sätze! Complete the sentences with a form of **derselbe** or **der gleiche,** as appropriate.

1. Wilfried und Gisela trainieren in _____ Sporthalle.

2. Alle Spieler dieser Mannschaft tragen _____ Tennisschuhe.

3. Bei uns spielt man Korbball und Volleyball im _____ Stadion.

4. Wir kaufen immer _____ Fußbälle.

E. Übersetzen Sie die folgenden Sätze!

1. Jürgen, do you know the new swimmer? Man (**Mensch**), that one is really good!
2. Mr. Schneider, do you like the new rackets? —No, with those you can't play too well.
3. Rita, do you like the new car? —Yes, that one really drives well!
4. Miss Spanner, do you know the names of those who want to play chess?
5. Don't buy any more tickets. We have enough of them.
6. Were those the ice skaters from Sweden?
7. Toni and I practice in the same gymnasium.
8. All the players wear the same shoes.

F. Sportgegenstände. Konrad and Gertrud are shopping for sporting equipment but they can never agree on what to buy. Complete their conversation following the model.

Zum Beispiel: Diese Tennisschuhe sind gut.
Vielleicht, aber die da sind noch besser.

Man kann mit diesen Bällen gut Tischtennis spielen.
Vielleicht, aber mit denen da kann man noch besser spielen.

Diesen Badeanzug (*women's swimsuit*) finde ich schön.
Vielleicht, aber den da finde ich noch schöner.

1. Dieser Schläger ist sehr preiswert (*reasonable in price*).
2. Dieses Netz ist sehr stark.

3. Diesen Tennisschläger finde ich gut.
4. Diese Skier sind sehr schön.
5. Mit diesen Fahrrädern können wir sehr schnell fahren.
6. Dieses Zelt hätte ich gern.

Indefinite Pronouns and Adjectives

The following are indefinite pronouns and adjectives:

1. alle

   Alle waren beim Fußballspiel.
   All were at the soccer game.

2. ein bißchen   (wenig)

   Könnten wir noch *ein bißchen* länger hierbleiben? Ich möchte noch *ein bißchen* schwimmen.
   Could we stay here a little longer? I'd like to swim a little more.

3. ein paar*

   Vor *ein paar* Wochen sind wir zu einem Schachturnier gegangen.
   A few weeks ago we went to a chess tournament.

4. etwas

   Hast du *etwas* gekauft?   (pronoun)
   Did you buy something?

   Hast du *etwas* Kaffee gekauft?   (adjective)
   Did you buy some coffee?

   Ich habe so *etwas* noch nie gesehen.
   I've never seen anything like that.

5. jeder(mann)[+]

   Jedermann sollte ein Hobby haben.
   Everyone should have a hobby.

   Das ist fast *jedermanns* Lieblingssport.
   That is almost everyone's favorite sport.

---

*__Ein paar__ (*a few*) is invariable and should not be confused with __ein Paar__ (*a pair*).
[+]The indefinite pronoun __jeder__ also occurs in the accusative case (__jeden__) and the dative (__jedem__): __Der Schiedsrichter sollte jedem gerecht sein.__ *The umpire should be fair to everyone.*

6. jemand

Jemand hat mir Eintrittskarten für die Sportveranstaltung verkauft.
Somebody sold me tickets to the sports event.

7. man

Wie kommt *man* zum Stadion?
How does one (how do you) get to the stadium?

Man hat mich gefragt, wie das Spiel steht.
They asked me what the score was.

The pronoun **er** cannot be used in place of **man: Man bekommt gute Noten, wenn man** (not **er**) **fleißig lernt.** The other case forms of **man** are:

Hans macht *einen* verrückt!   (accusative)
Hans drives one (you) mad.

Das Rauchen schadet *einem*.   (dative)
Smoking is bad for you.

8. nichts

Sammelst du etwas?   —Nein, ich sammle *nichts*.
Do you collect anything?   —No, I don't collect anything.

9. niemand (keiner)*

Niemand (keiner) konnte den Schiedsrichter verstehen.
No one could understand the referee.

10. viel (vieles)†

Sie hat *viel (vieles)* für die Party gekauft.   (pronoun)
She bought many things for the party.

Heute habe ich *viel* Arbeit.   (adjective)
Today I have a lot of (much) work.

Viele Amerikaner spielen Racketball.   (adjective)
Many Americans play racketball.

Ich interessiere mich für *viele* Sportarten.   (adjective)
I'm interested in many types of sports.

Notice that the adjective **viel** is usually invariable in the singular and means *much*; it is declinable in the plural and means *many*.

---

*The indefinite pronoun **keiner** also occurs in the accusative (**keinen**) and the dative (**keinem**): **Mit keinem kann ich so gut Tennis spielen wie mit dir.**

†When **viel** takes the prefixes **zu** or **wie** it forms one word with these prefixes: **zuviel** (*too much*), **wieviel** (*how much*). As soon as an ending is added, however, **viel** must be written as a separate word: **Wie viele Karten hast du?** *How many cards do you have?* **Ich habe eine zuviel.** *I have one too many.*

11. wenig

Heute habe ich *wenig* Arbeit. Endlich kann ich mal ausspannen.
I have little (not much) work to do today. Finally I can relax.

Wenige Leute können gut segeln.
Few people know how to sail well.

Notice that **wenig** is usually invariable in the singular, just like **viel.**

Many indefinite pronouns can be used in conjunction with adjectives, including **etwas, nichts, viel, wenig,** and **alles.** While adjectives following **alles** take weak endings, adjectives following other indefinite pronouns usually take strong endings. Such adjectives are usually capitalized.*

Wir haben über *etwas Interessantes* gesprochen.   (accusative)
We spoke about (discussed) something interesting.

Sie haben von *nichts Interessantem* gesprochen.   (dative)
They mentioned nothing interesting (didn't mention anything interesting).

Kurt hat *wenig Wichtiges* gesagt.
Kurt said little of importance.

Marie hat *viel Wichtiges* geschrieben.
Marie wrote much of importance.

Alles Gute!   (weak ending)
Good luck!   (All things good!)

The indefinite **anders** (*else*) may be used in conjunction with **jemand** or **niemand** (although in formal German the declined adjective **anderer** is preferred).

Jemand anders (anderer)—nicht Werner—hat ein Tor geschossen.
Someone else—not Werner—scored a goal.

Ich habe mit *niemand anders (anderem)* gesprochen.†
I didn't talk to anyone else.

The neuter form **anderes** is declined strong and may be used with many other indefinites.

Wir haben über *etwas (nichts) anderes* gesprochen.
We talked about something (nothing) else.

Ingrid hat von *nichts anderem* gesprochen.
Ingrid didn't mention anything else.

---

*Non-descriptive adjectives and a few others are not capitalized: **Der Trainer hat alles übrige erklärt.** *The coach explained all the rest.*
†**Anders** may also be used as an adverb meaning *differently;* **Er spielt anders als du; er ist viel agressiver.** *He plays differently than you do; he is more aggressive.*

Many indefinites can be intensified by the use of **irgend:**

> Wissen Sie *irgend etwas* über Autorennen?
> Do you know anything at all about car racing?

> *Irgend jemand* hat meinen Schläger genommen.
> Someone or another took my racket.

> Rebekka, du solltest *irgendwann* einmal ausspannen.
> Rebekka, you ought to relax sometime.

Übungen

°A. **Richard ist Pessimist.** Complete his answers to these questions following the model.

Zum Beispiel: Hat unsere Mannschaft viel gelernt?
Nein, sie hat nichts gelernt.

Glaubst du, daß jemand ein Tor schießen wird?
Nein, niemand wird ein Tor schießen.

1. Hast du etwas Interessantes über Schach gelesen?
2. Glaubst du, daß jedermann heute gut gespielt hat?
3. Sind alle heute sehr gut geschwommen?
4. Hältst du viel von dem neuen Trainer?

B. **Ergänzen Sie die folgenden Sätze!** Complete each sentence first with the correct form of **viel** and then with the correct form of **wenig.**

1. _____ Leute waren im Stadion.

2. Wir haben mit dem Trainer über _____ gesprochen.

3. Mein Vater trinkt Kaffee mit _____ Zucker.

4. Erika ist in _____ Sportarten begabt.

5. Ich kenne _____ Berufsspieler persönlich.

C. **Angelika gibt Ratschläge.** Give advice as Angelika would.

Zum Beispiel: Ich habe Hunger.
Wenn man Hunger hat, sollte man etwas essen.

Diese Jacke im Schaufenster gefällt mir.
Wenn eine Jacke einem gefällt, sollte man sie kaufen.

Schach macht mich nervös.
Wenn Schach einen nervös macht, sollte man es nicht spielen.

1. Ich habe Durst.
2. Ich bin müde.
3. Sportsendungen gefallen mir.

4. Ich finde Golf langweilig.
5. Volleyball interessiert mich.
6. So ein Schläger gefällt mir.

D. **Übersetzen Sie die folgenden Sätze!**

1. We stayed at (**in**) the swimming pool a little too long.
2. Heinrich, please buy a few tennis balls.
3. Someone or another took my new racket.
4. Everyone should do something just for fun (**nur zum Spaß**).
5. Too much coffee is bad for you (*one*).
6. Nobody else wanted to say anything at all about the game.

E. **In einem exklusiven Klub.** Complete the sentences in this conversation with the appropriate indefinite pronouns or adjectives.

—Wie oft spielt _____ Tennis hier?

—Solche Spiele finden jedes Wochenende statt.

—Kann _____ hier spielen; oder muß _____ zu einem

Tennisklub gehören?

—_____ darf hier nur spielen, wenn _____ zu diesem

Tennisklub gehört. _____ anders darf hier spielen. Übrigens (*by the*

way), irgend _____ hat mir _____ Interessantes über diesen

Klub gesagt: im Sommer spielen _____ Berufsspieler auf diesen

Tennisplätzen. Nun, wohin gehen Sie jetzt?

—Ich gehe auch Tennis spielen. Ich bin auch Berufsspieler.

—Tatsächlich! _____ Gute!

A. Zur Wiederholung. Übersetzen Sie die folgenden Sätze!

1. Frank, who did you go to the show with?
2. What kind of a ball do they (**man**) play with?
3. These are our table tennis rackets. Which one do you want, Anna?
4. Where did you meet the coach who works in this stadium, Miss Braun?
5. The girl whose father is a coach sits next to me.
6. Are those the swimmers whom the coach helped yesterday?
7. That is the tennis court on which we played with somebody from Bonn.
8. Whoever plays soccer has to be strong.
9. A few days ago Ute told me something interesting about the new team.
10. One should always relax before a game.

B. Zur Gesamtwiederholung. Übersetzen Sie die folgenden Sätze!

1. Are there many Americans who don't watch television?   (Chapter 6)
2. What kind of games do they (**man**) usually broadcast?
3. In which new stadium do you prefer (like better) to play, Rudi?   (Chapter 7)
4. Are those the young Canadian players about whom the German coach was talking?
5. If our team had only won we could have flown to Mexico for a couple of days.   (Chapters 8 and 11)
6. What a poor game! I wish(ed) somebody or another had scored a goal.   (Chapter 8)
7. The reporter claimed that Pelé is the most popular player in soccer.   (Chapter 9)
8. It says (**steht**) in the newspaper that somebody else scored the most goals.
9. Which hockey player (**Hockeyspieler**) hurt himself last night?   (Chapter 10)
10. Everybody except that young (female) athlete practices in this gymnasium.   (Chapter 11)
11. There is nothing in the newspaper about this game between our team and the French one.   (Chapters 7 and 11)

13
Kunst und Leben

Ein Bildhauer in seinem Studio in West-Berlin

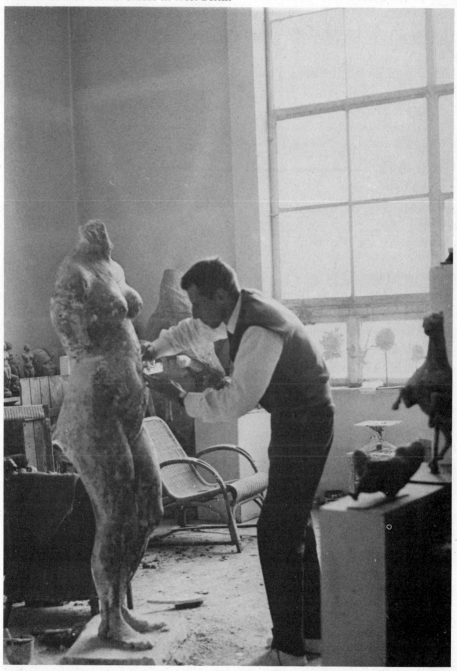

The Passive Voice: Present Tense and Past Tense

The Passive Voice: Future and Perfect Tenses

The Statal Passive

The Passive with Modal Verbs; Alternatives to the Passive

The Use of *es* with Verbs That Do Not Take an Object

Wortschatz

das Bild (-er) picture

der Bildhauer (-), die Bildhauerin (-nen) sculptor

der Dichter (-), die Dichterin (-nen) poet

die Dichtung (-en) poetry

der Dirigent (-en, -en), die Dirigentin (-nen) conductor

das Drama (-en) drama

die Erzählung (-en) tale, narration

das Gedicht (-e) poem

die Geige (-n) violin

das Gemälde (-) painting

das Klavier (-e) piano

die Komödie (das Lustspiel) comedy

der Komponist (-en, -en), die Komponistin (-nen) composer

das Konzert (-e) concert

die Kunst (¨e) art

der Künstler (-), die Künstlerin (-nen) artist

das Kunstwerk (-e) work of art

das Lied (-er) song

der Maler (-), die Malerin (-nen) painter

der Musiker (-), die Musikerin (-nen) musician

die Oper (-n) opera

das Orchester (-) orchestra

die Orgel (-n) organ

der Roman (-e) novel

der Sänger (-), die Sängerin (-nen) singer

der Schauspieler (-), die Schauspielerin (-nen) actor, actress

der Schriftsteller (-), die Schriftstellerin (-nen) writer

das Stück (-e) play, work, piece

die Symphonie (-n) symphony

das Theater (-) theatre

die Tragödie (das Trauerspiel) tragedy

die Trompete (-n) trumpet

der Walzer (-) waltz

auf · führen	to perform	malen	to paint
entdecken	to discover	schaffen*	to create
entwerfen*	to design	vergleichen*	to compare
komponieren	to compose	veröffentlichen	to publish

A. *Answer the following questions, choosing a word from the list given.*

1. Was kann man nicht komponieren?

   Lied / Symphonie / Konzert / Oper / Komödie

2. Worauf kann man keine Musik spielen?

   Geige / Dichtung / Klavier / Trompete / Orgel

3. Was gibt es nicht in einem Theater?

   Drama / Komödie / Theaterstück / Roman / Tragödie

4. Was kann man nicht in einem Buch oder als Buch veröffentlichen?

   Gedicht / Roman / Orchester / Erzählung

5. Was hat nichts mit Musik zu tun?

   Konzert / Lied / Oper / Bild / Walzer

B. *What profession do you associate with each of the following people?*

1. Virginia Woolf
2. Zubin Mehta
3. Henry Moore
4. Katherine Hepburn
5. Pablo Picasso
6. Artur Rubinstein
7. Emily Dickinson
8. Beverly Sills

C. *Write five sentences, choosing one word from each column.*

Zum Beispiel: Ein Maler malt Gemälde.

Maler	singt	Oper
Sänger	spielt	Symphonie
Musiker	dichtet	Roman
Schriftsteller	malt	Gedichte
Dichter	schreibt	Gemälde

---

*Verbs marked with an asterisk are strong verbs; see the appendix for principal parts of strong verbs.

D. *Choose the most logical response on the left for each statement or question on the right.*

1. Nun, Doris, hat man dich schon entdeckt?

2. Haben Sie ihr Haus selbst gebaut?

3. Heute abend sehen wir uns "Othello" an.

4. Paul Klee schuf sehr viele Gemälde.

a. Ja, aber wir haben es von einem Architekten entwerfen lassen.

b. Ja, und ich finde sie alle interessant.

c. Nein, noch nicht. Aber ich werde bestimmt ein Star.

d. Das ist ein gutes Stück. Es wurde letztes Jahr in Berlin aufgeführt.

The Passive Voice: Present Tense and Past Tense

Look at the following examples of the passive and active voices in English. The subjects are in italics.

Passive Voice

Germany is visited by many Americans.

The Statue of Liberty was made by the French.

Active Voice

Many Americans visit Germany.

The French made the Statue of Liberty.

You can see that the subject of the sentence in the passive voice is the direct object of the corresponding sentence in the active voice. While in the active voice the subject performs the action of the verb, in the passive voice the subject usually *receives* the action of the verb.

Formation

Notice that in the English sentences, the passive is formed with *to be* and the past participle of the main verb. In German the passive voice is formed with **werden**, *to become*, and the past participle of the main verb. The passive voice can occur in a variety of tenses, depending on the tense of the auxiliary **werden**. For now let's consider only the most common tenses, the present and the past.

Dieses Orgelstück *wird* oft gespielt.   (present)
This piece for organ (organ music) is often played.

Dieses Orgelstück *wurde* oft gespielt.   (past)
This piece for organ was often played.

Notice that the past participle occurs at the end of the clause. Notice also that the auxiliary **werden** is singular to agree with the singular subject, **dieses Orgelstück.** But if the subject is plural, a plural form of **werden** must be used.

Bachs Orgelstücke *werden* oft gespielt.   (present)
Bach's pieces for organ are often played.

Bachs Orgelstücke *wurden* oft gespielt.   (past)
Bach's pieces for organ were often played.

To use another example:

Dieser Roman *wurde* im neunzehnten Jahrhundert geschrieben.
This novel was written in the nineteenth century.

Solche Romane *wurden* im neunzehnten Jahrhundert geschrieben.
Such novels were written in the nineteenth century.

The verb must agree with the subject not only in number but also in person:

Ich *wurde* zum Konzert eingeladen.
I was invited to the concert.

Du *wurdest* auch zum Konzert eingeladen.
You were also invited to the concert.

The Agent of the Action

In English the agent of the action—that is, the person or thing that motivates the action—is expressed using the preposition *by*. In German the agent (person or thing) is expressed by **von**.

Viele schöne Symphonien wurden *von Mozart* komponiert.
    (agent = Mozart)
Many beautiful symphonies were composed by Mozart.

Dieser Holzschnitt wurde *von Albrecht Dürer* gemacht.
    (agent = Dürer)
This woodcut was made by Albrecht Dürer.

Dieses tiefe Tal wurde *vom Fluß* geformt.   (agent = **Fluß**)
This deep valley was formed by the river.

Das Getreide wurde *vom Regen* verdorben.*   (agent = **Regen**)
The grain was ruined by the rain.

---

*With inanimate agents, *by* can also be expressed with **durch: Das Getreide wurde durch den Regen verdorben.**

The Force Through Which an Action Is Brought About

In German there is a distinction between the agent of an action, introduced by the preposition **von**, and a force that implies a personal agent. Such a force is expressed by the preposition **durch**.

> Der Hirsch wurde *durch einen Schuß* (vom Jäger) gefällt.
> The stag was felled by a shot (from the hunter).

> Die Straßen wurden *durch den Verkehr* beschädigt.
> The streets were damaged by the traffic.

Notice that the preposition **von** takes the dative case but that **durch** takes the accusative.

Übungen

A. **Übersetzen Sie das Verb *werden*!** The verb **werden** has three uses: (1) used with adjectives and nouns, it is the equivalent of *to become*; (2) used with the infinitive, it expresses the future tense; (3) used with the past participle, it expresses the passive voice. Translate the following sentences and tell when **werden** is used to express the passive voice.

1. Hier wird Deutsch gesprochen.
2. Im Sommer werden die Schauspieler Urlaub machen.
3. *Die Dreigroschenoper* wurde von Bertolt Brecht geschrieben.
4. Die *Kinder- und Hausmärchen* werden oft von Eltern erzählt.
5. Wir werden zu den Salzburger Festspielen reisen.
6. Rebekka wird Sängerin, aber ihr Bruder wird Kunst studieren.
7. Dieses Orchester wurde gestern von seinem Dirigenten verlassen.
8. Wann wurde *Die Leiden des jungen Werthers* geschrieben?
9. Ricarda Huchs Erzählungen werden von vielen Leuten gelesen.
10. Ich werde mit Rosemarie und Otto ins Konzert gehen.

°B. **Ersetzen Sie die Pronomen!** Replace the pronouns in italics with the pronouns in parentheses and change the verbs accordingly.

1. *Ich* wurde von Cornelia begrüßt.   (er, sie *pl.*, du, wir, sie *sing.*)
2. Wird *sie* oft zum Abendessen eingeladen?   (du, sie *pl.*, ihr, Sie)
3. *Wir* werden morgen vom Konzert abgeholt.   (er, du, Sie, sie *sing.*)
4. *Ich* wurde von Sara nach dem Bild gefragt.   (wir, du, sie *sing.*, ihr)
5. *Er* wurde von dem Schriftsteller angerufen.   (ich, du, ihr, Sie)

C. **Bilden Sie Sätze im Präsens!** Rearrange the words to form sentences in the present tense of the passive voice.

Zum Beispiel: Händels *Messias* / werden / singen / oft in Amerika
Händels *Messias* wird oft in Amerika gesungen.

1. die Trompete / werden / spielen / von vielen Musikern
2. die *Brandenburgischen Konzerte* / werden / übertragen / oft in Amerika

---

3. in welchen Ländern / Deutsch / werden / sprechen
4. Helga Novaks Erzählungen / werden / lesen / von manchen Amerikanern
6. Goethes *Faust* / werden / aufführen / sehr oft

D. **Finden Sie den passenden Satz!** The sentences on the left are in the active voice. *Some* of the sentences on the right are in the passive voice. Match the active sentences on the left with the corresponding passive sentences on the right and translate.

Zum Beispiel: Rembrandt hat dieses schöne Bild gemalt.
Dieses schöne Bild wurde von Rembrandt gemalt.
This beautiful picture was painted by Rembrandt.

1. Rembrandt hat dieses schöne Bild gemalt.

2. In der Schweiz spricht man Deutsch, Italienisch und Französisch.

3. Kolumbus hat Amerika im Jahr 1492 entdeckt.

4. Heinrich von Kleist schrieb viele berühmte Dramen.

5. Im neunzehnten Jahrhundert sammelten die Brüder Grimm viele Märchen.

6. Balthasar Neumann entwarf viele herrliche Bauten.

7. Wer schrieb *Tristan und Isolde*?

8. Viele Musiker spielen die *Brandenburgischen Konzerte*.

9. Man hat diese Komödie gestern aufgeführt.

10. Viele Amerikaner besichtigen (*view*) das Brandenburger Tor.

a. Viele Musiker werden die *Brandenburgischen Konzerte* spielen.

b. Diese Komödie wurde gestern aufgeführt.

c. Das Brandenburger Tor wird von vielen Amerikanern besichtigt (*viewed*).

d. Dieses schöne Bild wurde von Rembrandt gemalt.

e. Wir werden Deutsch, Italienisch und Französisch in der Schweiz sprechen.

f. Viele Amerikaner werden das Brandenburger Tor besichtigen.

g. Viele berühmte Dramen wurden von Heinrich von Kleist geschrieben.

h. Im neunzehnten Jahrhundert wurden von den Brüdern Grimm viele Märchen gesammelt.

i. Die *Brandenburgischen Konzerte* werden von vielen Musikern gespielt.

j. Viele herrliche Bauten wurden von Balthasar Neumann entworfen.

k. Deutsch, Italienisch und Französisch werden in der Schweiz gesprochen.

l. Amerika wurde im Jahr 1492 von Kolumbus entdeckt.

m. Von wem wurde *Tristan und Isolde* geschrieben?

E. **Bilden Sie Sätze in der Vergangenheit!** Rearrange the words to form sentences in the past tense of the passive voice.

Zum Beispiel: *Die Blechtrommel (The Tin Drum)* / werden / schreiben / von
Günter Grass
Die Blechtrommel wurde von Günter Grass geschrieben.

1.   diese Musik / werden / komponieren / von Beethoven
2.   im Mittelalter / viele Dome / werden / bauen
3.   wann / dieses Bild / werden / malen?
4.   *Faust* / werden / schreiben / von Goethe
5.   Amerika / werden / entdecken / im Jahre 1492 von Kolumbus

F. **Schreiben Sie Sätze im Passiv!** Change the following sentences to the passive voice; use the present or past tense as appropriate.

Zum Beispiel: Mozart komponierte einundvierzig Symphonien.
Einundvierzig Symphonien wurden von Mozart komponiert.

1.   Schumann schrieb viele Sonaten.
2.   In der Schweiz spricht man Deutsch, Französisch und Italienisch.
3.   Golo Mann veröffentlichte viele Werke über deutsche Geschichte.
4.   Die Religion beeinflußte viele Künstler.
5.   Marie Curie entdeckte das Radium.
6.   Viele amerikanische Studenten besuchen Deutschlands Kunstmuseen.

G. **Ergänzen Sie die folgenden Sätze mit *durch* oder *von*!**

1.   Viele gothische Dome wurden ＿＿＿＿＿＿ unbekannten Architekten

errichtet.

2.   Unser Garten wird oft ＿＿＿＿＿＿ starken Winden beschädigt.

3.   Die *Chromatische Phantasie* wurde ＿＿＿＿＿＿ Johann Sebastian Bach

komponiert.

4.   Glaubst du, daß das ganze Universum ＿＿＿＿＿＿ Gott geschaffen

wurde?

5.   Die alten Gebäude wurden gestern ＿＿＿＿＿＿ eine Explosion zerstört.

6.   Die Autobahn wurde ＿＿＿＿＿＿ den vielen Verkehr abgenutzt und

mußte ＿＿＿＿＿＿ den Arbeitern erneuert werden.

H. **Übersetzen sie die folgenden Sätze!**

1.   These symphonies were composed by Beethoven.
2.   Many pretzels (**Brezeln**) are eaten at the Oktoberfest.
3.   The bridge was destroyed by an explosion.
4.   These songs were written by Paul McCartney and John Lennon.
5.   These rooms were designed by Walter Gropius.

6. Radium was discovered by Marie Curie.
7. *Parzifal* was written by Richard Wagner.
8. The roads were damaged by the traffic.

I. **Warum sind diese Leute berühmt?** For each drawing, create a sentence in the passive voice; use the following persons' names: Hermann Hesse, Paul McCartney and John Lennon, Leonardo da Vinci, Kapitän James Cook, Frank Lloyd Wright.

The Passive Voice: Future and Perfect Tenses

The Present Perfect Tense

Since **werden** takes the auxiliary **sein** (not **haben**), **sein** is used to form the perfect tenses of the passive voice. **Worden**, shortened from **geworden**, is used as the past participle of **werden**. The word order in the present perfect tense is:

subject + present tense of **sein** + *past participle of main verb +* **worden**

> Dieses Buch *ist* von vielen Deutschen *gelesen worden.*
> This book has been read by many Germans.

> Diese Oper *ist* letztes Jahr von vielen Menschen *gehört worden.*
> This opera was heard by many people last year.

> Diese Platten *sind* von vielen Leuten *gekauft worden.*
> These records were bought by many people.

The Past Perfect Tense

This tense differs from the present tense only in that the past tense of **sein** is used:

subject + past tense of **sein** + *past participle of main verb +* **worden**

> Dieses Buch *war* von vielen Deutschen *gelesen worden.*
> This book had been read by many Germans.

> Diese Oper *war* von vielen Menschen *gehört worden.*
> This opera had been heard by many people.

> Diese Platten *waren* von vielen Leuten *gekauft worden.*
> These records had been bought by many people.

The Future Tense

In the future tense of the passive voice, which rarely occurs, the auxiliary **werden** appears twice. The word order is:

subject + present tense of **werden** + *past participle of main verb +* **werden**

> Dieses neue Buch *wird* von vielen Deutschen *gelesen werden.*
> This new book will be read by many Germans.

> Diese Oper *wird* bald von vielen Menschen *gehört werden.*
> This opera will soon be heard by many people.

> Diese Platten *werden* von vielen Leuten *gekauft werden.*
> These records will be bought by many people.

Summary of Tenses of the Passive Voice

All tenses of the passive voice use **werden** in combination with the past participle of the main verb.

Present:	wird . . . gekauft
Past:	wurde . . . gekauft
Present perfect:	ist . . . gekauft worden
Past perfect:	war . . . gekauft worden
Future:	wird . . . gekauft werden

Word Order in the Passive Voice

The same principles of word order discussed in Chapters 1 and 2 apply to the passive voice. The present or past tense of the auxiliaries **werden** or **sein** functions as the finite verb and is positioned accordingly.

Dieses Volkslied wurde im neunzehnten Jahrhundert entdeckt.   (normal word order)

Dieses Volkslied ist im neunzehnten Jahrhundert entdeckt worden.

Im neunzehnten Jahrhundert wurde dieses Volkslied entdeckt.   (inverted word order)

Im neunzehnten Jahrhundert ist dieses Volkslied entdeckt worden.

Ich glaube, daß dieses Volkslied im neunzehnten Jahrhundert entdeckt wurde.   (transposed word order)

Ich glaube, daß dieses Volkslied im neunzehnten Jahrhundert entdeckt worden ist.

Ein Schritt weiter _____

There is another passive tense, the future perfect, which is rarely used. As in the future tense of the passive, the future perfect contains the auxiliary **werden** twice. Normal word order in the future perfect of the passive is:

subject + present tense of **werden** + past participle of main verb + **worden sein**

Dieses neue Buch wird von vielen Deutschen gelesen worden sein.
This new book will have been read by many Germans.

Diese Oper wird bis September von vielen Menschen gehört worden sein.
This opera will have been heard by many people by September.

Diese Platten werden bis Ende des Jahres von vielen Leuten gekauft worden sein.
These records will have been bought by many people by the end of the year.

Schöne Klänge im Freien

Übungen

A. **Verändern Sie die Sätze!** Change the following sentences to the past tense of the passive voice.

Zum Beispiel: *Hamlet* und *Macbeth* sind von Shakespeare geschrieben worden.
Hamlet und *Macbeth* wurden von Shakespeare geschrieben.

1. Die Oper *Tannhäuser* ist von Richard Wagner komponiert worden.
2. Ich glaube, daß beim Oktoberfest viel Bier getrunken worden ist.
3. Von wem ist die Berliner Mauer errichtet worden?

4. *Faust* und *Hermann und Dorothea* sind von Goethe geschrieben worden.
5. Wir sind gestern vom Bahnhof abgeholt worden.
6. Der Friedens-Nobelpreis ist 1979 von Mutter Theresa gewonnen worden.
7. Viele Wiener Walzer sind von Johann Strauß komponiert worden.

°B. **Verändern Sie die Sätze!** Change the following sentences from the past to the present perfect tense.

Zum Beispiel: Das Drama *Don Carlos* wurde von Friedrich Schiller
                      geschrieben.
                      Das Drama *Don Carlos* ist von Friedrich Schiller geschrieben
                      worden.

1. Diese Symphonien wurden von Haydn komponiert.
2. Wissen Sie, von wem *Buddenbrooks* geschrieben wurde?
3. Die Kaiser-Wilhelm-Gedächtniskirche wurde im Zweiten Weltkrieg zerstört.
4. Die Lieder "I Want to Hold Your Hand" und "She Loves You" wurden ins Deutsche übersetzt.
5. *Die Brücke* wurde von Emil Nolde gemalt.

C. **Übersetzen Sie die folgenden Sätze ins Englische!** Then change the italicized clauses to the active voice.

Zum Beispiel: *Welche Symphonien waren von Beethoven komponiert worden,*
                      bevor er taub wurde?
                      Which symphonies had been composed by Beethoven before
                      he became deaf?
                      Welche Symphonien hatte Beethoven komponiert, bevor er
                      taub wurde?

1. *Das erste Auto war von Daimler und Benz gebaut worden,* bevor Diesel den Dieselmotor konstruierte.
2. *Dieses Bild war von Dürer gemalt worden,* bevor er nach Italien reiste.
3. *Das erste Lied war von der Sängerin schon gesungen worden,* als sie plötzlich ihre Stimme verlor.
4. *Das Gedicht war von der Dichterin schon vorgelesen worden,* als ich ankam.

D. **Übersetzen Sie die folgenden Sätze ins Englische!** Tell which are in the future tense of the passive voice.

1. Leider wird es bestimmt kälter.
2. Morgen kann ich nicht ins Konzert mitgehen, denn ich werde zu viele Hausaufgaben haben.
3. Werden noch mehr Stücke von Stockhausen komponiert werden?
4. Wirst du diese Gedichte von Rilke lesen?
5. Glaubt ihr, daß das Klavierkonzert übertragen werden wird?
6. Will Paula Musikerin oder Bildhauerin werden?
7. Stefan wird Literatur und Linguistik studieren.

1. This picture was painted by Paul Klee. (present perfect tense)
2. This artwork had been made before the artist was thirty years old.
3. I don't believe that more songs will be composed by those singers.
4. When was the Cologne Cathedral (**Kölner Dom**) built? (present perfect tense)
5. Will the museum be visited by many tourists?
6. This tale was written by Elisabeth Langgässer.
7. *Egmont* had already been written when Goethe wrote *Hermann und Dorothea.*

F. **Vorhersagen.** What do you think will happen in the near future? Write three sentences, following these models.

Zum Beispiel: Gemälde werden von Robotern gemalt werden.
Musik wird von Computern gespielt werden.

The Statal Passive

You have seen that the passive formed with the auxiliary **werden** expresses an action, a subject being acted upon by an agent or force. This is quite different from the use of **sein** in combination with a past participle to express the result of an action, a construction called the statal passive. Compare the following sentences.

True Passive	*Statal Passive*
Die Tür *wurde* um vier Uhr geschlossen. (action) The door was (being) closed at four o'clock.	Die Tür war den ganzen Tag geschlossen. (state) The door was closed all day.
Diese Platte *wurde* bei der Party zerbrochen. (action) This record was broken at the party.	Wir konnten die Platte nicht spielen, denn sie war zerbrochen. (state) We couldn't play the record because it was broken.
Das Haus *wurde* gestern grün gestrichen. (action) The house was painted green yesterday.	Das Haus, in dem wir wohnten, war grün gestrichen. (state) The house we lived in was (painted) green.

The passive auxiliary **werden** is used to indicate action; the verb **sein** is used to describe a state resulting from actions no longer in progress.

Übungen

A. **Ergänzen Sie die folgenden Sätze!** Complete the following sentences with the correct auxiliary verb in parentheses and translate.

1. Die Türen des Museums _____ pünktlich um neun Uhr aufgemacht. (wurden / waren)

2. Der Bus blieb stehen, denn die Achse (*axle*) _____ gebrochen. (wurde / war)

3. Ich kann die Musik nicht hören, weil sie zu leise (*softly*) gespielt _____. (wird / ist)

4. Gestern _____ das ganze Haus in nur fünf Stunden gestrichen. (wurde / war)

5. Rebekka kauft einen neuen Mantel, weil der alte abgetragen (*worn out*) _____. (wurde / ist)

6. Shakespeares Dramen _____ sehr oft in Deutschland aufgeführt. (werden / sind)

7. Diese Landschaft _____ sehr oft gemalt. (wird / ist)

B. **Übersetzen Sie die folgenden Sätze!** Be careful to distinguish between the true passive and the statal passive.

1. Is this art museum visited often in the summer?
2. The house is painted blue.
3. Is the bank closed today?
4. No, the doors are opened at nine o'clock.
5. Was this building designed by Frank Lloyd Wright?
6. The record was already sold. So (**daher**) we couldn't buy it.

The Passive with Modal Verbs; Alternatives to the Passive

The Passive with Modal Verbs

Modal verbs can be used with a combination of the auxiliary **werden** and the past participle of the main verb to express the passive voice. The modals are usually in the present or past tense. Compare:

	Past Participle of Main Verb	Passive Auxiliary	
Diese Geschichte darf nicht von jedem	gelesen	werden.	(present)

Diese Geschichte darf nicht von jedem   gelesen   werden.   (present)
This story must not be read by everyone.

Dieser Walzer sollte heute   gespielt   werden.   (past)
This waltz was supposed to be played today.

Das Theaterstück mußte in Berlin   aufgeführt   werden.   (past)
The play had to be staged in Berlin.

Diese Sonate kann auf dem Klavier   gespielt   werden.   (present)
This sonata can be played on the piano.

Notice in the above examples that the last two elements of the clause are the past participle and the passive auxiliary **werden**.

Alternatives to the Passive

The true passive voice, a form of **werden** used in combination with a past participle, occurs less frequently in German than English, but there are various other ways to express the passive.

Man + Verb in the Active Voice

The pronoun **man** used as the subject of the main verb in the active voice is especially common in conversational German. Compare:

> Solche Statuen werden oft in Ausstellungen gezeigt.   (passive voice)
> Man zeigt solche Statuen oft in Ausstellungen.   (**man** + active voice)
> Such statues are often shown in exhibitions.

> Deutsche Opern werden auch in Amerika aufgeführt.   (passive voice)
> Man führt deutsche Opern auch in America auf.   (**man** + active voice)
> German operas are staged in America, too.

> Das Schloß Neuschwanstein wurde im neunzehnten Jahrhundert
>   erbaut.   (passive voice)
> Man hat das Schloß Neuschwanstein im neunzehnten Jahrhundert
>   erbaut.   (**man** + active voice)
> The castle Neuschwanstein was built in the nineteenth century.

The Reflexive

The reflexive pronoun **sich** is sometimes used with the verb in place of the passive with inanimate subjects; the reflexive is never used with people in this manner.

Die Arbeit kann leicht gemacht werden.   (passive voice)
Die Arbeit macht sich leicht.   (reflexive)
The work can be done easily.

Die Arbeit konnte leicht gemacht werden.   (passive voice)
Die Arbeit hat sich leicht gemacht.   (reflexive)
The work could be done easily.

Dieses Buch kann schnell gelesen werden.   (passive voice)
Dieses Buch liest sich schnell.   (reflexive)
This book can be read quickly.

This construction is usually the equivalent of *can be* in English. The construction *can be* used in combination with the past participle can also be expressed in German with the auxiliary **lassen** together with the reflexive and the main verb.

Das kann leicht erklärt werden.   (passive voice)
Das läßt sich leicht erklären.   (**lassen** + reflexive)
This can be easily explained.

Diese Sache kann schnell erledigt werden.   (passive voice)
Diese Sache läßt sich schnell erledigen.   (**lassen** + reflexive)
This matter can be disposed of quickly.

Diese Sache konnte schnell erledigt werden.   (passive voice)
Diese Sache ließ sich schnell erledigen.   (reflexive)
This matter could (was able to) be disposed of quickly.

The use of **sein** as an auxiliary in combination with **zu** and the infinitive of the main verb is equivalent to *can be, should be* or *must be* followed by the past participle of the main verb.

Dieses Buch muß bis morgen gelesen werden.   (passive voice)
Dieses Buch ist bis morgen zu lesen.   (**sein zu** + infinitive)
This book must (should) be read by tomorrow. (This book is to be read by tomorrow.)

Solche Fehler sollen nicht gemacht werden.   (passive voice)
Solche Fehler sind nicht zu machen.   (**sein zu** + infinitive)
Such errors must not (should not, are not to) be made.

So ein Gemälde kann leicht verkauft werden.   (passive voice)
So ein Gemälde ist leicht zu verkaufen.   (**sein zu** + infinitive)
Such a painting can be sold easily.

Die Arbeit konnte nicht schnell gemacht werden.   (passive voice)
Die Arbeit war nicht schnell zu machen.   (**sein zu** + infinitive)
The work could not be done quickly.

Übungen

A. Übersetzen Sie die folgenden Sätze ins Englische!

1. Dieser Roman muß bis morgen gelesen werden.
2. Leider durfte das Drama nicht aufgeführt werden.
3. Meine Mutter meint, daß dieses Theaterstück aufgeführt werden soll.
4. Zigaretten dürfen in der Oper nicht geraucht werden.
5. Die Symphonie muß heute abend gespielt werden.
6. Die Erzählung konnte von den Studenten nicht verstanden werden.

°B. Bilden Sie Sätze mit *man*! Change the following sentences to the active voice using **man** as the subject.

Zum Beispiel: Dieses Volkslied wird oft gesungen.
Man singt oft dieses Volkslied.

Wann wurde der Kölner Dom errichtet?
Wann hat man den Kölner Dom errichtet?

1. Das Brandenburger Tor wird oft fotografiert.
2. Diese Dichtung wurde im achtzehnten Jahrhundert geschrieben.
3. Shakespeares Dramen wurden in Deutschland öfter aufgeführt als in England.
4. Im neunzehnten Jahrhundert wurden solche Erzählungen geschrieben.
5. Ich wurde sehr früh angerufen.
6. Diese Komödien werden selten aufgeführt.

Zum Beispiel: Die Berichte müssen nächste Woche geschrieben werden.
Man muß die Berichte nächste Woche schreiben.

Die Berichte mußten letzte Woche geschrieben werden.
Man mußte die Berichte letzte Woche schreiben.

1. Zigaretten dürfen hier nicht geraucht werden.
2. Solche Straßen müssen repariert werden.
3. Dieser Roman kann sehr schnell gelesen werden.
4. Das teure Bild konnte nicht gefunden werden.
5. Die alten Bücher durften nicht aus der Bibliothek entfernt werden.
6. Diese Tragödie soll aufgeführt werden.

°C. Bilden Sie Sätze mit *sich*! Change the following sentences to the active voice using the reflexive **sich**.

Zum Beispiel: Dieser Bericht kann schnell geschrieben werden.
Dieser Bericht schreibt sich schnell.
This report can be written quickly.

Dieser Bericht konnte schnell geschrieben werden.
Dieser Bericht hat sich schnell geschrieben.
This report could be written quickly.

1. Dieser Fehler kann leicht gemacht werden.
2. Dieses Klavierstück kann leicht gespielt werden.
3. Dieser Roman konnte gut verkauft werden.
4. Die Fenster können nicht leicht zugemacht werden.
5. Die Statue konnte nicht gefunden werden.

°D. **Bilden Sie Sätze mit *lassen*!** Change the sentences of Exercise C to the active voice using the auxiliary verb **lassen.**

    Zum Beispiel: Dieser Bericht kann schnell geschrieben werden.
                        Dieser Bericht läßt sich schnell schreiben.

                        Dieser Bericht konnte schnell geschrieben werden.
                        Dieser Bericht ließ sich schnell schreiben.

°E. **Bilden Sie Sätze mit *sein zu*!**

    Zum Beispiel: Dieses Gedicht kann leicht verstanden werden.
                        Dieses Gedicht ist leicht zu verstehen.

1. Diese Oper kann nicht leicht gesungen werden.
2. Dieses Gemälde soll kopiert (*copy*) werden.
3. Dieses Drama darf in Berlin nicht aufgeführt werden.
4. Diese Künstlerin muß gut behandelt werden.
5. Diese Sonate kann leicht gespielt werden.

F. **Übersetzen Sie die folgenden Sätze!**

1. This film should be seen by everyone.
2. This book can be read in an hour.   (Translate with the passive, **sich lassen**, and **sein zu**.)
3. This music was composed in Germany.   (Use **man**.)
4. Was this drama often performed in Austria?   (Use **man**.)
5. The work could be done easily.   (Translate three ways.)
6. The poem is to be discussed tomorrow.
7. The statue was nowhere to be found.

G. **Was man nicht kann, muß man eben erlernen!** Hans always has excuses for not doing things. Counter each of his excuses using **man**, **sich (lassen)**, and **sein zu**.

    Zum Beispiel: Dieses Gedicht ist zu schwer zu verstehen!
                        Man kann dieses Gedicht sehr leicht verstehen.
                        Dieses Gedicht versteht sich leicht.
                        Dieses Gedicht läßt sich leicht verstehen.
                        Dieses Gedicht ist leicht zu verstehen.

1. Das alte Volkslied ist zu schwer zu singen!
2. Das Museum ist zu schwer zu finden!
3. Dieser Roman ist zu schwer zu lesen!
4. So ein Bericht ist zu schwer zu schreiben!

The Use of *es* with Verbs
That Do Not Take an Object

You have seen that the *subject* of a passive sentence is the same as the direct (*accusative*) *object* of the corresponding active sentence:

> *Shakespeares Dramen* werden oft von deutschen Theatern aufgeführt. (passive)
> Shakespeare's dramas are often performed by German theaters.

> Deutsche Theater führen *Shakespeares Dramen* oft auf. (active)
> German theaters often perform Shakespeare's dramas.

Many verbs that take dative rather than accusative objects (verbs like **danken**, **helfen** and **folgen**) can be put in the passive voice through the use of the artificial subject **es**.

> Wir danken dem Musiker für das Konzert. (active—no accusative object)
> We are thanking the musician for the concert.

> Es wird dem Musiker für das Konzert gedankt. (passive with **es**)
> The musician is being thanked for the concert.

> Sie halfen den alten Schauspielern. (active—no accusative object)
> They helped the elderly actors.

> Es wurde den alten Schauspielern geholfen. (passive with **es**)
> The elderly actors were helped.

The same principle applies to many verbs such as **fahren**, **tanzen**, **trinken**, **singen**, and **klopfen** (*to knock*).

> Die Deutschen tanzen, singen und trinken sehr viel beim Oktoberfest. (active—no accusative object)
> The Germans dance, drink, and sing a lot during the Oktoberfest.

> Es wird sehr viel beim Oktoberfest getanzt, getrunken und gesungen. (passive with **es**)
> There is a lot of dancing, drinking, and singing during the Oktoberfest.

> Die Zuschauer klatschten lange am Ende der Aufführung. (active— no accusative object)
> The audience applauded for a long while at the end of the performance.

> Es wurde am Ende der Aufführung lange geklatscht. (passive with **es**)
> There was a lot of applause at the end of the performance.

Jemand klopfte an die Tür.   (active—no accusative object)
Somebody knocked at the door.

Es wurde an die Tür geklopft.   (passive with **es**)
There was a knock at the door.

Usually such passive sentences occur in types of word order where the artificial subject **es** does not immediately precede the finite verb. In such constructions the artificial subject **es** must be dropped. Nevertheless, the verb must always agree with the artificial subject, **es**:

Inverted Word Order:	Am Ende der Aufführung wurde ~~es~~ lange geklatscht.
Transposed Word Order:	Der Kritiker schrieb, daß ~~es~~ am Ende der Aufführung lange geklatscht wurde.
Question:	Wurde ~~es~~ am Ende der Aufführung lange geklatscht?

Übungen

°A. **Bilden Sie Sätze mit es!** The following sentences contain only verbs that do not have accusative objects. Change them to the passive voice using the artificial subject **es**.

Zum Beispiel: Man fliegt oft nach Berlin.
   Es wird oft nach Berlin geflogen.

   Man hat den armen Kindern geholfen.
   Es wurde den armen Kindern geholfen.

1. Man antwortet nicht auf solche Fragen.
2. Man hat dem Orchester für das schöne Konzert gedankt.
3. Man folgt nicht immer dem Rat der Eltern.
4. Man hat laut an die Tür geklopft.
5. Man hilft mir bei den Hausaufgaben.

B. **Übersetzen Sie die folgenden Sätze!** Use the passive voice.

1. There is always a lot of dancing and singing at Martin's parties.
2. Was there a knock at the door?
3. I was told yesterday that the orchestra is very good.
4. I know that people drive fast in Germany.

C. **Was für eine Party!** Describe a party you might have attended, using **es** and some of the following verbs, plus whatever other verbs you might want to include.

Zum Beispiel: Es wurde viel geflirtet.

1. flirten
2. über andere Leute sprechen
3. trinken
4. singen
5. Kartoffelchips essen
6. wild tanzen
7. Komplimente machen
8. Musik hören

Rückblick

A. **Zur Wiederholung. Übersetzen Sie die folgenden Sätze!**

1. Many fairy tales were collected in the nineteenth century. (past tense)
2. Wagner's operas are often performed at (**in**) Bayreuth.
3. German is spoken in Liechtenstein. (Translate with the passive and with **man**.)
4. Why is the art museum closed today?
5. I don't know. It was closed at precisely (**pünktlich um**) three o'clock and it is still closed.
6. Such a novel cannot be written quickly. (Translate four ways: with the passive, with **man**, with **sich**, and with **sich lassen**.)
7. That report had to be written yesterday. (Translate three ways: with the passive, with **man**, and with **sein zu**.)
8. Why wasn't the singer thanked? (Translate with the passive and with **man**.)
9. I believe that all young musicians should be helped. (Translate with the passive and with **man**.)

B. **Zur Gesamtwiederholung. Übersetzen Sie die folgenden Sätze!**

1. Such interesting tales were collected by the German Romantics (**Romantiker**). (Chapter 7)
2. The narrow (**eng**) streets were damaged by the heavy (**stark**) traffic.
3. I wished my record hadn't gotten (been) broken! (Chapter 8)
4. The musician claimed that this piece had never before (**noch nie**) been played. (Chapter 9)
5. According to the newspaper this art museum is visited by many tourists.
6. Toni, were you helped with your homework? (Chapter 10)
7. These novels were discussed at the lecture. (Chapter 11)
8. Do people often fly from here (**von hier aus**) to Switzerland? (Translate with the passive.)
9. Are those the artists who were invited to the performance (**Aufführung**)? (Chapter 12)
10. I like these poems. Which one was written by Heinrich Heine?

14
Handel und Wirtschaft

Eine Bank in Bonn

Conjunctions

Particles

Numbers

Expressions of Time

Extended Adjectives

Wortschatz

die Arbeit work, employment

der Arbeiter (-), die Arbeiterin (-nen) worker, laborer

die Fabrik (-en) firm, business

das Geld money, cash

das Geschäft (-e) business, trade, store

die Kreditkarte (-n) credit card

der Reisescheck (-s) traveler's check

der Scheck (-s) check

das Scheckkonto (-s) checking

das Sparbuch (¨er) savings book; **das Sparkonto (-s)** savings account

der Verkäufer (-), die Verkäuferin (-nen) vendor, salesperson

ab · heben: Geld abheben* to withdraw money

ab · zahlen to pay off, finish payments on

an · stellen to employ

bar · zahlen to pay cash

ein · lösen to redeem, to cash

ein · zahlen to deposit (money)

eröffnen to open (an account, a store)

führen to carry (merchandise)

mieten to rent (from)

reparieren to repair

sparen (auf etwas) to save (for something)

um · gehen* to handle; **mit Geld gut umgehen** to handle money well

verdienen to earn

vermieten to rent (to)

auf Raten kaufen to buy on an installment plan

jemandem etwas schuldig sein to owe someone something

hundert Mark klein haben to have change for one hundred marks

---

*Verbs marked with an asterisk are strong verbs; see the appendix for principal parts of strong verbs.

A. *Match each of the nouns on the left with one of the verbs on the right.*

1. Scheck
2. Arbeiter
3. Geld
4. Auto
5. Waren
6. Geschäft

a. abzahlen
b. führen
c. einlösen
d. einzahlen
e. eröffnen
f. anstellen

B. *Complete the sentences.*

1. Rolf hält überhaupt nichts von Kreditkarten oder Schecks. Er meint, man soll

   immer _____.

2. Hast du nur ein Scheckkonto oder auch ein _____?

3. Frau Lippmann geht immer nur im Kaufhaus Müller einkaufen.

   Sie meint, dort wären die _____ besonders freundlich.

4. Kann ich Ihnen vielleicht jetzt zweihundert Mark geben und dann den

   Fernseher jeden Monat mit fünfzig Mark _____?

5. Ich gehe auf die Bank, weil ich etwas Geld _____ will;

   ich muß heute viele Dinge kaufen.

C. *Match each statement on the left with the correct answer on the right.*

1. Hast du vielleicht fünfzig Mark klein?

2. Mensch, ich bin total pleite (*broke*)!

3. Ach du liebe Zeit, wo sind denn unsere Reiseschecks?

4. Guten Tag. Ich möchte gern eine Konto eröffnen.

5. Wie gefällt es dir bei deiner neuen Firma?

6. Na, wie geht das Geschäft?

7. Was wird in dieser Fabrik eigentlich gemacht?

8. Ist die Wohnung noch frei oder haben Sie sie schon vermietet?

a. Hast du wirklich überhaupt kein Geld mehr auf dem Sparbuch?

b. Besser als bei der alten. Meine Arbeit ist interessanter, und ich verdiene mehr Geld.

c. Ach, Sie wissen ja, das erste Jahr ist immer etwas schwierig.

d. Soviel ich weiß, machen sie dort Fernsehapparate.

e. Nur nicht nervös werden, Rita. Ich habe sie im Hotelsafe gelassen.

f. Ja, das tut mir leid, aber ich habe sie gerade vor 10 Minuten vermietet.

g. Ein Scheck- oder ein Sparkonto?

h. Nein, ich habe auch nur großes Geld.

1. Sparen Sie im Augenblick auf etwas?
2. Was könnten Sie reparieren, wenn Sie müßten?
3. Haben Sie schon einmal etwas auf Raten gekauft?
4. Ist Ihnen jemand Geld schuldig?
5. Was würden Sie gern mieten?
6. Kennen Sie jemand, der nicht gut mit Geld umgehen kann?

Conjunctions

Coordinating Conjunctions

A coordinating conjunction joins words, phrases or entire clauses and generally has no effect on word order. **Aber** (*but*) is a common coordinating conjunction:

Ich kaufe nie auf Raten, *aber* mein Bruder macht das immer.
I never buy on the installment plan, but my brother always does that.

Rita sagt, daß sie mit Geld gut umgeht, *aber* daß ihr Mann damit schlecht umgeht.
Rita says that she handles money well but that her husband doesn't.

The other coordinating conjunctions are **denn** (*for*), **doch** (*but*), **oder** (*or*), **sondern** (*but rather*), and **und** (*and*):

Ute will ein Scheckkonto bei dieser Bank eröffnen, *denn* sie hat schon sowieso ein Sparbuch da.
Ute wants to open a checking account at that bank, for she already has a savings account there anyway.

Karla geht heute einkaufen, *doch* gestern mußte sie im Bett bleiben.*
Karla is going shopping today, but yesterday she had to stay in bed.

Wir machen heute einen Schaufensterbummel, *oder* wir gehen ins Kino.
We'll go window shopping today, or we'll go to the movies.

Mein Vater zahlt nie bar, *sondern* er benutzt immer seine Kreditkarte.†
My father never pays cash, but rather he uses his credit card.

Ich habe mir einen neuen Wagen gekauft, *und* jetzt muß ich ihn abzahlen.
I bought myself a new car and now I have to pay it off.

---

*As a conjunction, **doch** is equivalent to **aber.**
†**Sondern** is always preceded by a negative.

Two-Part Conjunctions (Correlatives)

Correlatives are phrases that function as coordinating conjunctions. The most important are **entweder . . . oder** (*either . . . or*), **nicht nur . . . sondern auch** (*not only . . . but also*), and **weder . . . noch** (*neither . . . nor*).

> *Entweder* Inge zahlt die Rechnung, *oder* Hans zahlt sie.
> Either Inge will pay the bill (check), or Hans will pay it.

> *Entweder* Inge *oder* Hans zahlt die Rechnung.
> Either Inge or Hans will pay the bill.

> *Nicht nur* Eduard *sondern auch* seine Schwester ist uns Geld schuldig.
> Not only Eduard but also his sister owes us money.

> *Weder* die Krawatte *noch* der Hut paßt zum Anzug.
> Neither the tie nor the hat goes with the suit.

Sentence Adverbs

In the sentence, **Ja, ich spreche Deutsch, ja** functions as a separate sentence; for this reason, it is separated from the main clause by a comma and has no effect on the word order in the main clause. Other common sentence adverbs are **bitte** (*please*), **danke** (*thank you*), **doch** (*however*), **nein** (*no*), and **nun** (*now*).

> *Bitte*, könnten Sie diesen Reisescheck einlösen?
> Could you please cash this traveler's check?

> *Danke*, haben Sie auch 100 Mark klein?
> Thank you, do you also have change for a hundred marks?

> In Deutschland zahlt man keine Steuern. —*Doch*, man zahlt sie.*
> In Germany they don't pay any taxes. —On the contrary, they do.

> *Nein*, ich kann mir keinen neuen Wagen leisten.
> No, I can't afford a new car.

> *Nun*, ich kann mir vielleicht nächstes Jahr einen neuen leisten.
> Well, maybe I can afford a new one next year.

Note that when the adverb **nun** means *now* rather than *well*, it is not separated from the main clause by a comma and causes inversion of the subject and verb:

> Ich habe mein Sparbuch endlich gefunden. *Nun* kann ich etwas
>   Geld abheben.
> I finally found my savings book. Now I can withdraw some money.

As the preceding example shows, **nun** always implies a conclusion. The adverb **jetzt** must be used if reference is strictly to time.

> Es ist *jetzt* 9 Uhr 30.
> It's now 9:30.

---

*Note that **doch** negates a previous negation.

Subordinating Conjunctions

A subordinating conjunction joins a subordinate clause to another clause. In a subordinate clause (which cannot stand alone as a sentence), the finite verb appears last, as discussed in Chapter 1. **Daß** is one of the most common subordinating conjunctions.

Margot sagt, *daß* die Schuhe ihr gut passen.
Margot says that the shoes fit her well.

In the preceding example, **Margot sagt** is a main clause and **daß die Schuhe ihr gut passen** is a subordinate clause. The most common subordinating conjunctions are:

1. als   *when*

   Als ich in der Stadt war, bin ich auch auf die Bank gegangen.
   When I was downtown I went to the bank, too.

Als, wenn, and **wann** all mean *when* but have different uses. **Als** means *when* referring to one uninterrupted period or single event in the past: **Als ich in der Stadt war . . . , Als Hans in Deutschland lebte . . .** Wenn is less frequently used to refer to the past; when it is used in the past it always means **whenever:**

Jedesmal, *wenn* wir in München waren, haben wir Leberkäse mit
   Senf bestellt.
Every time (whenever) we were in Munich, we ordered Leberkäse and mustard.

Wenn (never **als**) is also used in future or present time and is the equivalent of *when, whenever,* or *if:*

Wenn ich Geld habe, kaufe ich mir immer eine neue Platte.
Whenever (if) I have money, I always buy a new record.

Wenn Marie kommt, gehen wir auf den Markt.
When Marie comes we are going to the (open) market.

Wann is only used in direct and indirect questions:

Hildegard, *wann* hast du dein
   Haus verkauft?''
Hildegard, when did you sell your
   house?

Ich fragte Hildegard, *wann* sie
   ihr Haus verkauft hat.
I asked Hildegard when she sold
   her house.

2. als ob   *as if*

   Hartmut benimmt sich, *als ob* er viel Geld hätte.
   Hartmut acts (behaves) as if he had a lot of money.

---

3. bevor *before*

Herr Friedemann hatte in einer Fabrik gearbeitet, *bevor* man ihn hier anstellte.
Mr. Friedemann had worked in a factory before he was hired here.

4. bis *until*

Helmut hat auf einen Farbfernseher gespart, *bis* er ihn sich leisten konnte.
Helmut saved for a color t.v. set until he could afford it.

5. da *since (because)*

Da du dich so krank fühlst, solltest du nicht zur Arbeit gehen.
Since you feel so sick, you shouldn't go to work.

When **da** causes transposed word order, it is equivalent to *since* in English, or *given the fact that*, as in the preceding example. When **da** functions as an adverb it causes inverted word order and is equivalent to *there* or *then*:

Ich suchte nach meiner Katze, und *da* lag sie hinter dem Ofen.
I looked for my cat, and there it lay behind the stove.

Unser Reifen platzte auf einmal. *Da* hatten wir alle wirklich Angst!
Our tire burst all of a sudden. Then we were all really afraid!

6. damit *in order that*

Richard mietete einen größeren Wagen, *damit* seine Freunde mitfahren könnten.
Richard rented a larger car in order that his friends could go along.

7. daß* *that*

Inge sagt, *daß* Petra sich einen neuen Wagen gekauft hat.
Inge says that Petra bought a new car.

Note that if **daß** is omitted, normal word order is used. This often happens with the subjunctive of indirect discourse (discussed in Chapter 9): **Inge sagte, Petra habe sich einen neuen Wagen gekauft.**

8. indem (implies intention and simultaneity)

Rolf verbringt seine Freizeit, *indem* er alte Wagen repariert.
Rolf spends his free time by repairing old cars.

Marie verbessert ihre Deutschkenntnisse, *indem* sie an einem Konversationskurs teilnimmt.
Marie is improving her German by taking a conversation course.

---

*The relative pronoun **das** has an antecedent; the conjunction **daß** does not: **Rita kauft das Gerät, das wir gesehen haben.** *Rita is buying the (radio, t.v., stereo) set that we saw yesterday.*

9. nachdem *after*

Herr Meyer eröffnete ein neues Geschäft, *nachdem* er sein altes
geschlossen hatte.
Mr. Meyer opened a new store after he had closed his old one.

10. ob *whether (if)**

Der Kunde fragte die Verkäuferin, *ob* man in diesem Geschäft auch
Stereoanlagen führt.
The customer asked the saleswoman whether (if) they also carried stereo sets
in that store.

11. obgleich, obwohl *although*

Regina will eine neue Stellung finden, *obgleich* (*obwohl*) sie hier
einen guten Gehalt bekommt.
Regina wants to find a new job although she receives a good salary here.

12. seitdem *since (the time)*

Seitdem ich die neue Stellung habe, verdiene ich viel mehr Geld.
Since I've had the new job, I've been earning a lot more money.

13. während *while (during the time)*

Heute geht Frank zum Zahnarzt, *während* wir einen
Schaufensterbummel machen.
Frank is going to the dentist's today while we go window shopping.

14. weil *because*

Ich gehe heute auf die Bank, *weil* ich etwas Geld einzahlen will.
I'm going to the bank today because I want to deposit some money.

Interrogative Words as Subordinating Conjunctions

Question words (interrogatives) function as subordinating conjunctions
when they are used in indirect questions.

Wieviel Geld verdient deine Schwester?   —Ich weiß nicht, *wieviel*
   sie verdient.
How much money does your sister earn?   —I don't know how much she earns.

Wem haben Sie Ihr Haus   Herr Scheel fragte mich, wem ich
   vermietet?   mein Haus vermietet habe.
To whom did you rent your house?   Mr. Scheel asked me to whom I rented
                                         my house.

As the examples show, interrogatives generally act as subordinators after
verbs of communication or knowledge, like **sagen, fragen,** or **wissen.**

Ob is only used in indirect questions—that is, after verbs of communication or
knowledge.

Subordinate and Main Clause

An introductory subordinate clause functions as the first element of the sentence and causes inversion in the main clause:

> *Da mein altes Sofa abgenutzt ist, kaufe ich mir ein neues.*
> Since my old sofa is worn out I'm buying myself a new one.

A quoted sentence introducing a main clause also causes inversion.

> „Ich gehe im Supermarkt einkaufen," *sagte Irene.*
> "I'm going shopping at the supermarket," said Irene.

> „Muß man hier barzahlen?" *fragte Lore.*
> "Do you have to pay cash here?" asked Lore.

Übungen

A. **Ergänzen Sie die folgenden Sätze!** Complete each sentence with the appropriate conjunction in parentheses.

Zum Beispiel: Heinrich arbeitet in der Bank, _____ er wird nicht gut bezahlt. (sondern, aber, wenn, weil)
Heinrich arbeitet in der Bank, aber er wird nicht gut bezahlt.

1. _____ ich in der Stadt war, habe ich mir einen neuen Hut gekauft. (wann, wenn, als, und)

2. _____ bist du geboren? (wann, wenn, weil)

3. Rita arbeitet nicht bei der Bank, _____ im Reisebüro. (aber, sondern, bis, entweder)

4. _____ Sonja _____ ihre Schwester ist in dieser Fabrik angestellt. (aber ... sondern, entweder ... oder, erstens ... zweitens)

5. Ich gehe mit dir einen Schaufensterbummel machen, _____ du willst. (ob, wenn, nachdem, bis)

6. _____ wir Zeit hätten, würden wir nach Deutschland reisen. (obwohl, wenn, wann, als)

7. Ich gebe Heinrich kein Geld mehr, _____ er ist mir schon zweihundert Mark schuldig. (weil, denn, oder)

8. Rudi will etwas Geld abheben, _____ die Bank ist heute geschlossen. (sondern, doch, obgleich)

9. _____ die Schreibmaschine _____ der Fernseher funktioniert gut. (entweder ... oder, weder ... noch)

10. Paul Johnson spricht Deutsch, _____ er Deutscher wäre. (doch, wenn, als ob)

11. _____ ich keine Kreditkarte habe, muß ich immer barzahlen. (da, damit, indem)

12. Helga wartet auf uns auf dem Markt, _____ wir fertig sind. (damit, bis, bevor)

13. Erich geht heute nicht zur Arbeit, _____ er Besuch aus Deutschland hat. (obgleich, weil, ob)

14. Wir kaufen uns einen neuen Farbfernseher, _____ wir uns die olympischen Spiele ansehen können. (nachdem, daß, indem, damit)

15. Jetzt spart Inge auf eine Reise nach Österreich, _____ sie jede Woche fünfzig Mark aufs Sparkonto bringt. (bevor, denn, weil, indem)

16. Herr Schneider will wissen, _____ wir einen Reisescheck einlösen dürfen. (wenn, ob, wie)

17. _____ ich ein Sparkonto eröffnet hatte, sparte ich auf meine Deutschlandreise. (bevor, vor, nachdem)

B. **Ergänzen Sie die folgenden Sätze mit dem passenden Adverb!** Complete the following sentences with **bitte, danke, doch, nein,** or **nun,** as appropriate.

1. Haben wir noch Brot?—_____, wir haben kein Brot mehr. Ich muß zum Bäcker.

2. Möchtest du noch ein Stück Kuchen? _____, aber ich habe wirklich schon genug gegessen.

3. So ein Wagen kann sicher nicht sehr teuer sein.—_____!

4. _____, können Sie mir diesen Scheck einlösen?

C. **Ergänzen Sie die folgenden Sätze mit *nun* oder *jetzt!***

1. Mein Wagen startet nicht. _____ werden wir zu spät kommen.

2. Ich möchte auf die Bank, aber _____ ist es zu früh.

3. Ich habe nicht genug Geld bei mir. _____ muß ich meine Kreditkarte benutzen.

4. Gestern hat es geregnet, und _____ regnet es wieder.

D. **Bilden Sie Sätze!** Rearrange the words and phrases to form sentences.

Zum Beispiel: bevor Ursula einkaufen ging / sie / angerufen / eine Freundin / hatte

Bevor Ursula einkaufen ging, hatte sie eine Freundin angerufen.

1. Herr Kronstadt will wissen / wann / aufmacht / man / das Geschäft
2. entweder / ich / kaufe / eine neue Schreibmaschine / oder / ich / meine alte reparieren / lasse
3. Richard und Monika / immer / eine Kreditkarte / benutzen / wenn / einkaufen / sie / gehen
4. nachdem Frau Ziemann diese Firma gekauft hatte / sie / noch mehr Arbeiter / stellte / an
5. „Warum kannst du mit Geld nicht besser umgehen?" / Fräulein Thiele / ihre Schwester / fragte.

E. **Verbinden Sie die folgenden Sätze!** Join the two clauses with an appropriate subordinating conjunction (or interrogative). Translate the sentence.

Zum Beispiel: Man benutzte Gaslichter, _____ Edison die Glühbirne (*lightbulb*) erfand.

Man benutzte Gaslichter, bis Edison die Glühbirne erfand.
They used gas lights until Edison invented the lightbulb.

1. Die Kommunisten errichteten die Berliner Mauer, _____ Berlin in vier Zonen geteilt worden war.

2. Man kann auf etwas Teueres sparen, _____ man jeden Monat ein bißchen Geld auf ein Sparkonto einzahlt. (two possibilities)

3. Wolfgang hat ein Scheckkonto bei der Kölner Bank, _____ er immer barzahlt.

4. Frau Biermann fragte den Verkäufer, _____ die neuen Schuhe zu ihrem Kleid passen.

5. Der Tourist wollte wissen, _____ es in Westdeutschland so viele Gastarbeiter gibt.

6. Ich glaube, daß Gertrud ihrer Tochter eine Schreibmaschine kauft, _____ sie ihre Hausaufgaben schneller machen kann.

7. Diese Schuhe sind zu eng (*narrow*), _____ diese hier zu weit (*wide*) sind.

Übersetzen Sie die folgenden Sätze!

1. I never buy on the installment plan, but rather I always pay cash.
2. Silvia wants to rent (**mieten**) this house, but Mr. Lederer doesn't want to rent it out. (**vermieten**)
3. Either Gretchen or her brother went shopping with Krista.
4. That is not a traveler's check.—Yes (it is)!
5. I sold my old car. Now I have to buy a new one.
6. When we went window-shopping I saw a beautiful suit.
7. Please take (**bringen**) that check along when you go to the bank, Miss Becker.
8. Marianne lived in Ulm until she was thirteen years old.
9. Tina bought me this book so (in order that) I could (can) learn German.
10. One receives good grades by working hard.
11. Joseph wants to know whether this coat is expensive.
12. Mrs. Klemperer, could you tell me who paid the bill?

G. **Gehen Sie mit Geld gut um?** Are you a wise shopper? Answer the following questions.

1. Kaufen Sie immer auf Raten, zahlen Sie immer bar, oder benutzen Sie immer eine Kreditkarte?
2. Haben Sie nur ein Scheckkonto oder auch ein Sparbuch?
3. Sie gehen im Kleidergeschäft einkaufen. Folgen Sie immer dem Rat des Verkäufers (der Verkäuferin), oder sehen Sie selber, ob Ihnen die Kleider wirklich gut passen?
4. Sparen Sie auf etwas Wichtiges wie ein Haus oder einen Wagen?
5. Sind Sie jemand Geld schuldig? Wieviel schulden Sie ihm (ihr)?
6. Wie schnell zahlen Sie ihre Rechnungen ab, wenn Sie auf Raten kaufen?
7. Die wichtigste Frage: Geben Sie mehr Geld aus als Sie verdienen? (Wenn Sie „ja" antworten, so sind Sie bei dieser Prüfung durchgefallen!)

Particles

Particles (such as **auch, bloß, denn,** and **nämlich**) occur mainly in the predicate of a sentence and express the speaker's attitude toward the statement made. They are especially common in conversational German. Here are some of the most common uses:

Max hatte *aber* recht!
Max was right after all! (surprise)

Das hätte ich *aber* nicht erwartet!
I really wouldn't have expected that.

Du willst *also* nicht ins Kino gehen. (*Also*, du willst nicht ins Kino gehen.)
So (I was right), you don't want to go to the movies.

Was du *auch* (*immer*) willst, ich gebe es dir.
Whatever you want, I'll give it to you.

Wie konntest du so etwas *bloß* glauben?
How could you even believe such a thing?

Wenn Sara *bloß* ein bißchen lernen würde!
If Sara would just (merely) study a little!

Woher hast du *denn* so eine alte Schreibmaschine gefunden?
Where in heaven's name did you find such an old typewriter?

Du willst *doch* nicht ins Kino gehen?
You *mean* you *really* don't want to go to movies after all? (disappointment)

Du willst also nicht ins Kino gehen? —*Doch!**
So you don't want to go to the movies? —On the contrary, I do want to.

Komm *mal* mit!
Why don't you come along? (emphasis)

Wir gehen ins Museum. Es gibt *ja* eine interessante Ausstellung.
We're going to the museum. There's an interesting exhibition, you know.

Ich muß fleißiger arbeiten. Ich will *nämlich* bessere Noten bekommen.
I have to work harder. After all, I want to get better grades.

Marie will sich einen Wagen kaufen und kann *nicht mal* Auto fahren!
Marie wants to buy a car and can't even drive! (surprise)

Nun gut, ich komme mit.
Okay, okay (all right), I'm coming. (concession)

Nun laß das doch!†
Stop that now! (impatience)

Du hast den ganzen Tag gespielt. Nun machen wir Schluß!
You have played all day. Now that's enough. (conclusion)

Schon gut!
Okay, okay (all right)! (concession)

Schon wieder?
What, again? (annoyance)

Komm *schon* mit!
Why don't you come along? (encouragement)

---

*Note that **doch** negates the negation of a previous statement.
†**Doch** (unstressed) emphasizes impatience: **Nun, iß doch!** *Will you just eat now?*

Übungen

A. **Welche Übersetzung paßt am besten?** Choose the most appropriate translation of each sentence.

1. Walter, du hättest deinem Bruder aber etwas Geld geben sollen!

   a. Walter, okay, okay, so you should have given your brother some money!
   b. You really should have given your brother some money, Walter!

2. Schon gut! Ich zahle bar, Herr Valentiner!

   a. Okay, okay! I'll pay cash, Mr. Valentiner!
   b. On the contrary, I'll pay cash, Mr. Valentiner!
   c. I'll pay cash, you know, Mr. Valentiner!

3. Warum benutzt du denn immer deine Kreditkarte?

   a. After all, why do you always use your credit card?
   b. In heaven's name, why do you always use your credit card?
   c. On the contrary, why do you always use your credit card?

4. Sie führen hier also tragbare Geräte.

   a. So you do carry portable sets, as I expected.
   b. You mean, you do carry portable sets after all.
   c. Okay, okay! So you do carry portable sets.

5. Veronika hat ein neues Sofa gekauft und hat nicht einmal hundert Mark auf der Bank!

   a. Veronika bought a new sofa and doesn't have a hundred marks in the bank after all!
   b. Veronika bought a new sofa and doesn't even have a hundred marks in the bank!
   c. You know, Veronika bought a new sofa and doesn't even have a hundred marks in the bank!

6. Probier mal diesen Kuchen! Mutti hat ihn ja gebacken.

   a. Why don't you try this cake? Mom made it, you know.
   b. So, you're going to try this cake. Mom made it, in heaven's name!

B. **Ein Schaufensterbummel.** Cornelia and her husband Max are window-shopping for clothes. Complete their conversation with one of the particles indicated in parentheses.

CORNELIA: Schau dir _____ diese Schuhe an! (mal, schon, auch)

MAX: Ich habe _____ schon viele gute Schuhe. (nun, ja, mal)

CORNELIA: _____ gut, aber du hast gar keine Anzüge, zu denen die

Schuhe passen! (schon, doch, aber)

MAX: Wie kannst du so etwas _____ sagen! (ja, nun, bloß)

Ich habe _____ wenigstens vier Anzüge, zu denen meine

Schuhe passen! (auch, also, doch)

CORNELIA: _____ gut, das stimmt. (bloß, aber, nun) Ich meine ja nur,

daß du dir _____ wirklich mal wieder etwas Neues kaufen

solltest. (aber, schon, denn)

MAX: Meinst du das wirklich? Willst du vielleicht morgen mit mir einkaufen

gehen? Ich tue das _____ nicht gern allein. (schon, aber,

nämlich)

CORNELIA: _____ gerne! (mal, aber, bloß)

Numbers

Cardinal Numbers

0	null	11	elf	30	dreißig
1	eins*	12	zwölf	40	vierzig
2	zwei	13	dreizehn	50	fünfzig
3	drei	14	vierzehn	60	sechzig
4	vier	15	fünfzehn	70	siebzig
5	fünf	16	sechzehn	80	achtzig
6	sechs	17	siebzehn	90	neunzig
7	sieben	18	achtzehn	100	hundert
8	acht	19	neunzehn	101	hunderteins[†]
9	neun	20	zwanzig	200	zweihundert
10	zehn	21	einundzwanzig		

1000 tausend
2001 zweitausendeins
100 000 hunderttausend
1 000 000 eine Million
3 600 000 drei Millionen[‡] sechshunderttausend
1 000 000 000 eine Milliarde (*billion*)
1 000 000 000 000 eine Billion (*trillion*)

---

*Germans write the numeral 1 as 1; they write 7 as 7.

[†]Notice from the table that, contrary to English usage, **und** is not usually used between **hundert** or **tausend** followed by any other number: **hundertvier, zweitausendzwanzig**.

[‡]Contrary to English usage the plural of **Million** (**Milliarde**, and **Billion**) is used when followed by numbers or nouns.

Pronunciation of Cardinal Numbers

1. The **-echs** of **sechs** is pronounced as in **ex**tra, but the **-ech** of **sechzehn** and **sechzig** is pronounced as in **Recht**.

2. The **ie** of **vier** is pronounced as written, but the **ie** of **vierzehn** and **vierzig** is pronounced short as in **Wirt**.

3. **Dreißig** contains an **ß**, not a **z** as in the other tens: **zwanzig, vierzig, fünfzig,** etc.

4. **Zwei** is sometimes pronounced **zwo** where there is a danger of misunderstanding; for instance, in telephone conversations. It is always written **zwei**.

Cardinal Numbers in Writing

Numbers from one to one million are written as one word, including the conjunction **und**.

> Letztes Jahr waren *vierundzwanzig* Gastarbeiter hier angestellt.
> Last year there were twenty-four guest workers employed here.

But:

> Es sind über eine Million fünfhunderttausend Einwohner in dieser Stadt.
> There are over 1,500,000 inhabitants in this city.

Numbers in German are written out in most of the same situations as when they are written out in English, except that all numbers are written out in approximations.

> Ich habe *zehn* Bücher.
> I have ten books.

> Ich fahre um *10.00* ab.
> I'm leaving at 10:00.

> Es gibt über *zehntausend* Angestellte in dieser Fabrik.   (approximation)
> There are over 10,000 employees in this factory.

Commas are used in German where a decimal point is used in English; a period or space is used in German where commas are used in English.

DM 1,30 = eine Mark dreißig
1.30 marks

DM −,22 = zweiundzwanzig
Pfennig*
.22 marks

1 500 000 or 1.500.000
1,500,000

---

*Both **Mark** and **Pfennig** are always singular in prices.

-er, mal

The suffix **-er** is often added to numbers to indicate decades. No other endings may be added to this suffix.

> Der Zweite Weltkrieg fand in den dreißiger und vierziger Jahren statt.
> The Second World War took place during the thirties and forties.

The plural numbers **Hunderte** and **Tausende** are capitalized and used much as in English.

> Wir haben *Tausende* von Jugendlichen beim Rockkonzert gesehen.
> We saw thousands of young people at the rock concert.

The adverbs *once, twice, three times,* etc. are formed through the addition of **-mal** to the cardinal numbers.

> Brigitte mußte ihre Schreibmaschine *dreimal* in die Reparatur bringen.
> Brigitte had to take her typewriter to the repair shop three times.

Je, pro, beide

Je before numbers indicates an equal distribution:

> Der Professor stellte den Studenten je vier Fragen.
> The professor asked the students four questions each.

Pro is equivalent to *per* after numbers.

> Diese Würste kosten DM 10.— pro Kilo.
> These sausages cost ten marks per kilogram.

The definite article may also be used to mean *per*:

> Diese Würste kosten DM 10.— *das* Kilo.

Beide (plural) means *both*. **Beides** is the singular and refers to concepts or inanimate objects.

> Josef hat seine *beiden* Autos verkauft.
> Josef sold both of his cars.

> *Beide* Männer waren da.
> Both men were there.

> *Die beiden* waren da.
> Both of them were there.

> Sagt man „Brüderlein" oder „Brüderchen"?   —*Beides ist* richtig.
> Does one say "Brüderlein" or "Brüderchen"?   —Both are right.

Adjectives following **beide** are usually declined weak.

> Ute hat drei gute Bücher gekauft. Ute hat *beide* guten Bücher gekauft.
> Ute bought three good books. Ute bought both good books.

Ein(s)

When unstressed, **ein** is the indefinite article *a* or *an*; when stressed, it is the number *one*. In both cases it is declined as an **ein**-word.

Ich sehe einen neuen Wagen da.
I see a new car there.

Ich sehe nur einen neuen Wagen da.
I see only one new car there.

Just as do other **ein**-words, **ein** takes the endings of the **der**-words when it is not followed by a noun:

Ich habe fast alle meine Reiseschecks eingelöst. Nur einer ist übrig.
I've cashed almost all of my traveler's checks. Only one is left.

Ich zähle: eins, zwei, drei, vier . . .
I'll count: one, two, three, four . . .

No ending is added to **ein** if it is followed by **und** as part of another number.

einundzwanzig   But: hunderteins

Ordinal Numbers

der, das, die	erste
	zweite
	dritte
	vierte
	fünfte
	sechste
	sieb(en)te
	achte
	neunte
	zehnte
		der, das, die	elfte
			zwölfte
			dreizehnte,
			   vierzehnte, etc.
			zwanzigste
			einundzwanzigste,
			   etc.
			hundertste
			hundert(und)erste
			hundertzweite, etc.
			tausendste, etc.

Ordinal numbers are formed from cardinal numbers by adding the suffix **-t** or **-st** and the appropriate adjective endings. The suffix **-t** is added to the cardinals from two to nineteen. All other cardinals take the suffix **-st**. The ordinals **erste**, **dritte**, **siebte** (**siebente**), and **achte** are irregular.

zweite   zwanzigste
zehnte   fünfundvierzigste
neunzehnte   hundertste

Barbara arbeitet am zweiten Schalter in der Bank.
Barbara works at the second window in the bank.

Wir müssen bis zum fünfundzwanzigsten Kapitel lesen.
We must read up to the twenty-fifth chapter.

Das ist die vierte Kreditkarte, die Hans verloren hat.
That is the fourth credit card Hans has lost.

The numerical adverbs **erstens, zweitens**, and so forth are formed by attaching the suffix **-ens** to ordinal numbers.

> *Erstens* kann ich mir keinen neuen Wagen leisten, und *zweitens* bin ich mit meinem alten zufrieden.
> First (in the first place), I can't afford a new car, and second (in the second place) I'm satisfied with my old one.

Fractions

Fractions are formed from ordinal numbers through the addition of **-el**. They are neuter and do not change in the plural.

ein Drittel	ein Viertel	ein Fünftel
a third	a fourth	a fifth
drei Viertel	ein Fünfundzwanzigstel	
three-fourths	a twenty-fifth	

The fraction *one-half* is not derived from any numeral: **eine Hälfte**. *Half a* is expressed by **halb.**

> Möchtest du einen Apfel? —Bitte, gib mir nur *eine Hälfte.*
> Would you like an apple? —Please give me just a half.

> Ich möchte einen halben Apfel.
> I would like half an apple.

Note the following expressions based on **half**; such expressions cannot be declined.

anderthalb	zwei(und)einhalb	drei(und)einhalb
one and a half	two and a half	three and a half

> In *anderthalb* Jahren kaufe ich mir einen neuen Wagen.
> In a year and a half (one and a half years) I'll buy a new car.

Common Mathematical Expressions

Here are some common mathematical expressions in German:

$2 + 8 = 10$	Zwei und (plus) acht ist zehn.
$8 - 2 = 6$	Acht weniger (minus) zwei ist sechs.
$4 \times 5 = 20$	Vier mal fünf ist zwanzig.
$(4.5 = 20)$	
$40 : 8 = 5$	Vierzig geteilt durch acht ist fünf.
$\sqrt{64} = 8$	Quadratwurzel aus vierundsechzig ist acht.
$4^3 = 64$	Vier hoch drei ist vierundsechzig.
$\dfrac{n}{2}$	n über zwei
n_7	n sieben
$x(a + b)$	x mal Klammer *a* plus *b*

Übungen

A. **Lesen Sie die folgenden Zahlen vor!** Read the following numbers aloud.

1. 1	6. 70
2. 14	7. 101
3. 16	8. 489
4. 20	9. 1 008
5. 31	10. 300 009

B. **Lesen Sie die folgenden Sätze vor!** Read the following sentences aloud.

1. Der römische Historiker Tacitus, der 120 nach Christi starb, schrieb viel über die germanischen Stämme (*tribes*).
2. Karl der Große lebte zwischen 768 und 814.
3. Im Jahre 1517 veröffentlichte Martin Luther seine 95 Thesen.
4. Der große deutsche Maler Albrecht Dürer starb im Jahre 1528.
5. Johann Sebastian Bach lebte zwischen 1685 und 1750.
6. Der größte Dichter der deutschen Sprache, Johann Wolfgang von Goethe, wurde im Jahre 1749 geboren.
7. Ludwig van Beethoven wurde im Jahre 1770 geboren.
8. Westdeutschland (die BRD) ist 248 542 Quadratkilometer groß.
9. Ostdeutschland (die DDR) ist 108 173 Quadratkilometer groß.
10. Der Rhein ist 865 Kilometer lang.
11. Die Zugspitze (in den Alpen) ist 2963 Meter hoch.
12. Die Bevölkerung (*population*) der heutigen BRD beträgt (*amounts to*) 61 350 000; die der heutigen DDR beträgt 16 720 000; die des heutigen Österreichs beträgt 7 500 000, und die der heutigen Schweiz beträgt 6 345 000.
13. Zwischen 1820 und 1978 sind fast 6 977 000 Deutsche in die USA eingewandert (*immigrated*).
14. Zwischen 1951 und 1960 allein sind 477 765 Deutsche in die USA eingewandert.

C. **Ergänzen Sie diese Serien!** Complete each series of numbers with the missing number and read the series in German.

1. 2, 4, 6, ____

2. 5, 10, 15, ____

3. 2, 5, 8, 11, ____

4. 3, 4, 6, 9, ____

5. 34, 17, 36, 18, ____

D. **Schreiben Sie die folgenden Zahlen!** Write out the following numbers.

1. 42
2. 1016
3. 416

4. 101
5. 61
6. 3 500 000
7. 20 002

E. **Schreiben Sie die folgenden mathematischen Ausdrücke!** Write the following mathematical expressions in words.

Zum Beispiel: $60 : 12 = 5$
Sechzig geteilt durch zwölf ist fünf.

1. $14 \times 2 = 28$
2. $1000 + 405 = 1405$
3. $36 - 20 = 16$
4. $\sqrt{144} = 12$
5. $5^2 = 25$
6. $\dfrac{a}{3}$
7. p_9
8. $y(a + b)$

F. **Übersetzen Sie die folgenden Sätze!**

1. There are over 4,550 employees in this factory.
2. The Beatles wrote many songs in the sixties and seventies.
3. Thousands of guest workers live in this town.
4. Why did the professor repeat that word four times?
5. This coffee costs eleven marks per kilogram.
6. Do you like these cars, Mr. Wagner? —Yes, both are beautiful.
7. Where are your brothers, Marie? —Both went to the movies.
8. Does Ulrike work at the first window? —No, she works at the third one.
9. The seventh chapter in this book is harder than the eighth.
10. Only a half of these stores carry portable sets.
11. Toni, would you like half a piece of cake?
12. I have to pay my car off in two and a half years.
13. I'm not buying that hat. In the first place it is too expensive. In the second place, I don't need it.

G. **An welche Zahl denken Sie?** What number do you associate with each of the following?

1. eine Minute
2. Kolumbus
3. ein Jahr
4. die Vereinigten Staaten
5. das Alphabet
6. die Planeten
7. Beethovens Symphonien
8. eine amerikanische Fußballmannschaft
9. eine Baseballmannschaft
10. Februar

Expressions of Time

Telling Time: Twelve-hour System

In conversational German, time is told on a twelve-hour basis using the prepositions **nach** and **vor**.

Wieviel Uhr ist es?   (Wie spät ist es?)

Es ist 8.05.*	Es ist 12.55.
Es is fünf (Minuten) nach acht.	Es ist fünf (Minuten) vor eins.
Es ist 8.10.	Es ist 7.50.
Es ist zehn (Minuten) nach acht.	Es ist zehn (Minuten) vor acht.
Es ist 8.15.	Es ist 7.45.
Es ist Viertel nach acht.	Es ist Viertel vor acht.

The half hour is commonly stated in two ways:

Es ist 5.30.	Es ist 1.30.
Es ist fünf Uhr dreißig.	Es ist ein Uhr dreißig.
Es ist halb sechs.	Es ist halb zwei.

To avoid ambiguity, the following expressions may be included:

8 Uhr *morgens*	8 Uhr *abends*
8:00 A.M.	8:00 P.M.
12 Uhr *mittags*	12 Uhr *mitternachts*
12:00 noon	12:00 midnight

Other useful time expressions include:

gegen 8 Uhr	um *(pünktlich)* 8 Uhr
around eight o'clock	at (exactly) eight o'clock

Wieviel Uhr haben Sie?   —Ich habe 8 Uhr.
What time do you have?   —I have eight o'clock. (My watch says eight o'clock.)

Telling Time: Twenty-four-hour System

In official use (transportation schedules, theater ads, and so forth), time is told on a twenty-four-hour basis (as it is in the U.S. armed services). In this system, qualifications such as A.M. and P.M. are avoided by designating the hours after noon as "thirteen" instead of "one P.M.," "fourteen" instead of "two P.M.," and so on until "twenty-four"—i.e., midnight.

---

*A period is used in time expressions where a colon is used in English: *It is 8:05.*

Was gibt zum Ausverkauf (What's on sale)?

Es ist 1.15.*	Es ist 12.40.
Es ist ein Uhr fünfzehn.	Es ist zwölf Uhr vierzig.
Es ist 19.55.	Es ist 24.00.
Es ist neunzehn Uhr fünfundfünfzig.	Es ist vierundzwanzig Uhr.

Dates

Names of days of the week, months of the year, and seasons are masculine:

ein schöner Sonntag	ein warmer Juni	ein kurzer Sommer
a beautiful Sunday	a warm June	a short summer

Dates are written and read in the following manner:

am 22. Juli 1979 / den 22. Juli 1979 / (more formally) 22.VII.79
am (den) zweiundzwanzigsten Juli neunzehnhundertneunundsiebzig

Goethe wurde am (den) 28. August 1749 geboren.
Goethe was born on August 28, 1749.

---

*When time is told using the twenty-four-hour system, **Viertel** and **halb** are not used.

Dates in the heading of letters are written after the place of origin: Hamburg, den 22. Juli 1979. To say *in* a certain year (*in 1832*) one must either say **im Jahre 1832** or use no preposition at all.

Goethe ist *im Jahre 1832* gestorben. (Goethe ist *1832* gestorben.)

The prepositional phrase **am** may be used with a day of the week or with any part of the day except **die Nacht**. **Im** is used with most other time expressions.

(am) Freitag	am Abend
am 22. März	am Nachmittag
im März	im Jahre 1920
im Winter	im 19. Jahrhundert

But: in der Nacht

To ask about the date, one can say:

Welcher Tag ist heute?
Welchen Tag haben wir heute? }—Heute ist Freitag.

Der wievielte ist heute?
Den wievielten haben wir heute? }—Heute ist der 20. März.

Adverbs of Time

Many adverbs of time are formed from nouns by attaching the suffix **-s**. Such forms refer to recurring time periods and are capitalized only if they are derived from days of the week.

tags (am Tag)	morgens
during the day	in the morning
vormittags	mittags
in the forenoon (late morning)	at noon
nachmittags	abends
in the afternoon	in the evening
nachts (in der Nacht)	Montags (am Montag)
at night	on Monday(s)
Sonntags (am Sonntag)	
on Sunday(s)	

These adverbs may be used after other expressions of time: **Dienstag nachmittags gehe ich immer einkaufen**. *I always go shopping on Tuesday afternoon.*

Morgen (Vor-, Nach-), **Mittag**, and **Abend** can be used after other expressions of time to express a specific period; in that case, they are not capitalized.

heute morgen	Montag morgen	gestern nachmittag
this morning	Monday morning	yesterday afternoon
gestern abend	Dienstag vormittag	
last night	Tuesday forenoon (late morning)	

When **morgen** occurs alone or before another time expression it means *tomorrow*.

morgen	morgen abend
tomorrow	tomorrow evening
morgen nachmittag	morgen früh
tomorrow afternoon	tomorrow morning

Days of the week, months, seasons, and the nouns **Tag**, **Woche**, and **Monat** are in the accusative case when modified by adjectives.

Hans war *letzten Donnerstag* nicht bei der Arbeit.
Hans wasn't at work last Thursday.

Nächsten Januar bin ich in Berlin.
I'll be in Berlin next January.

Letzten Sommer habe ich für dieses Geschäft gearbeitet.
Last summer I worked for this business (store).

Wir haben *jeden Tag* Unterricht.
We have class every day.

Diese Woche muß ich auf die Bank.
This week I have to go to the bank.

Frau Schmidt fährt *nächsten Monat* in die Schweiz.
Mrs. Schmidt is going to Switzerland next month.

Duration of time is expressed with the definite article and the appropriate noun (time expression) in the accusative case.

Klara hat *den ganzen Tag* gearbeitet.
Klara worked all day long.

Wir haben fast *die ganze Nacht* Karten gespielt.
We played cards almost all night long.

Karsten hat *das ganze Jahr* Fußball gespielt.
Karsten played soccer all year long.

An indefinite point in time is expressed by the genitive expression **eines . . . (e)s**.

Eines Tages fahren wir zusammen nach Wien.
One of these days we'll drive to Vienna together.

Eines Tages begegneten wir einigen alten Freunden im Park.
One day we met some old friends in the park.

Here are some other useful time expressions:

vor einer Stunde (vor drei Tagen, vor fünf Jahren)
an hour ago (three days ago, five years ago)

in einer Stunde in an hour	heute in acht Tagen a week from today
vorgestern the day before yesterday	morgen in einem Monat a month from tomorrow
übermorgen the day after tomorrow	(schon) seit drei Stunden* for three hours
gestern vor acht Tagen a week ago yesterday	frühmorgens early in the morning

Übungen

A. **Wann fährt der Zug ab?** Given below are the departure times of various trains from the Frankfurt railroad station. The hours are given according to the official twenty-four-hour system. Read them in German aloud, then restate them in conversational German.

Zum Beispiel: 13.10
Der Zug fährt um dreizehn Uhr zehn ab.
Der Zug fährt nachmittags um zehn Minuten nach eins ab.

1.	01.45		4.	11.35
2.	12.00		5.	24.00
3.	05.15		6.	15.42

B. **Übersetzen Sie den folgenden Brief!**

August 18, 1981

Dear Marie-Luise,

 I received your letter Friday afternoon. Last night I began to write you this letter, but an old friend called me at around 9:30 and we talked for a long time **(lange)**. Then I was too tired to continue writing. I work well in the day but not at night because I become too sleepy. Well, tomorrow morning I'm leaving for Germany for **(auf)** a couple of months. I have been packing my things **(meine Sachen)** all day long until now. Two months from today I'll be back home again. Maybe one day we can go to Germany together.

Give my regards to your parents. **(Grüß deine Eltern von mir!)**

Your Wolfgang

---

*This expression is used with the present tense, as discussed in Chapter 1.

C. **Beschreiben Sie das Leben eines Studenten!** Describe Kurt's day, telling what time he does each of the following. Use expressions such as **morgens**, **nachmittags**, and **abends**.

Zum Beispiel: Kurt steht morgens um zehn Minuten nach sieben Uhr auf.

1.

2.

3.

4.

5.

6.

7.

Now describe your own daily schedule.

Extended Adjectives

Compare the sentences on the left, which contain relative clauses (in italics), with those on the right, which contain extended adjectives (also in italics).

Relative Clause	*Extended Adjective*
Das Flugzeug, *das gestern auf dem Frankfurter Flughafen landete,* war voll besetzt. The airplane that landed at the Frankfurt airport yesterday was completely full.	Das *gestern auf dem Frankfurter Flughafen landende* Flugzeug war voll besetzt.

Relative Clause	Extended Adjective
Man sprach über ein Gedicht, *das von Rilke kurz vor seinem Tod geschrieben wurde.* They spoke about a poem that was written by Rilke shortly before his death.	Man sprach über ein *von Rilke kurz vor seinem Tod geschriebenes* Gedicht.
Diese Erfindung, *die für die Kernforschung so wichtig ist,* wurde von einem Deutschen gemacht. This discovery, which is so important for atomic research, was made by a German.	Diese *für die Kernforschung so wichtige* Erfindung wurde von einem Deutschen gemacht.
Diese uralte Schrift, *die von Linguisten immer noch nicht zu entziffern ist,* bleibt ein Rätsel. This ancient script, which still cannot be deciphered by linguists, remains a riddle.	Diese *von Linguisten immer noch nicht zu entziffernde* uralte Schrift bleibt ein Rätsel.

Most modern writers avoid lengthy extended adjectives, although they are quite common in modern technical literature, especially in the natural sciences, and in older literature. For this reason you should develop a facility to read them.

Study hint: If you find it difficult to comprehend an extended adjective, try the following procedure: (1) think of the introductory **ein-** or **der**-word as joined to the final noun of the phrase—for instance, in the first example: **das . . . Flugzeug;** (2) insert the appropriate relative pronoun and continue with the extended adjective making any other necessary changes in the final verb form: **das . . . Flugzeug,** *das* **gestern auf dem Frankfurter Flughaven** *landete.* . . .

Übungen

Übersetzen Sie die folgenden Sätze! The following vocabulary may be new to you:

leider	*unfortunately*	fliehen	*to flee*
eigentlich	*actually*	streichen	*to paint*
befolgen	*to follow (a law)*	Schwierigkeit	*difficulty*
vertreiben	*to drive out*	Auskünfte (pl.)	*information*

1. Man findet überall in Europa schöne von den Römern errichtete Bauten.
2. Leider trennt die im Jahre 1961 von der Regierung der DDR gebaute Mauer die Stadt Berlin.

3. Dieses in sechs Monaten abzuzahlende tragbare Gerät ist eigentlich zu teuer.
4. Die neu gewählten Politiker haben das von manchen Bürgern nicht befolgte Gesetz besprochen.
5. Nach dem Zweiten Weltkrieg sind viele von den Kommunisten vertriebene Flüchtlinge in die BRD geflohen.
6. Das vor zwei Jahren gestrichene Haus sah immer noch sehr neu aus.
7. Endlich ging die mit Schwierigkeiten zu verstehende Ausländerin zur Polizeiwache (*police station*), um Auskünfte über die Stadt zu holen.

Rückblick━━━━━━━━━━━━

A. **Zur Wiederholung. Übersetzen Sie die folgenden Sätze!**

1. We would like to rent that big house, but we have to pay too many taxes (**Steuern**).
2. I don't go to that store because they don't cash checks.
3. I can't buy a stereo set until I withdraw some money.
4. They will call us when they repair our car.
5. When did you order that book, Tina?
6. Martin wants to know if you have change for 500 marks.
7. There are about 1066 workers in this factory.
8. Is Rudi only 21 years old?
9. My parents were just (only) teenagers (**Teenager**) in the forties.
10. Veronika and Michael, what do you do Friday afternoons?
11. Goethe died in 1832.
12. Last summer I rented a house at the beach (**am Strand**).

B. **Zur Gesamtwiederholung. Übersetzen Sie die folgenden Sätze!**

1. Those brown shoes don't fit me. —My new shoes don't fit me either (**auch nicht**). (Chapter 7)
2. Helena is employed in that Swiss bank.
3. If I could only handle money better! (Chapter 8)
4. Krista, you shouldn't have bought that car on the installment plan.
5. My parents claim that everything costs too much. (Chapter 9)
6. The saleswoman said that they had never before (**noch nie**) carried those sets.
7. Mrs. Sommer, did you decide to buy the first sofa? (Chapter 10)
8. Was this street damaged by the traffic or the workmen? (Chapter 11)
9. Do you know the addresses of those who have not paid off their bills, Miss Schröder? (Chapter 12)
10. When was this third check cashed, Mr. Rauschning? (Chapter 13)
11. We didn't go shopping in that store because the doors were closed when we arrived.

Appendix, Vocabularies, Index

Appendix

Principal Parts of Strong and Irregular Verbs

The following chart shows the principal parts of strong and irregular verbs. Most verbs with prefixes are not listed; for example, the principal parts of the verbs **anfangen** and **beschreiben** are given under the verbs **fangen** and **schreiben**. The past participles of verbs that form their perfect tenses with the auxiliary **sein** are preceded by **ist**. Irregular third-person singular forms of the present indicative are also listed.

Infinitive	Past Stem	Past Participle	Third-Person Singular
backen *to bake*	buk	gebacken	bäckt
befehlen *to command*	befahl	befohlen	befiehlt
beginnen *to begin*	begann	begonnen	
beißen *to bite*	biß	gebissen	
betrügen *to deceive*	betrog	betrogen	
biegen *to bend*	bog	gebogen	
bieten *to offer*	bot	geboten	
binden *to bind*	band	gebunden	
bitten *to ask*	bat	gebeten	
blasen *to blow*	blies	geblasen	bläst
bleiben *to remain*	blieb	ist geblieben	
braten *to roast*	briet	gebraten	brät
brechen *to break*	brach	gebrochen	bricht
brennen *to burn*	brannte	gebrannt	
bringen *to bring*	brachte	gebracht	
denken *to think*	dachte	gedacht	
dringen *to press*	drang	gedrungen	
dürfen *to be allowed*	durfte	gedurft	darf
empfehlen *to recommend*	empfahl	empfohlen	empfiehlt
erschrecken* *to be frightened*	erschrak	ist erschrocken	erschrickt
essen *to eat*	aß	gegessen	ißt
fahren *to drive, ride, go*	fuhr	ist gefahren	fährt
fallen *to fall*	fiel	ist gefallen	fällt
fangen *to catch*	fing	gefangen	fängt
finden *to find*	fand	gefunden	
fliegen *to fly*	flog	ist geflogen	
fliehen *to flee*	floh	ist geflohen	

---

*The transitive verb **erschrecken,** *to frighten,* is weak.

Infinitive	Past Stem	Past Participle	Third-Person Singular
fließen to flow	floß	ist geflossen	
fressen to eat (of animals)	fraß	gefressen	frißt
frieren to freeze	fror	gefroren	
geben to give	gab	gegeben	gibt
gehen to go	ging	ist gegangen	
gelingen to succeed	gelang	ist gelungen	
gelten to be worth	galt	gegolten	gilt
genießen to enjoy	genoß	genossen	
geschehen to happen	geschah	ist geschehen	geschieht
gewinnen to win, gain	gewann	gewonnen	
gießen to pour	goß	gegossen	
graben to dig	grub	gegraben	gräbt
greifen to seize	griff	gegriffen	
haben to have	hatte	gehabt	hat
halten to hold	hielt	gehalten	hält
hangen to hang (intr.)	hing	gehangen	hängt
heben to lift	hob	gehoben	
heißen to be named; order	hieß	geheißen	
helfen to help	half	geholfen	hilft
kennen to know	kannte	gekannt	
klingen to sound	klang	geklungen	
kommen to come	kam	ist gekommen	
können to be able	konnte	gekonnt	kann
laden to invite (usually einladen)	lud (or ladete)	geladen	ladet (or lädt)
lassen to let	ließ	gelassen	läßt
laufen to run	lief	ist gelaufen	läuft
leiden to suffer	litt	gelitten	
leihen to lend	lieh	geliehen	
lesen to read	las	gelesen	liest
liegen to lie	lag	gelegen	
lügen to (tell a) lie	log	gelogen	
meiden to avoid	mied	gemieden	
messen to measure	maß	gemessen	mißt
mögen to like; may	mochte	gemocht	mag
müssen to have to, must	mußte	gemußt	muß
nehmen to take	nahm	genommen	nimmt
nennen to name	nannte	genannt	
pfeifen to whistle	pfiff	gepfiffen	
quellen to gush forth	quoll	ist gequollen	quillt
raten to advise; guess	riet	geraten	rät
reiben to rub	rieb	gerieben	
reißen to tear	riß	gerissen	
reiten to ride	ritt	ist geritten	

Infinitive	Past Stem	Past Participle	Third-Person Singular
rennen *to run*	rannte	ist gerannt	
riechen *to smell*	roch	gerochen	
rufen *to call*	rief	gerufen	
saufen *to drink* (of animals)	soff	gesoffen	säuft
schaffen* *to create*	schuf	geschaffen	
scheiden *to part*	schied	ist geschieden	
scheinen *to seem; shine*	schien	geschienen	
schieben *to shove*	schob	geschoben	
schießen *to shoot*	schoß	geschossen	
schlafen *to sleep*	schlief	geschlafen	schläft
schlagen *to strike*	schlug	geschlagen	schlägt
schließen *to shut*	schloß	geschlossen	
schmelzen *to melt*	schmolz	ist geschmolzen	schmilzt
schneiden *to cut*	schnitt	geschnitten	
schreiben *to write*	schrieb	geschrieben	
schreien *to cry*	schrie	geschrie(e)n	
schreiten *to stride*	schritt	ist geschritten	
schweigen *to be silent*	schwieg	geschwiegen	
schwimmen *to swim*	schwamm	ist geschwommen	
schwinden *to vanish* (usually **verschwinden**)	schwand	ist geschwunden	
schwingen *to swing*	schwang	geschwungen	
sehen *to see*	sah	gesehen	sieht
sein *to be*	war	ist gewesen	ist
senden *to send*	sandte (*or* sendete)	gesandt (*or* gesendet)	
singen *to sing*	sang	gesungen	
sinken *to sink* (intr.)	sank	ist gesunken	
sitzen *to sit*	saß	gesessen	
sollen *to be supposed to; shall* (denoting obligation)	sollte	gesollt	soll
sprechen *to speak*	sprach	gesprochen	spricht
springen *to jump*	sprang	ist gesprungen	
stechen *to prick*	stach	gestochen	sticht
stehen *to stand*	stand	gestanden	
stehlen *to steal*	stahl	gestohlen	stiehlt
steigen *to climb*	stieg	ist gestiegen	
sterben *to die*	starb	ist gestorben	stirbt
stoßen *to push*	stieß	gestoßen	stößt
streichen *to stroke*	strich	gestrichen	
streiten *to contend*	stritt	gestritten	

***Schaffen** meaning *to work* is weak.

Infinitive	Past Stem	Past Participle	Third-Person Singular
tragen *to carry*	trug	getragen	trägt
treffen *to meet; hit*	traf	getroffen	trifft
treiben *to drive*	trieb	getrieben	
treten *to step*	trat	ist getreten	tritt
trinken *to drink*	trank	getrunken	
tun *to do*	tat	getan	tut
verderben* *to ruin, spoil*	verdarb	verdorben	verdirbt
vergessen *to forget*	vergaß	vergessen	vergißt
verlieren *to lose*	verlor	verloren	
verzeihen *to pardon*	verzieh	verziehen	
wachsen *to grow*	wuchs	ist gewachsen	wächst
waschen *to wash*	wusch	gewaschen	wäscht
wenden *to turn*	wandte (*or* wendete)	gewandt (*or* gewendet)	
werben *to woo*	warb	geworben	wirbt
werden *to become*	wurde (*or* ward)	ist geworden	wird
werfen *to throw*	warf	geworfen	wirft
wiegen *to weigh*	wog	gewogen	
winden *to wind*	wand	gewunden	
wissen *to know*	wußte	gewußt	weiß
wollen *to wish, want*	wollte	gewollt	will
ziehen† *to pull*	zog	gezogen	
zwingen *to force*	zwang	gezwungen	

---

*As an intransitive verb, **verderben** is conjugated with the auxiliary **sein.**

†As an intransitive verb, **ziehen** (*to move*) is conjugated with **sein.**

Vocabularies

The nominative plural and unusual singular endings are indicated. The following symbols and abbreviations are used:

*	strong verb	*fam.*	familiar
•	separable prefix	*gen.*	genitive
sein	verb requiring auxiliary **sein** in perfect tenses	*insep.*	inseparable
		int.	interjection
acc.	accusative	*intr.*	intransitive
adj.	adjective	*pl.*	plural
adv.	adverb	*p.p.*	past participle
conj.	conjunction	*prep.*	preposition
dat.	dative	*pron.*	pronoun
en-*masc.*	**en**-masculine (weak masculine) nouns (see Chapter 4)	*sing.*	singular

---

German-English

ab off; down; away; **ab und zu** now and then

der **Abend, -e** evening; **gestern abend** last night; **heute abend** tonight; **Silvesterabend** New Year's Eve

das **Abendbrot, -e** supper, evening meal

das **Abendessen, -** dinner, evening meal

aber but; however

*ab • fahren (sein)** to leave, depart

die **Abfahrt, -en** departure

*ab • fliegen (sein)** to take off

*ab • heben** to remove; **Geld abheben** to withdraw money

ab • holen to pick up; to call for

das **Abitur** final examination that entitles one to go from **Gymnasium** to a university

ab • kürzen to shorten

*ab • nehmen** to lose (weight); to take off

ab • nutzen to use up; to wear out

ab • schalten to switch off

die **Abschlußprüfung -en** final examination

*ab • schreiben** to copy

ab • schwindeln to swindle

das **Abteil, -e** compartment

*ab • tragen** to wear out

ab • zahlen to pay off, finish payments on

Ach (*int.*) ah

die **Achse, -n** axle

acht eight

achte- eighth

achtzehn eighteen

achtzig eighty

das **Adjectiv, -e** adjective

die **Adresse, -n** address

der **Adventskranz, ⁼e** Advent wreath

das **Adverb, -ien** adverb

(das) **Afrika** Africa

aggressiv aggressive; belligerent

ähnlich (*dat.*) similar (to); **ähnlich *sehen** to resemble

aktiv active

die   **Aktivität -en** activity
    all all; **alle Leute** everyone; **alle**
      vier Jahre every four years
    alle (*pl.*) everyone, all
    allein alone
    allerbeste- best of all
    allerfriedlichste- most peaceful
      or tranquil
    allerklügste- smartest, cleverest
    alles everything, all; **Alles**
      Gute! The best to you!

die   **Alpen** (*pl.*) the Alps
    als when; than; as; **als Kind** as
      a child; **als ob** as if
    also so; therefore
    alt old

das   **Alter, -** age
    altmodisch old-fashioned

die   **Ameise, -n** ant

(das)   **Amerika** America

der   **Amerikaner, -; die**
      Amerikanerin,-nen American
    amerikanisch American
    an (*dat. or acc.*) at; on; to;
      of; **am besten** best; **am Tag**
      by day
    ander- other; different; **etwas**
      anderes something else;
      jemand anders someone else;
      another; **niemand anders** no
      one else
    ändern to change
    anders otherwise, differently
    anderthalb (*indeclinable*) one and
      a half

der   **Anfang, -̈e** beginning
    ***an · fangen** to begin

der   **Anfänger, -; die Anfängerin, -nen**
      beginner
    ***an · gehen (sein)** to begin; to
      approach
    ***an · halten** to stop
    ***an · kommen (sein)** to arrive,
      reach

die   **Ankunft, -̈e** arrival
    an · reden to speak to; to address
    ***an · rufen** to telephone; to call up
    an · schalten to turn on
    an · schauen to look at, watch
    an · schnallen to strap on; **Bitte**
      anschnallen! Fasten seat belts!
    ***an · sehen** to look at
    (an) statt (*gen.*) instead of
    an · stellen to undertake; to hire

der   **der Anthropologe (en-*masc.*);**
      die Anthropologin, -nen
      anthropologist

die   **Antwort, -en** answer
    antworten (*dat.*) to answer
    ***an · ziehen** to put on; to dress;
      sich anziehen (*dat.*)
      to get dressed

der   **Anzug, -̈e** suit; clothing

der   **Apfel, -̈** apple

der   **Apfelsaft** apple juice

die   **Apotheke, -n** pharmacy

der   **Apotheker, -; die Apothekerin,**
      -nen pharmacist
    arabisch Arabic

die   **Arbeit** work; job; employment
    arbeiten to work

der   **Arbeiter, -; die Arbeiterin,-nen**
      worker, laborer

der   **Architekt (en-*masc.*) die**
      Architektin, -nen architect

die   **Architektur** architecture
    ärgern to annoy; to anger; **sich**
      ärgern über (*acc.*) to be
      annoyed (angry) at (about)
    arm poor

der   **Arm, -e** arm

der   **Artikel, -** article

der   **Arzt, -̈e; die Ärztin, -nen** doctor

der   **Aschenbecher, -** ashtray

der   **Aschermittwoch** Ash Wednesday

(das)   **Asien** Asia

der   **Astronom (en-*masc.*); die**
      Astronomin -nen astronomer
    atmen to breathe

die   **Atombombe, -n** atom bomb
    auch also, too; **auch nicht** neither;
      nicht nur. . .sondern auch
      not only . . . but also
    auf (*dat. or acc.*) on; to; in; at;
      auf einmal all at once;
      auf dem Lande in the country;
      aufs Land to the countryside
    auf · führen to perform

die   **Aufführung, -en** performance
    ***auf · geben** to give up; to deliver
    auf · machen to open
    auf · räumen to clean up

der   **Aufsatz, -̈e** essay; paper

das   **Aufsatzthema, pl. -themen**
      theme, subject
    auf · setzen to put on
    ***auf · stehen (sein)** to get up, rise

der   **Augenblick, -e** moment

das	**Äuglein, -** little eye (*diminutive*)		**bauen** to build
	aus (*dat.*) from; out of	der	**Bauer (en-***masc.***); die Bäuerin,**
	aus · beuten to exploit		**-nen** farmer, peasant
der	**Ausdruck, ̈-e** expression	der	**Bauernhof, ̈-e** farm
	aus · drücken to express	der	**Baum ̈-e** tree
der	**Ausgang, ̈-e** exit	der	**Baustein, -e** brick
	ausgezeichnet outstanding,	die	**Bauten** (*pl.*) buildings
	excellent	(das)	**Bayern** Bavaria
die	**Auskunft, ̈-e** information		**bayrisch** Bavarian
das	**Ausland** foreign country; **im (ins)**	der	**Beamte** (*declined adj.*); **die**
	Ausland abroad		**Beamtin, -nen** official, civil
der	**Ausländer, -; die Ausländerin,**		servant
	-nen foreigner		**beantworten (eine Frage)** to
	aus · machen to turn off, put out;		answer (a question)
	nichts ausmachen (*dat.*)		**bedecken** to cover
	not to matter		**bedienen** to serve; **sich**
	aus · probieren to try (out), test		**bedienen** to make use of; to
	aus · reden (*dat.*) to talk		serve oneself
	(someone) out of (doing	sich	**beeilen** to hurry
	something)		**beeinflussen** to influence, affect
der	**Ausruf, -e** interjection		**beenden** to complete, finish
sich	**aus · ruhen** to rest		***befehlen** (*dat.*) to order, command
	***aus · sehen** to appear, look		**befolgen** to follow
	außer (*dat.*) except; besides		**begabt** gifted
	außerhalb (*gen.*) outside; beyond		**begegnen (sein,** *dat.*) to meet
	aus · spannen to relax		***beginnen** to begin
	***aus · sprechen** to pronounce		**begrüßen** to greet
	***aus · steigen (sein)** to get out		**behaupten** to claim; to maintain
	(off)		**bei** (*dat.*) next to; with; at (the
die	**Ausstellung, -en** show; exhibition		home of); **bei mir** at my
der	**Ausweis, -e** pass; identification		house; **beim Lesen** while
sich	***aus · ziehen** (*dat.*) to get		reading
	undressed; to take off		**bei · bringen (brachte . . . bei,**
das	**Auto, -s** car, auto		**beigebracht)** to teach; to show
die	**Autobahn, -en** freeway, highway		how to
das	**Autorennen** car race		**beide** both; **die Beiden** the two
	autoritär authoritarian		of them
der	**Autor, -en; die Autorin, -nen**	das	**Bein, -e** leg
	author, writer	das	**Beispiel, -e** example; **zum**
			Beispiel (z.B.) for example
der	**Bach, ̈-e** creek, stream		***beißen** to bite
	***backen** bake		***bei · stehen** (*dat.*) to help, assist
der	**Bäcker, -** baker		**bei · stimmen** (*dat.*) to agree
die	**Bäckerei, -en** bakery		(with)
das	**Bad, ̈-er** bath; bathroom		**bei · wohnen** (*dat.*) to attend
der	**Badeanzug, ̈-e** swimming suit		**bekannt** known; well-known
	baden to bathe		***bekommen** to get, receive
der	**Bahnhof, ̈-e** railroad station	(das)	**Belgien** Belgium
	bald soon		**beliebt** popular, beloved
der	**Ball, ̈-e** ball		**bemerken** to notice
das	**Band, ̈-er** ribbon, tape	sich	***benehmen** to behave
der	**Band, ̈-e** book, volume		**benutzen** to use, utilize
die	**Band, -s** band (music)		**beobachten** to watch, observe
die	**Bank, -en** bank		**bequem** comfortable
	bar · zahlen to pay cash	der	**Berater, -** advisor, counselor

der **Berg, -e** mountain
der **Bericht, -e** report, account
　　berichten to report
der **Beruf, -e** occupation, profession, job
der **Berufsspieler, -; die Berufsspielerin, -nen** professional player
der **Berufssport** pro sports
　　berühmt famous
　　berühren to touch; **nicht berühren** don't touch
　　beschädigt injured, damaged
　　*****beschreiben** to describe
　　besetzt occupied
　　besichtigen to view, look at
　　besonders especially
　　*****besprechen** to discuss
　　besser better
　　*****bestechen** to bribe
　　*****bestehen** to pass (an exam); **bestehen aus** to consist of
　　bestellen to order
　　bestimmt certain(ly), sure(ly)
der **Besuch, -e** visit
　　besuchen to visit
　　beten to pray
　　*****betragen** to amount to
　　*****betreten** to enter, trespass; **nicht betreten** stay off (the grass)
das **Bett, -en** bed
der **Bettler, -; die Bettlerin, -nen** beggar
die **Bevölkerung** population
　　bevor (*conj.*) before
　　bewachen to guard, watch over
　　*****beweisen** to prove
sich *****bewerben (um)** to apply (for)
　　bezahlen to pay
die **Bezahlung, -en** payment
　　bezaubernd charming, lovely
die **Beziehung, -en** relations; connection
die **Bibliothek, -en** library
die **Biene, -n** bee
das **Bier** beer
der **Bierwagen, ⸚** horse-drawn beer cart
das **Bierzelt, -e** beer tent or pavillion
　　*****bieten** to offer
das **Bild, -er** picture; painting
　　bilden to form
der **Bildhauer, -; die Bildhauerin, -nen** sculptor
　　billig cheap

die **Billion, -en** trillion
　　*****binden** to bind, unite
der **Biologe (en-***masc.***); die Biologin, -nen** biologist
　　bis (*prep., acc.*) to; as far as; by; (*conj.*) until
　　bisher until now
　　bißchen: ein bißchen a little
　　bitte please
　　*****bitten um** to ask for
　　bitterlich bitterly
　　*****blasen** to blow
　　blau blue
die **Blechtrommel, -n** tin drum
　　*****bleiben (sein)** to stay, remain
der **Bleistift, -e** pencil
　　blitzen to flash; **es blitzt** it is lightning
　　bloß simply, just
das **Blümchen** little flower
die **Blume, -n** flower
die **Blumenfrau, -en** flower lady
die **Bluse, -n** blouse
der **Boden, ⸚** floor
der **Bogen, -** (or ⸚) sheet (of paper)
das **Bonbon, -s** hard candy
das **Boot, -e** boat
　　böse angry; evil; **böse sein (auf,** *acc.*) to be angry (with)
der **Bote (en-***masc.***)** messenger
die **Bowle, -n** punch; punch bowl
das **Boxen** boxing
　　brasilianisch Brazilian
(das) **Brasilien** Brazil
　　*****braten** to roast
　　brauchen to need; **du brauchst das nicht zu machen** you don't need to do that
　　braun brown
　　brav good; well-behaved
　　*****brechen** to break (**sein** with *intr.*)
　　breit wide, broad
　　brennen (brannte, gebrannt) to burn
die **Brezel, -n** pretzel
der **Brief, -e** letter
die **Briefmarke, -n** stamp
　　bringen (brachte, gebracht) to bring
das **Brötchen, -** roll
das **Brot, -e** bread
die **Brücke, -n** bridge
der **Bruder, ⸚** brother
das **Brüderchen, -, das Brüderlein, -** little brother

die **Brüderlichkeit** fraternity
die **Brust, ⁻e** breast; chest
das **Buch, ⁻er** book
das **Bücherregal, -e** bookshelf
die **Buchhandlung, -en** bookstore
das **Büchlein, -** booklet
der **Buchstabe (en-*masc.*)** letter
    (alphabet)
die **Bühne, -n** stage
der **Bund, ⁻e** organization; band
der **Bundeskanzler, -; die**
    Bundeskanzlerin, -nen
    chancellor, head of government
die **Bundesrepublik Deutschland**
    Federal Republic of Germany
der **Bundestag** German parliament
    bunt colorful; multicolored
der **Buntstift, -e** colored pencil
die **Burg, -en** castle, fortress
der **Bürger, -; die Bürgerin, -nen**
    citizen
der **Bürgermeister, -** mayor
die **Burgruine (*sing.*)** castle ruins
das **Büro, -s** office
der **Bus, -se** bus
die **Butter** butter

das **Chemiegebäude, -** chemistry
    building
    chemisch chemically; **chemisch**
    reinigen to dry clean
    chinesisch Chinese
    chromatisch chromatic
die **Computerwissenschaft** computer
    science
der **Computerwissenschaftler, -; die**
    Computerwissenschaftlerin,
    -nen computer scientist

    da (*adv.*) there; then; (*conj.*) since;
    because
    dabei at the same time
    dadurch thereby; that way
    dafür for it
    dagegen against it
    dahin (to) there
    dahinter behind it
    damals then, in those days
die **Dame, -n** lady
    damit with it; (*conj.*) so that
    danach after that, later on
    daneben next to it
(das) **Dänemark** Denmark
    Danke (*pl.*) thanks
    danken (*dat.*) to thank

    dann then
    daran on it
    darauf on it; **sich freuen darauf**
    to be happy about it
    darüber over that (it); about that
    daß (*conj.*) that
    dauern to last
    davon about it
    davor in front of it
    dazwischen in between
die **Debatte, -n** debate
    debattieren to debate
    decken to cover; **den Tisch**
    decken to set the table
    dein your (*fam. sing.*)
    deinethalben, deinetwegen on
    your account; as far as you're
    concerned; **um deinetwillen**
    for your sake
    dekorieren to decorate
die **Demokratie, -n** democracy
    demokratisch democratic
    denken (dachte, gedacht) (an)
    (*-acc.*) to think (about, of)
    denn (*conj.*) for, because
    derselbe, dasselbe, dieselbe the
    same
    deshalb therefore
    deutsch German
der **(die) Deutsche** (*declined*
    adj.) German
die **Deutschkenntnisse** (*pl.*)
    knowledge of German
(das) **Deutschland** Germany
    deutschsprachig
    German-speaking
der **Dezember** December
das **Dia, -s** slide (photographic)
der **Dichter, -; die Dichterin, -nen**
    poet; writer
    dichten to write (poetry)
die **Dichtung, -en** poetry
    dick thick, fat; **das macht dick**
    that's fattening
der **Dieb, -e** thief
der **Dienstag, -e** Tuesday
der **Dieselmotor, -en** diesel engine
    dieser, dieses, diese (*adj.*) this;
    (*pron.*) this one
    diesseits (*gen.*) on this side of
das **Ding, -e** thing
der **Dirigent (en-*masc.*); die**
    Dirigentin, -nen director,
    manager
    diskutieren to discuss

doch still, however, but; **Doch!** Yes. (in reply to negative question)

der **Doktor, -en** doctorate; doctor

das **Dokument, -e** document

der **Dom, -e** cathedral

die **Donau** Danube

der **Donnerstag, -e** Thursday

donnern to thunder

das **Dorf, -̈er** village

dort there; **dort drüben** over there

dorthin there; to that place

der **Dotter, -** yolk (of an egg)

das **Drama, pl. Dramen** drama

drängen to press, shove

draußen outside

drei three

dreimal three times

dreißig thirty

dreizehn thirteen

dreizehnte thirteenth

drinnen inside

dritt-e third

das **Drittel, -** third

drohen (*dat.*) to threaten

drüben over there

drucken to print

dumm stupid

die **Dummheit, -en** stupidity; foolishness

dunkel dark, dim

die **Dunkelheit** darkness

durch (*acc.*) through; by

*durch • backen** to bake thoroughly; **durchgebacken** well-done

*durch • dringen (sein)** to penetrate; to come through; (*insep.*) to penetrate (as sound)

*durch • fallen (sein)** to fail, flunk

durchsuchen to search (through)

dürfen (durfte, gedurft; darf) to be allowed; may

der **Durst** thirst; **Durst haben** to be thirsty

das **Dutzend, -e** dozen

eben just, even

ebenso equally; **ebenso ... wie** just as ... so

die **Ecke, -n** corner

die **Ehe, -n** marriage

ehrlich honest

die **Eiche, -n** oak

der **Eiffelturm** Eiffel Tower

eigen- own

eigentlich really, actually

einfach simple; simply

der **Einfluß, -̈sse** influence

einflußreich influential

der **Eingang, -̈e** entrance

die **Einheit, -en** unity

einige some, several

ein • kaufen to buy; to shop; **ein • kaufen *gehen** to go shopping

*ein • kommen (sein)** come in

*ein • laden** to invite

die **Einladung, -en** invitation

ein • lösen to cash (a check)

einmal once, formerly; **auf einmal** suddenly; **es war einmal** once upon a time

ein • packen to pack (up)

ein • reichen to turn in

eins one

ein • schalten to switch on

*ein • schlafen (sein)** to fall asleep

*ein • steigen (sein)** to get on, board

die **Eintrittskarte, -n** ticket

ein • wandern (sein) to immigrate

der **Einwohner, -** inhabitant, resident

einzig single, only

das **Eis, die Eiskrem** ice cream

die **Eisenbahn, -en** railway

eiskalt ice cold

der **Eisläufer, -; die Eisläuferin, -nen** ice skater

der **Elefant** (en-*masc*) elephant

elektronisch electronic

elf eleven

elfte- eleventh

die **Eltern** (*pl.*) parents

*empfehlen** (*dat.*) to recommend

das **Ende, -n** end, conclusion; **zu Ende *gehen** to come to an end

enden to end

endlich finally, at last

die **Endung, -en** ending

die **Energiekrise, -n** energy crisis

eng strict; narrow

der **Engländer, -; die Engländerin, -nen** Englishman (woman)

(das) **Englisch** English

der **Englischlehrer, -; die Englischlehrerin, -nen** English teacher

das **Enkelkind, -er** grandchild
entdecken to discover
***entfallen (sein)** to escape
entfernt remote, distant
entgegen against; toward
entgegen · eilen (sein) to hurry to meet
***entgegen · kommen (sein)** to come to meet; to cooperate
***entgegen · laufen (sein)** to run to meet; to run counter to
enthüllen to expose, reveal
entlang (*acc.*) along
***entlang · gehen (sein)** to go along
sich ***entschließen** to decide, make up one's mind
entschuldigen to excuse; **sich entschuldigen** to apologize
***entsprechen** (*dat.*) to correspond to
***entstehen (sein)** to originate
entweder either; **entweder . . . oder** either . . . or
***entwerfen** to design, sketch
entziffern to decipher
die **Epoche, -n** era, epoch
erbauen to construct
erben to inherit
***erbrechen** to break open
die **Erdbeere, -n** strawberry
***erfahren** to learn; to discover; to experience
***erfinden** to invent
die **Erfindung, -en** discovery; invention
ergänzen to complete
***erhalten** to receive
erinnern to remind; **sich erinnern an** (*acc.*) to remember
sich **erkälten** to catch cold
die **Erkältung, -en** cold
erkennen (erkannte, erkannt) to recognize
erklären to explain, account for
die **Erklärung, -en** explanation
sich **erkundigen** to inquire
erlauben (*dat.*) to permit, allow
erledigen to settle; to take care of
erlernen to acquire; to learn
erobern to conquer
eröffnen to open, start (an account, store)
errichten to found, erect
die **Erscheinung, -en** appearance

***erschießen** to shoot; to kill by shooting
ersetzen to substitute
erst (*adv.*) not until; **erste-** (*adj.*) first
***erstechen** to stab
erstens in the first place
erwähnen to mention
erwarten to expect
erwürgen to strangle
erzählen to tell, relate
die **Erzählung, -en** narrative, story
***essen** to eat; **gern Fleisch essen** to like meat; **zu Abend essen** to have dinner; **zu Mittag essen** to have lunch
das **Essen** eating; meal
der **Eßlöffel,-** tablespoon
etwas (*pron.*) something; **irgend etwas** anything; **so etwas** such a thing; (*adv.*) somewhat, a little
euer your (*fam. pl*)
(das) **Europa** Europe
europäisch European
das **Examen, -** comprehensive exam at the end of a course of study
exklusiv exclusive
der **Exorzist (en-***masc.***)** exorcist
die **Fabrik, -en** factory
das **Fach, ⸚er** subject; department
***fahren (sein)** to go; to drive; to travel; **Fahrrad fahren** to ride a bicycle; **in die Ferien fahren** to go on vacation; **mit dem Zug fahren** to take the train
der **Fahrer, -; die Fahrerin, -nen** driver
die **Fahrkarte, -n** ticket
der **Fahrkartenschalter, -** ticket counter
der **Fahrplan, ⸚e** (train, bus) schedule; timetable
das **Fahrrad, ⸚er** bicycle; **Fahrrad *fahren** to ride a bicycle
die **Fahrt, -en** trip, drive
der **Fall, ⸚e** case; fall
***fallen (sein)** to fall
falsch false
die **Familie, -n** family
der **Fang, ⸚e** capture; prey
***fangen** to catch
die **Fantasie, -n** fantasy
die **Farbe, -n** color

der	**Farbfernseher, -** color television	der	**Fluß, ⁼sse** river, stream
der	**Farbfilm, -e** color film	die	**Flüssigkeit** liquid
der	**Fasching** carnival, Mardi Gras		**folgen (sein,** *dat.***)** to follow
	faschistisch fascist		**folgend** following, next
	fast almost		**formen** to form
	fasten to fast		**fort** away
	faul lazy, rotten		**fort · dauern** to continue, last
der	**Februar** February		***fort · fahren (sein)** to go on; to
die	**Feder, -n** feather; pen (quill)		continue
der	**Federball** badminton; birdie	das	**Foto, -s** photo
der	**Federballplatz, ⁼e** badminton	der	**Fotoapparat, -e** camera
	court		**fotografieren** to photograph
der	**Fehler, -** error	die	**Frage, -n** question
die	**Feier, -n** celebration; holiday,		**fragen (nach)** to ask (about)
	festival	(das)	**Frankreich** France
	feiern to celebrate	der	**Franzose (en-***masc.***); die**
das	**Feld, -er** field		**Französin, -nen** French
das	**Fenster, -** window		person
die	**Ferien (***pl.***)** vacation; **in die**		**französich** French
	Ferien *fahren to go on	die	**Frau, -en** woman; wife; Mrs.
	vacation	das	**Fräulein, -** young lady; Miss
der	**Fernsehapparat, -e** television set		**frei** free
	***fern · sehen** to watch TV		**freigebig** liberal, generous
das	**Fernsehen** television; **im**	die	**Freigebigkeit** liberality, generosity
	Fernsehen on TV	die	**Freiheit, -en** liberty, freedom
die	**Fernsehsendung, -en** telecast,	der	**Freitag, -e** Friday
	TV broadcast	die	**Freizeit** spare time; leisure
	fertig finished; ready	die	**Fremdsprache, -n** foreign
das	**Fest, -e** festival, holiday		language
	festlich festive		***fressen** to devour; to eat (of
das	**Festspiel, -e** festival performance		animals)
der	**Festwagen, -** float	sich	**freuen (auf) (***acc.***)** to look forward
das	**Feuer, -** fire		to; **(über) (***acc.***)** to be happy
die	**Figur, -en** shape, figure		about
	filmen to film	der	**Freund, -e; die Freundin,**
	***finden** to find; to consider; to		**-nen** friend; **mein Freund** my
	discover		boyfriend; **meine Freundin** my
die	**Firma,** *pl.* **Firmen** firm, company		girlfriend
der	**Fisch, -e** fish		**freundlich** kind; friendly
	fischen to fish	die	**Freundlichkeit** kindness;
der	**Fischer, -** fisherman		friendliness
die	**Flasche, -n** bottle	die	**Freundschaft, -en** friendship
das	**Fleisch** meat	der	**Friede (***acc., dat., sing.* **-en,** *gen.*
der	**Fleiß** diligence, industry		*sing.* **-ens)** peace; **der**
	fleißig hard-working, diligent		**Friedens Nobelpreis** Nobel
	***fliegen (sein)** to fly		Peace Prize
	***fliehen (sein)** to flee, escape		**friedlich** peaceful
	flirten to flirt		**frisch** fresh
	***fließen (sein)** to flow	der	**Friseur, -e; die Friseurin, -nen**
	fließend fluent(ly)		hairdresser, barber
der	**Flüchtling, -e** refugee		**froh** happy, glad
der	**Flug, ⁼e** flight	die	**Frucht, ⁼e** fruit
der	**Flügel, -** wing		**früh** early; **früher** earlier;
der	**Flughafen, ⁼** airport		formerly
das	**Flugzeug, -e** airplane		

der **Frühling, -e** spring
frühmorgens (*pl.*) early in the morning
das **Frühstück, -e** breakfast
frühstücken to have breakfast
sich **fühlen** to feel
führen to lead; to carry (merchandise)
der **Führerschein, -e** driver's license
fünf five
fünfte- fifth
das **Fünftel, -** fifth part
fünfzehn fifteen
fünfzig fifty
funktionieren to work; to operate
für (*acc.*) for; **was für . . .** what kind of . . .
furchtbar awful, terrible
sich **fürchten (vor)** (*dat.*) to be afraid (of)
der **Fuß, -̈e** foot; **zu Fuß *gehen** to walk, go on foot
der **Fußball** soccer; football
die **Fußballmannschaft, -en** soccer team
der **Fußballplatz, -̈e** soccer field
das **Futur** future tense

die **Gabel, -n** fork
die **Gallerie, -n** gallery
der **Gang, -̈e** walk; gait
ganz all, complete(ly)
das **Ganze** (*declined adj.*) the whole thing; total
gar quite; **gar kein** not a single; **garnichts** nothing at all
der **Garten, -̈** garden
das **Gaslicht, -er** gas light
der **Gastarbeiter, -; die Gastarbeiterin, -nen** foreign worker
der **Gastgeber, -; die Gastgeberin, -nen** landlord; landlady
das **Gasthaus, -̈er;** restaurant, inn, tavern
der **Gastwirt, -e; die Gastwirtin, -nen** innkeeper
das **Gebäude, -** building, structure
***geben** to give; **es gibt** there is (are); **Was gibt es Neues?** What's new?
das **Gebiet, -e** territory, district
das **Gebirge, -** mountains, mountain range

geboren born, née; **Wann sind Sie geboren?** When were you born?
gebrauchen to use
der **Geburtstag, -e** birthday
das **Gebüsch, -e** bushes
die **Gedächtniskirche, -n** memorial church
der **Gedanke** (*acc., dat. sing.* **-n**; *gen. sing.* **-ns**, *pl.* **-n**) thought, idea; plan
das **Gedicht, -e** poem
gefährlich dangerous
***gefallen** to please; **Es gefällt mir.** I like it.
das **Gefieder, -** plumage, feathers
das **Gefilde, -** fields
das **Geflügel** poultry, fowl
gegen (*acc.*) against; into; **gegen zwei Uhr** around two o'clock
gegenüber (*dat.*) opposite
der **Gegner, -** opponent
das **Gehalt, -̈er** salary
geheimnisvoll mysterious
***gehen (sein)** to go; to walk; to be in working order; **auf die Nerven gehen** to be irritating; **Wie geht es Ihnen?** How are you? **zu Ende gehen** to come to an end
das **Gehör** sense of hearing
gehören (*dat.*) to belong to
die **Geige, -n** violin
der **Geist, -er** spirit
das **Gelände, -** tract of land
das **Geld** money, cash
die **Gelegenheit, -en** opportunity
***gelingen** to succeed; **es ist dir gelungen** you succeeded
***gelten** to carry weight; to be valid
das **Gemälde, -** picture; painting
das **Gemüse, -** vegetable(s)
gemütlich comfortable, pleasant
genau careful; exact(ly); **genau so** just as
***genießen** to enjoy
genug enough
der **Genuß, -̈sse** pleasure
der **Geologe** (**en**-*masc.*); **die Geologin, -nen** geologist
das **Gepäck** baggage
gerade right now; just; straight
das **Gerät, -e** tool; apparatus; set
gerecht fair, just
die **Gerechtigkeit** justice, fairness

das   **Gericht, -e** dish, course
    germanisch Germanic
die   **Germanistik** German philology
    gern gladly, willingly; **gern haben**
      to like; **gern machen**
      to like to do
    gesamt entire, complete
das   **Geschäft, -e** business, trade;
      store
die   **Geschäftsleute** (*pl.*)
      businesspeople
    ***geschehen (sein)** to happen
das   **Geschenk, -e** gift
die   **Geschichte, -n** story; history
das   **Geschichtsbuch, ̈er** history book
das   **Geschlecht, -er** gender
die   **Geschwister** (*pl.*) brothers and
      sisters
die   **Gesellschaft, -en** company,
      society
das   **Gesetz, -e** law, statute
    gesetzlich legal
das   **Gespräch, -e** conversation; talk
    gestern yesterday; **gestern**
      abend last night; **gestern vor**
      acht Tagen a week ago
    gestrichen (*p.p. of* **streichen**)
      painted
    gesund healthy
die   **Gesundheit** health
das   **Getränk, -e** drink, beverage
das   **Getreide** grain, corn
das   **Gewehr, -e** rifle; weapon
    ***gewinnen** to win
sich   **gewöhnen an** (*acc.*) to get
      used to
    gewöhnlich usually
    gewohnt accustomed to; **Ich bin**
      gewohnt es zu tun. I'm
      accustomed to doing it.
    ***gießen** to pour
der   **Gipfel, -** peak, summit
das   **Glas, ̈er** glass
der   **Glaube** (*acc., dat. sing.* **-n,** *gen.*
      sing. **-ns,** *pl.* **-n**) faith, belief
    glauben (*dat.*) to think; to believe
    gleich (*adj.*) same, alike; (*adv.*)
      right now, just
die   **Gleichheit** equality
das   **Glück** luck; happiness
    glücklich happy; lucky
die   **Glühbirne, -n** electric bulb
    gnädig kind; gracious
    gotisch gothic

der   **Gott, ̈er** god; **Gottseidank!**
      Thank God! **Um Gottes**
      willen! For heaven's sake!
    ***graben** to dig
das   **Gramm, -e** gram
das   **Gras, ̈er** grass
    grau gray
    grauen to be afraid of; **es graut**
      mir I dread
    ***greifen** to grasp
die   **Grenze, -n** border; limit
der   **Griff, -e** hold
    groß tall, big; important, great
die   **Großeltern** (*pl.*) grandparents
die   **Großmutter, ̈** grandmother
die   **Großstadt, ̈e** large town, city
      (over 100,000)
der   **Großvater, ̈** grandfather
der   **Gruselfilm, -e** horror movie
    grüßen to greet
die   **Grube, -n** ditch
    grün green
der   **Grund, ̈e** bottom; basis; **im**
      Grunde at the bottom
    gründen to found, establish
die   **Grundschule, -n** elementary
      school
    gut well, good
das   **Gute** (*declined adj.*) the good, that
      which is good; **Alles Gute!**
      The best to you!
    gutmütig good-natured
die   **Gutmütigkeit** good nature
das   **Gymnasium,** *pl.* **Gymnasien**
      secondary school

das   **Haar, -e** hair
    haben (hatte, gehabt; hat) to
      have; **Durst haben** to be
      thirsty; **gern haben** to like;
      Hunger haben to be hungry;
      Lust haben to want to;
      recht haben to be right
der   **Hafen, ̈** port, harbor
    halb half; **Es ist halb sechs.** It's
      five-thirty.
die   **Halle, -n** court; market
der   **Hallensport** indoor sport
der   **Hals, ̈e** neck, throat
    ***halten** to hold; to detain; **halten**
      von to think of
das   **Halteschild, -er** stop sign
die   **Haltestelle, -n** (bus, streetcar)
      stop

die **Hand, -e** hand; handwriting
der **Handschuh, -e** glove
die **Handtasche, -n** purse
der **Hang, -e** slope
*hängen (*intr.*) to hang, suspend; (*transitive, weak verb*) to hang, suspend
hart difficult, hard
der **Hase (en-**-*masc.*) hare
das **Hauptgebäude, -** main building
die **Hauptschule, -n** intermediate school
die **Hauptstraße, -n** main street
das **Haus, -er** house; **nach Hause gehen** to go home; **zu Hause** at home
die **Hausarbeit, -en** housework
die **Hausaufgaben** (*pl.*) homework
das **Häuschen** little house; cottage, cabin
die **Hausfrau, -en** housewife
hebräisch Hebrew
das **Heft, -e** notebook
das **Heftchen, -** booklet
die **Heide, -n** heath, moor
heidnisch pagan
heim home(ward)
die **Heimat, -en** homeland
die **Heimstadt, -e** home town
*heim · gehen (sein) to go home
*heim · kommen (sein) to come home
heiraten to marry; to get married
heiß hot
*heißen to be called; **ich heiße** my name is
*helfen (*dat.*) to help
das **Hemd, -en** shirt
her here, this way
*herauf · steigen (sein) to climb, mount
*heraus · finden to discover, find out
*heraus · geben to issue, publish
*heraus · kommen (sein) to come out
*heraus · ziehen to pull out, remove
her · bringen (brachte . . . her, hergebracht) to bring here
der **Herbst, -e** fall
*herein · kommen (sein) to come in
*her · geben to give away; to deliver

*her · kommen (sein) to derive from
der **Herr (en-**-*masc.; sing.* **-n,** *pl.* **-en)** gentleman; sir; Mr.
herrlich splendid, wonderful
*herum · fahren (sein) to drive around
*herum · gehen (sein) to go around; to wander
*herum · laufen (sein) to run about
*herunter · lassen to lower
das **Herz (***dat. sing.* **-en,** *gen. sing.* **-ens,** *pl.* **-en)** heart; **Hand aufs Herz!** Honest to God!
heute today
heutig present, modern
heutzutage nowadays
hier here
hierher right here
die **Hilfe, -n** help
hilflos helpless
der **Himmel, -** sky
hin there
*hinauf · steigen (sein) to ascend; to climb up
*hinaus · gehen (sein) to go out
sich **hinaus · lehnen** to lean out
hinaus · schauen to look out
*hinein · gehen (sein) to go into, enter
*hin · fallen (sein) to fall down, decay
*hin · gehen (sein) to go there
hinten at the back
hinter (*dat. or acc.*) behind
*hinunter · gehen (sein) to go down
der **Hirsch, -e** stag, hart
der **Historiker, -; die Historikerin, -nen** historian
die **Hitze** heat
hoch high; to the power of
hoch · achten to respect
höchstens at most
die **Hochzeit, -en** wedding
hoffen to hope
hoffentlich hopefully, I hope
höflich polite
holen to get; to go for
das **Holz, -er** wood
der **Holzschnitt, -e** woodcut
hören to hear, listen to (music, etc.)
das **Hormon, -e** hormone

der	Hörsaal, -säle auditorium; lecture room
die	Hose, -n pants, trousers
der	Hubschrauber, - helicopter
das	Huhn, -er fowl; chicken
	hüllen to wrap (up); to hide
der	Hund, -e dog
	hundert hundred
	hundertste- hundredth
der	Hunger hunger; Hunger haben to be hungry
	hungrig hungry
	husten to cough
der	Hut, -e hat

der	Idealismus idealism
	idealistisch idealistic
die	Idee, -n idea
	ihr her, their
	Ihr your (polite)
	immer always, more and more; immer besser better and better
der	Imperativ imperative mood
das	Imperfekt imperfect tense
	in (dat. or acc.) in; to; into
	indem while; by
	indirekt indirect
	informiert informed
der	Ingenieur, -e; die Ingenieurin, -nen engineer
das	Ingenieurwesen engineering
	innerhalb (gen.) within
	interessant interesting
sich	interessieren (für) to be interested (in)
	inzwischen meanwhile
	irgend some; any; irgend jemand anyone; someone; irgendwann sometime
sich	irren to be wrong, make a mistake
(das)	Italien Italy
	italienisch Italian

	ja yes; indeed
das	Jachtrennen yacht racing
die	Jacke, -n jacket
der	Jägerhut, -e hunting hat
das	Jahr, -e year
die	Jahreszeit, -en season
das	Jahrhundert, -e century
der	Januar January
	japanisch Japanese

	je ever je . . . desto the more . . . the more . . . ; je früher je lieber the earlier the better
	jeder, jedes, jede each
	jedermann everyone
	jedesmal every time
	jemand someone; anyone
	jener, jenes, jene that
	jenseits (gen.) on that side of; beyond
	jetzt now
	jiddisch Yiddish
der	Journalismus journalism
der	Journalist (en-masc.) die Journalistin, -nen journalist
die	Jugend youth
die	Jugendherberge, -n youth hostel
der	Juli July
	jung young
der	Junge (en-masc.) boy
der	Juni June
die	Jura (pl.) law
der	Jurist (en-masc.); die Juristin, -nen lawyer

der	Kaffee, -s coffee; eine Tasse Kaffee a cup of coffee
der	Kaffeeklatsch afternoon tea party
der	Kaiser, - emperor
die	Kaiserin, -nen empress
	kalt cold
der	Kampf, -e fight, battle
	kämpfen to fight
(das)	Kanada Canada
	kanadisch Canadian
der	Kanzler, - chancellor
die	Kapelle, -n band
der	Kapitalismus, - capitalism
	kapitalistisch capitalistic
der	Kapitän, -e captain
das	Kapitel, - chapter
	kaputt broken, ruined
der	Karneval, -s carnival, Mardi Gras
die	Kartoffel, -n potato
der	Kartoffelsalat, -e potato salad
der	Kasten, - box, chest
das	Kätzchen, - kitten
die	Katze, -n cat
	kaufen to buy; auf Raten kaufen to buy on time
das	Kaufhaus, -er department store
	kegeln to bowl
	kein (adj.) no; not any; überhaupt kein none at all

keiner (*pron.*) no one; not any; none

der **Kellner, -** waiter

die **Kellnerin, -nen** barmaid, waitress

*__kennen (kannte, gekannt)__ to know; to be acquainted with

*__kennen · lernen__ to meet, make the acquaintance of

die **Kernforschung, -en** atomic research

die **Kerze, -n** candle

keusch pure

das **Kilogramm, -e** kilogram

das **Kind, -er** child

das **Kinderhüten** childcare

die **Kindheit** childhood; infancy

das **Kino, -s** movies, cinema

die **Kirche, -n** church

der **Kirchturm, ¨e** church tower

die **Kirschtorte, -n** cherry tart

klagen to complain

die **Klammer, -n** bracket; parenthesis

klar clear

klären to clarify, purify

die **Klasse, -n** class

das **Klassenzimmer, -** classroom

klatschen to gossip; to applaud

das **Klavier, -e** piano

das **Klavierstück, -e** piano piece

das **Kleid, -er** dress; (*pl.*) clothes

sich **kleiden** to dress

die **Kleidung** clothing

klein small; **hundert Mark klein haben** to have change for 100 marks

(das) **Kleinasien** Asia Minor

die **Kleinstadt, ¨e** small town (under 20,000)

das **Klima, -s** climate

klopfen to knock

das **Kloster, ¨** monastery

der **Klub, -s** club

klug clever, smart

die **Klugheit** intelligence; shrewdness

der **Kniestrumpf, ¨e** knee socks

der **Koch, ¨e; die Köchin, -nen** cook

das **Kochbuch, ¨er** cookbook

kochen to cook

der **Koffer, -** suitcase

Köln Cologne

die **Kolonie, -n** colony

Kolumbus Columbus

komisch funny, strange

der **Kommandant (en-*masc.*); die Kommandantin, -nen** commander

*__kommen (sein)__ to come

der **Kommunismus, -** communism

der **Kommunist (en-*masc.*); die Kommunistin, -nen** communist

kommunistisch communist

die **Komödie, -n** comedy

der **Komparativ** comparative (degree)

kompetent competent

komponieren to compose

der **Komponist (en-*masc.*); die Komponistin, -nen** composer

die **Konditoriei, -en** pastry shop

der **König, -e** king

die **Königin, -nen** queen

die **Konjunktion, -en** conjunction

der **Konjunktiv** subjunctive mood

können (konnte, gekonnt; kann) to be able; to know how; to understand; can

der **Konservatismus** conservatism

kontrollieren to check, inspect

das **Konzert, -e** concert

der **Kopfschmerz, -en** headache

das **Kopfweh** headache

kopieren to copy

der **Korb, ¨e** basket

der **Korbball, ¨e** basketball

kosten to cost

das **Kostüm, -e** costume, dress

das **Kostümfest, -e** costume ball

krank sick

der **(die) Kranke** (*declined adj.*) patient, sick person

das **Krankenhaus, ¨er** hospital

die **Krankenschwester, -n** nurse

die **Krankheit, -en** illness, disease

der **Kranz, ¨e** wreath

die **Krawatte, -n** tie

die **Kreditkarte, -n** credit card

der **Krieg, -e** war

kriegerisch warlike, martial

der **Kritiker, -; die Kritikerin, -nen** critic

die **Küche, -n** kitchen

der **Kuchen, -** cake, tart; **ein Stück Kuchen** a piece of cake

der **Kugelschreiber, -** ballpoint

die **Kuh, ¨e** cow

kühl cool

sich **kümmern (um)** to care (for)

der **Kunde (en-*masc.*)** customer

die	**Kunst, ̈e** art		der	**Lehrer, -; die Lehrerin, -nen** teacher
der	**Künstler, -; die Künstlerin, -nen** artist		der	**Leib, -er** body
das	**Kunstmuseum, -museen** art gallery			**leicht** light; easily
das	**Kunstwerk, -e** work of art			**leid** painful, disagreeable; **Tut mir leid.** I'm sorry.

die **Kunst, ̈e** art
der **Künstler, -; die Künstlerin,** **-nen** artist
das **Kunstmuseum, -museen** art gallery
das **Kunstwerk, -e** work of art
kursiv italic
kurz short, a short time
kürzlich recently
die **Kusine, -n** cousin
der **Kuß, ̈sse** kiss
küssen to kiss
die **Küste, -n** coast

das **Labor, -s** laboratory, lab
laden to load; to invite
die **Lage, -n** situation
die **Lampe, -n** lamp
das **Land, ̈er** country; region; **auf dem Lande** in the country; **aufs Land *fahren** to go to the country
landen (sein) to land
die **Landkarte, -n** map
die **Landschaft, -en** landscape, scenery
lang long
lange (adv.) a long time; **schon lange** for a long time
die **Langweile** tedium, boredom
langsam slow(ly)
langweilig boring, tedious
der **Lärm** noise
lassen to let; to leave (behind); **rufen lassen** to send for; **sich die Haare schneiden lassen** to have one's hair cut
der **Lastwagen, -** truck
laufen (sein) to run
der **Läufer, -; die Läuferin, -nen** runner
laut loud
lauten to sound
das **Leben, -** life
leben to live
das **Lebensjahr, -e** year (of one's life)
das **Lebensmittel, -** food, provisions
das **Lebensmittelgeschäft, -e** grocery store
der **Leberkäse, -** liver loaf
lecker delicious
die **Lederhose, -n** leather shorts
legen to lay; to put; **sich legen** to lie down
lehren to teach

der **Lehrer, -; die Lehrerin, -nen** teacher
der **Leib, -er** body
leicht light; easily
leid painful, disagreeable; **Tut mir leid.** I'm sorry.
das **Leid, -en** pain; grief
leiden to suffer; to bear; to permit
leider unfortunately
leise softly
sich **leisten** (dat.) to afford
lernen to learn; to study
lesen to read; **(über)** (acc.) to lecture (about)
letzt- last, latest
die **Leute** (pl.) people
das **Lexikon,** pl. **Lexiken** dictionary
der **(die) Liberale** (declined adj.) liberal
der **Liberalismus** liberalism
das **Licht, -er** light
lieb dear, beloved; **Ach du liebe Zeit!** Oh my goodness! **ich trinke lieber** I prefer to drink; **je früher je lieber** the earlier the better
die **Liebe, -n** love
lieben to love
die **Liebesenttäuschung, -en** unhappy love affair
der **Liebling, -e** dear; favorite
das **Lieblingsfach, ̈er** favorite subject
das **Lied, -er** song, tune
liefern to deliver
die **Lieferung, -en** delivery, issue
liegen to lie; to be situated
die **Limonade** lemonade
die **Linguistik** linguistics
die **Linie, -n** line; route
links (adv.) left, to the left
die **Literatur, -en** literature
das **Loch, ̈er** hole
der **Löffel, -** spoon
los loose
los · kaufen to ransom; to redeem
los · lassen to set free, release
die **Lösung, -en** solution
der **Löwe (en-**masc.**)** lion
die **Luft, ̈e** air
lügen to (tell a) lie
die **Lust, ̈e** desire; **Lust haben** to feel like

das **Lustspiel, -e** comedy

machen to make; to do; **das macht ihm nichts aus** that's nothing to him; **dick machen** to be fattening; **eine Prüfung (Reise) machen** to take a test (trip); **gern machen** to like to do; **sich leicht machen** to be easy to do; **sich Sorgen machen um** (*dat.*) to worry about; **Urlaub machen** to go on vacation

die **Macht, ⁻e** power

mächtig strong, powerful

das **Mädchen, -** girl

der **Mai** May

mal once; just; **schau mal!** just look! **vier mal fünf** four times five

das **Mal, -e** time; **zum ersten Mal** for the first time

malen to paint

der **Maler, -; die Malerin, -nen** painter

man (*acc.* **einen**, *dat.* **einem**) one; you; they

mancher, manches, manche many a; (*pl.*) many, some

manchmal sometimes, occasionally

der **Mann, ⁻er** man; husband

die **Mannschaft, -en** team

der **Mansch, -e** mixture

der **Mantel, ⁻** overcoat

das **Märchen, -** fairy tale

das **Marionettentheater, -** puppet theatre

die **Mark, -** mark (currency)

der **Markt, ⁻e** market; **auf den Markt *gehen** to go to the market

der **Marktplatz, ⁻e** marketplace

der **März** March

die **Maske, -n** ask

der **Maskenball, ⁻e** costume ball

das **Maß, -e** measure

die **Mäßigkeit** moderation

die **Mathematik** mathematics

der **Mathematiker, -; die Mathematikerin, -nen** mathematician

mathematisch mathematical

die **Mauer, -n** wall

die **Maus, ⁻e** mouse

die **Medizin, -en** medicine

das **Meer, -e** sea, ocean

das **Mehl** flour

mehr more

mehrere several

die **Meile, -n** mile

mein my

meinen to mean, to think

meinetwillen: um meinetwillen for my sake

die **Meinung, -en** opinion, belief

meist- most

meistens usually

die **Mensa, Mensen** (*pl.*) student restaurant

der **Mensch** (**en-***masc.*) human being, person, man; **Mensch!** Man!

menschlich human

merken to notice

das **Messer, -** knife

(das) **Mexiko** Mexico

mieten to rent (from)

die **Milch** milk

mild kind, generous

die **Milliarde, -n** billion

mißbilligen to disapprove, object to

***mißverstehen** to misunderstand

mit (*dat.*) with

mit · bringen (brachte . . . mit, mitgebracht) to bring along

miteinander together

***mit · fahren (sein)** to ride along

***mit · gehen (sein)** to go along

das **Mitglied, -er** member

***mit · kommen (sein)** to accompany, come along

***mit · nehmen** to take along

das **Mittagessen** lunch, noon meal

mittags at noon, noons

das **Mittelalter** Middle Ages

mitten midway; **mitten in** (*dat.*) in the middle of

der **Mittwoch, -e** Wednesday

das **Möbel** furniture

mögen (mochte, gemocht; mag) to like; to care for; may

der **Monat, -e** month

monatelang for months

der **Montag, -e** Monday

der **Mörder, -; die Mörderin, -nen** murderer

der **Morgen, -** morning

morgen tomorrow; **morgen früh** tomorrow morning; **morgen in einem Monat** a month from tomorrow; **morgens** in the morning, mornings

das	**Motorrad, ⁻er** motorcycle
	müde tired
(das)	**München** Munich
die	**Musik** music; band
der	**Musiker, -; die Musikerin, -nen**
	musician
der	**Musikkenner, -** connoisseur of
	music
	muskulös muscular
	müssen (mußte, gemußt; muß)
	to have to; must
die	**Mutter, ⁻** mother
die	**Mutti** mom, mama

	na (*int.*) well, now
	nach (*dat.*) to; after; according to;
	nach Hause *gehen to go
	home; **nach oben** upstairs;
	nach unten downstairs
der	**Nachbar, -n; die Nachbarin, -nen**
	neighbor
die	**Nachbarschaft, -en**
	neighborhood, vicinity
	nachdem (*conj.*) after
	nach · eilen (sein) (*dat.*) to
	pursue, hurry after
	*nach · laufen (sein) (*dat.*) to run
	after
der	**Nachmittag, -e** afternoon; **heute**
	nachmittag this afternoon,
	nachmittags in the afternoon,
	afternoons
die	**Nachricht, -en** news, report
	*nach · schlagen to look
	(something) up
	nächst- next, nearest
die	**Nacht, ⁻e** night
der	**Nachtisch, -e** dessert
	nachts in the night
	nah near, close
die	**Nähe** closeness; neighborhood
	nähen to sew, stitch
die	**Näherin, -nen** seamstress
der	**Name** (*acc., dat. sing.* **-n**; *gen.*
	sing. **-ns**, *pl.* **-n**) name
	namens called, by the name of
	nämlich namely
der	**Nationalsozialismus** national
	socialism
die	**Natur** nature
	natürlich naturally, of course
	neben (*dat. or acc.*) next to,
	beside
	nebenan (*adv.*) next door

	nebeneinander side by side
	negativ negative
	*nehmen (nahm, genommen) to
	take
	nein no
	*nennen (nannte, genannt) to name;
	to call
der	**Nerv, -en** nerve; **auf die Nerven**
	gehen to get on someone's
	nerves
	nervös nervous
	nett kind, nice
das	**Netz, -e** net
	neu new, recent; **Was gibt es**
	Neues? What's new?
	neulich recently, a week or so
	ago
	neun nine
	neunte- ninth
	neunzehn nineteen
	neunzig ninety
	nicht not; **nicht nur . . . sondern**
	auch not only . . . but also;
	nicht wahr? right?;
	noch nicht not yet
	nichts nothing; **gar nichts**
	nothing at all
	nie never; **noch nie** never before
	nieder down, low
	nieder · brennen (brannte . . .
	nieder, niedergebrannt)
	to burn down
	*nieder · schießen to shoot down
	niedrig low
	niemand no one; **niemand**
	anders no one else
der	**Nikolaus** St. Nicholas
der	**Nikolaustag** St. Nicholas Eve
	noch still; yet; in addition; **noch**
	ein another; **noch einmal**
	once more; **noch etwas** some
	more; **noch nicht** not yet;
	noch nie never (before);
	weder . . . noch neither . . . nor
das	**Nomen, -** noun
der	**Norden** north
	nördlich north, northerly
die	**Nordseeküste** North Sea Coast
	normalerweise normally
(das)	**Norwegen** Norway
die	**Note, -n** grade
das	**Notengeben** giving grades
	null zero
	nun now, well
	nur only; **wenn nur** if only

---

die   **Nuß, ⁻sse** nut
       nützlich useful

       ob whether; **als ob** as if
       oben above; **nach oben** upstairs
der   **Ober, -** (head) waiter; **Herr Ober!**
         Waiter!
       oberhalb (*gen.*) above
       obgleich although
das   **Objekt, -e** object
das   **Obst** fruit
       obwohl although
       oder or
der   **Ofen, ⁻** stove
       offen open
       öffnen to open
       oft often
       ohne (*acc.*) without
das   **Oktoberfest, -e** Bavarian autumn
         festival
die   **Olympiade** Olympics
       olympisch olympic
die   **Oma, -s** grandma
der   **Onkel, -** uncle
der   **Opa, -s** grandpa
die   **Oper, -n** opera
der   **Orangensaft** orange juice
das   **Orchester, -** orchestra
die   **Organisation, -en** organization
die   **Orgel, -n** organ
der   **Ort, -e** place
der   **Osten** east
(das)   **Österreich** Austria
der   **Österreicher, -; die**
         Österreicherin, -nen Austrian
       östlich east, easterly
der   **Ozean, -e** ocean

das   **Paar, -e** pair
       packen to pack
das   **Paket, -e** package
das   **Papier, -e** paper
der   **Papierkorb, ⁻e** wastebasket
das   **Parlament, -e** parliament
       parlamentarisch parliamentary
die   **Partei, -en** political party; faction
der   **Passagier, -e; die Passagierin,**
         -nen passenger
der   **Paß, ⁻sse** pass, passport
       passen (*dat.*) to fit; **passen zu** to
         match
       passend appropriate, suitable
der   **Passiv** passive
       pauken to cram

       peinlich embarrassing; painful
       perfekt perfect
das   **Perfekt** perfect tense
       persisch Persian
       persönlich personally
der   **Pfeffer, -** pepper
       ***pfeifen** to whistle
der   **Pfennig, -e** cent, 1/100 mark
das   **Pferd, -e** horse
das   **Pferderennen, -** horserace
der   **Pfiff, -e** whistle
die   **Pflanze, -n** plant
       pflanzen to plant
das   **Pfund, -e** pound; **drei Pfund**
         Äpfel three pounds of apples
der   **Philosoph (en-***masc.***) die**
         Philosophin, -nen philosopher
die   **Philosophie, -n** philosophy
die   **Physik** physics
der   **Physiker, -; die Physikerin, -nen**
         physicist
das   **Picknick, -s** picnic
das   **Plattdeutsch** Low-German
die   **Platte, -n** record
der   **Plattenspieler, -** record player
der   **Platz, ⁻e** place; room
       platzen to burst, blow out
       pleite broke
       plötzlich suddenly
das   **Plusquamperfekt** past perfect
         tense
die   **Politik** politics
der   **Politiker, -; die Politikerin, -nen**
         politician
die   **Politikwissenschaft**
         political science
der   **Politikwissenschaftler, -; die**
         Politikwissenschaftlerin, -nen
         political scientist
       politisch political
die   **Polizei** police
die   **Polizeiwache, -n** police station
der   **Polizist (en-***masc.***); die Polizistin,**
         -nen policeman (women)
der   **Portier, -s** porter
die   **Post** mail; post office
die   **Postkarte, -n** post card
das   **Präfix, -e** prefix
die   **Präposition, -en** preposition
das   **Präsens** present tense
der   **Präsident (en-***masc.***)** president
der   **Preis, -e** price; prize
       preiswert good value; reasonable
         in price
(das)   **Preußen** Prussia

der	**Prinz (en**-*masc.*) prince	
die	**Prinzessin, -nen** princess	
	pro per	
	probieren to try	
das	**Pronomen, -** pronoun	
	protestantisch protestant	
die	**Prüfung, -en** test, exam	
der	**Psychologe (en-**masc.**); die**	
	Psychologin, -nen	
	psychologist	
die	**Psychologie** psychology	
das	**Publikum** public	
	pünktlich punctually	
die	**Puppe, -n** doll	
das	**Puppenhaus, ⁻er** dollhouse	

der	**Quadratkilometer, -** square kilometer
die	**Quadratwurzel, -n** square root
die	**Qualität, -en** quality
die	**Quelle, -n** spring, well

die	**Rache** revenge
das	**Rad, ⁻er** bike
der	**Rasen, -** lawn, grass
der	**Rat** advice, counsel
die	**Rate, -n** installment; **auf Raten kaufen** to buy on time
	*raten (*dat.*) to advise; to guess
das	**Rathaus, ⁻er** city hall
das	**Rätsel, -** riddle, puzzle
	rauchen to smoke
das	**Rauchen** smoke, smoking; **Nicht Rauchen** No smoking
der	**Raum, ⁻e** room; space
	Raus! Get out!
die	**Realschule, -n** secondary school
die	**Rechnung, -en** bill
	recht (*adv.*) right; **recht haben** to be right
	rechts to the right; right
der	**Rechtsanwalt, ⁻e; die Rechtsanwältin, -nen** lawyer
die	**Rede, -n** speech
das	**Referat, -e** lecture; report
das	**Reformhaus, ⁻er** health food store
die	**Reformkost** health food
der	**Reformkostfanatiker, -; die Reformkostfanatikerin, -nen** health food fanatic
das	**Regal, -e** bookshelf
die	**Regel, -n** rule; **in der Regel** usually
	regelmäßig regularly
der	**Regen** rain

der	**Regenschirm, -e** umbrella
	regieren to rule, reign
die	**Regierung, -en** government
der	**Regierungschef, -s** head of the government
	regnen to rain
	regnerisch rainy
das	**Reh, -e** deer
	reich rich
das	**Reich, -e** state, realm, empire
der	**Reifen, -** tire
die	**Reihe, -n** row
	rein clean
	reinigen to clean; **chemisch reinigen** to dry clean
die	**Reise, -n** trip; **Gute Reise!** Have a good trip!; **eine Reise machen** to take a trip
das	**Reisenbuch, ⁻er** travel book
das	**Reisebüro, -s** travel agency
	reisen (sein) to travel
der	**(die) Reisende** (*declined adj.*) traveler; tourist
der	**Reisescheck, -s** traveler's check
	*reißen to rip, tear
	*reiten (sein) to ride (a horse)
	reizend charming, attractive
der	**Rekord, -e** (sports) record
der	**Rekordbrecher, -; die Rekordbrecherin, -nen** record breaker
das	**Rennen** racing
die	**Reparatur, -en** repair; **in die Reparatur bringen** to have repaired
	reparieren to repair
	reservieren to reserve
das	**Rezept, -** recipe
	richten to arrange
	richtig correct; real
der	**Ritter, -** knight
der	**Rock, ⁻e** coat, skirt
die	**Rockgruppe, -n** rock group
das	**Rohr, -e** pipe
die	**Rolle, -n** role, part
das	**Rollschuhlaufen** roller skating; **Rollschuhlaufen *gehen** to go roller skating
der	**Roman, -e** novel
der	**Römer, -; die Römerin, -nen** Roman
	römisch Roman
der	**Rosenmontag, -e** Monday before Lent
das	**Röslein, -** little rose; rosebud

das	**Roß, -sse** steed			

das **Roß, -sse** steed
    rot red
der **Rückblick, -e** glance back
der **Rücken, -** back
der **Rucksack, ̈e** knapsack
der **Ruf, -e** call, cry
    *rufen to call; **rufen *lassen** to send for
    ruhen to rest
    ruhig quiet, still; **sei(d) ruhig!** be quiet
die **Ruine, -n** ruin
    russisch Russian
(das) **Rußland** Russia

die **Sache, -n** thing; matter
der **Saft, ̈e** juice
    sagen to say; to tell
das **Salz** salt
    sammeln to gather, collect
der **Samstag, -e** Saturday; **samstags** Saturdays
die **Sandburg, -en** sand castle
der **Sänger, -; die Sängerin, -nen** singer
der **Satz, ̈e** sentence
    sauber clean
    sauer sour
    *saufen to drink (of animals)
das **Schach** chess
das **Schachbrett, -er** chessboard
die **Schachfigur, -en** chess piece
    schaden (*dat.*) to harm
    *schaffen to create
der **Schaffner, -** train conductor, steward
die **Schaffnerin, -nen** stewardess
die **Schallplatte, -n** record
der **Schalter, -** counter
der **Schatten, -** shadow
der **Schatz, ̈e** sweetheart, darling; treasure
    schauen to look (at)
das **Schaufenster, -** store window
der **Schaufensterbummel, -** window shopping; **einen Schaufensterbummel machen** to go window shopping
der **Schaum** foam
der **Schauspieler, -** actor **die Schauspielerin, -nen** actress
der **Scheck, -s** check
das **Scheckkonto, -s** checking account

    *scheiden to separate; to get divorced
    *scheinen to appear; to shine
    schenken to give
der **Schi, -er** ski; skiing
    schicken to send
der **Schiedsrichter, -; die Schiedsrichterin, -nen** referee
    *schießen to shoot; **ein Tor schießen** to score
das **Schild, -er** sign; notice
der **Schlaf** sleep
    *schlafen to sleep
das **Schlafzimmer, -** bedroom
der **Schlag, ̈e** blow
    *schlagen to beat; to hit
der **Schlager, -** racket
    schlank slim, thin
    schlecht bad, poor; **Mir ist schlecht.** I feel ill.
    *schließen to close
das **Schlittschuhlaufen** ice skating
das **Schloß, ̈sser** castle; lock
der **Schluß, ̈sse** end; **Schluß machen** to finish
der **Schlüssel, -** key
    schmecken to taste
der **Schmetterling, -e** butterfly
    schmücken to decorate
    schmuggeln to smuggle
der **Schmuggler, -; die Schmugglerin, -nen** smuggler
der **Schnee** snow
    *schneiden to cut; **sich die Haare schneiden *lassen** (*dat.*) to have one's hair cut
    schneien to snow
    schnell fast, quickly
der **Schnitt, -e** cut, slice
das **Schnitzel, -** cutlet
die **Schokolade, -n** chocolate; **eine Tafel Schokolade** chocolate bar
    schon already; indeed; **Ich lerne schon seit drei Monaten.** I have been studying for three months. **schon gut** all right; **schon lange** long ago; **schon wieder** again
    schön beautiful
    schrecklich terrible
    *schreiben to write
die **Schreibmaschine, -n** typewriter
der **Schreibtisch, -e** desk

die	**Schrift, -en** handwriting	der	**Senf** mustard
der	**Schriftsteller, -;** die		**servieren** to serve
	Schriftstellerin, -nen writer	der	**Sessel, -** armchair
der	**Schritt, -e** step		**setzen** to set, place; **sich setzen**
der	**Schuh, -e** shoe		to sit down
	schulden to owe		**sicher** certainly
	schuldig guilty		**sieben** seven
die	**Schule, -n** school		**siebte-** seventh
das	**Schuljahr, -e** school year		**siebzehn** seventeen
die	**Schulpflicht** compulsory	das	**Silber** silver
	education	der	**Silvesterabend** New Year's Eve
das	**Schulwesen, -** educational system		***singen** to sing
der	**Schuß, ̈sse** shot	die	**Sitte, -n** custom
	schwach weak		***sitzen** to sit
das	**Schweden** Sweden	der	**Sitzplatz, ̈e** seat
	schwedisch Swedish	der	**Ski, -er** ski; **das Paar Skier** pair of
	***schweigen** to be quiet		skis
die	**Schweiz** Switzerland		***ski · laufen (sein)** to ski
der	**Schweizer, -;** die **Schweizerin,**	der	**Skiläufer, -;** die **Skiläuferin, -nen**
	-nen Swiss		skier
	schwer difficult; heavy; serious		**so** as; so; thus; **so . . . wie** as . . .
die	**Schwester, -n** sister		as; **so etwas** such a thing
	schwierig hard, difficult	die	**Socke, -n** sock
die	**Schwierigkeit, -en** difficulty	das	**Sofa, -s** couch, sofa
das	**Schwimmbad, ̈er** swimming		**sofort** immediately
	pool		**sogar** even
	***schwimmen (sein)** to swim	der	**Sohn, ̈e** son
der	**Schwimmer, -;** die **Schwimmerin,**		**solange** as long as
	-nen swimmer		**solcher, solches, solche** such
	sechs six	der	**Soldat (en-***masc.***)** soldier
	sechste- sixth		**sollen (sollte, gesollt; soll)** to be
	sechzehn sixteen		supposed to; to have to; to be
	sechzig sixty		said to; should
der	**See, -n** lake	der	**Sommer, -** summer
die	**See, -n** ocean; sea	die	**Sonate, -n** sonata
	segeln to sail		**sondern** but, on the contrary;
das	**Segeln** sailing		**nicht nur . . . sondern**
	***sehen** to see, watch; **ähnlich**		**auch** not only . . . but also
	***sehen** to resemble	die	**Sonne, -n** sun
	sehenswert remarkable	der	**Sonnenschein** sunshine
	sehr very, very much		**sonnig** sunny
	sein his, its	der	**Sonntag, -e** Sunday; **sonntags** on
	***sein (sein)** to be		Sunday
	seit (*dat.*) since, for; **seit fünf**	die	**Sorge, -n** worry; **sich Sorgen**
	Jahren for the last five years		**machen um** (*dat.*) to be
	seitdem since then, ever since		worried about
	selbst (selber) even; self; myself,		**soviel** so much, many
	etc.		**sowieso** in any case
	selbständig independent	die	**Sowjetunion** Soviet Union
	selten seldom		**sowohl** the same as
	senden (sandte, gesandt *or*	der	**Sozialismus, -** socialism
	sendete, gesendet) to send,		**sozialistisch** socialistic
	broadcast	(das)	**Spanien** Spain
die	**Sendung, -en** broadcast; (TV,		**spanisch** Spanish
	radio) program		**spannend** exciting

das	**Sparbuch, ̈er** savings book		die	**Stelle, -n** position, place
	sparen to save			**stellen** to put, place; **eine Frage**
das	**Sparkonto, -s** savings account			**stellen** to ask a question
	spät late		die	**Stellung, -en** position, job
	spazieren (sein) to take a walk,			**stemmen** to lift
	stroll			***sterben (sein)** to die
	*spazieren · gehen (sein) to take a			**sterblich** mortal
	walk, hike		die	**Stereoanlage, -n** stereo set
der	**Spaziergang, ̈e** walk; **einen**		der	**Stern, -e** star
	Spaziergang machen to take		die	**Steuer, -n** tax
	a walk		die	**Stimme, -n** voice
die	**Speisekarte, -n** menu			**stimmen** to tune
	speziell especially		der	**Stock, ̈e** stick; story (house)
sich	**spiegeln** to be reflected			**stören** to disturb
das	**Spiel, -e** game; sport		der	**Strand, ̈e** beach, shore
der	**Spielbeginn** beginning of the		die	**Straße, -n** street
	game		die	**Straßenbahn, -en** streetcar
	spielen to play		der	**Strauch, ̈er** shrub; brush
der	**Spieler, -; die Spielerin, -nen**			***streichen** to paint
	player			***streiten** to argue, dispute
der	**Spielplatz, ̈e** playing field			**streng** strict, stern
das	**Spielzeug, -e** toy		die	**Strenge** strictness; severity
der	**Sport** sports; **Sport *treiben**			**stricken** to knit
	to take part in sports		der	**Strumpf, ̈e** sock; stocking
die	**Sportart, -en** type of sport		das	**Stück, -e** piece; play; work
der	**Sportgegenstand, ̈e**		das	**Stückchen, -** little piece
	sporting goods		der	**Student (en-*masc.*); die**
die	**Sporthalle, -n** gymnasium			**Studentin, -nen** student
der	**Sportler, -; die Sportlerin, -nen**			**studieren** to study
	athlete		das	**Studium, *pl.* Studien**
die	**Sportveranstaltung, -en**			postsecondary school
	sporting event			studies lasting about five years
die	**Sprache, -n** language			(master's degree equivalent)
	*sprechen to speak; **sprechen**		der	**Stuhl, ̈e** chair
	über (*acc.*) to discuss		das	**Stühlchen, -** little chair
das	**Sprichwort, ̈er** saying, proverb		die	**Stunde, -n** hour
	*springen (sein) to jump		der	**Sturm, ̈e** storm
der	**Staat, -en** state, country		das	**Subjekt, -e** subject
das	**Stadion, *pl.* Stadien** stadium			**suchen** to seek, look for
die	**Stadt, ̈e** town, city		(das)	**Südafrika** South Africa
die	**Stadtmitte** city center		der	**Süden** south
der	**Stamm, ̈e** stem; tribe			**südlich** south, southerly
der	**Stand, ̈e** position, state		der	**Supermarkt, ̈e** supermarket
	stark strong, numerous, heavy		die	**Suppe, -n** soup
	(rain)			**süß** sweet, charming
	statt (*gen.*) instead of		die	**Süßigkeiten** (*pl.*) sweets, candy
	stattdessen instead of that			**sympathisch** likeable, congenial
	*statt · finden to take place		die	**Symphonie, -n** symphony
	stecken to put, place			
	*stehen to stand; to be		die	**Tablette, -n** pill
	*stehlen to steal		die	**Tafel, -n** blackboard; bar
	*steigen (sein) to climb			(chocolate)
der	**Stein, -e** stone		der	**Tag, -e** day; **am Tag** by day; **den**
				ganzen Tag all day; **vor acht**
				Tagen a week ago

das	**Tagebuch, ¨er** diary, journal		**trainieren** to train
die	**Tageszeitung, -en** daily		**trauen** (*dat.*) to trust
	newspaper	das	**Trauerspiel, -e** tragedy
das	**Tal, ¨er** valley	der	**Traum, ¨e** dream
	tanken to fill up		**träumen** to dream
die	**Tanksstelle, -n** gas station		**traurig** sad
die	**Tante, -n** aunt		***treffen** to meet
	tanzen to dance		***treiben** to drive; to practice;
die	**Tanztruppe, -n** dance troupe		**Sport treiben** to take part
die	**Tasche, -n** pocket		in sports
die	**Tasse, -n** cup		**trennen** to separate
der	**Täter, -; die Täterin, -nen** culprit		***treten (sein)** to walk; to step
	tätig active		**treu** faithful, loyal
die	**Tatsache, -n** fact		***trinken** to drink
	tatsächlich really		**trocken** dry
	taub deaf		**trocknen** to dry (**sein** with
das	**Tausend, -e** thousand		*intr.*)
	tausendst- thousandth	die	**Trompete, -n** trumpet
der	**Teddybär (en-*masc.*)** teddy bear		**trotz** (*gen.*) in spite of
der	**Tee, -s** tea		**trotzdem** nevertheless
der	**Teich, -e** pond		**tschechisch** Czech
	teilen to divide	die	**Tschechoslowakei**
	***teil · nehmen (an)** (*dat.*) to take		Czechoslovakia
	part, participate (in)		***tun** to do; to make; **Tut mir leid.**
	telefonieren to telephone		I'm sorry. **weh tun** to hurt
der	**Teller, -** plate	die	**Tür, -en** door
der	**Tennisplatz, ¨e** tennis court	die	**Türkei** Turkey
der	**Tennisschläger, -** tennis racket		**türkisch** Turkish
der	**Teppich, -e** rug; carpet	der	**Turm, ¨e** tower
	teuer expensive	das	**Turnen** gymnastics
das	**Theaterstück, -e** play, drama	das	**Turnier, -e** contest, tournament
das	**Thema,** *pl.* **Themen** theme,		
	subject		
der	**Thron, -e** throne		
	tief deep		**üben** to practice; to exercise
das	**Tier, -e** animal		**über** (*dat. or acc.*) over; above;
	tippen to type		(*acc.*) about
der	**Tisch, -e** table		**überall** everywhere
das	**Tischtennis** ping pong		**überhaupt** at all; **überhaupt**
die	**Tochter, ¨** daughter		**kein** none at all
der	**Tod, -e** death		***über · laufen (sein)** to overflow
die	**Tomate, -n** tomato		**übermorgen** day after tomorrow
der	**Topf, ¨e** pot, jar		**übernachten** to spend the night
das	**Tor, -e** goal; gate; **ein Tor**		**überqueren** to cross
	***schießen** to score		**übersetzen** to translate
die	**Torte, -n** cake; tart	die	**Übersetzung, -en** translation
	total completely		***übertragen** to broadcast
die	**Tracht, -en** traditional costume,	die	**Übertragung, -en** broadcast
	dress		**überzeugen** to persuade,
	tragbar portable, wearable		convince
	***tragen** to wear; to carry		**übrig** left over, remaining
die	**Tragödie, -n** tragedy		**übrigens** by the way
der	**Trainer, -; die Trainerin, -nen**	die	**Übung, -en** exercise
	coach	die	**Uhr, -en** watch; clock; o'clock

um (*acc.*) about, around; for; **Um Gottes willen!** For God's sake! **um . . . herum** round about; **um sechs Uhr** at six o'clock; **um . . . zu** in order to

umarmen to embrace

umflattern to flutter around

die **Umgebung** surroundings, neighborhood

*um · gehen (sein) to handle; **mit Geld gut um · gehen** to handle money well.

sich **um · kleiden** to change clothes

der **Umschlag, -̈e** envelope

*um · schreiben to rewrite

*um · steigen (sein) to change trains (buses)

der **Umzug, -̈e** change of dwelling, move

unabhängig independent

die **Unabhängigkeit** independence

unbedingt without fail; unconditional

unbekannt unknown

unbestimmt indefinite

und and

unehrlich dishonest

der **Unfall, -̈e** accident

unfreundlich unfriendly

ungefähr about, almost

ungerecht unfair

ungern reluctantly

die **Uni, -s** university

die **Universität, -en** university

das **Universum** universe

unser our

unsretwillen: um unsretwillen for our sake

unten below; **nach unten** downstairs

unter (*dat. or acc.*) under, beneath; **unter die Studenten** among the students

*unterbrechen to interrupt

*unter · gehen (sein) to sink

unterhalb (*gen.*) under, below

*unterlassen to neglect; to refrain (from)

der **Unterricht, -e** instruction, classes

unterrichten to teach (a subject)

der **Unterschied, -e** difference

unterwegs en route

ununterbrochen uninterrupted

uralt ancient

der **Urlaub** vacation; **auf (in) Urlaub *gehen** to go on vacation

der **Ursprung, -̈e** origin

der **Vater, -̈** father

der **Vati** papa

der **Vegetarier,-; die Vegetarierin, -nen** vegetarian

sich **verabreden** to agree; to make an appointment

verabschieden to pass (law); **sich verabschieden** to say goodbye

veranstalten to organize

die **Veranstaltung, -en** show, performance

verantwortlich responsible

die **Verantwortung, -en** responsibility

verbessern to improve

*verbieten (*dat.*) to forbid

*verbinden to join

verboten forbidden

der **Verbrecher, -; die Verbrecherin, -nen** criminal

verbringen (verbrachte, verbracht) to spend (time)

*verderben to spoil, ruin (**sein** with *intr.*)

verdienen to earn

der **Verein, -e** club; association

die **Vereinigten Staaten** United States

sich ***verfahren** to get lost

die **Vergangenheit** past

*vergeben (*dat.*) to forgive

*vergehen (sein) to pass away; to disappear

*vergessen to forget

*vergleichen to compare

verheiraten to marry

verkaufen to sell

der **Verkäufer, -; die Verkäuferin, -nen** vendor; salesperson

der **Verkehr** traffic

verkleinern to reduce, diminish

die **Verkleinerung, -en** reduction; diminution

verlangen to demand; to ask for

*verlassen to leave, abandon

verlernen to forget

sich **verletzen** to injure oneself

sich **verlieben (in)** (*acc.*) to fall in love (with)

*verlieren to lose

verlorengegangen lost
vermieten to rent out; to lease
vermissen to miss
verneinen to deny
veröffentlichen to publish
verpassen to miss
verrückt crazy
verschieden various; different
*verschwinden (sein) to disappear
versetzen to move, transfer
versorgen to care for
verspäten to delay; **sich
verspäten** to be late
*versprechen (*dat.*) to promise;
sich versprechen to say the
wrong thing
verstecken to hide
*verstehen to understand
versuchen to try
verteidigen to defend
verteilen to distribute
vertrauen (*dat.*) to trust
*vertreiben to expel, banish

der (die) **Verwandte** (*declined adj.*)
relative
verwenden (verwandte, verwandt
or verwendete; verwendet)
to use
verzollen to pay duty on

der **Vetter, -n** cousin
viel much, many
vielleicht perhaps, maybe
vier four
viert- fourth

das **Viertel, -** fourth; quarter; **Viertel
vor acht** quarter of eight
vierzehn fourteen
vierzig forty

der **Vogel, ⸚** bird
das **Volk, ⸚er** people; nation
das **Volkslied, -er** folksong
die **Volkspolizei** East German police
voll completely
vollbracht finished, completed
voll · tanken to fill up completely
von (*dat.*) from; of; about; by
vor (*dat. or acc.*) before; in front
of; on account of; **vor zwei
Wochen** two weeks ago
vorbei past
*vorbei · kommen (sein)
to come by
vor · bereiten to prepare

der **Vorgang, ⸚e** process
vorgestern day before yesterday

vor · haben (hatte ... vor,
vorgehabt) to intend, plan
to do

der **Vorhang, ⸚e** curtain
*vor · lesen to read aloud
die **Vorlesung, -en** lecture
der **Vormittag** late morning;
vormittags in the late morning,
mornings
der **Vorname** (*acc., dat. sing.* **-n**; *gen.
sing.* **-ns**; *pl.* **-n**) Christian
name (first name)
vorne in front
*vor · schlagen to suggest
vorsichtig cautious, careful
vor · stellen to present, introduce;
sich vor · stellen to introduce
oneself; (*dat.*) to imagine
das **Vorurteil, -e** prejudice
vor · zeigen to show

wach awake
*wachsen (sein) to grow
der **Wagen, -** car; vehicle
die **Wahl, -en** election, choice
wählen to choose, elect
wahr true; **nicht wahr?** isn't it?
das **Wahre** (*declined adj.*) truth, that
which is true
während (*prep. with gen.; conj.*)
while, during
währenddessen meanwhile
die **Wahrheit** truth; reality
wahrscheinlich probably
der **Wald, ⸚er** forest, wood
der **Walzer, -** waltz
die **Wand, ⸚e** wall
der **Wanderer, -** traveler, hiker
wandern (sein) to hike; to walk
wann when
die **Waren** (*pl.*) goods
warten (auf) (*acc.*) to wait (for)
warum why
was what, whatever; **was für
ein** what kind of
die **Wäsche, -n** laundry; washing
*waschen to wash; **sich die Hände
waschen** to wash one's hands
das **Wasser** water
der **Wasserfall, ⸚e** waterfall
wecken to waken
der **Wecker, -** alarm clock
weder ... noch neither ... nor
der **Weg, -e** way; road
weg away, gone

wegen (*gen.*) on account of

*weg · gehen (sein) to leave, go away

weg · machen to take away

*weh tun (*dat.*) to hurt; sich weh tun to hurt oneself

(die) Weihnachten Christmas; zu Weihnachten at Christmas

der Weihnachtsbaum, ¨-e Christmas tree

das Weihnachtslied, -er Christmas carol

weil because

der Wein, -e wine

weinen to cry

das Weinfest, -e wine festival

weiß white

weit wide; weit weg far away

*weiter · lesen to continue reading

*weiter · sprechen to continue speaking

welcher, welches, welche which

die Welt, -en world

der Weltkrieg, -e world war; der Erste Weltkrieg World War I

wenden (wandte, gewandt *or* wendete, gewendet) to turn

wenig little, few

wenigstens at least

wenn when; whenever, if; wenn nur if only

wer who

*werden (sein) to become

*werfen to throw

das Werk, -e work

weshalb why, on account of which

der Westen west

westlich west, westerly

weswegen why, on account of which

das Wetter, - weather

der Wettkampf, ¨-e contest, match

wichtig important, serious

wider (*acc.*) against

*widerfahren (sein) to happen

wider · hallen to echo

sich wider · spiegeln to be reflected

*widersprechen (*dat.*) to contradict

wie as, how

wieder again

*wieder · bekommen to get back

wiederholen to repeat; (·) to retrieve

die Wiederholung, -en repetition

*wieder · sehen to see again

(das) Wien Vienna

die Wiese, -n meadow

wieviel how many, how much; Der wievielte ist heute? What's the date today? Wieviel Uhr ist es? What time is it?

der Wille (*acc., dat. sing.* -n; *gen. sing.* -ns, *pl.* -n) will, volition; Um Gottes willen! For Heaven's sake!

wirklich really

die Wirtschaft economics; business

wissen (wußte, gewußt; weiß) to know

die Wissenschaft, -en science

wissenschaftlich scientific

der Witwer, - widower

wo where (at)

die Woche, -n week

das Wochenende, - weekend

wodurch whereby

wofür for what

wogegen on the other hand

woher how; from where

wohin which way; to what place, where (to)

wohinter behind what

wohl probably, perhaps

wohnen to live, reside

die Wohnung, -en apartment, dwelling

das Wohnzimmer, - living room

wollen (wollte, gewollte; will) to want; to intend to; to claim to

womit with what

wonach after what

woran about what; on what

worauf for what; on what

woraus out of what

das Wort, ¨-er word

der Wortschatz vocabulary

worüber about what

wunderbar wonderful

sich wundern (über) (*acc.*) to be surprised (at)

wunderschön lovely

wünschen to wish

der Wurf, ¨-e throw

der Wurm, ¨-er worm

die Wurst, ¨-e sausage

die Zahl, -en number, figure

zahlen to pay

der Zahn, ⸚e tooth
der Zahnarzt, ⸚e; die Zahnärztin, -nen dentist
das Zahnweh toothache
zehn ten
zehnte- tenth
zeigen to show
die Zeit, -en time; Ach du liebe Zeit! Oh my goodness! die alten Zeiten the old days
das Zeitalter, - age, era
die Zeitschrift, -en magazine
die Zeitung, -en newspaper
*zerbrechen to shatter, smash (sein with intr.)
die Zeremonie, -ien ceremony
*zerfallen (sein) fall into ruin
*zerreißen to tear up
zerstören to disrupt, destroy
*ziehen to pull; (sein) to move
das Ziel, -e goal
ziemlich fairly, rather
die Zigarette, -n cigarette
das Zimmer, - room, apartment
der Zoll customs; duty
der Zollbeamte (declined adj.); die Zollbeamtin, -nen customs officer
die Zollkontrolle customs inspection
zu (prep. with dat.) to; at; for; (adv.) too; ab und zu now and then; zu Hause at home
der Zucker sugar
zuerst first, at first
zufrieden content, pleased
der Zug, ⸚e parade; train

der Zugang, ⸚e access, entry
zu · hören (dat.) to listen to; to audit
zuletzt finally; at length
zu · machen to shut; to fasten
zunächst first
*zu · nehmen to put on; to gain (weight)
zurück back
*zurück · bleiben (sein) to stay behind
zuruck · führen to lead back
zuruck · kehren (sein) to return
*zurück · kommen (sein) to return, come back
zusammen together
*zusammen · bringen (brachte . . . zusammen, zusammengebracht) to join, bring together
*zusammen · fallen (sein) to fall down, collapse
*zusammen · halten to hold together
der Zuschauer, - spectator
*zu · schließen to lock up
zuviel too much
zwanzig twenty
zwanzigste- twentieth
zwei two
zweite- second
zwischen (dat. or acc.) between, among
zwölf twelve
zwölfte- twelfth

Abitur: to take the — das Abitur machen

able: to be — können, konnte, gekonnt, kann (*see pp. 109–115*)

account: on — of *prep.* wegen (*gen.*)

according to *prep.* nach (*dat.*)

across from *prep.* gegenüber (*dat.*)

address die Adresse, -n

Advent wreath der Adventskranz, ¨e

afford sich (*dat.*) leisten

afraid: to be — of sich fürchten vor (*dat.*)

after *prep.* nach (*dat.*)

after *conj.* nachdem

afternoon der Nachmittag, -e **this —** heute nachmittag

after that *adv.* danach

against *prep.* gegen (*acc.*)

ago *prep.* vor (*dat.*)

alarm clock der Wecker, -

all alle

along *prep.* entlang (*acc.*); **— the street** die Straße entlang

along *adv.* auch

Alps die Alpen

also *adv.* auch

always *adv.* immer

animal das Tier, -e

answer *noun* die Antwort, -en; *verb* antworten (*with dat. of the person*)

anything etwas; **— at all** irgend etwas

arrive *an · kommen (*sein*)

art: art museum das Kunstmuseum, -museen; **art work** das Kunstwerk, -e

artist der Künstler, -, die Künstlerin, -nen

as *conj.* wie; **— if** als ob

ask fragen; **to — for something** um etwas (*acc.*) *bitten; **to — about,** fragen nach (*dat.*)

athlete der Sportler, -; die Sportlerin, -nen

attend (*school*) besuchen; (*performances, events*) bei · wohnen (*dat.*)

aunt die Tante, -n

at *prep.* in, bei, auf (*all with dat.; see pp. 238–252*)

backpack der Rucksack, ¨e

bad: to be bad for schaden (*dat.*)

bank die Bank, -en; **to go to the —** auf die Bank *gehen (*sein*)

be *sein (*sein*) (*see p. 11*)

because *conj.* weil; **— of** *prep.* wegen (*gen.*)

become *werden (*sein*)

beer (das) Bier

before *conj.* bevor

before *prep.* vor (*dat. or acc.; see pp. 249–252*)

behind *prep.* hinter (*dat. or acc.; see pp. 249–252*)

believe glauben (*with dat. of the person*)

belong (to) gehören (*with dat. of the person to express ownership*); gehören zu (*with dat. to express membership*)

better besser

between *prep.* zwischen (*dat. or acc.; see pp. 249–252*)

big groß

bill die Rechnung, -en

bird der Vogel, ¨

blouse die Bluse, -n

blue blau

book das Buch, ¨er

bookstore die Buchhandlung, -en

border die Grenze, -n

boring langweilig

both: — things beides *pron.*; beide (die beiden) Kinder

bottle die Flasche, -n; **a bottle of milk** eine Flasche Milch

boy der Junge (*weak masc.; see p. 93–94*)

bread das Brot

break *brechen

bridge die Brücke, -n

bring bringen, brachte, gebracht

broadcast *übertragen

brother der Bruder, ¨

brown braun

build bauen

building das Gebäude, -

bus der Bus, Busse; **by bus** mit dem Bus

but aber; **— on the contrary** (*used to negate negatives*) sondern (*see p. 15*)

buy kaufen

by *prep.* von (*personal agent*), mit (*transportation*), bei (*proximity to structures or places; all with dat.*); durch (*means or instrument, with acc.*); an, neben (*both with dat. or acc.*); (*up to, until*) bis (*with acc.; see pp. 245–252*)

cafe das Café, -s
cake der Kuchen, -
call *rufen; **to be called** *heißen
can können, konnte, gekonnt, kann (*see pp. 109–115*)
Canadian kanadisch-
candy; (hard) — das Bonbon, -s
capital die Hauptstadt, ̈e
capitalistic kapitalistisch
car der Wagen, -; das Auto, -s
carry *tragen; (*sell*) führen
cash ein • lösen
castle das Schloß, Schlösser
catch cold sich erkälten
cathedral der Dom, -e
century das Jahrhundert, -e
ceremony die Zeremonie, -n
change: to have — for klein haben; **Do you have change for 50 Marks?** Haben Sie fünfzig Mark klein?; (*noun*) das Kleingeld
chancellor der Bundeskanzler, -
chapter das Kapitel, -
check: traveler's check der Reisescheck, -s
chef der Küchenchef, -s
chemistry building das Chemiegebäude, -
chess: to play chess Schach spielen
child das Kind, -er
Christmas: — card die Weihnachtskarte, -n; — tree der Weihnachtsbaum, ̈e
church die Kirche, -n
city die Stadt, ̈e
claim behaupten
close (a building) *schließen
coach der Trainer, -; die Trainerin, -nen
coffee (der) Kaffee
cold kalt
collect sammeln
come *kommen (*sein*); — from, *kommen (*sein*) aus (*dat.*); **come again** *wieder • kommen (*sein*); **come over** *vorbei • kommen (*sein*)
completely ganz
compose komponieren
conclusion: in conclusion zum Schluß
conservative konservativ
contradict *widersprechen (*with dat. of the person*)
cook kochen; *noun* der Koch, ̈e; die Köchin, -nen
copy *ab • schreiben
corner die Ecke, -n; **at the** — an der Ecke

cost kosten
costume das Kostüm, -e; — **ball** das Kostümfest, -e
cousin (*male*) der Vetter, -n; (*female*) die Kusine, -n
cram pauken
cup die Tasse, -n; **a cup of coffee** eine Tasse Kaffee
current aktuell
customs inspection die Zollkontrolle; **to stop for the** — zur Zollkontrolle *an • halten
customs official der Zollbeamte (*declined adjective, see pp. 167–168*)
cut *schneiden

damage schaden (*dat.*)
dance tanzen
daughter die Tochter, ̈
day der Tag, -e
decide sich *entschließen
dentist der Zahnarzt, ̈e; die Zahnärztin, -nen
department store das Kaufhaus, ̈er
describe *beschreiben
design *entwerfen
desk der Schreibtisch, -e
destroy zerstören
die *sterben (*sein*)
difficult schwer
dirndl das Dirndl, -
discover entdecken
discuss *besprechen
dishonest unehrlich
do *tun; machen
doctor der Arzt, ̈e; die Ärztin, -nen
doctorate: to receive a doctorate den Doktor machen
door die Tür, -en; **to knock at the** — an die Tür klopfen
drama das Drama, Dramen; das Schauspiel, -e
drink *trinken
drive (*travel*) *fahren (*sein*)

each other einander (*see p. 229*)
early früh
easily leicht
eat *essen; **to** — **breakfast** frühstücken
eighth acht-
either . . . or entweder . . . oder (*see p. 321*)
eleven elf
embarrassing peinlich
embrace umarmen

emperor der Kaiser, -
empire das Reich, -e
employ an · stellen
empress die Kaiserin, -nen
enough genug
erect errichten
essay der Aufsatz, ⁻e
Europe (das) Europa
evening der Abend, -e; **in the —** am
   Abend; **evening meal** das
   Abendessen, -
ever je
everyone jedermann
everything alles
exam das Examen, -
except *prep.* außer (*dat.*)
expensive teuer
explain erklären
exposition die Ausstellung, -en

fair gerecht
fairy tale das Märchen, -
family die Familie, -n
famous berühmt
farmer der Bauer, -n; die Bäuerin, -nen
fast schnell
father der Vater, ⁻
festival das Fest, **at the —** beim Fest;
   wine — das Weinfest, -e
few wenig; **a —** ein wenig; ein bißchen
fight kämpfen
film der Film, -e
find *finden
first erst-; **at —** zuerst
fish der Fisch, -e
fit passen (*with dat. of the person*)
five fünf
flower die Blume, -n; **little —** das
   Blümchen (Blümlein), -
flunk *durch · fallen (*sein*); **He flunked
   the test.** Er ist in (bei) der Prüfung
   durchgefallen.
fly *fliegen (*sein*)
follow folgen (*dat.*)
forbid *verbieten (*with dat. of the person*)
for *prep.* für (*acc.*); **— Christmas** zu
   Weihnachten; **I have been studying
   German for two years.** Ich lerne
   schon seit zwei Jahren Deutsch.; **I'm
   going to Germany for two years.** Ich
   fahre (fliege) auf zwei Jahre nach
   Deutschland.
foreign word das Fremdwort, ⁻er
forest der Wald, ⁻er
forget *vergessen

forgive *vergeben (*with dat. of the
   person*)
fork die Gabel, -n
former jener, jenes, jene (*see p. 77*)
fortress die Burg, -en
four vier
France (das) Frankreich
freedom die Freiheit, -en
French *adj.* französich
Frenchman der Franzose (*weak masc.;
   see pp. 93–94*)
fresh frisch
Friday der Freitag; **on —** am Freitag;
   — afternoon Freitag nachmittag
friend der Freund, -e; die Freundin, -nen
front: in — of *prep.* vor (*dat. or acc.; see
   pp. 249–252*)
fruit das Obst; die Frucht, ⁻e

game das Spiel, -e
garden der Garten, ⁻; **little —** das
   Gärtchen (Gärtlein), -
gas station die Tankstelle, -n
German *adj.* deutsch; **West —**
   westdeutsch
get (*become*) *werden (*sein*); (*receive*)
   *bekommen; **— up** *auf · stehen (*sein*);
   — used to sich gewöhnen an (*acc.*)
girl das Mädchen, -
girlfriend die Freundin, -nen
give *geben; **— up** *auf · geben; **giving
   grades** das Notengeben
glass das Glas, ⁻er; **a glass of water** ein
   Glas Wasser; **two glasses of
   water** zwei Glas Wasser
go *gehen (*sein*); **— down** (*ship*)
   *unter · gehen (*sein*); **— along**
   *mit · gehen (*sein*)
goal: to score a — ein Tor *schießen
golf (das) Golf
good gut; **goods** die Waren
goodnaturedness die Gutmütigkeit
government die Regierung, -en
grade die Note, -n
grandchild das Enkelkind, -er
grandfather der Großvater, ⁻
grandparents die Großeltern
green grün
groceries die Lebensmittel
grocery store das Lebensmittelgeschäft, -e
grow *wachsen (*sein*); (*transitive*) *ziehen;
   züchten; **Do you grow roses in your
   garden?** Ziehst (züchtest) du Rosen in
   deinem Garten?

hair das Haar, -e; **to get a haircut** sich (*dat.*) die Haare *schneiden *lassen

half *adj.* halb; **one and a —** anderthalb (*indeclinable*); **two and a —** zweieinhalb (*indeclinable*); (*see p. 335*)

hand die Hand, ⸚e

handle: — money mit Geld *um · gehen (*sein*)

happen *geschehen (*sein*)

hard: to work hard fleißig arbeiten

have haben (*see p. 8*); **— something done** etwas machen *lassen (*see pp. 117–118*); **— to** müssen, mußte, gemußt, muß (*see pp. 109–115*)

health food store das Reformhaus, ⸚er

hear hören

help *helfen (*dat.*); *noun* die Hilfe, -n

her *possessive adj.* ihr, ihr, ihre (*see pp. 81–84*)

here her; **come —** : Komm her!

hide verstecken

high hoch (*see p. 156*)

hike wandern (*sein*)

hiker der Wanderer, -

his *possessive adj.* sein, sein, seine (*see pp. 81–84*)

history die Geschichte, -n

hold *halten; **— together** *zusammen · halten

holiday der Feiertag, -e

home: at — zu Hause; **(toward) —** nach Hause

homework die Hausaufgaben (*pl.*)

hot heiß

hotel das Hotel, -s

hour die Stunde, -n

house das Haus, ⸚er

how wie; **— much** wieviel; **— many** wie viele

hungry: to be — Hunger haben

hurry sich beeilen

hurt (oneself) (*sich*) verletzen

husband der Mann, ⸚er

ice cream das Eis; die Eiskrem

ice skater der Eisläufer, -; die Eisläuferin, -nen

if wenn; **as —** als ob; (*whether*) ob

important wichtig

in *prep.* in (*dat. or acc.; see pp. 249–252*); **— 1981** im Jahre 1981; **— German** auf deutsch; **— spite of** *prep.* trotz (*gen.*)

influence beeinflussen; *noun* der Einfluß, -flüsse

inside drinnen; **come —** *herein · kommen (*sein*)

installment: to buy on the — plan auf Raten kaufen

instead of *prep.*, (an)statt (*gen.*); **— going home** anstatt nach Hause zu *gehen

intelligence die Klugheit

interested: to be — in sich interessieren für

interesting interessant

interrupt *unterbrechen

into *prep.* in (*acc.*)

invite *ein · laden

its *possessive adj.* sein, sein, seine (*see pp. 81–84*)

jacket die Jacke, -n

Jägerhut der Jägerhut, ⸚e

just *adj.* gerecht

just *adv.*: **— as** ebenso; **just as old as I** ebenso alt wie ich

kilogram das Kilogramm; das Kilo, -s; **three kilograms of coffee** drei Kilo Kaffee

kind: what — of was für; **What kind of a tree is that?** Was für ein Baum ist das?

king der König, -e

knock klopfen; **to — at the door** an die Tür klopfen

knife das Messer, -

knight der Ritter, -

know (*a fact*) wissen, wußte, gewußt, weiß; (*to be acquainted with*) kennen, kannte, gekannt; **(know how) know** (*languages and things learned through memorization*) können, konnte, gekonnt, kann (*see pp. 123–124*)

laboratory das Labor, -s

landscape die Landschaft, -en

language die Sprache, -n

large groß

last *adj.* letzt

last dauern

late spät

latter: the latter diese- (*see p. 77*)

laugh lachen

law das Gesetz, -e

lay legen

learn lernen

leave *ab · fahren (*sein*); (*abandon*) *verlassen

lecture die Vorlesung, -en; **at the** — bei
der Vorlesung; **lecture hall**
der Hörsaal, -säle
less weniger
let *lassen; **Let's go to the movies.** Laß
(laßt, lassen Sie) uns ins Kino *gehen!
*Gehen wir ins Kino! (*see pp. 20, 22*)
letter der Brief, -e
library die Bibliothek, -en
lie (*recline*) *liegen
light das Licht, -er
like *gefallen (*dat.*) **I like these records.**
Diese Schallplatten gefallen mir.
listen to *zu • hören (*dat.*); — **music**
Musik hören
little klein
live leben
lock *zu • schließen
long *adj.* lang; *adv.* lange
look: — for suchen (nach, *dat.*);
— **forward to** sich freuen auf (*acc.*);
— **like** ähnlich, (*dat.*) *sehen; — **up**
(*consult a book*) *nach • schlagen;
— **well** gesund aus • sehen
lose *verlieren; — **weight** *ab • nehmen
lot: a — of viel (*indeclinable in sing.*),
viele (*pl.*); **a lot of time** viel Zeit; **a lot
of friends** viele Freunde
love: in — with verliebt *sein in (*acc.*)
luggage das Gepäck

magazine die Zeitschrift, -en
make machen
man (*male*) der Mann, ̈-er; (*human being*)
der Mensch (*weak masc.;*
see pp. 93–94)
many viele
market der Markt, ̈-e; **to the —** auf den
Markt
married *adj.* verheiratet
marry heiraten
mask die Maske, -n
mathematics die Mathematik
may (*be permitted*) dürften, durfte,
gedurft, darf (*see pp. 109–115*)
mayor der Bürgermeister, -
meantime: in the — inzwischen
meat das Fleisch
meet sich *treffen
member das Mitglied, -er
Mexico (das) Mexiko
Middle Ages das Mittelalter
milk die Milch
miss (das) Fräulein, -

Monday der Montag, -e;
on — am Montag
money das Geld
month der Monat, -e; **next —** nächsten
Monat
more and more immer (*with comparative*);
the more . . . the more je . . . desto
most die meisten
mother die Mutter, ̈
mountain der Berg, -e
movies das Kino; **to the —** ins Kino
Mr. Herr (*weak masc.; sing.* -n, *pl.* -en;
see pp. 93–94)
Mrs. (die) Frau, -en
Munich (das) München
museum das Museum, -seen
music die Musik; **rock —** die Rockmusik
musician der Musiker, -; die Musikerin,
-nen
my *possessive adj.* mein, mein, meine
(*see pp. 81–84*)

name der Name (*acc., dat. sing.* -n; *gen.*
sing. -ns; *pl.* -n; *see p. 94*)
nature die Natur, -en
nauseated: I'm nauseated. Mir ist
schlecht.
need brauchen; **You don't need to do
that.** Du brauchst das nicht zu machen.
neighbor der Nachbar, -n; die Nachbarin,
-nen
never nie(mals)
new neu
New Year's Eve der Silvesterabend;
on — am Silvesterabend
newspaper die Zeitung, -en
next nächst-; — **month** nächsten Monat;
— **year** nächstes Jahr
next (door) to *prep.* neben (*dat. or acc.;*
see pp. 249–252)
night die Nacht, ̈-e; **last —** gestern abend
nine neun
nineteenth neunzehnt-
no *adj.* kein, kein, keine (*see pp. 26,*
81–84); **no one** keiner; niemand
no *adv.* nein
nobody niemand; — **else** niemand
anders
not nicht; — **a(ny)** kein, kein, keine (*see*
pp. 26, 81–84); — **anything** nichts
notebook das Heft, -e
nothing nichts
novel der Roman, -e
now jetzt
nowhere nirgendwo

o'clock: It is one o'clock. Es ist ein Uhr.
office das Büro, -s
often oft
on prep. auf, an (dat. or acc.; see pp.
249–252); — Monday am Montag
only nur
open adj. offen
open auf • machen; öffnen
opera die Oper, -n; to the — in die Oper
orchestra das Orchester, -
order (food, etc.) bestellen; in — that
damit; in — to um . . . zu
outside draußen; to go —
*hinaus • gehen (sein)
old alt
over prep. über (dat. or acc.)

pack packen; I'm packing my suitcase.
Ich packe meinen Koffer.
paint *streichen
paper das Papier
park der Park, -s
parents die Eltern
parliament das Parlament
party (political) die Partei, -en; (social
gathering) die Party, -s
pass (an exam) *bestehen; (a law)
verabschieden
passport der Paß, Pässe
pay bezahlen (with dat. of the person);
— cash bar • zahlen; — duty
on verzollen; — off ab • zahlen
pencil der Bleistift, -e
people die Leute; man (indefinite pron.
with sing. vb.; see p. 310)
per pro; How much do eggs cost per
dozen? Wieviel kosten Eier pro
Dutzend?
perform auf • führen
permitted: to be — dürften, durfte,
gedurft, darf (see pp. 109–115)
pharmacy die Apotheke, -n
photograph auf • nehmen; fotografieren;
noun das Foto, -s; die Aufnahme, -n
physics building das Physikgebäude, -
picture das Bild, -er
piece das Stück, -e; a piece of cake ein
Stück Kuchen
place: in the first — erstens; in the
second — zweitens
plan der Plan, ⁻e
plane das Flugzeug, -e; by — mit dem
Flugzeug
play spielen
player der Spieler, -; die Spielerin, -nen

please bitte; Please speak slower. Bitte,
sprechen Sie langsamer!
pocket die Tasche, -n
poem das Gedicht, -e
policeman der Polizist (weak masc.; see
pp. 93–94)
politician der Politiker, -; die Politikerin,
-nen
politics die Politik
poor (of — quality) schlecht
popular beliebt
portable set das tragbare Gerät, -e
postcard die Postkarte, -n
post office die Post; to the —
auf die Post
potato salad der Kartoffelsalat, -e
practice üben
present das Geschenk, -e
president der Präsident (weak masc.; see
pp. 93–94)
probably wahrscheinlich; wohl; It is
probably ten o'clock. Es wird wohl
zehn Uhr sein. It was probably ten
o'clock. Es wird wohl zehn Uhr
gewesen sein.
problem das Problem, -e
professor der Professor, -en
pronounce *aus • sprechen
put (in a horizontal position) legen; (in a
standing position) stellen; — on sich
(dat.) *an • ziehen

quality die Qualität, -en
queen die Königin, -nen
question die Frage, -n
quickly schnell

racket der Schläger, -
radium (das) Radium
railroad station der Bahnhof, ⁻e
rain regnen; noun der Regen
read *lesen
really wirklich
receive *bekommen
recipe das Rezept, -e
recognize erkennen, erkannte, erkannt
recommend *empfehlen
record die Schallplatte, -n
reelect wieder • wählen
referee der Schiedsrichter, -
relative der (die) Verwandte (declined
adj.; see pp. 167–168)
relax aus • spannen
remain *bleiben (sein)
remember sich erinnern an (acc.)
repair reparieren

repeat wiederholen
report der Bericht, -e
reporter der Reporter, -; die Reporterin, -nen
rewrite *um • schreiben
rest sich aus • ruhen
restaurant das Restaurant, -s; **student —** die Mensa, Mensen
Rhine der Rhein; **on the —** am Rhein
right recht; **He is —.** Er hat recht.; **to the —** nach rechts; **on the —** rechts
rock music die Rockmusik
road der Weg, -e
room das Zimmer, -
ruins die Ruine, -n
rule: as a — zur Regel

sake: for . . . sake um . . . willen; **for my sake** um meinetwillen (*see pp. 216, 261*)
salad der Salat, -e
saleswoman die Verkäuferin, -nen
salt das Salz, -e
same: the — derselbe, dasselbe, dieselbe (*see p. 286*)
sausage die Wurst, ⁼e; **little —** das Würstchen (Würstlein), -
say sagen
school die Schule, -n; **to —** in die Schule
score: to — a goal ein Tor *schießen
seamstress die Näherin, -nen
search through durchsuchen
see *sehen
self (*see pp. 222–226*)
sell verkaufen
sentence der Satz, ⁼e
set (*apparatus*) das Gerät, -e
seventh siebt-
several mehrere
ship das Schiff, -e
shoe der Schuh, -e
shop ein • kaufen; **to go shopping** ein • kaufen *gehen (*sein*)
short kurz
show *noun:* **to the —** ins Kino
show zeigen
side: on the other — of *prep.* jenseits (*gen.*); **on this — of** *prep.* diesseits (*gen.*)
sign das Schild, -er
sing *singen
singer der Sänger, -; die Sängerin, -nen
sister die Schwester, -n
sit *sitzen
six sechs

skirt der Rock, ⁼e
sleep *schlafen; **to go to —** *ein • schlafen (*sein*)
small klein
smart klug
smoke rauchen
so so; **— much** soviel; **— many** so viele
soccer (der) Fußball; **to play —** Fußball spielen
socialistic sozialistisch
sofa das Sofa, -s
some etwas (*with sing. noun*); einige (*with pl. noun*)
someone or another irgend jemand
son der Sohn, ⁼e
song das Lied, -er
soon bald
Spanish spanisch
spite: in spite of *prep.* trotz (*gen.*)
stadium das Stadion, -dien
stand *stehen; **— up** *auf • stehen (*sein*)
statue das Standbild, -er; die Statue, -n
stay *bleiben (*sein*); **— behind** *zurück • bleiben (*sein*); **— overnight** übernachten
stereo set die Stereoanlage, -n
stocking der Strumpf, ⁼e
stop *stehen • bleiben (*sein*); **— for the customs inspection** zur Zollkontrolle *an • halten
store der Laden, ⁼; das Geschäft, -e
story die Geschichte, -n
strawberry die Erdbeere, -n
street die Straße, -n
strict streng
strong stark
student der Student (*weak masc.; see pp. 93–94*); die Studentin, -nen
studies das Studium
study studieren
style: out of — altmodisch
subject das Thema, -men
such solcher, solches, solche; **— a** so(lch) ein, ein, eine
suggest *vor • schlagen
suit der Anzug, ⁼e
suitcase der Koffer, -
summer der Sommer; **in the —** im Sommer
sun die Sonne, -n
supposed: to be — to sollen, sollte, gesollt, soll (*see pp. 109–115*)
sweater der Pullover, -
swim *schwimmen (*sein*)
swimmer der Schwimmer, -; die Schwimmerin, -nen

swimming pool das Schwimmbad, ˵er
Swiss schweizerisch
Switzerland die Schweiz; **to —** in die Schweiz
symphony die Symphonie, -n

table der Tisch, -e; **— -tennis racket** der Tischtennisschläger, -
take *nehmen; **— the Abitur** das Abitur machen
tale die Erzählung, -en
talk noun die Rede
talk *sprechen; **— to** *sprechen mit
tax die Steuer, -n
taxi das Taxi, -s
tea (der) Tee
teacher der Lehrer, -; die Lehrerin, -nen
team die Mannschaft, -en
tear up *zerreißen
television: to watch — *fern · sehen
tell sagen; (relate) erzählen
ten zehn
tennis (das) Tennis; **to play —** Tennis spielen; **— ball** der Tennisball, ˵e; **— court** der Tennisplatz, ˵e
terrific furchtbar
terrified: to be grauen; **I'm terrified of snakes.** Es graut mir vor Schlangen.
test die Prüfung, -en
than als; **Kurt is stronger than his brother.** Kurt ist stärker als sein Bruder.
thank danken (dat.)
that conj. daß; **so —** damit; relative pron. der, das, die (see pp. 277 –279)
their possessive adj. ihr, ihr, ihre (see pp. 81–84)
there da, dort; **— is (are)** es gibt (acc.; see pp. 231 –233)
third dritt-
thirteen dreizehn
thirty dreißig
this dieser, dieses, diese
thousand das Tausend, -e; **two —** zweitausend; **— s of** Tausende von
three drei
throne der Thron, -e
ticket die Fahrkarte, -n; **admission —** die Eintrittskarte, -n
time die Zeit, -en; **at that —** damals; **for a long —** lange; **one time (once)** einmal; **two times (twice)** zweimal
tired müde
to prep. zu, nach (both with dat.): **to the university** zur Universität; **to**

Berlin nach Berlin; auf, in (both with acc.); **to the bank (post office)** auf die Bank (Post); **in order —** um . . . zu
today heute
tomato die Tomate, -n
tomorrow morgen; **— morning** morgen früh
tonight heute abend
too auch; **— much** zuviel; **— many** zu viele
tourist der Tourist (weak masc.; see pp. 93–94); die Touristin, -nen
town die Stadt, ˵e; **to go downtown** in die Stadt *fahren (sein); **town hall** das Rathaus, ˵er
tower der Turm, ˵e
train station der Bahnhof, ˵e
translate übersetzen
travel reisen (sein); **— agency** das Reisebüro, -s
traveler's check der Reisescheck, -s
tree der Baum, ˵e
trip die Reise, -n; **to take a—** eine Reise machen
turn: — in ein · reichen; **— out** (lights) aus · schalten
two zwei

uncle der Onkel, -
under prep. unter (dat. or acc.; see pp. 249–252)
understand *verstehen
university die Universität, -en; (colloquial) die Uni, -s; **to attend the —** die Uni besuchen, auf die Uni *gehen (sein)
until prep. bis (acc.)
untruthful unehrlich
use gebrauchen
useful brauchbar, nützlich
usually gewöhnlich

vacation: on — in (auf) Urlaub
vegetable das Gemüse (sing.); **vegetable soup** die Gemüsesuppe
vegetarian der Vegetarier, -; die Vegetarierin, -nen
Vienna (das) Wien
village das Dorf, ˵er
visit besuchen

wait for warten auf (acc.)
waiter der Kellner, -; **—!** Herr Ober!
waitress die Kellnerin, -nen

walk: to take a — einen Spaziergang
machen, *spazieren · gehen (*sein*)
wall die Wand, ⸚e; (*outside*) die Mauer, -n
want wollen, wollte, gewollt, will (*see pp.*
109–115)
warm warm
watch: — television *fern · sehen
weak schwach
wear *tragen
weather das Wetter
week die Woche, -n
well gut; (*healthy*) gesund
what was
when wann (*in direct and indirect*
questions); (*whenever*) wenn; (*relating*
to one past action or period) als
(*see p. 322*)
where wo; **(to)** — wohin
whether ob
which welcher, welches, welche
while *conj.* während; **while reading** beim
Lesen
who wer
whoever wer auch
win *gewinnen
window das Fenster, -; (*counter*) der
Schalter, -; **at the ticket window** am
Schalter; **to go window-shopping**
einen Schaufensterbummel machen

wine der Wein; **— festival**
das Weinfest, -e
winter der Winter; **in —** im Winter
wish wünschen
with *prep.* mit (*dat.*)
withdraw (*money*) *ab · heben
without *prep.* ohne (*acc.*); **without eating**
breakfast ohne zu frühstücken
woman die Frau, -en
word das Wort, ⸚er; **foreign —** das
Fremdwort, ⸚er
work arbeiten
worker der Arbeiter, -; die Arbeiterin, -nen
workman der Arbeiter, -
world die Welt, -en
worry about sich (*dat.*) Sorgen
machen um
wreath der Kranz, ⸚e

year das Jahr, -e; **next —** nächstes Jahr
yes ja
yesterday gestern
yet schon; **not —** noch nicht
young jung
your *possessive adj.* dein, dein, deine
(*sing. familiar*); euer, euer, eu(e)re (*pl.*
familiar); Ihr, Ihr, Ihre (*formal, see pp.*
81–84)
youth hostel die Jugendherberge, -n

Index